AUGUSTINE

Modern Studies in Philosophy is a series of anthologies presenting contemporary interpretations and evaluations of the works of major philosophers. The editors have selected articles designed to show the systematic structure of the thought of these philosophers, and to reveal the relevance of their views to the problems of current interest. These volumes are intended to be contributions to contemporary debates as well as to the history of philosophy; they not only trace the origins of many problems important to modern philosophy, but also introduce major philosophers as interlocutors in current discussions.

Modern Studies in Philosophy is prepared under the general editorship of Amelie Oksenberg Rorty, Livingston College, Rutgers University.

Dr. Robert A. Markus is currently teaching at The University of Liverpool, England.

MODERN STUDIES IN PHILOSOPHY

AMELIE OKSENBERG RORTY

GENERAL EDITOR

Augustine

A Collection of Critical Essays

EDITED BY

R. A. MARKUS

Anchor Books

DOUBLEDAY & COMPANY, INC.

GARDEN CITY, NEW YORK

1972

Contents

Introduction

Few thinkers have left as deep a mark on Western intellectual history as Augustine of Hippo, and yet he is not much studied by philosophers. Although his age was not one in which philosophy flourished, it was still held in high respect. Philosophy was the quest of wisdom; it held the key to the meaning of life and it provided men with a rule to live by. The traditional figure of the philosopher furnished late antiquity with one of its cherished models, since for both pagans and Christians the philosopher represented an ideal of intellectual culture. The philosophic life was as near as one could get on earth to the good life, and it pointed the way to its full realization in another world. The idealized figure of the philosopher was one of the most popular of the images utilized in late Roman funerary art: men liked to think of themselves as dedicated to the pursuit of wisdom; but the actual activity of the philosopher was very much less popular. It was confined to a very small number of centers and carried on by a small number of people—after Plotinus, the great Neoplatonist of the third century A.D.—in the main by thinkers within the Neoplatonic tradition (though profoundly modified by Aristotelian logic), and very largely in the form of commentaries on the philosophical classics. Among them were thinkers of importance and, sometimes, originality;[1] but the philosophic thought of late antiquity is generally markedly derivative in character.

If the philosophy of the philosophers bore the stamp of the past, the philosophy of the dilettante—and this must include most of the "philosophy" of late antiquity—was even more thoroughly derivative. At its most superficial, it might amount to no more than a smattering of neatly codified and summarized doctrines taught by the thinkers of classical antiquity and the views associated with the various philosophic schools. Compendious and easily accessible, such summaries were a normal component of every cultivated man's education. Plato and Parmenides took their place in his intellectual equipment alongside snippets from Virgil and Livy. The spectrum between this antiquarian and literary interest in philosophy at one extreme and the professional interest of Alexandrian or Athenian Neoplatonists at the other was wide. Somewhere along it we must place Augustine's.

Both Christian and pagan underwent the same education in late antiquity. We should expect their knowledge of philosophy and their approach to it to differ little. For the most part, our expectations are borne out by fact. Among Christian writers we find much the same range of interest in philosophy as among pagans. The one chief difference is that the spectrum here is shortened, the fully professional end being cut off. The reason for this is simple. It is that "philosophy" as generally understood was held to be a body of teaching concerned with the ultimates of human life. Christianity offered such a body of doctrine and was often referred to as a "philosophy." How could a Christian, whose understanding of God, the world, and man was necessarily drawn from the Gospel, who had his own "Christian philosophy," share the preoccupations of a pagan philosopher? On whatever level he found something in common with Plotinus or Plato or Aristotle, it could not be on the level of insight into the ultimate truth. *Ex hypothesi*, on the generally current conception of philosophy, that of a Christian could not be identical with that of a pagan. In the sense of the all-embracing intellectual activity concerned with everything relevant to the realization of the ultimate purposes of human life, Christian and pagan "philosophy" had necessarily to be mutually exclusive. Some Christian thinkers, especially in earlier centuries, had thus come simply to contrast "Christian philosophy" with pagan, only to reject the latter out of hand as embodying the teachings of falsehood and idolatry. A more complex and more positive assessment had also, however, come into being long before Augustine, and the type of thinking carried on by pagan Greek philosophers had found a place in the minds of Christian thinkers. It had, naturally, to be a subordinate place. The concepts and procedures of the Greek philosophers had to be fitted into the preoccupations of minds committed to a "Christian philosophy," into a wisdom structured in terms of the Christian Gospel. Neither Augustine nor any other Christian writer in this period could be a "philosopher" on the same terms and in the same sense as a pagan philosopher.

Augustine seems to have been conscious of a dilemma. Philosophy, he was clear, could be considered as a type of rational activity: on one occasion he pointed out that the central facts of the Christian message (the incarnation, death, and resurrection of Jesus) were historical facts and therefore not within the sphere of the distinctive procedure of philosophy, the abstract, analytical type of argumentation which is its proper method (*De Trinitate* IV. 16. 21). Augustine seems to be thinking of philosophy here as a type of intellectual activity, defined by its characteristic procedure. On another occasion, however, he described Christianity as "the one true philosophy" (*Contra Iulianum* IV. 14. 72), here tacitly identifying philosophy with the results of an intellectual activity —certain doctrines about the final truths of life—rather than thinking of it in terms of a distinctive type of activity. We might call the first of Augustine's conceptions the "technical," the second the "total," conceptions of philosophy. His dilemma, in these terms, was this: a Christian thinker could have no objection to philosophic thought taken in its "technical" sense, indeed needed to have recourse to it for his own purposes of clarifying the logic of some of the statements of his Christian beliefs and of solving some of the puzzles these gave rise to. In this sense, however, "philosophy" was not fully what it was generally understood to be: it was not concerned with the ultimate truths which were thought to be its proper realm. If, however, it did concern itself with such truths (i.e., understood in its "total" sense), then only the "Christian philosophy" could claim to be true, even though its essential basis lies not in rational reflection and analysis but in belief about a historical revelation; and no other philosophy could form the proper object of study for a Christian interested in the truth, except insofar as it happened to anticipate or to confirm the truths taught by Christianity. In practice, Augustine overcame the dilemma by confining his

interest in what we would recognize as philosophy to the
level he distinguished (in the term I have suggested) as "technical." He subordinated it rigidly to the study of the scriptures which contained the truths necessary for a Christian.
He thought of philosophy as a useful, even indispensable, aid
in a Christian thinker's search for a deeper understanding of
the truth about God, about man, and about the world in general. The fundamentals of this insight could never be furnished by philosophy (taken in this narrow, "technical"
sense). They would be disclosed to the Christian believer in
his faith in the Gospel message and in the teaching of the
Church. Philosophy would provide a useful means of analysis and clarification; it could not serve as the source of an
alternative body of teaching. Its function would be within
the framework and in the context of the Christian faith as a
datum. Thus Augustine's philosophical thought is always part
of what we would regard as a theological enterprise, and has
to be isolated from its setting and its avowed purpose if we are
to study it for itself. That the attempt is worth making is
a measure of Augustine's intellectual stature.

Other Christian theologians, Thomas Aquinas, most notably, have been acutely conscious of the difference between
philosophy and theology. Such a consciousness is largely la-
tent and incipient in Augustine. For this reason, among
others, his work lends itself less readily to philosophical study
than does the work of Aquinas who was, no less than Augustine, first and foremost a theologian. Augustine's philosophy has been less studied, and still less by scholars trained in
the philosophical tradition current since the last war in
Britain and in North America. There are, however, a number of themes represented in Augustine's vast literary output
which have been the subject of philosophical investigation in
this idiom. There are others which have not—at any rate so
far—been written about, or not in the idiom characteristic of
the dominant philosophical tradition of the English-speaking
world, which belong, nevertheless, to an area traditionally
within the sphere of philosophical interest. Studies of themes
in both groups have been included in this collection. Some of
the essays printed here may stimulate professional philosophers to extend the range of their attention to fields to which

historians and theologians have hitherto paid more attention.

The first two selections are concerned with Augustine's place in the history of Christian Platonism. Augustine derived from Neoplatonist thinkers the main bulk of the conceptual equipment which he used in diverse fields. Nevertheless, an investigation of at least some of Augustine's philosophical ideas (we shall encounter examples in the course of this book) is not by any means simply the examination of Neoplatonist ideas as they might be found in Plotinus or Proclus, in St. Ambrose or St. Gregory of Nyssa. As A. H. Armstrong points out, "Christian Platonism" is a rough shorthand for the interplay of two complex traditions. Augustine is most sharply divided from Plotinus—though not so much from Plato or later Neoplatonists—along with the other great Christian Platonists of his age by his views concerning the relationship between man's self and the transcendent or divine reality. R. J. O'Connell also studies one aspect of this relationship in tracing the development of Augustine's views on human life in terms of their Plotinian origins. From Plotinus, Augustine had learned to see life as a progressive liberation from the world of sense and from the body, its perfection achieved in contemplation of a "spiritual" truth. O'Connell's paper seeks to give an account of the ways in which Augustine came to modify and transform this initial view, without, however, ever liberating himself from its spell. The cognate theme of the attitude toward the body and the material universe forms the second of Armstrong's crucial points for characterizing Augustine's version of Christian Platonism. Pagan and Christian Platonism are both "other worldly," both reserved about the claims of the body and the material world, and also both opposed to a cosmological dualism such as would imply the rejection of the material world as evil. Armstrong distinguishes a variety of options open to Platonists on this point and argues that in comparison with either the great pagan Neoplatonists or with some strands in the tradition of Christian Platonism, Augustine greatly reduces the religious relevance of the material universe. Armstrong's third crucial case for assessing Augustine's place in the history of Christian Platonism, his views on God's grace and men's salvation, brings us into a distinctively theological area; it does, however, also provide a context for the discussions of human free will in the section, "God and Free Will."

Augustine was no logician or theorist of language, yet he did inherit a body of sophisticated logical and linguistic theory which he made his own and used for his own purposes. Essays 3 and 4 are concerned with his theories of signs and meaning. It was his interest in the methods of interpreting the images and figures of the scriptures that brought Augustine to take an interest in the logical and linguistic concept of sign. The stimulus for the conceptual clarification came from theology, and the philosophically clarified concept was deployed in theological discussion. Augustine's definitions and classifications of signs constitute a fine example of a distinctively philosophical discussion undertaken for specifically theological ends. (A parallel case could be cited from Augustine's discussions of the notions of image and likeness, models of lucid analysis, used in expounding (a) man's relationship to God, and (b) one of the relations between God the Father and the Son.)

Philosophical problems forced themselves on Augustine's attention in several ways. In addition to the ways exemplified in the second section, there is a variety of philosophical problems raised for Augustine by the nature of the philosophical concepts which he derived from his Neoplatonic sources. The essays in the third section indicate some of this variety. The argument, "If I am mistaken, I am," analyzed by Gareth B. Matthews, is a strictly philosophical one, and, alone of all the themes discussed in this volume, one in which Augustine's interest was entirely philosophical. The problem was raised for him by his need to answer the case for a philosophical skepticism of the "academic" type, and he tried to answer the case on its own ground. But Augustine's theory of knowledge abounds in arguments which were forced on him in quite different ways. His general account of knowledge was cast in the molds of Platonic philosophy. The difficulties he frequently encountered in rendering an acceptable account of knowledge were inherent in the explanatory framework he had adopted. In the second and third of his essays, Matthews deals with two such puzzles, both created for Augustine by his antecedent adoption of a dualistic theory of mental and

bodily activity. A. C. Lloyd explores a problem of another
kind, that involved in formulating the concept of a person.
In the task of elucidating the theology of the Trinity, Augustine turned to Aristotle's *Categories*. His difficulties in deploy-
ing the Aristotelian concepts sprang from the theological purpose to which they were harnessed; to the extent, indeed (as
Lloyd suggests) that incipient possibilities for the formulation
of a concept of the person were left unexplored, Augustine
being inhibited by (in the main) theological considerations.
If Lloyd is right, this constitutes an interesting example of
theology providing both the originating stimulus for a philosophical clarification and the chief frustrating limitation upon
it. William L. Rowe and John M. Rist (fourth section) both
consider Augustine's views on man's freedom, the one in relation to God's foreknowledge, the other in relation to God's
predestining choice: both cases illustrating philosophical difficulties raised for Augustine by his theological views.

Time is the one subject which of all the topics dealt with
by Augustine has been most frequently and most fully subjected to strictly philosophical discussion. Space and balance
have allowed the inclusion of only two essays concerned with
this subject (fifth section), but references to most of the other
important philosophical discussions will be found in Hugh M.
Lacey's paper (see below, p. 307 n. 30). The problem of time
was raised for Augustine by his belief in the creation of the
world by a creator, God, and his theory of time is part of his
account of the contingent nature of the created world. It is
in that context that Robert Jordan presents Augustine's views
on time. Augustine was acquainted with some ancient discussions of time, and was evidently deeply influenced by Plotinus'
reflection on this subject, as on so many others. But his own
relational theory of time—examined by Lacey—was his own
personal solution to the puzzles which arise from a theory of
time as substantial, such as Augustine seems to have ascribed
to the Manichees who wanted to know what there was before
time.

Historians and theologians have written a great deal on Augustine's views of society. His attitude toward the Roman Empire of his day, his views on the Christian Church in relation
to the secular world in which it was set, his theories on the

nature of political authority and obligation have been much studied.[2] His mind on these matters, as on so many others, did not stand still; it underwent unceasing development. This is one reason for the difficulty of attributing a "political philosophy" to Augustine. Another lies in the inevitable complications due to the fact that Augustine's views on this cluster of themes are too many-dimensional to constitute anything that can be read off in the simple dimension of theory. Social attitudes, political alignments, the facts of life of a provincial bishop in late Roman North Africa, and a variety of theological considerations contribute to the formation of a complex intellectual development to which it is impossible to render justice while confining oneself to the dimension of pure theory. The three essays included in the sixth section nevertheless point toward the gradual emergence in Augustine's mind of a coherent vision of the political order which would repay closer study by philosophers. Peter Brown suggests that the reason for the continued relevance of Augustine's political thought lies in its rejection of a "rational myth of the state": Augustine repudiates the attempt to derive the state, political arrangements, and obligations from the nature of a "rational man" extrapolated from our experience. F. E. Cranz, in the first of his papers reprinted here, traces the process whereby Augustine freed himself from the spell of the classical political myth of the state as the embodiment of a natural order among men, directed to the perfecting of man in the life of virtue and consummated in happiness. In the second of his papers, Cranz considers a facet of Augustine's mature view of society as irretrievably dislocated, as incapable of leading men to their true fulfillment, and perpetually subject to a radical tension between ultimately different and conflicting values and loyalties clung to by its members. There are pointers here to the possibility of a fruitful philosophic inquiry into Augustine's political theories. What, for instance, is the force of Augustine's denial that the state is ordained by nature? What are the implications of the models for political obligation which he rejects, of those he adopts? The three papers I have included in this section do not ask, still less answer, questions of this kind. I have included them as the three most distinguished studies known to me which discuss Augustine's views on questions connected with political life in a way such as could lead to a bridging of the gap between historical scholarship and philosophical analysis. This purpose the collection as a whole will, I hope, serve usefully.

For help in planning the volume I am very grateful to Amelie Rorty and Anthony Kenny; for help in executing my plan and dealing with the manifold difficulties on the way, to Paul H. Drymalski and Ronnie Shushan.

R.A.M.

Liverpool
January 1971

NOTES

1. See A. C. Lloyd, "The later neo-Platonists," Part IV of *Cambridge History of Later Greek and Early Medieval Philosophy,* ed. A. H. Armstrong (Cambridge, 1967).

2. For a recent discussion, see my *Saeculum: History and Society in the Theology of Saint Augustine* (Cambridge, 1970).

CHRISTIAN PLATONISM

1

St. Augustine and Christian Platonism

A. H. ARMSTRONG

Most people who have studied St. Augustine would be prepared to accept the description of him as a Christian Platonist,
indeed perhaps the greatest, and certainly the most influential,
of Christian Platonists. But this description, when we look at
it more carefully, raises a great many questions. What do
we mean by Christian Platonism? It is a term which has been
used, and misused, in a great variety of different ways, and
applied to a great variety of different people. Even if we confine our attention to the area of its use most relevant to the
theme of this lecture, that is, to the Christian thought of,
roughly, the first millennium A.D., we shall find too many
differences, and too complex an interaction of manifold and
various ideas, to make it possible to give an abstract, generalized, Aristotelian-type definition of Christian Platonism
which will be either truthful or helpful.[1] We are dealing with
the interplay of two great traditions, both of which have an
inexhaustible capacity for stimulating thought of a great
many different kinds. I need hardly remind this, or any other
intelligent audience, that 'Christianity' can mean a large number of different things, and that any statement that a particular doctrine or attitude to life is 'authentically Christian' or
'essential to Christianity' is liable to provoke disagreement,
even if its context is a scholarly discussion of a limited period
in the history of Christian thought. And 'Platonism' can mean
almost as many different things. The thought of St. Augus-

The Saint Augustine lecture for 1966 (Villanova University Press,
1967), reprinted by permission of the author and publisher.

tine is, certainly, one kind of Platonically influenced Christian thought. But there are many other kinds, some very different from the Augustinian.[2] And there have been, and are, Christian Platonists, especially, I think, in the Christian East and the English-speaking world, who feel uneasy with Augustine, and are sometimes led precisely by their Platonism into quite violent opposition to Augustinian ways of thinking. It therefore seems worth while to explore the question of where St. Augustine stands within Christian Platonism, to enquire what he has in common with and where he differs from other Christian Platonists. In this lecture I propose to consider three topics, out of the many which might be chosen, to illustrate the variations possible within Christian and pagan Platonism, and the place of Augustine in this long and complex tradition of Christian Platonist thinking. An investigation of this kind, in the limited time of a single lecture, can only be a very tentative one, and I do not wish to claim any sort of finality for any conclusions at which I may arrive. For the purposes of this enquiry 'Christianity' will be taken to mean traditional Christianity, something, that is, which would be recognizable, as a version of the faith which they themselves held, to the great Fathers and Doctors of East and West, to St. Augustine himself and his predecessors, contemporaries, and successors during the next three or four centuries: though we may need to look beyond the bounds of the ancient Church for solutions to some of the very lively and contemporary problems which our investigation raises. And, though the name 'Platonism' can properly be given to any way of thinking which originates from a sympathetic reading of those most unusual, baffling, and endlessly fascinating philosophical documents, the Dialogues of Plato, we shall be mainly concerned here with that later Greek Platonism whose rise and development was roughly contemporary with that of Christianity, and which entered very early on an intimate, though at times uneasy and even hostile relationship with the new religion: the Platonism, that is, whose successive stages are rather misleadingly called by modern scholars Middle Platonism and Neoplatonism.[3]

The first topic which I propose to discuss is that of the natural divinity of the soul. The idea that the human soul is by its very nature in some sense divine and co-eternal with God still sometimes finds enthusiastic supporters among Christians both in East and West.[4] It is one of the central and most important doctrines of the Platonism of Plotinus and Porphyry, though not of all pagan Platonism. For Plotinus and his chief disciple man's soul is not only, as all pagan Platonists held, naturally immortal, living a life which had no beginning and can have no end. It is in its true, essential nature divine, though in a subordinate degree, in a sense which excludes any fundamental change, any real fall, corruption, sin or loss of its true nature, and therefore any need or possibility of redemption. The part of us which reasons, which Plotinus, when he is speaking most precisely, identifies as our true self, can direct its attention upwards or downwards, can be distracted by the concerns and needs of the body and the body-bound lower self or turn upwards and open itself to the light, which always plays upon it, of Intellect and its source, the Good, and so become fully and consciously that universal and eternal divine reality which in a sense it always is, and rise with it in the movement of self-transcendence in which the divine Intellect eternally returns to its source. The whole object of the philosophic life is to ensure that we turn the right way, upwards, and wake to and make our own the glory which is always ours by right. But it seems that for Plotinus our true self cannot sin or suffer; it cannot come down to the level of body or be completely involved in its life. That in us which sins and suffers and is ignorant and emotionally disturbed and in general is the subject of what we should regard as ordinary human experience is the lower self, the 'other man', which is an image or expression of the higher self on a lower level.[5] Now, though this doctrine, in much less nuanced and carefully limited forms than that in which Plotinus stated it, occasionally finds Christian defenders, it seemed to the great Christian thinkers of the fourth and fifth centuries, as it seems to most Christians today, quite incompatible with any sort of Christianity. They were very conscious of their opposition to the pagan Platonists on this point, and very careful to exclude any suggestion of natural divinity from their often Platonic-sounding accounts of the nature of man and his way to spiritual perfection and the vision of God.

Here St. Augustine appears as a fully representative Christian Platonist of his time, in complete accordance with the great thinkers of the Greek-speaking Christian East, and especially with the deepest thinker of them all, and the one most deeply influenced by Platonism, St. Gregory of Nyssa. Both Augustine and Gregory give very Plotinian-sounding accounts of the journey of the soul; and for both that journey is, as it is for Plotinus, a return to man's proper and original state and his own true country and Father.

Robert J. O'Connell, of Fordham University, in a series of extremely interesting articles, of which the last and most explicit appeared in the *International Philosophical Quarterly* in September 1964, has even maintained that Augustine still believed when he wrote the *Confessions* that we are fallen parts of a Plotinian universal soul, and that some baffling features of this great work can only be explained in the light of the Plotinian doctrine. His evidence and arguments do not seem to me conclusive, but the possibility that he is right needs a good deal of further consideration. But Father O'Connell does not maintain, and no one who knows the evidence could seriously maintain, that Augustine, or any other great Christian Platonist, held that the soul was naturally divine and intrinsically unfallen. Both Augustine and Gregory of Nyssa insist again and again that the soul is a creature, not a part of God, and stress the intrinsic mutability and peccability which is essential in being a creature and is to be seen even in the highest, angelic creation. The contrast between the immutability of God and the mutability of the creature is one of the great recurring themes in Augustine's thought. Creaturely mutability is not for him a defect or imperfection in the creature, an unnecessary falling short of an attainable ideal. It is intrinsic to creatureliness; it is the inescapable consequence of not being God and so being absolutely and continuously dependent on God for first existence and continuance in being. And I think that one reason why he insists on it so strongly, especially when he is considering the most exalted created spirits or human souls made perfect, is that he was so vividly conscious of the fundamental opposition here between Christianity and the pagan Platonism which he knew so well.[6]

The division on this point between Christians and pagans is indeed a fundamental one, and has far-reaching consequences for morality and religious behaviour. But, once we have clearly recognized this, we must be careful not to make it too sharp or too absolute: there are a number of necessary qualifications to be added to the simple statement of it. First, we must remember that 'divine' meant different things to pagans and Christians. For a pagan Greek, to say that the soul was not merely *theios,* divine, but *theos,* a god, did not necessarily mean more than that it was an immortal being. *Theos* is a word of very vague and various meaning, and certainly no pagan Platonist thought that all beings called *theoi* were identical with or parts of the Absolute Good, the Supreme Reality, the Creator (in the Christian sense) of heaven and earth. There was probably here a good deal of misunderstanding between pagans and Christians. Plotinus, as we have seen, gives his divine souls the qualities of immutability and impeccability, and regards their existence as necessary. But they are, none the less, eternally created, wholly dependent for their being and well-being on the One and its first expression or production, the Divine Intellect. They share, as parts of Universal Soul, in the production and administration of what is below them, the material world, but they do so with power and forms supplied to them from above: they are essentially derived and dependent beings. St. Augustine himself recognizes clearly what the true teaching of Plotinus on this point is, and states it admirably in a chapter of the *City of God* (X, 2) which is a good example of his generally fair and irenic attitude to pagan Platonism.[7] And, when we turn back from Plotinus to Plato, we find, first of all, that he expresses himself much more cautiously than his great third-century follower. Plato does not call the soul a *theos,* but at most asserts a kinship and likeness between it and the gods. And even if he had thought that man's soul, or at least its highest part, the intellect, was a *theos,* this would not necessarily have meant to him everything which it meant to Plotinus, whose thought at this point is deeply influenced by the noetic of Aristotle and later Aristotelians; he endows man's higher self with the impassibility of the Aristotelian 'separable' or 'active' intelligence. But this is not the Platonism of Plato, who was deeply influenced by the Orphic-Pythagorean tradition according to which the soul was indeed a god or spirit (*theos* or *daimon*), but a highly fallible and peccable one, punished for its primal sin by a fall into the cycle of reincarnation. And, though the *Phaedo,* the *Republic* and the *Phaedrus* present the soul as naturally immortal, we should not forget that the *Timaeus* shows the Demiurge not only making *theoi* but telling them explicitly that they, like everything else which he has made, are *not* immortal by nature but only by his unchanging good will (41 A-B); and, though this is myth, it does at the very least suggest that Plato did not feel himself committed to any doctrine of the natural immortality and immutability of all divine beings—he does not put details into his myths which flatly contradict his serious philosophical convictions.[8] Plotinus, then, is not a safe guide to the thought of Plato on this point. And the later Neoplatonists, Iamblichus and Proclus, abandoned the uncompromising doctrine of the soul's divinity which they found in Plotinus and Porphyry, and held that it did 'altogether come down' and was capable of sin and ignorance. This abandonment of Plotinus was quite deliberate and conscious, and was closely connected with the later Neoplatonist development of Platonic thought about *Eros* into something very like the Christian doctrine of *Agape* and grace—a development which I believe to have started from elements genuinely present in the thought of Plato and to owe little to Christian influence.[9]

There are, then, good historical reasons for not making the contrast between pagan and Christian thought about the natural divinity of the soul too unqualified and sharp. And we must remember, too, that the Fathers of the fourth and fifth centuries, and those Christians since who have remembered and followed their teaching, have always held that God wills to give men by grace in Christ a created divinity by participation which they do not possess by nature. This is as true of the Christian West as of the Christian East; and St. Augustine expresses the doctrine with his own unsurpassable clarity and conciseness: "God wills to make you a god; not by nature, as his Son is, but by his gift and adoption." (Sermon 166. 4. 4).[10] What separates Plotinus and Augustine here is not a denial on the one side and an affirmation on

the other that all that we are and can be is given by God. For
Plotinus, as for Augustine, we have and are nothing which
we have not received. The differences lie in the ways of thinking about what God gives and how he gives it. Does he give
a fixed and unchanging nature only, or a nature open and
unfinished and a freely given life and love above nature in
which that nature can find its real, but unpredictable fulfilment? And does he give his gifts without Christ, or only in
Christ? To this I shall return, in a different context, later in
the lecture.

The investigation of our first topic has shown St. Augustine
as a thoroughly representative Christian Platonist, in full accordance with other Christian Platonists of his time, and after,
in making a stand against pagan Platonism which was neces-
sitated by his Christian belief. The next topic which I propose
to discuss is that of pagan and Christian Platonist attitudes to
the body and the material universe. The subject matter here
is very much more complex, and I must inevitably discuss it
at a high level of generalization, so that it is important to
stress that my conclusions here are very tentative. Both the
Platonist and the Christian ways of thinking about the body
and the world of sense-experience have had in them from
their beginnings, in the Dialogues of Plato and the New Testament respectively, certain tensions and variations of outlook.
But the tensions are never between completely inconsistent
positions, and the variations are only within certain limits,
and it seems to me that, at least if we confine our attention to
'traditional' Christianity, as I have earlier described it, these
limits to a great extent coincide: and it was this coincidence
which was one of the things which attracted the early Christians most powerfully to Platonism and did most to make
Christian Platonism possible. Neither Christians nor Platonists, if they are to be faithful to their deepest convictions,
can be simply negative in their attitude to the body and the
world, regarding them as wholly evil and alien. Their fundamental belief that the material world, with all that is in it,
is good, and made by a good divine power simply because of
his goodness, prevents them from becoming Gnostics or
Manichees, however much some representatives of both tra-

ditions, and particularly the Christian, might have liked to be.
For there appears in both traditions at certain points a very
strong drive towards an extreme dualism in the sphere of human life, a rejection and hatred, not primarily of the material
universe as a whole, but of the earthly, animal body of man.
In the Christians this sometimes went very much further than
in the pagans; and whatever precisely the origins may be of
the extreme asceticism and the tendency to hate and fear
sexual intercourse and even to depreciate marriage which
appear frequently in the early Church, they do not appear to
be Platonic or Hellenic.[11] It is notable that the great Christian
Platonists, from Clement of Alexandria to St. Augustine, are
generally opposed to this sort of extremism. Augustine in
particular is often more balanced and positive—and not, as
sometimes seems to be assumed, more unbalanced and negative—in his attitude to the body, sex and marriage than most
of his Christian contemporaries. He made two advances of
special importance towards a more positive and constructive
way of thinking about these matters. By his clear-cut insistence that the cause of sin lies in the will, not in the body (e.g.
City of God XIV, 3), he did a great deal to banish from
Western Christian thinking the shadow of the Pythagorean-
Platonic belief in the dark, recalcitrant element which is a
necessary constituent of the material world and the source of
evil to the soul which comes into contact with it; a belief
which persists in Plotinus, though the later pagan Neoplatonists abandoned it. And by his rejection of the doctrine of
that other great Christian Platonist, St. Gregory of Nyssa,
which persisted in later Greek Christian thought, that the
division of the human race into sexes was made *ratione peccati*, with a view to procreation only after the Fall, and was
no part of the original creation in the image of God, and his
insistence that there would have been begetting and birth of
children in Paradise (*City of God* XIV, 21 ff), Augustine took
at least the first step towards that positive, Christian valuation
of sex of which our own time has realized the necessity more
vividly than ever before.[12]

It should be noted that the Christian doctrine of the resurrection of the body did not make as much difference between
the Christian and pagan Platonist attitudes to our present

bodies as is sometimes assumed and as many modern Christians would be inclined to think it should have done. From the beginning the Christian tradition had stressed, not only the reality of the resurrection, but the difference of the glorified resurrection body from the body as we know it in this life (see especially St. Paul, I Corinthians 15). And the pagan Platonists believed in astral or celestial bodies which, like the glorified body for which Christians hope, were perfectly conformed and subordinated to the spirit, and many of them thought that the good and wise man's final destiny would be permanent embodiment in such a body. Here again St. Augustine was very well aware of the kinship between pagan Platonist and Christian thought, and bases on it a very powerful and effective attack on Porphyry for his total rejection of the Christian doctrines of the Incarnation and Resurrection, a rejection which he shows to be inconsistent with Neoplatonist teaching about the soul of the world and the astral gods (*City of God* X, 29, and XXII, 26).[13]

Neither pagan Platonists nor Christians, then, if they are to be true to some of their most deeply held beliefs, can utterly reject or despise the body or the material universe. But they cannot, either, regard the goods of the body and of this world as all the goods there are, or the most important goods. For neither of them can the world be self-sufficient or self-explanatory, the only world or the best world, or our present state, however much improved and developed on its own level, that in which we shall find our true and final happiness. Both are inevitably 'other-worldly,' though neither should hate this world. H. Crouzel, in his *Origène et la Philosophie,* indicates very well the sort of harmony between Platonism and Christianity which is possible here. Crouzel is much concerned to show that Origen is not as Platonist in an un-Christian or un-Biblical sense as he has been represented to be, but the last words of his book are as follows:

> All the same, there is a vision of the world, a cosmological point of view of Hellenic origin, which really dominates the thought of the Alexandrian. . . . It is the Platonic representation of a universe on two levels, of which the higher, that of the divine, is the model of the lower, its symbol, where

the world of the senses is to be found. This, because it is
symbol, is not self-sufficient and has no existence which is
not a means to an end and derived: its end, according to
God's plan, is to lead the soul to the divine, and sin consists
in stopping the movement of the intelligence at it, putting it
in place of the divine. Into this point of view, borrowed from
Platonism, the sacramental structure characteristic of the
time of the Church fits harmoniously.[14]

It hardly needs demonstration that St. Augustine, like the
great Greek Christian theologians of the fourth century, is
Platonically other-worldly in this sense.

So far our examination of this topic of the attitude to the
body and the material universe has shown Christian and
pagan Platonists rather closer to each other than is sometimes
supposed, with St. Augustine occupying, again, a central
position in the Christian Platonist tradition. But to leave the
discussion here would, it now seems to me, suggest an altogether unjustifiable complacency about the satisfactoriness of
the Christian Platonist position which I have sketched so
briefly and inadequately, and would not offer very much possibility of finding in ancient Christian tradition anything which
would even begin to help us to deal with the enormously
difficult, if also enormously hopeful, situation in which we
traditional Christians now find ourselves as we try to bring
our ancient faith into living and redemptive contact with our
drastically changed and vastly enlarged contemporary understanding of man and the universe. It does seem to me that St.
Augustine and, to a great extent, the other Christian thinkers
of his age, missed the chance of carrying out a much deeper
and more dynamic transformation of Platonism than they in
fact effected (they could not, and in my opinion should not,
have broken away from Platonism altogether): and that, in
one respect, their thought about the material universe shows
a certain regression in comparison with that of pagan Platonism, or at least fails to make the necessary Christian advance.
For a pagan Platonist, even one as other-worldly as Plotinus,
the cosmos was always religiously relevant. The continuing
sense of the divine presence and power always manifested in
the universe, and especially in its upper part, the region of

PROBLEM OF IDOLATRY !

the heavenly bodies; a veneration for those bodies as living cosmic divinities; and a strong awareness of kinship with the Soul of the World and membership in the living organic unity of all things; these are all essential parts, though for Plotinus not the most important parts, of Platonic philosophical religion. The universe for a pagan Platonist is not only good, but holy. One might almost, using Christianizing terms perhaps for once not altogether inappropriately, say that the cosmos is the one great sacrament for Plotinus and that he has a doctrine of the mystical body of the universe.[15] Now the Christians reacted strongly against this cosmic religion of the pagan philosophers. It provided, in fact, one of the main grounds of controversy between pagans and Christians. And I do not wish at all to suggest that the Christian reaction was wholly unjustifiable. Cosmic religion in its strongest form, the Stoic, was certainly from a Christian point of view idolatry —the Creator was identified with his creation. And, though I do not regard Platonist cosmic religion, in which star-gods and world-soul are created divinities, as necessarily pantheist or idolatrous, it was hardly acceptable to Christians as it stood. There is also a good deal to be said for Sambursky's view that if Christians in general, following the lead of John Philoponus in the sixth century, had rejected, not only the veneration of the heavenly bodies, but the astronomical belief which went with it, the belief, that is, in the intrinsic difference and superiority of the Upper Cosmos above the moon which found its extreme expression in Aristotle's doctrine of the aether or quintessence, the progress of science might have been accelerated and the new astronomy of the Renaissance might not have met with such bitter opposition in some Christian quarters. From both the Christian and the scientific point of view, the cosmic religion of late antiquity had to be rejected, and it might have been better if it had left a less deep mark on Christian thinking about the visible heavens than it did.[16]

But none the less, I think that in the rejection of the cosmic religion something important was in danger of being completely lost, and an opportunity was, in the fourth and fifth centuries, missed. What was in danger of being lost was the sense of the holiness, the religious relevance of the cosmos as a whole, and with it, inevitably, the sense of the holiness of ordinary human life and bodily activities. It is easy to find an expression of this more compatible with orthodox Christianity than the cosmic religion of late antiquity. The Christian can easily see in the whole universe the presence and power of the creative and life-giving Trinity: indeed he must see it if he is to have a properly vivid sense of the meaning of his own belief in creation. He can see the play of the Eternal Wisdom not only in the movements of the heavens but in the growth-patterns of trees and plants and the games of his puppy or kitten. He can be aware of the creative presence in all life, not of the world-soul, but of the Holy Spirit, the Lord and Life-Giver. This sense of holiness, of an intimate and immediate presence of God in the world, has not been absent from the Christian tradition, though it has all too often been much less prominent and widespread than it ought to have been. St. Hildegarde expresses it finely in her Sequence to the Holy Spirit, 'life of the life of every creature'; and it has played a particularly important part in the English and American Protestant tradition, and, sometimes at least, in the spirituality of the Eastern Orthodox.[17] But in the period with which we are immediately concerned it is very much in the background, when it is there at all. St. Basil the Great, in his early treatise *De Spiritu*, makes a good deal of use of a passage of Plotinus dealing with the world-soul in describing the working of the Holy Spirit. But in adapting Plotinus to his Christian purposes he is not led to say anything about the cosmic activity of the Spirit. A description of how the world-soul gives light and life to the cosmos and all things in it becomes a description of how the Holy Spirit sanctifies individual Christians. St. Augustine can speak magnificently of the beauty and order of the world as a witness to its Creator. But once this thought has served its purpose of leading the mind to the transcendent God, he turns away from the universe to concern himself with God's working in the soul or in the Church.[18] And Western Christianity has on the whole remained very much too Augustinian in this way. I am inclined to think that the lack of any broad human and humane interest and concern with the world around us, which is so often apparent in Christians and has alienated so many good and intelligent people from the Church and contributed so much to the present general rejection of Christianity, is due not so much to other-worldliness as to churchiness. It is not, that is, the result of that conviction that we are strangers and pilgrims in this world and that here we have no continuing city which is one of St. Augustine's great themes and which I believe he was right in thinking as essential to Christianity as to Platonism. Plato himself shows how other-worldliness can be combined with an intense concern for the reform of the human city. But what, I think, is mainly responsible for Christian narrowness and lack of humanity is the concentration of attention away from God's work in the world and in the life of ordinary people everywhere and the almost exclusive focusing on his work for souls in the Church: so that our personal prayer and the rites and sacraments of the Church have not, as they should, enhanced our sense of God's presence and work in the whole of his material creation, but distracted our attention from it; and the Church, instead of being, as she now declares herself in the great Council, the servant of mankind and the sacrament of the world's salvation, has been thought of as an exclusive institution whose often rather worldly interests are more important than the general welfare of mankind and the world which has been entrusted to man's care. The 'natural', we have thought, does not matter very much; only the 'supernatural' does, and there is no 'supernatural' worth considering outside the Church.

This churchiness, I must regretfully admit, seems to me generally apparent in the great thinkers of the 'golden age of the Fathers.' It is, perhaps, the main reason why a dynamic Christian transformation of Platonic thought about the cosmos somewhat analogous to the Christian transformation of Platonic thought about the soul which we have already discussed, a doctrine of the redemption of the whole universe in and through Christ, took so long to develop even in the Christian East, and has played very little part in Western Christian thinking until our own time. The foundations for such a doctrine had been well and truly laid in the earliest tradition of the Church. St. Irenaeus saw it clearly in the New Testament. He says of Christ: 'For the maker of the world is indeed the Word of God; and this is our Lord, who in the

last times was made man, existing in this world: Who invisibly
contains all things that were made, and is established in the
whole creation, as being God's Word, governing and disposing
all things; and therefore into his own he came invisibly, and
was made flesh and hung upon the tree, that he might sum up
all into himself' (*Adversus Haereses* V. 18. 2 tr. J. Keble):
and of the redemption of all creation: 'For God is rich in all
things, and all things are his. The creation therefore itself
must be renewed to its old condition and without hindrance
serve the righteous; and this the Apostle hath made evident
in the Epistle to the Romans thus speaking: "For the expectation of the creature waiteth for the revelation of the sons of
God. For the creature is made subject to vanity, not willingly,
but because of him who hath subjected it in hope: because
the creature itself also shall be delivered from the bondage of
corruption into the liberty of the glory of the sons of God." '
(*Adv. Haer.* V. 32. 1 quoting Romans 8:19–21–again in
Keble's translation; cp. 36. 1). This splendid teaching of
Irenaeus attracted all too little attention in the great age of
the Fathers, perhaps because of its millenarian context. (We,
though we cannot be millenarians, might be well advised to
pay some attention to the strange, and often beautiful, imagin-
ings of Book V. They will at least bring home to us that our
Christian hope is for a new earth which is still material, however glorified and transformed, in which none of the goodness and joy of this present life will be lost, and also that the
vision of God which is our true end is a spiritual vision transcending even the glory of the risen body and the renewed
creation.) [19]

The idea of cosmic redemption was, perhaps, always more
congenial to the Christian East than the Christian West. St.
Gregory of Nyssa mentions the restoration of all things (*De
Hominis Opificio*, chs. 22 and 23) but does not develop the
theme, and it does not seem in general to play any important
part in the thought of the Cappadocians. [20] The development
of the doctrine in the East is above all due to one of the greatest theologians of Christian antiquity, St. Maximus the Confessor (A.D. 580–662). By constructively criticizing Origen
and developing and, where necessary, correcting the thought
of the Cappadocians and Pseudo-Dionysius, and with a great

deal of help at important points from the sixth-century development of Aristotelian studies in the Greek Christian
world, he arrived at a way of thinking which still seems to
me to have something of value in it for our contemporary
world. Maximus, here developing Cappadocian thought but
also owing a good deal to Aristotle, sees movement as the law
of creation; but he does so without losing sight of the eternal
and unchanging, behind and beyond the movement of the
world. He remains a Christian Platonist. All created things
for him have to move towards their goal, which is not existent
in creation, but pre-exists as a *logos* in the *Logos,* an idea or
intention in the eternal Word of God. Christ the Word in
creating gives all things a dynamic being 'homed' on him and
brings them (all other things in man) back and on to him
by redemption and deification. In the thought of Maximus the
difference between spiritual and material is far less important
than the fact that both are created from nothing and both
designed to be brought back to God (though the material is
to return through and under the leadership of the spiritual).
There is no idea of escaping from the body, but only of reforming and transforming the carnal lusts and passions. There
is nothing in man, body, passions, natural powers, or even
that division of the sexes which Maximus, following Greek
tradition, cannot see as part of man's true nature, which is
destined to be destroyed. Transcendence means transformation. The lower is dominated by and brought to co-operate
with the higher. Ultimately the whole of man, body and passions included, is brought by the grace of God working on
man through his intellect to a union with God without confusion of created and uncreated. And in man, and through
his contemplation, the whole universe is brought back to God.
Man in himself unifies the material and intelligible, earth
and heaven, and brings it all back and presents it to God in
his glorification of him. And this is done only in and through
the Incarnation of Christ. All things were created in Him, and
man's sin is done away and he is redeemed and deified by
Christ's death, and he is brought back with all things to God
by the union without confusion of divine and human in the
Incarnation. The driving force of the whole process is love,

first God's for man and then, and in complete dependence
on God's love, man's love for God.

This is a magnificently dynamic, comprehensive and progressive view of the nature and destiny of man and the world,
in which the static, self-sufficient universe of pagan Platonism
which, like man's divine self, needs no redemption, is transformed into the moving, open, incomplete redeemed universe
of Christianity without loss of the Platonic awareness of the
eternal. We should not, of course, try to force it (or the
thought of St. Irenaeus) into an unreal conformity with our
inchoate contemporary theologies of cosmic redemption. St.
Maximus remains very much a Byzantine ascetic. His program for the reform and transformation of human nature is
austere: and it is in contemplation and mystic union, not by
any sort of human action on the material world, that Christ
in us brings back all creation to the Father: just as in St.
Irenaeus it is by a mysterious and miraculous action of Christ,
and not as the culmination of a long process of human action,
that the material world will finally be renewed and glorified.
Nor should we expect to find a solution in St. Maximus for
the enormous problems which our increased knowledge and
inevitably changed understanding of the universe and of human nature bring for traditional Christians. We must not
expect the Fathers and Doctors to do our own thinking for
us. But, none the less, there is room, at least in principle, in
St. Maximus' great vision of our life in Christ for all true
knowledge and all true love and their expressions.[21] It is a
tragedy that the theologies of Irenaeus and Maximus were
not better known and more influential in the West. Much of
the best of St. Augustine's thought, his theology of love and his
theology of history, would fit well into a Maximan framework. And if a doctrine of cosmic redemption had been a
living force in the centre of our theology and piety, and had
gone on developing according to the new needs and experiences of the centuries, the history of Western Christianity
might have been very different, and we might not have been
so ill equipped to deal with either Renaissance humanism or
modern thought. And even today our increasing knowledge
and appreciation of St. Maximus, and in general, of Eastern
Orthodox thought, in which his influence seems to be very

strong, may help us to deal with our contemporary problems.
If some theologian fully competent to do so were to bring St.
Maximus and Teilhard de Chardin together, the contact might
be fruitful, and the older Eastern tradition might help to suggest ways of correcting the defects, inevitable in a pioneer,
in the thought of the man who has restored to Western Ca-
tholicism a living (though by no means universally accepted)
belief in the holiness of the world and in cosmic redemption.[22]
And, certainly, a study of Eastern Christian theology will
prevent us from accepting uncritically the more aggressively
activist and this-worldly theologies of Christ's redeeming action, if, that is, we retain any respect at all for the ideas and
values of traditional Christianity.

My last topic is one which will show the reason why the
thought of St. Augustine and of Augustinians often arouses
uneasiness, and sometimes downright hostility, in other kinds
of Christian Platonists and in general of those pagans or Christians who have been influenced to some degree by Greek
humanism. It is that of God's universal will to save all mankind. In his anti-Pelagian writings Augustine, it must be admitted, takes a very dark view of the present state and future
destiny of the great majority of mankind, so dark a view that
his pessimism about man becomes a pessimism about God.
The doctrine of the *massa perditionis,* the intense emphasis
on inherited and personal guilt and sin, and the insistence
that God, for utterly mysterious reasons, selects from the mass
of men only a limited number for salvation from the deplor-
able present state with its appalling future consequences into
which he has allowed his creatures to get themselves, as they
appear in Augustine's own thought, even without the harden-
ing and exaggeration of later heterodox forms of Augustinian-
ism, are simply not compatible with the conclusions about
God and man to which the great majority of other serious
theists have come, especially those influenced by Platonism.[23]
For the pagan Platonist God is the Good, who diffuses his
good throughout the universe and to all mankind, giving it
to all to the limit of their capacity to receive it. In the thought
of Plotinus (though not of all pagan Platonists) the gift is
given without love or care, but equally without arbitrariness

or favouritism, as the sun shines. The belief that the divine powers which rule the universe are perfectly good is the fundamental tenet of the religion of Plato and his successors. And being good for Plato and the Platonists means doing good, and doing it with perfect wisdom and fairness. To theists of this sort, and to many Christian Platonists who have been led on by the revelation in Jesus Christ from their Platonic belief that God is good to believe that he is Love, and who understand this as meaning more, not less, goodness than Plato or any philosopher was able to conceive, the doctrine of Augustine is intolerable, and no appeal to mystery can justify it.[24] This rejection of any form of Augustinian selective predestination has, I think, been particularly characteristic of the English non-Calvinist and anti-Calvinist Christian tradition, which has, at times, been very deeply influenced by Platonism. The basic reason for the rejection, that this doctrine presents God as an arbitrary tyrant, and not really as supreme Goodness, Wisdom and Love, is magnificently expressed in the anti-Calvinist polemic of the great Cambridge Platonist, Cudworth:[25] and I must say here honestly and openly that, as a Cambridge man and a Platonist, and in spite of my genuine veneration for St. Augustine, I am compelled to share this view. It seems to me that any doctrine which restricts saving grace either to the elect or to those within the visible communion of the Church, and does not extend it effectively to all mankind, so that all are saved who do not freely persist to the end in refusing God's love, is an extreme example of that Christian narrowness of which I spoke earlier, which not only fails to pay sufficient attention to the goodness and holiness of the world and mankind outside the Christian limits, but supposes God to be equally narrow and selective in his love and care for his creation, and so presents him as a being worse, not better, than the God of the philosophers. Whenever and wherever the Gospel has been preached in this way, as very bad news, not good news, for the vast majority of mankind, it is not surprising that many pagans have scornfully rejected it and many Christians, finding it incompatible with their convictions about God's goodness and love for his creation, have reacted strongly against this presentation of Christianity, sometimes into untenable theological positions.

After this vigorously British piece of anti-Augustinianism, it may reasonably be asked whether I am advocating a return to the position of one of our few great British theologians, Pelagius. In fact, though I can sympathize to some extent with the Pelagian and 'semi-Pelagian' reactions against Augustine, I am certainly not a Pelagian, and wholeheartedly accept the present teaching of the Catholic Church, as magnificently expounded by the Second Vatican Council, and developed and applied by many contemporary theologians. The long wrestling of the mind of the Church through the ages with the problem of how to reconcile God's universal will to save all men in and through Christ, on which she has always insisted, with the absolute priority of grace and the fact that salvation can only be in some way through Christ in his Church, seems to me to have come, under the guidance of the Holy Spirit, to a successful issue of which we are only beginning to see and explore the implications. But we can already see how we can remain fully Augustinian on the most important point, that of the absolute priority of grace, while satisfying the legitimate demands of pagans and Pelagians.

Let us consider shortly what the main points of disagreement are between Plotinus, Pelagius, and Augustine. All agree that man has nothing which he has not been given, that he is wholly dependent for his being and his well-being upon God. For Plotinus, as we have seen, what God gives is a perfect higher self, impassible and impeccable, of which the lower self is a reflection or expression on a lower level of being. There is, therefore, no real question of salvation and no need for a redeemer. For Pelagius God gives man a nature equipped with everything that he needs for salvation in his creation, which is a real grace, a free and unmerited gift, and the primary and essential, though not the only grace. This nature is not impassible or impeccable; man can, and most men do, sin and will have to take the eternal consequences. The Pelagian view of the future destiny of mankind is nearly as grim as St. Augustine's. The Pelagians were, primarily, austere moralists, concerned to emphasize human responsibility and the need for human effort in the Christian life. And, like most ancient moralists, they took a grimly over-simplified, black-and-white view of human freedom and responsibility. There was no room in their thinking, any more than in Augustine's, for that proper attention to all the psycho-physical and social causes that may limit our free will and diminish our responsibility which our vastly increased modern knowledge of man forces upon us today. But, however disastrously most men may freely misuse what they have been given, the fault remains wholly theirs, not God's. He has given us all we need for our salvation, and given it to all men. Pelagius insists on the fact of real virtue, and even 'natural holiness' outside the Church (*Epistola ad Demetriadem*, chs. 3 and 4). But of course God can hardly be said to have given it to us through Christ Incarnate. In the Pelagian way of thinking Christ is our teacher, leader, helper, example and judge, but hardly in any real sense our redeemer.[26]

It was because they were primarily moralists that the Pelagians insisted so strongly, as they thought against Augustine, on human free will. Here their position (and still more that of the so-called 'semi-Pelagians') was very close to the Greek-Christian tradition, and especially to St. John Chrysostom, who was content, as the Christian East has generally been content (following in this a very ancient tradition of Greek thought) to assert both the necessity for God's grace and the necessity for man to co-operate with it freely without worrying too much about reconciling God's initiative and man's freedom. There is a *synergia*, a working together of God and his free creatures in the Christian life, and we cannot and should not investigate further.[27] Anti-Augustinians both in East and West have often been inclined to make the question of free will their central point of disagreement with St. Augustine, but I am prepared to believe that this may be largely due to misunderstanding and to accept the conclusion of Mother Mary Clark in her excellent book *Augustine, Philosopher of Freedom* (Paris, 1958) that Augustine really tried to maintain in his anti-Pelagian period his admirable earlier teaching on human free will and was to a great extent successful in reconciling it with his belief in predestination. But some recent English studies of Pelagianism have suggested that among the reasons for Pelagian opposition to Augustine may have been, not only the Pelagian and Eastern Christian conviction of the reality of free will, but also that which I have already suggested as the main point of difference between Augustine and other Christian Platonists, that the Augustinian account of God's dealings with mankind makes God so intolerably unfair. The most attractive feature of some at least of the Pelagians as Christian moralists is their passionate concern for social justice, in which, unfortunately, they stand almost alone among the Christians of their period. Pelagian voices are raised in revolutionary protest against that easy acceptance by Christians of the appalling social inequalities, injustices and cruelties of the late Roman Empire which is one of the worst scandals in the history of Christendom, and one from the effects of which we are still suffering. Now J. N. L. Myres has shown that in the legal language of the time *gratia* means judicial corruption and favouritism, and the phrase which Augustine uses of the Pelagians, *inimici gratiae,* would have meant to the ordinary man something like 'opponents of corruption in public life.' His examination of the Pelagian position in the light of the facts of contemporary life and language suggests very strongly that one thing which drove the Pelagians into such passionate opposition to Augustine was their conviction that God could not be in the least like a corrupt judge of the Roman Empire, their belief that the Augustinian doctrine presented the Lord in an all too human and contemporary light as a ruler of the most abominable injustice and cruelty.[28] St. Augustine upheld magnificently against pagans and Pelagians the fundamental Christian doctrines that the initiative is always and universally with God, that we can do nothing whatever towards our salvation of ourselves without or before his grace, and that saving grace is always and only given in and through the great redeeming act of Christ the Incarnate Word. But in upholding these doctrines he seems to have lost sight of, or at any rate failed to maintain, that simple belief in God's universal and equitable goodness which is the foundation of the faith of pagan Platonists and Pelagians, and very many more orthodox Christians. The present teaching of the Church as expounded in the Constitutions of the Second Vatican Council remains fully Augustinian on the vital points. But it also maintains, with a breadth and generosity most satisfying to those who cannot accept Augustine's teaching as it stands because of their belief that God is good, that the grace of Christ without which we cannot be saved is really offered to all men, and can be recognized at work beyond the bounds of the Church and even of Christianity; and that the whole universe is to share in the redemption of mankind.[29] We see in this teaching a supernatural giving as universal as the pagan Platonists conceived the self-diffusion of the Good. We see man, not as a changeless and self-sufficient eternal self, but as a creature unfinished, needing and receiving redemption. We see the universe, not as the static subordinate divinity of the old cosmic religion but as a great process guided by the Holy Spirit to share in the redemption which Christ has won for man. Plenty of problems and difficulties remain, but I believe that now after the Council we have a better chance than ever before of showing our religion as truly universal, free from narrowness or churchiness, the religion in which Platonism and all other great aspirations of the spirit of man to its eternal source and goal can find a glorious resurrection into a truth better than they could conceive, which offers hope to every man and to the whole world.

NOTES

These notes have been abbreviated. The interested reader is referred to the full text in the original publication.-Ed.

1. The *Cambridge History of Later Greek and Early Medieval Philosophy* (Cambridge, England, 1967; reprinted with corrections and additional notes and bibliography, 1971), of which I am editor, I hope, gives a fairly adequate idea of the variety and complexity of the pagan and Christian thought of the period. Parts II (by Henry Chadwick), *Philo and the Beginnings of Christian Thought;* V (by R. A. Markus), *Marius Victorinus and Augustine;* VI (by P. Sheldon-Williams), *The Greek Christian Platonist Tradition from the Cappadocians to Maximus and Erigena;* and VII (by H. Liebeschütz), *Western Christian Thought from Boethius to Anselm,* deal with various phases and aspects of Christian Platonism. Parts I, III, and IV (by P. Merlan, myself, and A. C. Lloyd) are concerned with pagan Platonism, and Part VIII (by R. Walzer) with early Islamic philosophy.

2. Eastern Christian and English Christian Platonism are touched on later in this lecture. One form of Christian Platonism which it has not been possible to deal with here, but which was extremely influential in the medieval Latin West and made a notable contribution to the formation of the European mind, is the simple Platonic Christian theism of the *De Consolatione Philosophiae* of Boethius. (The most generally accessible edition is that with English translation by H. F. Stewart and E. K. Rand in the Loeb Classical Library, last reprinted 1953.) The central and most influential idea of this is the great vision of the world as a whole which makes sense, a coherent unity held together and ruled in all its motions by an order which is also love, whose existence is due to and continually depends on the creative goodness of God, the Supreme Good. This vision, arrived at by reading Plato's *Timaeus* with Christian and late Platonist eyes without regard to the considerable divergences between Plato's thought in this dialogue and the Christian doctrine of creation, is particularly finely expressed in the ninth poem of Book III (the famous *O qui perpetua* on which so many commentaries were written in the early Middle Ages) and that great celebration of the love which orders the stars and the seasons, the sixth poem of Book IV. It is the foundation of the austerely encouraging moralizing of the *Consolation* about human destiny. The problem of the exact religious position of Boethius at the time when he wrote the *Consolation*

will probably never be completely solved. (One of the latest and best treatments of it, by H. Liebeshütz, will be found in the *Cambridge History* referred to in n. 1, Ch. 35D, pp. 550–55). There seem, however, to be two things worth saying about it which are relevant to our present theme of Christian Platonism. One is that Boethius, though of course in no way a naive or unscholarly person, represents, as has been indicated above, what may be called the 'naive' or 'concordist' kind of Christian Platonist, who finds no difficulty in assuming that Plato and the Bible are on all important points saying exactly the same thing. This sort of naive concordism has had a long history.

The other relevant point about the religious position of Boethius is that many Christians, before and after his time, who have come to know the teachings of the ancient moralists, have found their stern and clear vision of human destiny and true human values a source of strength and comfort in times of great suffering, and have turned to them, as Boethius did in prison, without any sense that they were doing anything contrary to their Christian profession. St. Augustine himself, who was certainly not a naive concordist, in his last days, during the Vandal invasion, used to comfort himself with a quotation from one of the finest examples of Stoic-Platonic moralizing on human destiny, the treatise *On Well-Being* of Plotinus (περὶ εὐδαιμονίας I 4[46]). According to his biographer, Possidius, 'amidst these calamities he used to console himself with the maxim of a certain wise man who said "no great man will think it a great matter when sticks and stones fall and mortals die"'. *Life of St. Augustine*, ch. 28, tr. F. R. Hoare in *The Western Fathers* (London, 1954)—a free translation of Plotinus I. 4. 7, 23–24.

3. The terms Middle Platonism and Neoplatonism are usually applied to the revived Platonism of the Roman Imperial period before Plotinus and to Platonism from Plotinus onwards respectively. But there is no breach of continuity between the two. Professor Merlan, in Part I of the *Cambridge History,* referred to in n. 1, shows clearly the close relationship of the thought of Plotinus to that of his predecessors. It is also important to remember that the influence of Platonism on Christian thought began well before the time of Plotinus (A.D. 204?–270). Philo of Alexandria, the precursor, and to a great extent the source of Christian Platonic thinking, was dead by A.D. 50. Justin and Clement of Alexandria belong to the second century (Clement was probably dead before A.D. 215) and Origen was a considerably older contemporary of Plotinus (born c. 184, died about A.D. 254). The pattern of Christian Platonism was well established before there

can be any question of Plotinian influence. This does not mean, of course, that Plotinus had no influence on Christian thought. There has been a tendency in some recent scholarship to play down his influence on later Christian Platonists, and even on later pagan Neoplatonists, unduly. But it is probable that philosophical teaching in the great Platonic schools of Athens and Alexandria was hardly influenced at all, directly or indirectly, by Plotinus till, at earliest, well on in the fourth century A.D. The philosophical education received by the Cappadocian Fathers, St. Basil of Caesarea, St. Gregory of Nyssa, and St. Gregory Nazianzen, was pre-Plotinian in character; which is not to say that they did not at some time read him and were not affected by what they read.

4. The idea that the human soul is in some sense by nature divine is to be found in Vladimir Solovyev (cf. his *Lectures on Godmanhood,* English translation, London, 1948, especially lecture 8) and Nicolas Berdyaev (cf. especially Ch. 8, "Manhood," of his *The Divine and the Human,* English translation, London, 1949); and it is sometimes asserted with remarkable recklessness by Western followers of the latter. It seems, as I have remarked below, incompatible with orthodox Christianity as this has been universally understood both in East and West: but I do not think that for this reason the whole thought of either of these two great Russian thinkers about God and man can simply be dismissed from serious consideration by Christians. There are in both of them some very profound insights, partially obscured by great ambiguity and lack of clarity in thought and expression. And Berdyaev's idea of divine humanity is very remote from the static incorruptible divinity of the Plotinian soul.

5. On this see further Part III, Ch. 14, of the *Cambridge History* referred to in n. 1. A rather different view of Plotinus' doctrine of the soul, presenting it as a good deal more compatible with the Christian position, will be found in *Eudaimonia,* by Wilhelm Himmerich (*Forschungen zur neueren Philosophie und ihrer Geschichte, neue Folge XIII,* Würzburg, 1959). The following are some of the most important passages from the *Enneads* dealing with man's higher self:

I. 1[53]10, 5–15; II. 9[33]2, 5–10; III. 4[15]3, 21–27; III. 6[26]5, 13–22; VI. 4[22]14, 16–31.

6. On the Christian opposition to the Plotinian doctrine of the divinity of the soul see E. L. Fortin, *Christianisme et Culture Philosophique au 5ème Siècle* (Paris, 1959) Ch. ii; R. A. Markus and P. Sheldon-Williams in the *Cambridge History* (see n. 1).

Part V, Ch. 22 and Part VI, Ch. 28. The articles by Fr. Robert J. O'Connell referred to in the text are:

'Enneads VI, 4 and 5 in the works of St. Augustine', *Revue des Études Augustiniennes*, IX, 1–2 (1963) pp. 1–39; 'The Enneads and St. Augustine's Image of Happiness', *Vigiliae Christianae*, 17 (1963), pp. 129–64; 'The Plotinian Fall of the Soul in St. Augustine', *Traditio*, XIX (1963), pp. 1–35; 'The Riddle of Augustine's *Confessions:* a Plotinian Key', *International Philosophical Quarterly*, IV, 3 (1964), pp. 327–72. Fr. O'Connell's two books, *St. Augustine's Early Theory of Man*, A.D. *386–391* (Cambridge, Mass., 1968) and *St. Augustine's Confessions: the Odyssey of Soul* (Cambridge, Mass., 1969) now seem to me to have established his position much more convincingly.

On St. Gregory of Nyssa's doctrine of creaturely mutability, see H. Urs von Balthasar, *Présence et Pensée* (Paris, 1942) and J. Daniélou, *Platonisme et Théologie Mystique* (2nd ed., Paris, 1953). It is clearly stated in *On the Creation of Man* (*De Hominis Opificio*), Ch. 16, *PG* 44, 184. The dynamic character of Gregory's thought about created, mutable human nature is well illustrated by *Life of Moses*, II, 3, p. 32, in the edition of J. Daniélou (Sources Chrétiennes, Paris, 1955), *PG* 44, 328B. The development of this doctrine by St. Maximus the Confessor is touched on later in this lecture.

One of the finest expressions of the doctrine of creaturely mutability to be found in patristic literature is one from St. Augustine's *Confessions* (XII, Ch. 11). St. Augustine is speaking here of the angelic creation, described in terms clearly reminiscent of the Neoplatonic intelligible world, which makes the contrast with Plotinus all the clearer.

7. Augustine is probably thinking here of such passages as V 3[49]8, 22–24 and 27–31; 17, 28–38; in this late treatise this side of Plotinus' thought is very much in evidence; the first deals with the illumination of the soul by the Second Hypostasis, Intellect, the second with its illumination by the One or Good.

There is ample evidence in the *Enneads* that Plotinus is not a pantheist, that he thought of the One or Good (which corresponds in his thought to what we mean by God) as the Wholly Other, totally different from the things which he produces. Perhaps the most striking passage is in chapters 9 and 10 of the treatise *On Contemplation*, III 8[30], where we find Plotinus not simply stating that the One is the Wholly Other, but demonstrating this at some length. It is also an inadequate and misleading account of his thought to represent the production of all things from the

One as an automatic and necessary process of 'emanation': on this see my contribution to the *Cambridge History* (see n. 1), Part III, Ch. 15. And when Plotinus, in the great treatise *On Free Will and the Will of the One* (VI 8[39]) brings himself to consider seriously whether the One is free, self-positing and with something analogous to (though far transcending) what we mean by will and personality, he answers firmly that he is, and speaks about him in fully theistic language.

It is relevant to quote here Plotinus' answer to Gnostic, and orthodox Christian, accusations that Hellenic philosophers are polytheists and idolaters, the sort of accusations, in fact, which recur frequently in St. Augustine and the other Fathers. It is in the great treatise *Against the Gnostics*, which is the concluding section of a major work, split up by Porphyry for his own editorial purposes, of which III 8, referred to above, is the first part. The essential sentence is as follows:

> It is not contracting the divine into one but showing it in that multiplicity in which God himself has shown it, which is proper to those who know the power of God, inasmuch as, abiding who he is, he makes many gods, all depending upon himself and existing through him and from him. (II 9[33]9, 35–39; my own translation from Plotinus II, Loeb Classical Library, 1966.)

8.   As always in dealing with Plato, I feel some doubt whether the general statements in the text, or any general statements, are not too dogmatic and absolute. There are tensions and possible contradictions in his thought as expressed in the Dialogues on this, as on all other points. But it does seem to me that a conviction of the fallibility and peccability of the human soul is basic to Plato's moral teaching (hence some of Plotinus' difficulties) and runs through all the great myths about the soul's nature and destiny in the *Gorgias, Phaedo, Phaedrus,* and *Republic,* which are imaginative presentations of the 'Orphic-Pythagorean' doctrine of man as a being fallen from the divine world as a result of some primal sin or flaw and needing purification and remedial punishment before he can return to his proper place. An earlier writer in the same tradition, Empedocles, combines in his poem *Purifications* (καθαρμοί) the strongest possible assertion of his own divinity with a sense of personal sin unparalleled in pagan Greek philosophical literature.

9.   The doctrine of the total descent of the soul is clearly stated, in conscious opposition to the teaching of Plotinus, in the last proposition (211) of the *Elements of Theology* of Proclus (pp. 184–85

of E. R. Dodds, Proclus, *The Elements of Theology*, 2nd ed., Oxford, 1963).

Cf. Proclus, *In Parmenidem*, 134A (V p. 948, 14–20, ed. Cousin, 1864). On the doctrine of 'descending' or 'providential' *Eros* in the later Neoplatonists see my article 'Platonic *Eros* and Christian *Agapé*' in *Downside Review*, No. 255 (Spring, 1961), pp. 115–21, and John M. Rist, *Eros and Psyche* (Toronto, 1964), *Epilogue* pp. 213–20.

10.   *Deus enim deum te vult facere: non natura sicut est ille quem genuit; sed dono suo et adoptione.*

Compare, e.g., St. Irenaeus, *Against Heresies*, III. 19. 1; St. Athanasius, *Orations against the Arians*, II. 70; Roman Liturgy, Preface of the Ascension: *ut nos divinitatis suae tribueret esse participes.*

11.   There should be no need to quote passages from the Bible and the Fathers to confirm that orthodox Christians have always believed that the material world is good. On the Platonic side the basic text is, of course, the *Timaeus*. For the attitude of Plotinus to the material world see my contribution to the *Cambridge History* (n. 1), Part III, Ch. 14, pp. 230–32. A passage (II 9[33]16, 48–55) from the treatise *Against the Gnostics* illustrates the positive side of it.

On extreme dualism and hatred of the body among Christians and pagans in the later Roman Empire, see E. R. Dodds, *Pagan and Christian in an Age of Anxiety* (Cambridge, 1965), Ch. I. For some possible clues to the origin of this sort of extremism, especially in matters of sex, among orthodox Christians as well as Gnostics, see J. Daniélou, *History of Early Christian Doctrine*, Vol. I, *The Theology of Jewish Christianity* (London, 1964), pp. 369–75 (Encratism) and the criticism of Daniélou's views by R. Murray in the *Heythrop Journal*, Vol. VI, No. 4 (October 1965) pp. 412–33 (*Recent Studies in Early Symbolic Theology;* see especially pp. 424–25 on the early Syriac Church). The Evil Female Āz, the principle of desire, especially sexual desire, who appears in Iran not only in Manichaean but in classical Zurvanite Zoroastrian theology, may also possibly be relevant here. She is fully discussed by R. C. Zaehner in *The Dawn and Twilight of Zoroastrianism* (London, 1961), Part II, Ch. 10, pp. 224–33. But the whole subject of the remoter origins of these attitudes to sex in some forms of Judaism in New Testament times and in early Christianity needs considerable further research.

12.   The teaching of Augustine on sin and the body is summed up in this sentence: 'The corruption of the body, which weighs down the soul, is not the cause but the penalty of the first sin. It

was not the corruptible flesh which made the soul sinful, but the sinful soul which made the flesh corruptible' (*City of God*, XIV, 3, 4–7; my own translation).

St. Gregory of Nyssa's doctrine of the 'double creation' is fully expounded in his *De Hominis Opificio*, Chapters 16 and 17 (*PG* 44, 177–91). It had a deep and lasting influence on Greek Christian thought. St. Augustine's lengthy refutation of it occupies Ch. 21 through 24 of Book XIV of the *City of God:* cf. St. Thomas, *Summa Theologiae*, I. 98. 2. St. Thomas here follows St. Augustine closely, with the significant addition that the pleasure in sexual intercourse felt by unfallen man would have been greater, not less, than that felt by fallen man, though remaining under perfect rational control (l.c., *ad tertium*).

13. On resemblances between pagan Platonist thought about astral bodies and the Christian doctrine of the resurrection body see further my Chapter 5 of *Christian Faith and Greek Philosophy*, by A. H. Armstrong and R. A. Markus (London, 1960; paperback edition, 1964; New York, 1965) pp. 47–49.

A characteristic passage from St. Augustine's polemic against Porphyry on this point is *City of God* X, 29: cf. Plotinus II 9[33]8, 30–37. The human astral body was of little importance to Plotinus, though he believed in it. On this and on the whole history of the idea of astral bodies in Platonism see E. R. Dodds, Appendix II, 'The Astral Body in Neoplatonism' to *Proclus: The Elements of Theology* (2nd ed., Oxford, 1963).

14. H. Crouzel, *Origène et la Philosophie* (Paris, 1962), p. 215. Some important differences, as well as resemblances, between pagan and Christian Platonist other-worldliness are well brought out by P. Sheldon-Williams in Part VI of the *Cambridge History* (see n. 1) Chapters 28 'Greek Christian Platonism' and 29 'The Cappadocians'. On Platonic other-worldliness in St. Augustine, see R. A. Markus in Part V of the same work, Ch. 22, 'Augustine Man: Body and Soul'. See also my Ch. 5 of *Christian Faith and Greek Philosophy*, referred to in n. 13. St. Augustine's own criticism of certain aspects of pagan Platonic other-worldliness is based on his insistence that the origin of sin lies in the will, not in the body (see n. 12); it is concisely stated in *City of God*, XIV, 5.

15. Plotinus speaks of the universe as 'holy' in a remarkable passage of the late treatise I 8[51], which is his fullest exposition of his doctrine that matter is the principle of evil. In speaking of the presence of soul to matter (which is the cause of its 'fall' he says: 'All the place is holy (πᾶς δὲ ὁ χῶρος ἱερός), and there is nothing which is without a share of soul' (I 8[51]14, 36–37, my own translation from Plotinus I, Loeb Classical Li-

brary, 1966). The quotation is from Sophocles, *Oedipus at Colonus*, 54 (cp. 16), and if Plotinus fully remembered the context of what he was quoting, the loving celebration of the holiness of Colonus with its many deities present in their local shrines, it is a very strong affirmation of his constant belief that the material world is not only the dwelling place but the expression or manifestation of soul (admittedly on the lowest possible level of being), and therefore holy, since soul is a god. For cosmic religion in Plotinus see further the passages quoted in notes 11 and 13. His polemic against the Gnostic despising of the material world in II 9[33] and his theory of beauty (for which see I 6[1] and V 8[31]) are based on his 'sacramental' view of material things (which are good and holy, though matter is evil, because all their limited reality is form and the activity of soul).

16.   On pagan cosmic religion and the Christian opposition to it see my Chapter 4 of *Christian Faith and Greek Philosophy* (n. 13), a chapter which now seems to me to need a great deal of correcting and supplementing on the lines of the following paragraphs of this lecture. On the radical criticism by John Philoponus of the astronomical theories which were an integral part of pagan cosmic theology, see the very full treatment of this important and neglected Christian thinker in Ch. VI, 'The Unity of Heaven and Earth,' of S. Sambursky, *The Physical World of Late Antiquity* (London, 1962).

17.   The Sequence of St. Hildegarde is printed in J. S. Phillimore, *The Hundred Best Latin Hymns* (London and Glasgow, 1926), pp. 58–59.

The best expressions of this sense of the holiness of the world in Christian literature are to be found in the spiritual writings of the seventeenth-century Anglican clergyman Thomas Traherne (1637–74). There are two good recent editions of these, the two-volume *Centuries, Poems and Thanksgivings*, ed. H. M. Margoliouth (Oxford, 1958) and the one-volume *Poems, Centuries and Three Thanksgivings*, ed. Anne Ridler (Oxford, 1966). The only work of Traherne's published in his lifetime was a polemical one entitled *Roman Forgeries*—a reminder that Traherne was vigorously Protestant, like the Cambridge Platonists, to whose thought his is closely related in many ways.

On the very unexpected part which the sense of the holiness of the world, already present in the Puritan Calvinist thought of the seventeenth century, may possibly have played in the evolution of ideas in New England, see Perry Miller's essay, 'From Edwards to Emerson' (*New England Quarterly* XIII, December 1940, pp. 589–617; reprinted in *Errand into the Wilderness* (Cambridge,

Mass., 1956: paperback edition New York, 1964) pp. 184–203).
On its importance in Eastern Orthodox spirituality see Ch. V,
'L'être crée' of Vladimir Lossky's Théologie Mystique de l'Église
d'Orient (Paris, 1944: English translation, London, 1956).

18.   On St. Basil's use in the De Spiritu of the first five chapters
of Plotinus V 1[10], and particularly the famous meditation on the
activity of the world-soul in Ch. 2, see H. Dehnhard, Das Problem
der Abhängigkeit des Basilius von Plotin (Patristische Texte und
Studien 3; Berlin, 1964). The parallel passages from Basil and
Plotinus which Dehnhard prints on pp. 6–13 show clearly the way
in which Basil adapts Plotinus to Christian purposes by substituting sanctification for creative activity in the cosmos.

The strong and vivid sense of the goodness of creation at which
St. Augustine arrived when he rejected Manichaeism is well illustrated by Confessions: VII, Chs. 12 (end)–14 (beginning).

19.   For the splendid materiality of the new earth according to
St. Irenaeus, see especially his account of what the 'Elders' had
heard the Apostle John say, Against Heresies V 33.3. The idea that
even after the Resurrection and the renewal of creation we shall
need further growth and training for the final vision of God appears in two passages, V 35.1 and 2.

20.   De Hominis Opificio 22.5 (PG 44 205C; cf. Ch. 23, PG 44
212C). This passage shows clearly that the idea of cosmic redemption was present to the minds of the Cappadocians, even if it is not
very prominent in their thought; so that the thought of St. Maximus is, as he himself believed, a genuine development of the earlier
Greek patristic tradition.

21.   The latest, and so far the best, work on the thought of St.
Maximus is, Microcosm and Mediator: the Theological Anthropology of Maximus the Confessor by Lars Thunberg (Acta Semi-
narii Neotestamentici Upsaliensis XXV: Lund, 1965). This is an
admirably complete and clear presentation, amply documented,
with a full Bibliography and an interesting survey of earlier literature in the Introduction. Two good short accounts of Maximus
are to be found in Polycarp Sherwood's introduction to his translation of the Ascetic Life and the Four Centuries on Charity (Ancient Christian Writers 21: Westminster, Maryland, and London,
1955) and the chapter in the Cambridge History (see n. 1) by P.
Sheldon-Williams (Part VI, Ch. 32). St. Maximus is a verbose
and voluminous writer in his theological works, and does not lend
himself easily to quotation; modern critical editions of at least his
major theological writings, the Quaestiones ad Thalassium and the
Ambigua, are very badly needed: they are at present only available
in the two volumes of Migne's Patrologia Graeca devoted to his

works (90 and 91). Reference, however, may be made to three
passages which may do something to illustrate the breadth of his
thought, to which I have drawn attention. The first, from the *Ad
Thalassium*, on the presence of the Holy Spirit in the whole created universe and in all mankind, should be compared with the
Sequence of St. Hildegarde (see n. 17): It is *Quaestiones Ad
Thalassium*, XIV, *PG* 90, 297 B.D. The second and third passages
illustrate the importance in St. Maximus' thought of the contemplation of the created universe as the way by which man returns to
God bringing all creation with him. The counsel which Maximus
gives here was admirably followed by Traherne (see n. 17), and
in a manner appropriate to our own times by Teilhard de Chardin:
they are *Ambigua* VI, *PG* 91, 1128 C-D and *Centuries on Charity*
I, 100.

22.   The contemplative side of Teilhard's thought which links
him with St. Maximus and Traherne is illustrated by *Le Milieu
Divin* I.3 A: pp. 30–33 of the English translation (London, 1960).
There are, of course, elements of at least equal importance in the
thought of Teilhard de Chardin which it is not easy to link with
the older Christian tradition. In particular, the central importance
of the idea of evolution is not something which one can expect to
find in the ancients or in the men of the seventeenth century.
Though I do think that the thought of St. Maximus and, indeed,
of St. Augustine, leaves room for the idea in principle and that
one can thoroughly accept evolution while retaining the fundamental Platonist awareness of the transcendent and eternal behind
and beyond the world of change, in its Christian form which has
always allowed a real value to time, movement, and human history.
One point of particular importance which appears in this passage,
in which Teilhard differs from the ancient Christian Platonist tradition, is his acceptance of the deep and all-pervading influence of
the body, and through it the whole material universe, on the soul.
This separates Teilhard particularly sharply from St. Augustine,
for whom (as for Plotinus) it was axiomatic that body cannot act
on spirit since body is inferior in the hierarchy of reality and soul
is superior, and the inferior cannot act on or affect that which is
superior to it: cf. E. Gilson, *The Christian Philosophy of St. Augustine* (London, 1961), Chapters III and IV; R. A. Markus in the
Cambridge History (see n. 1), Part V, Chs. 22 and 24.

23.   The doctrine of the *massa peccatrix* or *massa perditionis*,
with its consequences, is expounded in many places in St. Augustine's anti-Pelagian works. Passages which have struck me particularly are *De Correptione et Gratia* 16 and *Contra duas epistulas
Pelagianorum* II, vii, 13–16. The essentials of it are clearly stated

in the *De Natura et Gratia* written at an early stage in the Pelagian controversy (c. A.D. 413–15), e.g., IV 4–V 5. This passage brings out clearly (and cf. VIII 9–IX 10) the important part which St. Augustine's conviction that no salvation is possible without hearing the Gospel and sacramental baptism played, at least at this early stage in the controversy, in forming his doctrine of selective predestination.

To make clear my own position, and that of the many for whom I speak, and to show the relevance of the passages referred to in n. 25 from Cudworth attacking the Calvinist conception of arbitrary omnipotence (which I do not attribute to St. Augustine, but take as drawing the logical conclusion from his doctrine of predestination), it is necessary to state plainly:

(i) That the conception of 'justice' with which St. Augustine is operating in the *De Natura et Gratia* seems to me an almost supernaturally evil one: his 'justice' is to me a fine name for an arbitrary and vindictive cruelty which is the worst of vices, not a virtue, and which only a perverse theological logic could ever have attributed to the God who is ultimate Good and Love.

(ii) That the mercy shown to some seems to me to make the cruelty to the others worse by introducing an extreme arbitrariness which no allegation of the undoubted mystery of God's dealings with men can excuse.

(iii) That the great majority of mankind would have the best of all possible reasons for wishing that the God of the anti-Pelagian treatises did not exist and for doing everything possible to produce a convincing demonstration of his non-existence.

24. The Platonic doctrine of divine goodness is summed up in the famous text of the *Timaeus* about the motive of the Demiurge in making the world: 'He was good, and one who is good is always absolutely without any sort of selfish jealousy: so since he was quite free from this he wanted everything to be as nearly as possible like himself'.

The principle that god (ὁ θεός—a generalizing, not a monotheistic singular) is always the cause of good, never of evil is clearly expounded, as the reason for rejecting poetic mythology, in *Republic* II, 379. The way in which the Christian doctrine that God is Love should go on beyond, without contradicting, the philosophical conviction that God is the Good is very well illustrated by a passage from an impressive paper by Professor H. H. Price (Professor Price is not, of course, a Platonist), 'Faith and Belief', in *Faith and the Philosophers,* ed. John Hick (London and New York, 1964), p. 5.

25. Some characteristic passages from Cudworth, to be found in *Platonism and Cartesianism in the Philosophy of Ralph Cudworth* (Bern, 1962) by Lydia Gysi, are: 'Sermon before the House of Commons' 27; 'True Intellectual System of the Universe' 203; *ibid.* 202; *ibid.* 661. For Cudworth's passionate opposition to Calvinist predestination, cf. Ch. V of the book from which these references are taken (see above).

An interesting testimony to the strength of this sort of theism in the English-speaking world of the seventeenth century is the way in which some English and American theologians of the Calvinist tradition toned down their Calvinism without formally abandoning it and went as far as they could towards meeting the sort of objections brought against Calvinism by Cudworth and other contemporary opponents by developing the scriptural idea of God's covenant with men. On this 'federal' or 'covenant' theology see Perry Miller, *The Marrow of Puritan Divinity (Publications of the Colonial Society of Massachusetts,* February 1935; reprinted with an important introduction in *Errand into the Wilderness* (Cambridge, Mass., 1956; paperback edition New York, 1964) pp. 48–98).

26. On the thought of Pelagius see G. de Plinval, *Pélage, ses écrits, sa vie et sa réforme* (Lausanne, 1943) and the excellent short account by John Ferguson, *Pelagius, A Historical and Theological Study* (Cambridge, 1956).

A passage from the *Epistola ad Demetriadem* (Migne *PL* 30, 19B) is, in the context of its period, a remarkably strong assertion of the presence of real virtue among non-Christians. It is noteworthy that Pelagius includes contemporary pagan philosophers in his praise. The letter to Demetrias was preserved, and is printed by Migne, among the letters of St. Jerome! This passage should be compared with that from St. Maximus, *Ad Thalassium,* referred to in n. 21. It is perhaps significant that Pelagius attributes to 'nature' what St. Maximus attributes to the action of the Holy Spirit.

27. Some passages from the first of the recently discovered baptismal instructions of St. John Chrysostom, which follow each other fairly closely, show the characteristic Eastern Christian juxtaposition, without any sense of incongruity, of a fully Pauline theology of grace and baptismal regeneration through the Passion of Christ with a firm assertion of man's free will and responsibility for his own destiny. It should be remembered that Eastern Christian theology, except when under strong Western influence, has no room for the idea of original guilt and generally takes a less pes-

simistic view of the consequences of the Fall than St. Augustine.
There is a good and clear summary of orthodox teaching on this
point in the *The Orthodox Church,* by Timothy Ware (London,
1963) pp. 226–30.

For passages from John Chrysostom, see Paul W. Harkins, *St.
John Chrysostom: Baptismal Instructions (Ancient Christian Writers* 31: London and Westminster, Maryland, 1963) pp. 26–30.

For the theology of the 'semi-Pelagians,' i.e., the monks of the
Marseilles region, belonging very much to the Eastern monastic
tradition, who opposed the teaching of St. Augustine on grace and
predestination and tried, not very successfully, to work out a theologically satisfactory counter-position, see John Cassian, *Colla-
tiones* III and (especially) XIII. Very good short accounts of the
theological issues involved, especially the question of God's will to
save all men, which was a central point in this controversy, will
be found in the Introduction and notes by P. de Letter, S.J., to his
translations of Prosper of Aquitaine, *The Call of All Nations* and
Defense of St. Augustine (Ancient Christian Writers 14 and 32,
London and Westminster, Maryland, 1952 and 1963). I have not
discussed or illustrated the positions of Cassian and his opponent
Prosper here, as I think their attempted solutions are not very helpful, and confuse rather than clarify the main issues.

28.   The articles on which the view of Pelagianism adopted here
is based are: J. N. L. Myres, 'Pelagius and the End of Roman Rule
in Britain,' *Journal of Roman Studies,* 50 (1960) pp. 21–36; and
J. Morris, 'Pelagian Literature,' *Journal of Theological Studies*
N.S.16 (1965) pp. 26–60. (But see now Peter Brown, 'Pelagius and
His Supporters: Aims and Environment,' *ibid.,* N.S.19, (1968) pp.
93–114, which gives very serious reasons for doubting this interpretation.)

On the social record of the Church in the Christian Empire see
the authoritative, massively documented, and to a Christian reader
extremely depressing, account by A. H. M. Jones in Ch. XXIII of
his *Later Roman Empire* (Oxford, 1964) and Ch. XXIV of his
shortened and simplified version of this great work, *The Decline of
the Ancient World* (London, 1966).

29.   The breadth of Christian vision and concern characteristic
of the Council is well illustrated by *Constitution on the Church,*
II. 16, and *Decree on the apostolate of the laity,* II. 5 and 7.

2

Action and Contemplation

ROBERT J. O'CONNELL, S.J.

The generous array of studies already devoted to this topic illustrates the various angles of approach that can be taken.[1] The particular slant intended here is philosophical: this essay would hope to bring out the philosophical underpinnings of Augustine's early evaluation of action, contemplation, and their related forms of life; to point out how his thought on the question develops in successive phases of his career; and, finally, to suggest what modifications in the original philosophic underpinning might permit his more mature insights to unfurl more freely, and speak more tellingly to contemporary man.

"Now," Augustine asks Evodius in the *De Libero Arbitrio* (II, 25), "what are we to think of wisdom itself?" Evodius' reply comes in a set of questions, for men differ in their way of answering. The soldier thinks his soldiering the wise thing to do, the merchant his money-making, the farmer his farming; the contemplative considers it the part of wisdom to abstain from all such "temporal concerns" and gives himself up to the undivided search for truth in a life of leisure; still others choose to accept the "laborious cares and duties" that come with serving their fellow men and justly ruling in human affairs, thinking they have found the part of wisdom in doing so. A final group attempts to combine these latter two positions, devoting themselves alternately to contemplation and to the service of human society. Evodius, in short, can make

This paper was written especially for this volume.

no answer to Augustine's question until he comes to some
settled opinion on what "wisdom" is.

Augustine's immediate rejoinder might at first seem equally
non-committal (II, 26), but it merely shows that he respects
Evodius' assumption that one must know "what wisdom is"
before claiming to settle the matter satisfactorily. The ensuing
paragraphs of the dialogue take up this fundamental question, accordingly, and only in paragraph II, 35 does the confident answer come. Men's differing opinions on which style
of life is wise arise from their differing ways of envisaging the
"good" whose possession, they think, will make them happy,
—and the entire intervening argument is meant to prove that
it is the possession of truth that makes men happy: the possession of a subsistent Truth-Beauty we are urged to "em-
brace," "enjoy." Then, playing on the analogy of sense-
delights, he exhorts us to make it "meat and drink," delicate
perfume for the soul, to hearken with the inner, musical ear
to its "harmonious and creative silence," to gaze with rapture
on its splendorous "light" (II, 35).

A number of features of Augustine's argument are worth
noting, but a discussion of his view on action and contemplation compels our underlining four that are typical of his early
thinking: first, the eudaemonistic cast of the whole discussion;
second, the fact that the discussion of wisdom and happiness
moves swiftly into the question of the classic forms of life
(contemplative, active, and "mixed");[2] third, that Augustine
implies that the eudaemonistic quest for happiness can be fulfilled, and even during this "mortal life," on condition that
one adopt the purely contemplative form of life; and finally,
the relationship implied between the world of sense and the
supernal world of "Truth," a relationship that invites closer
investigation.

EUDAEMONISM

First, then, the strictly eudaemonistic cast of Augustine's
thinking. The phrase Evodius uses to describe those who devote themselves to active service of their fellows is piquing:
such men involve themselves in *laboribus officiosis, quos
humanae societati deberi putant. Deberi putant:* the more
deontological sense of duty is the mainspring of their choice.

It is significant that Augustine's subsequent argumentation
ignores entirely whatever force there may be in this type of
ethical motivation; he treats the question as though justice
could be done to it by viewing such engagement in the "active
life" from the standpoint of the quest for happiness. This must
seem all the more surprising in view of the extended experi-
mentation with Stoic themes (particularly that of the *bona
voluntas* and the associated *recta vita*) he has pursued
throughout the central sections of the *De Libero Arbitrio* I,[3]
but it is typical of his early procedure. Guardini's observations in this regard are much to the point; however much he
can be defended for it, the early Augustine does not show a
keenly developed sense of "duty."[4] And as principal proponents of the active life, particularly against their Epicurean
adversaries, the Stoics found themselves compelled to appeal
strongly to man's sense of duty to his fellow man and to human society as a whole.[5]

Augustine had attempted in Book I to forge a coincidence
between "living rightly" (*recte vivere*) and "living happily"
(*beate vivere*), but the coincidence broke down before his
eyes: he is compelled to admit in the end that the former is a
"condition" of the latter, our happiness being the concomitant
at best, perhaps more probably the reward of our living
rightly.[6] This has thrown him back into the register that dominated in the Cassiciacum dialogues: the motivation for leaving
the world of action and all its "cares" in order to adopt the
contemplative "life of philosophy" will henceforth be the
eudaemonistic one of "embracing" that Truth whose possession is the soul's happiness.

CONTEMPLATION AND THE CONTEMPLATIVE LIFE

Secondly, not only Evodius, but Augustine as well, tends to
slip from the "quest of wisdom" and the happiness it brings,
to the related issue of the form of life a man should choose
to that end. Despite the "innumerable sects" whose claims
one might weigh against each other, Augustine regularly feels
the alternatives can be simplified down to three: the "active"
life of involvement with (what he terms) the "temporal concerns" of human society; the thoroughly contemplative life;
and some alternating mixture of the two. The *De Libero*

Arbitrio passages alluded to above illustrate his value judgment in the matter. But that judgment did not have to wait on the composition of this work. Something very like it was represented by the *Hortensius* that Cicero had written upon retiring from public service, to which Augustine had responded so ardently at age nineteen;[7] his response, one reads, was still alive at Milan, where he and his friends discussed the practicalities of setting up a contemplative community;[8] it can only have been further stimulated by the reading of Plotinus' *Enneads*. Porphyry relates that his master had only the highest of praise for the Roman senator Rogatianus, who had abandoned politics entirely to devote himself unreservedly to the life of philosophy.[9]

I have attempted elsewhere to argue that this was precisely the issue that brought Augustine to ask counsel of the old Simplicianus; the choice facing him bore on the "way of life" he ought to choose among those open to him in the *Catholica*.[10] Whatever one thinks of that contention, this much is clear: the style of life at the Cassiciacum retreat, and the exhortations the Dialogues contain both to his pupils there and to his patron Romanianus, strongly suggest that Augustine had at last responded to the invitation embodied in Cicero's *Hortensius*—to leave the active life of secular ambitions and temporal cares in order to devote himself to the philosophic, i.e., the contemplative pursuit of "Truth."[11] That preference for the contemplative form of life and the theoretical supports of that preference run like a golden thread through Augustine's career from beginning to end.

The establishment of the community at Thagaste, on his return to Africa, witnesses to Augustine's hope that the contemplative interlude of Cassiciacum might take more permanent form; even as a bishop, he is concerned to gather a number of companions about him to provide as much of the studious and contemplative atmosphere as his episcopal duties will permit him. The *Confessions* suggest how strongly the contemplative nostalgia still grips him: he prays God to bestow on him "a time for meditation on the hidden things" of His Law, for "on nothing else would I want those hours to flow away which I find free from the need of replenishing

my body and my mental powers and the demands of such
service as we owe to other men. . .".[12]

HAPPINESS, NOW

That final phrase, however, indicates a shift in the winds of
Augustine's thinking. For one thing, it shows him far more
sensitive than earlier to the "demands of such service as we
owe to other men." But it also points indirectly to his abandonment of a conviction—at very least a hope—that ran
through his works at Milan and Rome: that total dedication
to the contemplative form of life would result, even while the
soul (properly disposed and "exercised") was still embodied,
in an enduring state of happiness. The closing paragraphs of
the *De Ordine* already point in this direction,[13] but the description of the seventh and highest state of the soul's ascent
in the *De Quantitate Animae* leaves little doubt upon the
matter: no longer a step on the way (*gradus*), it constitutes
a genuine dwelling place (*mansio*) of enjoyment, serenity,
and eternity, at which (Augustine believes) certain "great
and incomparable souls" have arrived even during this life.[14]

"THE LOST FUTURE"

Among the theoretical supports of Augustine's fascination
with the contemplative form of life, this will be the first to
break down. Peter Brown has brilliantly isolated what were
probably the chief factors leading to this breakdown,[15] but
the timing and the dynamics of it might well deserve closer
study. This much seems clear: the years from A.D. 391 until
the composition of the *Confessions* can be designated as the
decade of the "lost future," during which the protracted experience of the continued inaccessibility of his former ideal
and strenuous reflection on the residual evil in man brought
Augustine to conceive of life much more as an extended journey (*iter*) in and through time, much less as allowing for a
vertical ascent out of time and things sensible.

One factor in the breakdown alluded to may well be this:
Augustine's earlier evaluation of the contemplative life seems
strongly indebted to the Plotinian view of man as soul,
"fallen" into the world of body, sense, and time. The decade

from A.D. 391 onward may well have brought him to face
more squarely some of the difficulties in this view. The Cassiciacum dialogues regularly stress the side of this doctrine
that incriminates body and sense.[16] But as Augustine's early
thought develops, bringing him closer to the synthesis enclosed in the *De Vera Religione* (A.D. 391), he focuses more
and more firmly on that facet of the fall-teaching which attributes the fall to the soul's having turned away from "eternity" and into "time": the soul, cleaving to God in contemplative beatitude, enjoyed a participation of God's own
eternity; but then, yielding to a "restlessness" within itself, it
became "curious" to experience the power of its own activity
upon the temporal world of sense realities. Its plunge into
the temporal is at the same time a plunge into action: the
entire restless sphere of action, then, as contrasted with the
"rest" of contemplation, is logically speaking the sphere of
the "fallen."

THE IMAGE-WORLD AND THE REAL

This is the pivotal feature of the soul's fall that is stressed
in the *De Musica*—only begun at Milan, as Augustine twice
assures us, and for the most part written at Thagaste.[17] But
another of the work's interesting features is the way it brings
out the ambiguity that until now had haunted, and still continues to haunt, Augustine's way of relating the world of
sense, action, and time, to the "higher" world of intellect,
contemplation, and eternity. We saw him playing on this relationship in the *De Libero Arbitrio*: a long *manuductio* there
contrasted the way the lower senses "appropriate" their objects of enjoyment (I can, for example, enjoy a piece of
honeycomb by taste only on condition of making it my own,
my "private" and exclusive object of taste) with the way the
higher senses (hearing, seeing) and *a fortiori* the mind leave
the object enjoyed—the melody we both can hear, the sun we
both see, the "truth" we can both understand—intact and
"common" to all.[18] One is left with the thought that an as-
cending hierarchy, rising from the privacy of taste to the
commonness of sight, runs through the world of sense itself;
it might not do, then, to draw a flat contrast between sense
as the sphere of "private" enjoyment and intellect as the op-

posed sphere of "common" beatitude. Yet the finale of *De Libero Arbitrio* II indicates that Augustine has just such a contrast in mind.[19]

Similarly, Augustine describes the contemplative beatitude he has been leading up to as the "spiritual" counterpart of the five varieties of sense-delight: the latter, he suggests, are "images" of the "true" enjoyment of contemplative bliss. But here, too, the question arises, what is the ontological status of this entire image-world? Instead of stressing the positive value of the image, Augustine seems bent on so contrasting it with the "true" that an abrupt metaphysical discontinuity sets in to separate the sense-world from the world of Truth. Correlatively, an epistemological discontinuity warrants his urging us to "turn away" from the image-world in order to lift our soul's interior gaze to the realities above.

And yet there were elements in his thinking that might have led Augustine to attenuate this *chôrismos*. If he can describe the joys of embracing Truth in terms of the joys of sense, those joys of sense must be able to reveal to the human knower—that peculiar amalgam of sense and intellect—something of the true reality of which they are an analogue. And if, as the *De Libero Arbitrio* emphasizes, all sense-reality has been created "according to number," it must be accorded the capacity to reveal to man's knowledge something, at least, of the One from Whom all number proceeds.

At first, this seems the tack Augustine is taking in the *De Musica;* indeed, a work on esthetics might be expected to attribute to sense precisely the power hitherto denied it. The technique the "Master" uses throughout the first five books of that work is that of prompting his "disciple" first to "judge" on the rightness of various poetic meters *by ear*. The ear's tutored judgment is then checked, and regularly found to correspond to the mind's purely rational judgment of the numerical structure embodied in the particular meter under consideration.[20] Sense-perception has, accordingly, been granted a kind of insightful power into the "reality-structures" looked on as ingredient in the image-world—again, pretty much what a sensitive esthetic normally requires as its epistemological corollary.

The Sixth Book of the *De Musica* then proceeds to rank

the various levels of "number" required to account for the process of musical creation and appreciation, a ranking that leads the mind progressively upward to the very "sanctuary" of number.[21] Here the question is raised: how account for the soul's "distraction" from the One it must once have blissfully contemplated? Another way of putting the same question: how comes the soul to disperse itself in the "action" of creating all these lower-order numbers in imitation of the higher and the Highest?[22] The answer comes in the imagery of the Plotinian fall of the soul, but now described as the soul's turning from the rest of contemplation to the restless spending of its powers in the world of temporal action.[23]

In the logic of this position, once again "action" must be viewed as the continuation of the very movement of fall, the realm of action by definition the realm of fallenness. And the soul's "return" should logically impose on it a flight from the world of action to the life of contemplation. Nowhere, to my knowledge, does Augustine exploit Plotinus' own (however momentary) more benign judgment on action, viewing it as the weakened soul's first steps toward contemplation.[24] Instead, his rehabilitation of action takes a definite Christian twist.

ACTION AND CHARITY

For rehabilitate it he must. His previous judgment on it has been more severe than his Christianity will permit him. In the *De Quantitate Animae,* for example, surveying the entire realm of man's artistic accomplishments, he had pronounced them "great, and entirely human,"[25] but in the very next paragraph warned us that no true value could be found there.[26] The soul is bidden to hurry upward on the vertical ascent toward its contemplative mansion. Now, however, his tune has changed. The *De Moribus* especially has forced him to grapple with the central Christian injunction of charity. And while he is able to interpret charity with respect to God in terms coherent with the Plotinian intellectual *eros,* as the *appetitus beatitatis*—again, the eudaemonistic note still dominates—the command to love the neighbor does not fit into that scheme nearly so neatly. And Augustine does not fail to see and to admit, love of neighbor can and often does involve "action" on his behalf.[27]

Here, in the *De Musica*, the "intention" or "reference" of charity that had permitted him to defend the superiority of Catholic over Manichaean morality in the *De Moribus*, authorizes him to claim that action, even the symbol-making action that logically stands condemned in his variant of the Plotinian fall into time, can be a *gradus*, a step on the road to the soul's return, if undertaken to aid the neighbor to fulfill his own desire for contemplative bliss.

Here we have come to the first stages of Augustine's elaboration of the distinction between *uti* and *frui* that he will apply throughout his later works. God alone, the object of our contemplative beatitude, is so to be pursued as to be terminally "enjoyed"; every other reality the soul must "use" in its effort to attain that end.[28] Augustine is not beyond betraying an occasional discomfort at the corollaries this distinction imposes on him: the neighbor is made an object of "use," a hard word indeed.[29] So, in a certain sense, is God![30] But so strong is the eudaemonistic cast of his thinking that he sticks with it. And the result, for our purposes, is that the whole realm of action is now consigned to the category of the "useful." It has been rehabilitated to some extent; but given the centrality of charitable action in the Christian understanding of life, one cannot help wondering if Augustine was entirely satisfied with that rehabilitation.

PERSISTENCE OF THIS VIEW

It becomes tempting to hope, therefore, that his developing *intellectus fidei* would lead Augustine to test the frank eudaemonism that until now had presided over his thought; that his patent shift from a consideration of human life as a semi-Plotinian vertical ascent to the contemplative heights to one that sees life as an extended journey in and through time—that this shift would lead him to query more deeply the anthropology of "fallen soul" that underlay his former ideal; and that all of this would bring him around to establishing the bases of a fresh evaluation of the life of charitable action in human society. The "lost future" of contemplative serenity in this life might well have dawned on him in the light of searching doubts on Plotinus' uncompromisingly spiritual notion of man's true reality.

But however inviting such hopes, they are substantially disappointed in the sequel. Aside from the exception Brown has pointed to, the philosophical underpinnings of Augustine's original evaluation of action and the life of action remain essentially intact. The *Confessions* may or may not be Augustine's autobiographical illustration of his theory of man as "fallen soul," wandering away from, then pilgrimaging back to, the contemplative happiness of its eternal beginnings;[31] though that interpretation still appeals to me, one need not adopt it totally in order to acknowledge the nostalgia for contemplative "rest," "peace," and "recollection" that still breathes through Augustine's story. And the message of the Christian "return" contained in the thirteenth Book is hard to get around: we are meant to pass from the life of active "works" on behalf of our fellow men to the higher and more perfect "wisdom" of contemplative envelopment in God.[32] The inchoate "peace" of the Cassiciacum interlude has blossomed in the vision at Ostia with Monica, and Augustine longs to bring his whole soul where the two of them had left the "first-fruits" of their spirit.[33] Surely no one will fault the unstinting devotion Augustine brought to the active service of his flock at Hippo; nor is it easy to imagine that his experience with the life of charitable concern for others left his theoretical evaluation of it entirely untouched. We shall see some indications of that further on. But the substance of his view remains intact about this time: his *Contra Faustum* portrays a man willing to heed the call to the apostolic life, and yet, with the strong hankering still upon him for the quiet life of study he must leave behind.[34]

Both the *De Trinitate* and the *De Civitate Dei*, furthermore, show Augustine reiterating the conviction of the *De Beata Vita*: that the primary task of inquiry is to discover how men are to become happy.[35] And his answer there is substantially his earlier answer: man's happiness is found in the vision of God, that alone is to be "enjoyed," all else "used" in reference to that.[36] The Romans' complaints about the *Catholica* ultimately stem from their having located the source of their happiness elsewhere than in that Heavenly

City where the lyric peace and enjoyment of contemplation will be full.[37] And the task of coming to some "understanding" of the Trinitarian faith involves the correlated task of "understanding" the image-enigma of the Trinity that man himself is. What, then, is "man"?[38] That question must be answered by the thinker's answering another: wherein does the "image" of God reside? For man essentially is that, and no more than that, wherein the image of God resides.[39] The "negative" books of the *De Trinitate* are an *exercitatio animae,* granted, but one designed to get our minds to wrestle with the job of shearing off from our habitual notion of man what, after scrutiny, reveals itself as truly excrescence and accretion: the senses, the imagination, even the "lower reason" that presides over our "action" in this journey of human life.[40] The core of man, his central reality, is soul, and contemplative soul.[41] Consequently, even the corporeal aspects of man that make him the image of Christ in the fullness of resurrection are in the last analysis foreign to man's true and essential reality. For man as incarnate, image of the fullness that is Christ risen, is image "only of the Son." The image Augustine has been gradually uncovering is man as he responds to the creative idea of the triune God Who announced the intention of making man "to *our* image and likeness," an image that is to be found only "in the spirit of the mind."[42]

In the two great masterpieces of his later life, then, the spine of Augustine's earlier anthropology remains firm: basically eudaemonist, it locates the essence of man in soul considered as contemplative mind, placing man's end in beatifying contemplation and relegating all else to the category of the "useful."

Has nothing changed? No, some accents have shifted, and the business of the present-day Augustinian should be, I want to suggest, a fine sensitivity to those shifts of accent. The anti-Origenist controversy in the West, for one thing, has forced Augustine to re-examine one of the theses that may well have brought him originally to sympathize with the Plotinian theory of the fallen soul: the thesis that the evils of our present existence, and particularly those that afflict newborn children, may point to some sin committed before "this life" in the body. This is the difficulty he throws up insistently against Jerome's confident assertion of the individual-creation theory of the soul,[43] and it is one that Jerome never saw fit to answer, one to which Augustine himself may never have found an answer that fully satisfied him. When writing the *Retractations,* he censures a number of the corollaries he once drew from the soul-fall theory in his early works;[44] he neither formally admits nor formally denies having once held that theory;[45] his last word on the question is an almost weary *nec tunc sciebam, nec adhuc scio.*[46]

Again, one might think, Augustine would certainly investigate his anthropology from the ground up. And yet, in its essential elements, the pronouncedly spiritualist view of man that had grounded his earlier conviction that the contemplative was the most consonant form of life for man persists until the end.

MAN AND THE CONTEMPLATIVE DIMENSION

Few philosophic positions are less likely to win the favor of contemporary man than such a spiritualist anthropology. And, in an age that has rightly been called the world of "total work,"[47] the contention that man is essentially a contemplative creature rings almost like a perverse paradox. Even the thinker is expected to contribute what the frequently applied label requires of him, "intellectual work." Merleau-Ponty has acutely sketched the popular attitude of distrust toward the philosopher—that incurable stranger to his fellows, able in one instant to commit himself with seeming totality to their concerns, yet liable in the next instant, his eye become suddenly vacant, to voyage as far from the world of their frenetic action as the Socrates of the *Symposium,* or the guardian of the *Republic.* How can the cave dweller even guess at the sun that so absorbs him?[48]

They are right to suspect him, still. For despite the eclipse of that spiritualist view of man that grounded Augustine's contemplative preference, a great stream of philosophical tradition still runs strong, bearing with it the ancient reminder that man is not entirely a creature of "this world," and surely not of the world of total work. There is, as Josef Pieper reminds us, more than a remnant of archaeological crankiness in the connection between "Happiness and Contemplation."[49] And the contemporary tendency to set off Christian against Greek in this regard needs much of the correction that A. H. Armstrong, for one, has recently attempted to bring to it.[50]

RETRIEVING AUGUSTINE

The suggestion I wish to end with is this: the perennial appeal of Augustine and of Augustinianisms of every stamp is due, in part, to the persistence of man's mute, half-acknowledged affinity to contemplation, and to the "other world" to which it gives him access. But the effort to restate the enduring philosophic justification of contemplative man does not require acceptance of Augustine's entire anthropology, nor of his preference for the "contemplative" as a style of life consonant with man as he saw him.

Certain features of that anthropology I have singled out above for implicit criticism. Let me now be more explicit, and (as often as not abetted by suggestions from Augustine himself) to some degree constructive. How can one who has gone to Augustine's school re-express the central thrust of his position in terms that preserve its enduring value?

First, it should be said at the outset that certain contingent features of Augustine's view might well be shorn away. He himself came to criticize the contempt for body and sense that so often surfaced in his earlier works; one cannot help thinking that the Manichaean affect of his youthful years found only too resonant an expression in certain writings of Plotinus. The shift from considering the fall as into body and sense to viewing it as a plunge into action and temporal concerns has more than merely intellectual aspects to it: it does allow for a gentler attitude toward the sensible and corporeal aspects of man's composition. And yet, it can be wondered whether, to the very end of his life, Augustine's affect toward the incarnate features of human existence was not overly pessimistic. These are hard things to establish; "optimist" and "pessimist" are vague terms, and necessarily. Yet reading those repeated returns to the theme of the misery of mortal existence in the *De Civitate Dei*, the impression is difficult to avoid.[51]

Which is not to say that cheery, genial optimisms are the

only alternative: Augustine's destruction of the Stoic's stony-faced optimism as only putting a brave face on what genuine human misery is really *there* still gives us plenty to ponder.[52] But it also suggests that his victory may have been tainted on account of the very way his times compelled him to pose the question: is the Stoic's tight-lipped sense of "duty," his thorough deontologism that makes him a Kant before the letter, the only alternative to Augustine's own eudaemonism?

The answer to that Augustine has amply illustrated, without ever having taken full systematic advantage from the discovery: alongside the yearning for happiness that makes man a creature of desires, there works at his heart the sense of reverence that makes him a creature of wonder. Rudolph Otto has orchestrated the classic statement of this in respect to the religious experience: God is encountered not only as the *fascinosum* but also as the *tremendum*.[53] But, whether or not one agrees with Pieper that all contemplation is basically religious in character,[54] the same response to the *tremendum* emerges, in various and sometimes attenuated forms, in moments of "earthly contemplation" also, before the unexpected appearance of the spring wildflower, while suddenly rediscovering the look of questioning innocence in a child's eye, when gazing into the gaze of one who, his gaze tells us, quite unaccountably loves us.

That sense of "awe and reverence," to use Plato's terms from the *Phaedrus*,[55] lies in close neighborhood to the Stoic sense of duty. It can, in its own way, ground something of the same heroic carelessness of one's own yearning for happiness as marked the ancient sage's claim that the wise man could be happy, even on the rack. But it is not quite the same thing. For while it dimly supposes what the Stoic insisted was true, that the universe was to be trusted in its workings, that "though the universe slay us still may we trust,"[56] it encloses that trust in an atmosphere that the ancient Stoic only in his most desperate moments was driven to invoke: an atmosphere rising from the recognition that the Logos must be personal and could be addressed as a "Thou."[57] Further, it makes explicit what the Greeks and Romans were only vaguely coming to thematize, that the central experience from which this conviction of a personal universe is drawn is not that of ordered hierarchy in nature, vast impersonal design, inexorable and just in its workings. Rather, the universe of the *Phaedrus'* reverential wonder is most crucially disclosed in the quite peculiar, characteristically human experience of interpersonal encounter. It was a re-examination of the love of friendship that made Plato eventually speak of *eros* as instinct with "awe and reverence." It was the same phenomenon that persuaded Aristotle to attentuate momentarily the desire-aspect of love, to acknowledge that, in perfect friendship, the other is loved "for himself."[58]

Again, one has to admit, Augustine knew something of the experience of friendship. He knew a great deal, too, of the unaccountable goodness of a God whose gracious initiatives would, if only we paid attention to them, suffuse our hearts with wondering awe. Yet, one can perhaps justify a certain impatience with the rapidity with which he regularly reduces friendship to the eudaemonistic register, allowing his system to make the friend someone (or something?) to be "used" in our quest for contemplative happiness.[59] And alongside his injunction that the catechist first try to promote in his hearer a lively sense of, and grateful wonder at, God's prevenient love for us,[60] there stands that chilling reminder —triumph of system once more—that our relationship to God is to be envisaged less as that of "friend to friend," more after the fashion of the eye's relationship to the light whereby it sees, and for which it has a natural appetite.[61]

And yet, again, the later Augustine is not beyond throwing out hint after hint as to how his successors might bring into organic relation these two poles of the interpersonal. Of the "two commandments of love" it was said that the second was "like to the first"; alongside his insistence on seeing his childhood nurses and his mother as embodiments of God's own care wrapping him around on every side,[62] there are his repeated reminders to us not to miss the "everyday miracles" of our ordinary world,[63] and the progressively accentuated view of our eternal beatitude as delighted enjoyment, not only of God, but of our communion as fulfilled in God: the first person plural of the *De Civitate*'s climactic phrase is not wholly unintentional: "we shall rest and we shall see, we shall see and we shall love, we shall love and we shall praise. . .".[64] And finally, there is the *De Trinitate*'s vital admission that some human "enjoyment" may be dwelt in, though more as "refreshment, or even lodging for the traveler" than as permanent a stopping place.[65] The concession is somewhat weakened by the prevailing eudaemonism in which it is enclosed and the linear image of journey-toward-happiness in which it is expressed; but its very presence in Augustine's work suggests he may have felt that eudaemonism and its linear images might not do adequate justice to such peculiar disclosures of the "other world" as intersubjective love affords.

To capitalize on these disclosures, then, the present-day Augustinian might be well advised to complement his master's eudaemonism or, better, transform it, with a recognition of the reverential delight, the delighted reverence, that brings the spirit to a stillness of wondering awe before the "other", and before the other precisely as "embodiment," both *in and through* which the "receptive attention of assent"[66] is granted a glimpse of the "other world."

But this in turn would require—my penultimate suggestion—that Augustine's habitual manner of relating the "other" world to "this" might also undergo recasting. Instead of regarding the world of sense-experience as image, and all too often as "merely" image, of a higher world to be contemplated by the mind that turns within and away from sense, one ought frankly to regard *human* experience as never *either* purely sensual *or* purely intellectual, but as the quite peculiar interaction with reality that it is, a mode of receptive interaction that can best be explored in the æsthetic experience that functions in what Pieper has termed "earthly contemplation."[67] Once sense has been grasped as always to some degree "intellectualized," and "intellect" in its turn grasped as man's capacity to seize upon the "inscape" of things, processes, and persons, then "this world" becomes truly "embodiment" of the other world that glimmers both in its depths and at the same time infinitely beyond it. Or, to twist a pregnant phrase of Dewey's, human experience in its most heightened form then introduces us to "a world beyond this world, which is nevertheless the deeper reality of the world in which we live in our ordinary experiences."[68]

PHENOMENOLOGICAL
PROGRAM !!

At this point, a final readjustment comes into play. Augustine regularly connects the distracting quest for sense-experience and the disquieting immersion in temporal action, associating both under the heading of *curiositas*.[69] Contemplation, then, and the contemplative life are looked upon as the effort of the mind-soul to turn away from these connected pursuits, in order to achieve the "rest" and "peace" of cleaving to the purely intelligible. A revaluation of human sense-experience brings with it, then, a corresponding revaluation of action, and particularly of those forms of action in which human experience reaches its most heightened power.[70] Of the artist's activity is Plotinus' claim most truly verified;[71] but now it can be said that it is not merely inchoate contemplation, "attenuation or complement," but if truth were told, one of the most intense and powerful forms of contemplation man can know. Further, it is the form of human activity which best permits us, perhaps, to cut through the mutual exclusiveness of Augustine's all too habitual way of posing the action-contemplation question. For action here emerges naturally from the well of inner contemplative silences; in its deployment it returns upon the source from which it emerged, to nourish and enrich it even further; and that living cycle of mutual enrichment may illustrate the ideal our contemporary world of total work is mutely questing to rediscover, the true reality that is man, a creature born to be "contemplative in action."[72]

1. See the ample bibliographical suggestions in Aimé Solignac's Introduction to *Les Confessions*, Vol. 13 of *Les Oeuvres de Saint Augustin*, Paris, 1962, p. 186, note 2. One should add: pp. 45–84 of John Burnaby's *Amor Dei: A Study of the Religion of Saint Augustine*, London, 1938; Ragnar Holte's *Béatitude et Sagesse*, Paris, 1962; and most recently, A. Mandouze, *Saint Augustin: L'Aventure de la raison et de la grace*, Paris, 1968.

2. Sr. Mary Elizabeth Mason has argued for distinguishing between the *vis contemplativa* in each individual, and the *vita contemplativa* as an exterior form of life for some individuals: Augustine's appreciation of the former should be dissociated from his evaluation of the latter. See her *Active Life and Contemplative Life*, Marquette University, Milwaukee, 1961, pp. 38–43. I remain doubtful on whether this distinction holds as much force for Augustine as for her.

3. *De Libero Arbitrio* I, 21–28.

4. Romano Guardini, *Augustine's Conversion*, Westminster, Md., 1960, p. 53. The admission occurs within an eloquent defense of Augustine's eudaemonism, pp. 47–55.

5. See E. V. Arnold, *Roman Stoicism*, Cambridge, 1911, pp. 328–29; also Max Pohlenz, *Die Stoa, Geschichte Einer Geistigen Bewegung*, Göttingen, 1948–49, I, pp. 111ss.

6. *De Libero Arbitrio* I, 30.

7. *Confessions* III, 7–8.

8. *Confessions* VI, 24.

9. *Vita Plotini*, 7.

10. *Augustine's* Confessions: *The Odyssey of Soul*, Harvard University Press, 1969, pp. 90–94.

11. *Contra Academicos* I, 4 and II, 3–9; *De Ordine* I, 5, 8, 23–24.

12. *Confessions* XI, 2–3.

13. *De Ordine* II, 51.

14. *De Quantitate Animae* 76. See also *De Sermone Domini in Monte* I, 9, where Augustine expresses his belief that the Apostles had achieved, in this life, this tranquillity of the "consummate man of perfect wisdom."

15. See his *Augustine of Hippo*, University of California Press, 1967, pp. 146–57. The chapter is entitled "The Lost Future."

16. *Labes, viscum, tenebrae, sordes,* such are the terms the Augustine of Cassiciacum feels entitled to apply to the body.

17. See *Retractationes* I, vi, *inchoaveram tantummodo* (at Milan); I, xi, 1, *deinde* (in Africa) *sex libros De Musica scripsi.*

18. *De Libero Arbitrio* II, 15–33.

19. *Ibid.* II, 53. But see II, 38 for advance warning of this.

20. *De Musica* II, 20–25; III, 16; IV, 2–3, 30–31, 37.

21. *De Musica* VI, 35.

22. *De Musica* VI, 39.

23. *De Musica* VI, 40–41. See my *St. Augustine's Early Theory of Man,* Harvard University Press, 1968, pp. 173–83.

24. *Ennead* III, 8, 4.

25. *De Quantitate Animae* 72.

26. *Ibid.* 73.

27. *De Musica* VI, 46.

28. For firm articulation of this, see *De Doctrina Christiana* I, iii, 3–v, 5. See also the treatment in Burnaby's *Amor Dei* (cited in n. 1 above) pp. 85–137.

29. *De Doctrina Christiana* I, xxii, 20.

30. *De Trinitate* X, 17.

31. See my *Augustine's* Confessions: *The Odyssey of Soul* (cited in n. 10 above).

32. *Ibid.,* pp. 164–72. The pertinent section is *Confessions* XIII, 20–32.

33. Compare *Confessions* IX, 23–26, and XI, 39.

34. *Contra Faustum* XXII, 56–60.

35. *De Trinitate* XIII, 3–11; *De Civitate* VIII, 3. See Étienne Gilson, *The Christian Philosophy of Saint Augustine,* New York, 1960, pp. 3–10.

36. *De Trinitate* I, 20–21; *De Civitate Dei* VIII, 8.

37. This I propose as a condensed summary of the *De Civitate Dei.*

38. I take it that the question "where does the image of God reside in man" amounts, for Augustine, to asking what man, in God's creative idea, essentially *is.* This is Augustine's preoccupation from Books VIII to XIV.

39. *De Trinitate* XIV, 4–14.

40. *Ibid.* XI–XIII.

41. *Ibid.* XII, 25, and XIV, 4–14.

42. *Ibid.* XIV, 24–25.

43. *Ep.* 166; note how insistently Augustine comes back to this point.

44. *Retractationes* I, 1–4, *passim.* The bulk of Augustine's criticisms of his Cassiciacum Dialogues centers about the hard words he had for our senses and our body.

45. This is not quite to say he still *held* this theory at the time of the *Retractationes*.

46. *Retractationes* I, 1, 3.

47. See Josef Pieper, *Leisure, the Basis of Culture,* New York, 1952, pp. 25–29.

48. See *In Praise of Philosophy,* Northwestern University Press, 1963, pp. 33–41; 58–64.

49. See Pieper's work under that title, Chicago, 1966.

50. See his articles in *Downside Review,* "Salvation, Plotinian and Christian" (1957), pp. 126–39; "Platonic *Eros* and Christian *Agape*" (1961), pp. 105–21; "Platonic Love" (1964), pp. 199–208. Admitting the great justice in Armstrong's remarks, I would be tempted to re-express his main point differently: instead of saying that Plato's eudaemonism admits of generous elements, I would say that Plato is too sensitive to the variety of the forms of love to remain a thorough eudaemonist.

51. *De Civitate Dei* IX, 14; XIII, 10; XIX, 4.

52. *De Trinitate* XIII, 10.

53. Rudolph Otto, *The Idea of the Holy,* New York, 1923.

54. See his pregnant remarks on "earthly contemplation" in *Happiness and Contemplation* (cited in n. 49, above), pp. 76–88.

55. *Phaedrus* 254B and E. I could wish Armstrong's treatment had brought this feature of the *Phaedrus* into more prominence.

56. John Dewey, *Experience and Nature,* New York (Dover ed.), 1958, p. 420. There is much to gain in this connection from Dewey's notion of "natural piety."

57. See Cleanthes' *Hymn to Zeus,* and for one of many examples in Epictetus, *Discourses* III, xxiv, 95–113.

58. *Nicomachean Ethics* VIII, 3–4.

59. The most glaring example of this is his treatment of friendship in the *Soliloquies* I, 7, and 17–20. But the cast of thought persists so long as the later *uti-frui* distinction operates.

60. *De Catechizandis Rudibus* I, iv, 7.

61. *De Civitate Dei,* VIII, 8.

62. *Confessions,* I, 7.

63. See, for example, *De Civitate Dei* XXII, 24.

64. *Ibid.* XXII, 30. See the growth of this theme in Augustine's insistence on the social character of the Heavenly City, XIX, 5, 13, 17, 19.

65. *De Trinitate* XI, 10. Cf. IX, 13, where Augustine permits us to "enjoy" our neighbor, but "in God."

66. Dag Hammarskjöld, *Markings,* New York, 1964, p. 122.

67. See note 54 above.

68. *Art As Experience,* New York (Capricorn ed.) 1958, p.

195. Compare the observations of Jacques Maritain in his *Creative Intuition in Art and Poetry*, New York (Meridian ed.) 1955, pp. 75–98.

69. See my *Saint Augustine's Early Theory of Man*, pp. 173–83.

70. See Augustine's speculation on this point in *De Civitate Dei* XXII, 19.

71. See note 24 above.

72. In *De Civitate Dei* XIX, 2–19, Augustine rings some fresh variations on the "mixed-life" theme; significantly, they come connected with his explicit recognition of the social character of the Heavenly City; see note 64 above.

LANGUAGE AND MEANING

3

St. Augustine on Signs

R. A. MARKUS

Many of the topics of Augustinian theology and philosophy
in which the notion of 'signs' is central have received a good
deal of attention. This is true, above all, of Augustine's sacramental theology. His definition of *sacramentum* in terms of
signum became classical. His definition of *signum* is rarely
mentioned by later writers except in the context of sacramental theology; nevertheless, the notion plays an important
part in other contexts. Chief among these is Augustine's discussion of the meanings of Scripture,[1] but the concept enters
into such diverse fields of his interests as his theory of language, his discussion of miracles, of the relation of the world
to God, and of man's way of acquiring knowledge, not least
knowledge of himself. Notwithstanding the focal interest of
the notions of sign and of meaning in Augustine's thought,
they have, so far as I know, not received treatment as such.
This essay is, therefore, an attempt to disentangle what Augustine thought about signs, in particular, about words and
meaning. At the risk of ascribing to him preoccupations which
he would scarcely have recognised, no attempt is made here
to deal with any of the applications made by Augustine of
the notion.

A survey of the relevant background of discussion, here
as in general,[2] serves to throw into relief the originality of

Reprinted from *Phronesis* 2 (1957), pp. 60–83, by permission of the
author and the publisher. I have to thank Professor A. H. Armstrong
(Liverpool) and Professor Christine Mohrmann (Nijmegen) for valuable suggestions in writing this paper.

Augustine's contribution. From Aristotle onwards, the theme
of 'signs' recurs regularly in Greek philosophy; indeed, Philodemus in his *de Signis* and Sextus Empiricus suggest that the
question of signs was one of the focal points of the Stoic-
Epicurean debate.[3] The broad terms of reference for the
debate had been set by Aristotle's discussion of arguments
ἐξ εἰκότων and ἐκ σημείων. This is the context in which
he defines σημεῖον as πρότασις ἀποδεικτικὴ ἤ ἀναγκαία
ἤ ἔνδοξος (*Anal. Prior.* II. 27. 70a7). Anything which involves in its being the being of something else, either at
the same time or before or later, is a 'sign' of that thing
or event. The classification of the types of argument from
signs which Aristotle goes on to give, and their analysis,
do not concern us here. It should be noted, however, that
this is the concept of sign which recurs in rhetorical contexts,
first in Aristotle (cf. *de Soph. Elench.* 167b9; *Rhet.* I. 1357
a32–b36), and after him in almost every ancient work on
rhetoric.[4]

Notwithstanding important variations, the Aristotelian
theory of signs as a means of inference sets the general framework for the Stoic and Epicurean treatment. In both schools,
signs are the means of inference from what is empirically
given (πρόδηλον) to what is non-apparent (ἄδηλον). The
slightly different classifications of ἄδηλα given by the two
schools, and the different kinds of inference admitted by them
as legitimate, need not detain us here,[5] as we are not concerned
with the differences of opinion about the reach of knowledge or the means of obtaining it. Stoic logic (διαλεκτική)
was defined, in one way, as the science 'about signs and
things signified' (περὶ σημαίνοντα καὶ σημαινόμενα—Diog.
Laert. vii. 62). Its definition of 'sign' as 'a proposition in
sound condition which is antecedent and revelatory of the
conclusion' (Sext. Emp. *adv. Math.* viii. 245) is cast in propositional terms[6] in accordance with the Stoic view of reason
and the metaphysical structure of the world. The latter is a
deterministic system in which things are connected by rational necessity. Events are logically connected with other
events, and the sign therefore analytically entails the thing or
event signified.[7] Hence the Stoic insistence on the intervention of a conceptual intermediary between the sign and the

thing signified in the sign-relation: a sign signifies its object in virtue of a concept which applies to the object signified (Sext. Emp. *adv. Math.* viii. 11–12).

The Epicurean theory does away with this conceptual intermediary,[8] (*ibid.*, 13), and in this denial is centred its opposition to the intellectualised character of the sign in Stoic logic. Sextus Empiricus states the divergence between the two schools as lying in the fact that one conceives signs as intellectual, the other as sensible entities (*ibid.*, 177). Accordingly, for Epicurean logic, the relation of sign to thing signified is not a logical nexus; the inference from one to the other is based on πρόληψις (Diog. Laert. x. 33–34), and this kind of mental association is likewise the source of words having fixed meanings. Simple empirical sequence is at the root of the sign-signified relation: a regular and observed sequence establishes the πρόληψις which enables an inference to be made from one to the other, and such inference is valid only where there is a possibility of verification in sense (ἐπιμαρτύρησις —cf. Sext. Emp. *adv. Math.* vii. 212–16). By this means inference can extend the bounds of knowledge beyond the limits of what is given in present sense-experience to what may be verified in the future.

The Epicurean theory of signs, which derived their meaning from πρόληψις had no difficulty in accounting for the phenomena of language as well as of naturally expressive activity such as instinctive cries of beasts and men, gesture, and their like.[9] It is not clear to what an extent the Stoic theory of signs was meant by its adherents to provide a theory of language; at any rate, Diogenes Laertius is able to call the Stoic logic (διαλεκτική), defined by Chrysippus, as he notes, as the study of signs and things signified, their 'theory of language' (ἡ περὶ φωνῆς θεωρία—vii. 62). Its inadequacy in this field—in so far as it is pressed into service to furnish a theory of language—is apparent. Thus one line of attack made on the Stoic theory of signs by Sextus Empiricus is the observation that it cannot account for instinctive and non-discursive response to and interpretation of signs, being exclusively propositional and inferential in character (*adv. Math.* viii. 269–71), and that it is therefore unsuitable for any theory of language which would take into account

behaviour of this type. For his own part, Sextus Empiricus
is quite ready to include words among 'admonitive signs'
(σημεῖα ὑπομνηστικά—*adv. Math.* viii. 289–90). These, admitted by him as a legitimate basis for inferring 'temporarily
non-apparent things' (πρὸς καιρὸν ἄδηλα), bring to mind
the thing signified on experiencing its sign, in virtue of their
regularly observed association. The 'indicative sign' (σημεῖον
ἐνδεικτικόν),[10] however, is never observed in conjunction
with the object signified—which is φύσει ἄδηλον and hence
never observed along with its sign—and cannot therefore
serve as the basis of an inference.[11] It is only this latter
kind of sign that he attacks, and as he is careful to note, his
attack leaves the kind of sign of which language consists
untouched.

This brief outline must serve as a summary of a sustained
debate, of which Augustine can have had little first-hand
knowledge. Nevertheless, it is against its background that
his theory of signs must be assessed. Although the logical
acumen brought to bear on the problems of inference from
signs by Stoic and Epicurean writers was to be eclipsed by
other interests, the general outlines of their discussion served
to define the scope of 'signs' in the scraps of theory about
them to be found in later writers, secular and ecclesiastic
alike. The definition, for instance, given by Cicero in the
context of an examination of 'probable arguments' is a direct
echo of the Aristotelian definition[12] combined with the Epicurean insistence on the need for verification: *signum est
quod sub sensum aliquem cadit et quiddam significat quod
ex ipso profecto videtur, quod aut ante fuerit aut in ipso
negotio aut post sit consecutum, et tamen indiget testimonii
et gravioris confirmationis. . .* (*de Inv.* i. 30).[13] Quintilian,
likewise, in his classification of *probationes artificiales* defines signs as one of the possible bases of inference (*Inst. Or.*
v. 9). In general it may safely be asserted that this is the
sense which *signum* and σημεῖον actually bear in the contexts where they are used. According to the particular field
of application, they can normally be translated by 'evidence',
'symptom', 'portent'[14]—a 'sign' always allows something else
to be inferred. The same general acceptance is found again
in ecclesiastical writers;[15] a notable and frequently recurring

instance is the usage of 'signs' in reference to Scriptural events seen by the writers as pointing to other events. A strand of complexity is, however, often discernible in the application of the word 'sign' to the biblical miracles. Origen, in his comment on why σημεῖον rather than τέρας is the appropriate word for these, suggests the reason why this class of instances forms no exception to the rule: οὐκ ἔστι τι παράδοξον γενόμενον ἐν τῇ Γραφῇ, ὃ μὴ ἔστι σημεῖον καὶ σύμβολον ἑτέρου παρὰ τὸ αἰσθητῶς γεγενημένον (*in Joann.* 13. 60, *PG.* 14. 521): miracles are 'signs' and not mere 'wonders' precisely because by their marvellous nature they direct the mind to their author and his meaning in bringing them about. Another passage from Origen is worth quoting, if only because it is sometimes suggested that this may have been the source of Augustine's definition of signs: *signum namque dicitur, cum per hoc quod videtur aliud aliquid indicatur . . .* (*in Rom.* 4. 2, *PG.* 14. 968).

Some of the contexts, then, in which ecclesiastical writers used the notion of signs, though radically new, were still built around the notion understood in the general sense as current from Aristotle onwards. In the typological exegesis of the Bible by St Hilary and St Ambrose—above all a formative influence on Augustine—*signum* acquired a whole range of new resonances.[16] Nonetheless, the usage still remained within the scope of the definitions we have noticed in Cicero, Quintilian, and Origen.

It will have appeared from this summary survey of Hellenistic reflection about signs and its traces in Roman rhetoric and Christian theology, that the theory of signs is conceived primarily as a theory of inference. Language is hardly mentioned in this context,[17] and when it is explicitly recognised as relevant—since words *signify* and are therefore inescapably signs—the linguistic interest is only incidental. We have noted, for instance, that when Sextus Empiricus defines words as belonging to the class of σημεῖα ὑπομνηστικά, he does so in order to forestall the objection that his rejection of σημεῖα ἐνδεικτικά would involve the rejection of verbal signs, an obvious absurdity (*adv. Math.* viii. 289–90, cf. above, pp. 63–64). Aristotle, in defining words in terms of σύμβολον (*de Int.* I. 16a), may have been concerned to avoid the term σημεῖον, already in the process of becoming a technical word in his discussion of inference; though a few lines further on he does use σημεῖον in reference to verbs (16 b7–10). In general, no one would dispute that words are signs; but for no writer is the theory of signs primarily a theory of language, nor is reflection on language carried on in terms of 'signs'.

Before Augustine, I have found only one hint of an attempt to bring the notion of 'signification' to a central place in a theory of language. It occurs in a brief suggestion made by Plotinus which might well have been known to Augustine.[18] In his discussion of the categories of being, Plotinus asks to what category do words belong. His account is a criticism of Aristotle's statement (*Categ.* VI. 4 b32–35) that since speech is measured by syllables, it is a ποσόν. Plotinus admits that it is μετρητόν, but denies that, as λόγος, it is a ποσόν. The reason he gives is that, as such, it is significant (σημαντικόν). He then goes on to suggest that from the material point of view, speech consists of the disturbance set up by the voice in the surrounding air, and therefore falls into the category of action, so that it should be defined as 'meaningful action' (ποίησις σημαντική–*Enn.* VI. 1. 5).

It is scarcely possible—and, in view of Augustine's preoccupation with language of which he tells us in the first Book of his *Confessions,* scarcely necessary—to trace back to this hint the central place he gives to language in his reflection on signs. A more powerful influence which would tend to suggest a theory of language conceived in terms of a theory of signs was, in all probability, the primacy in Augustine's interests of Scriptural 'signs'. A theory of language as a system of signs must have been tempting, since it secured the possibility of bringing under one head, that of 'signs', the two enquiries into the literal meaning and the figurative or typological sense of Scripture. At any rate, whatever the reasons, words are for Augustine, signs *par excellence,* and his theory of signs is meant to be, from the start, a theory of language as well as of other types of sign. In this consists the originality of his reflection on meaning, and its ability to focus so many of his interests.

1. THE INTERPRETING OF SIGNS: THE INTERIOR TEACHER

Augustine's first *ex professo* discussion of the meaning of signs occurs in the early *De Magistro*. This work, dated about 389, is a dialogue, genuine and historical as Augustine claims in the *Confessions*,[19] between himself and his son Adeodatus.[20]

The enquiry concerns the meaning of signs, and of spoken words in particular, which are the most common and most important sort of sign. Why do we use signs?—is Augustine's opening question. The purpose of all speaking, we are told, is 'either to teach or to remind others or ourselves' (*de Mag.* I. 1). Other apparent purposes, such as, for instance, asking questions in order to learn, can all be brought under these two heads: for in asking questions we do no more than teach other people what we want to know. But there are more serious objections to be answered, the answers to which give some hint of how wide a range of functions will be ascribed to 'reminding' and to *memoria* (which I am content, for the present purpose, to render by the word 'memory'). Thus the objection has to be met that Christ taught his disciples to pray in set forms of words, whereas God can have no need of being taught or reminded of men's needs and desires. This difficulty is solved by agreeing that Christ 'did not teach them words, but realities by means of words. Thus they were to remind themselves to whom to pray and what to pray for . . .' (*de Mag.* I. 2). With such a broad acceptance of *memoria* nothing is in the way of establishing as a conclusion to Chapter I that 'even when we merely strain our minds towards something, although we utter no sound, yet because we ponder the words themselves, we do speak within our own minds. So, too, speech is a recalling to mind, since the memory in which the words are stored, by considering them, brings to mind the realities themselves of which the words are signs' (*ibid.*). Thus speech puts before the mind what was previously either altogether absent from it, or at least not present to it in the sense of being actually thought about.

This then is the common ground from which proceeds the enquiry begun in Chapter II of what words 'signify' (*ibid.*, II. 3). The first part of the argument, extending over the following five chapters and summarised in Chapter VIII, is designed to establish, first, that signs are the indispensable means of directing the mind's attention to things, and that nothing, therefore, can be learnt without the use of signs (*ibid.*, III. 6; cf. X. 29–31). The meaning of a sign, what it 'signifies', can only be expounded and established by means of further signs, as it were by giving synonyms; by circumlocution; by pointing or gesture; or by pictorial representation. The only exceptions granted at this stage in the discussion are words standing for actions, the meaning of which can be illustrated by actually performing the actions named by the words, for instance by walking or by speaking when one is asked for the meaning of *ambulare* or *loqui*. But even this is taken back later on, when these results established in the first part of the dialogue are recapitulated in the course of the argument of the second part. Adeodatus there rightly points out that such direct illustrative performance cannot be understood as giving the meaning of a word without any sign whatsoever: for it involves that the particular bit of walking done be performed and understood precisely as signifying any instance of walking, at any speed, by anybody, for any distance, etc. (*ibid.*, X. 29). Even at this point, however, Adeodatus is inclined to except the case of teaching and of speaking, both of which, he thinks, can be directly exemplified; but Augustine induces him to take the final step: 'we have as yet found nothing which can be shown directly by itself except speech, which also signifies itself along with other things. But since speech itself consists of signs, there is still nothing that can be taught without signs' (*ibid.*, X. 30). To establish this conclusion is the main burden of the first part of the work, and the rest of this part is taken up with a bewildering and often sophistical discussion of the ways in which 'speech also signifies itself along with other things'. To mark the end of this first part of the discussion, Augustine apologises for all this seemingly childish playing with words, but defends it as a prelude intended 'to exercise the power and keenness of our minds (*vires et mentis aciem*) and so to prepare ourselves not only to be able to support, but also to love the warmth and light of the blessed life' (*ibid.*, VIII. 21). And so we pass to the second part of the dialogue which deals with signs

signifying not other signs, but things which are not themselves signs but *significabilia* as they had agreed to call
them.[21]

This part begins with the long overdue distinction between
use and mention, that is to say between, for example, 'man'
as being a noun and man as being an animal (*ibid.*, VIII. 24).
To solve the puzzles which arise from neglecting this distinction Adeodatus points out that 'the things we speak of, we
signify; and what comes forth from the mouth of the speaker
is not the reality signified but the sign by which it is signified'
(*ibid.*, VIII. 23). Neither of the speakers seem to be aware
of the relevance of this observation to the first part of the
discussion. Adeodatus goes on to deny the applicability to
words of the distinction just drawn between use and mention:
'the exception [to this rule] is when it is the signs themselves
that are signified, a class we treated of a little while ago'
(*ibid.*, VIII. 23). These exceptions apart, then, in general we
use words to talk about the things they stand for, in order to
gain and to communicate knowledge about them (*ibid.*, IX.);
and indeed, as the first part of the argument claims to have
established already, nothing can be learnt without signs, not
even things which can be directly illustrated by the teacher
(*ibid.*, X. 29–31).

What happens, then, in the course of a conversation when
a word or phrase crops up whose meaning is not understood
by one of the parties? 'Thus when I read the words *et saraballae eorum non sunt immutatae*, the word *saraballae* does
not manifest to me the reality which it signifies. If it is head
coverings of some sort that are called by this name, did I
upon hearing this learn either what a head or what coverings are? These I had known before; and my knowledge of
them was gained not when they were called such by others
but when they were seen by myself. The first time the two
syllables *caput* struck my ears, I was just as ignorant of what
they signified as when I first read *saraballae*. But when the
word *caput* was repeatedly pronounced, I discovered that it
was the word for a thing which was already most familiar to
me from sight. Before I made that discovery, this word was a
mere noise to me; but I learned that it was a sign, when I
discovered what it was a sign of. And that reality I got to

know, as I said, not from being signified to me, but by seeing
it (*non significatu sed aspectu didiceram*). Therefore, it is
the sign that is learnt from the thing rather than the thing
from the sign given' (*ibid.*, X. 33). Failure in communication, the argument runs, can only be remedied by an explanation of the word or sign which fails in its task of manifesting
the reality it signifies; but as the example of *saraballae* shows,
such explanation must ultimately reach a point at which direct
acquaintance with the *significata* of primitive words is presupposed. In the following paragraph Augustine goes on to
generalise this conclusion: 'What I am above all trying to con-
vince you of, if I can, is that we do not learn anything by
means of the signs we call words. For, on the contrary, as I
have said, we learn the meaning of the word (*vim verbi*)—
that is to say the significance that is hidden in the sound—
only after recognising the reality which it signifies; we do not
first perceive this reality by means of such signification' (*ibid.*,
X. 34). The pointing with the finger (*intentio digitis*) whereby
we establish the meaning of primitive signs, he maintains, is
not a sign of the reality pointed to, nor of the word which is
being explained by this means, but rather of the indication
(*demonstrationis*) itself. In this way it resembles the function of the adverb *ecce*. 'By means of the pointing, then, I
cannot get to know either the thing [the head], since I already
know that, nor the sign [the word *caput*] for the finger is not
pointed at that' (*ibid.* X. 34).

The conclusion that we cannot get to know the meaning
of signs without knowing the realities they stand for appears
to contradict the conclusion of the first part of the work,
namely that we require signs in order that we may get to
know things. But Augustine means both these positions to be
taken quite seriously, and indeed reiterates the conclusions
of the first part in the course of this argument. His thesis is
precisely that no knowledge can either be acquired or communicated on the basis of the account so far given: in order
that I may know the meaning of signs, I have to know, in
the last resort, the things they stand for. On the other hand,
I have to rely on the words and signs of teachers to receive
the direct experience of these things—*ut attenderem . . . id
est, ut aspectu quaererem quid viderem* (*ibid.*, X. 35). 'The

value of words, to state the most that can be said for them, consists in that they bid us look for things. These they do not display to us for our knowledge' (*ibid.*, XI. 36). Either, Augustine seems to be arguing, we get to know the meaning of words together with the things which exemplify that meaning, or we have a mere mass of unorganised experience on the one hand, and a mere series of meaningless noises on the other. The enquiry after the meaning of symbols is at the same time the enquiry into the reality they speak of: 'If we know [the meaning of words together with the things signified] we recall rather than learn; but if we do not know, we do not even recall, though perhaps we may be prompted to enquire' (*ibid.*, XI. 36). Human teachers, on the one hand, can only teach us the meanings of words and signs, and experience, on the other hand, only furnishes us with brute givenness. Only the Interior Teacher, which is Christ dwelling in the mind, can teach by at once displaying to the mind the reality to be known and providing the language for its understanding. He is the source of both the objects encountered and the light which illuminates them for our understanding. This is the teacher whose activity is presupposed by all learning. The remaining three chapters are devoted to showing that this Interior Teacher is the source of all truth and knowledge; that he is the invisible light 'which we confessedly consult in regard to visible things, that it may manifest them to us to the extent that we are able to perceive them' (*ibid.*, XI. 38).

This discussion of signs has, in Augustine's hands, by a metaphysical *tour-de-force*, become one of the buttresses of the doctrine above all associated with his name. The very purpose of the work, as he tells us at the end of his life, had been to show that 'there is no teacher to teach man knowledge but God, according to the teaching of the Gospel: "one is your master, Christ".' (*Retract.* I. 12). This is the avowed concern of the *de Magistro*—so much so, that in reviewing it in his *Retractations*, Augustine does not feel called upon even to allude to the theory of signs and meaning which, after all, does form the bulk of it. In trying to isolate and examine this theory it is, therefore, as well to be on one's guard against attributing to it an importance in itself which it would certainly not have had in Augustine's estimation. But it is his theory of signs we are considering, and if we are to do this at all, we must do so on its own merits.

Augustine concluded from the argument of the dialogue that nothing external to the mind can, in the last resort, be regarded as the source of its knowledge. Neither the crude data of experience nor the 'pointers' to it in language and gesture can give knowledge without what M. Gilson has called[22] the mind's 'irreducible spontaneity'. In the *de Magistro* Augustine is content to short-circuit an examination of what this spontaneity consists in by invoking his favourite theory in one of its forms at the crucial point. A further exploration here might have brought him face to face with the inadequacy of a theory of language conceived, as it is in this work, as running parallel to the stream of experience and alongside it, so to speak, rather than within it. There is, indeed, a hint of another view of linguistic expression even in this work, the pursuit of which might have led Augustine to question the adequacy of the picture which is implicit in the rest of the dialogue. This is the suggestion he throws out that certain signs, linguistic or gestural, might be signs of indication, not of objects signified. On this suggestion, a system of signs might contain in itself the 'pointing to' (*intentio*) its objects for which Augustine could find no place in language. But this hint is not developed because, as Augustine says *à propos* of this suggestion, he is not interested in it precisely for the reason, as he puts it, that this pointing is 'only a sign of the indication itself rather than of any things indicated' (*de Mag.* X. 34; cf. above, p. 70). The further development of such a suggestion would have broken through the barrier between signs and *significata,* the mutual externality to each other of language and experience, related only by conventional rules of 'signification'. But by invoking the interpretative activity of the Interior Teacher, Augustine was able to escape the difficulties of this view of language and felt absolved from subjecting it to further scrutiny, at any rate, for the present.

2. SYMPTOM AND SYMBOL

At the end of the *de Magistro* Augustine makes the promise that 'another time, if God wills, we shall examine the whole question of the utility of words, which, properly considered, is not small' (XIV. 46). There can be little doubt that the work in which he gives us the fulfilment of this promise is the *de Doctrina Christiana,* Books II–IV. In this work, largely written some eight years after the *de Magistro,* but not completed until thirty years later,[23] Augustine's discussion is conceived of as introductory to and part of his treatise on Scripture interpretation. The work begins with a reminder of what is already familiar from the *de Magistro:* 'All knowledge (*doctrina*) is of things or of signs; but things are learnt by means of signs. Here I call *res* primarily only such things as are not used to signify other things, like wood, stone, beast and so on; not, however, the stone on which Jacob rested his head, or the beast sacrificed by Abraham instead of his son. For these, though things, are also signs of further things' (*de Doctr. Christ.* I. 2. 2). *Res,* in other words, is what a sign signifies directly, even if this *res* should itself happen to be a sign, though in this latter case Augustine prefers not to speak of it as *res* to avoid confusion. Signs, too, he goes on to observe, are *res,* or they would be nothing; but not all *res* are signs. Thus there are things which may be treated under the heads both of *res* and of *signa* according to whether we are interested in them in their own right or in their 'signification'. Certain things, however, have little or no interest in themselves, but their whole importance lies in their being used as signs: such are above all words. This is a considerable advance on the terminology of the various types of sign and of *significabilia* agreed in the *de Magistro.*[24]

Book I is *de rebus fidem continentibus,* the rest, as we are told, *de signis* (*de Doctr. Christ.* I. 40. 44). Augustine's remarks concerning the latter are again prefaced by the warning that we are not to forget that signs, too, are things: but we are now to attend to them in their bearings on other things (*ibid.,* II. 1. 1). A sign, then, in a definition destined to become classical throughout the Middle Ages, is said to be 'a thing which, in addition to what it is perceived to be by the

senses (*praeter speciem quam ingerit sensibus*) also brings
something else to mind (*in cogitationem*)' (*ibid.*, II. 1. 1).
A sign, to paraphrase this definition in more modern language, is an element in a situation in which three terms are
related. These we may call the object or *significatum* for
which the sign stands, the sign itself, and the subject to whom
the sign stands for the object signified.[25] It may be noted in
passing that Augustine appears to be the first to have stressed
this triadic nature of the relation of 'signifying': it had been
noticed before that signs belong to the category of relation
(πρὸς τι—cf. Sext. Emp. *adv. Math.* viii. 164); but in all
previous discussions the relation of sign to *significatum* is
conceived as a straightforward dyadic relation. The Stoic
theory, admittedly, insisted on the presence of a third element
in the sign-relation, the σημαινόμενον or concept signified;
the τυγχάνον or 'object' is signified only indirectly, in so far
as this concept applies to it.[26] But no stress was laid on the
subject or interpreter *to* whom the sign means or stands for
its object.

A thing is a sign, for Augustine, precisely in so far as it
stands *for* something *to* somebody. This three-term relation
is essential to any situation in order that one element in it
should function as a sign. A sign-situation is simply a situation in which, among others, this relation obtains. Whatever
element in such a situation functions as a sign, may also be
related to other elements in the situation in a large variety of
other ways. A sign-situation presupposes some of these
simpler, two-term relations in which the sign-thing or sign-
event must stand to other things or events in order that it
may function as a sign. For instance, that smoke may be a
sign of fire, its causal dependence on fire independent of any
observer is presupposed. Likewise, in order that a noise made
by a living organism may be a sign, it must be a product of
its activity; and it has to stand in a specific relation to it if it
is to be a word with meaning. The triadic relation of 'signifying' is built upon such dyadic relations, and different types
of 'signifying' may be distinguished according to what these
presupposed two-term relations are in each case.

Augustine distinguishes two fundamental types of sign according to whether the relation of dependence is between the

sign and the object, or between the sign and the subject. The first type he calls *signa naturalia*, and defines these as things (or events) 'which from themselves make known something other than themselves without any desire on anybody's part of "signifying"; as, for instance, smoke signifies fire. For smoke is not made by someone wanting to "signify" something, but on being apprehended and noted as a thing experienced, makes known the presence of fire . . .' (*de Doctr. Christ.* II. 1. 2). As further examples of this class he refers to footprints left by an animal passed out of sight, of facial expressions registering emotions like pain or anger without the person's wishing to show his feelings, and their like. For convenience, and without begging any of the questions that this terminology may suggest, I shall call this type of sign 'symptoms'.[27] A 'symptom', on this usage, which implies a certain extension of its sense in normal usage, is anything which 'goes together with' that of which it is taken to be the sign. It may be a 'symptom' in the conventional sense, a 'portent', or 'evidence' in a more general sense; it might depend on its *significatum* as an effect on its cause, as, for instance, smoke depends on fire; it might be part of a total condition as a rash is of measles; or it might give rise to its *significatum*, as a southwesterly wind may both bring and signify rain. The sign may be contemporaneous with its *significatum*, or occur before or after it, and the sign-relation may be reversible according to circumstances and observers, and it may be more or less tenuous. But Augustine, as he says, is not concerned with this type of sign, except to distinguish it from the second type, which he calls *signa data*.

These he defines as 'signs which living organisms make to each other in order to indicate, as far as they are able, what they feel or perceive or understand. The only reason we have for "signifying", that is, for giving signs, is to bring forth (*ad depromendum*) what is going on in the mind of the sign maker and to communicate it (*ad traiciendum*) to another's mind' (*ibid.*, II. 2. 3). Here the thing or event which is the sign is the product of the sign maker's activity and owes its significance entirely to this. What it means, or more precisely, what he means by it, it means in virtue of what he is doing with it. Let us call signs of this kind 'symbols'.[28] The most

important class of 'symbols' is, of course, that of words: not
because they differ fundamentally from gesture, facial expression and other forms of expressive activity—all these are *quasi
quaedam visibilia verba* (*ibid.*, II. 3. 4)—but because words
are used solely for the purpose of 'signifying' (*ibid.*, I. 2. 2).
They are, so to speak, diaphanous and do not distract attention from what they are employed to mean by claiming attention to what they are in their own right. The sign-signified
relation is not here reversible, as it is in the case of 'symptoms,'
nor is there a causal relation between them on which an inference could be based of the occurrence of the one from the
other. On the other hand, a 'symbol' has the determinate
meaning or range of meanings which the sign maker's activity
bestows on it. These ways in which 'symbols' differ from
'symptoms' are fundamental, and must not be allowed to be
blurred by the fact that there are signs which look as if they
might belong to either one or the other class. Instances of such
signs are, as Augustine notes in this connection, sounds
whereby animals communicate to one another their desires,
their perceptions of food or danger and so forth, and also signs
like the facial expressions of a man in pain. Whether these
are to be treated in the class of 'symbols' or of 'symptoms',
that is to say, whether they are to be treated as the products of
intentional expressive activity or as involuntary reactions to
stimulus and states of feeling, this, he observes, 'is another
question and is not relevant to what we are now dealing
with' (*ibid.*, II. 2. 3).

'What we are now dealing with' is the distinction between
the two fundamentally different types of sign. The question
of fact, as to which of the two types certain doubtful cases
belong, is, admittedly, a different question. But it is surely not
as irrelevant to an enquiry into language as Augustine seems
inclined to think that something which looks so very much
like language might in fact be something *toto coelo* different.
For clearly, although human speech cannot be thought of as
a succession of signs in the sense we have called 'symptoms'
—for understanding a speaker is not diagnosing from vocal
symptoms 'what is biting him'—yet, a good deal of human
behaviour is to be understood in more or less this way; and
speech as it is actually spoken, or better, acted, in a context

of posture, facial expression, gesture, vocal colour, stress, and rhythm, involves a good deal of what looks from the outside just like 'symptoms' of feeling. Indeed, it may well be argued that the key to understanding the emergence of the more sophisticated, conventional expressive activity of articulate language is to be found in the primitive 'naturally' meaningful activity of instinctive response: the foundations of deliberate meaningful activity are laid in the growth of awareness of the nexus of feeling (or stimulus) and response and of the possibility of the response being reproduced voluntarily.[29] The two types of sign distinguished in Augustine's dichotomy describe, on the one hand, what happens when we interpret a reaction to a stimulus, and on the other what we do when we interpret, say, a message in Morse Code or a page of the *Principia Mathematica:* but is what we do when listening to human speech very much like either of these activities, or even like a mixture of the two?

Unfortunately, beyond distinguishing the two types of sign and noting their precarious margins, Augustine does not discuss the importance of these cases which may, *prima facie,* be treated as either symptomatic or symbolic in their meaning. He seems to have been content to fall back on the traditional bifurcation of meaning—'by nature' and 'by convention', although he applies this in a novel way within the framework of his theory of the two kinds of sign. The classical discussion of the question in Plato's *Cratylus* stands in the background[30]; the Stoic and Epicurean divergences on this topic were, again, a commonplace of which Augustine probably had information at second hand.[31] Having brought the two discussions, that of signs as bases of inference and that of language, under one heading, that of signs, and distinguished the two main types of them, Augustine seems not to have concerned himself further with the question whether words had their meaning φύσει or θέσει. He merely assumes that in so far as signs have their meaning φύσει, they are *signa naturalia,* and not, properly speaking, language. His unified treatment of signs of all kinds seems to have been purchased at the cost of over-simplifying the problem of linguistic meaning: the distinction between alternative foundations for meaning within language became identified, in his mind, with the distinction between linguistic and extra-linguistic meaning.

Having dismissed *signa naturalia*, Augustine is thus led to describe the meaning of *signa data* as exclusively conventional in nature. He argues, for instance, when discussing the mysterious efficacy of magical invocations, that any expression, to be meaningful, presupposes a social solidarity between users of the same language. The language they both use has meaning *non natura, sed placito et consensione significandi*, and is understood just in so far as this *societatis consensio* is accepted and shared by both speaker and hearer. No thing or event, therefore, is a 'symbol,' no expression meaningful, *nisi consensus observantis accedat;* magical invocations, to be effective, presuppose a solidarity between magician and the demons which lend magic its efficacy. 'Nor have men established conventions of using signs with determinate meanings because signs already had been meaningful (*quia iam valebant ad significationem*) but they are meaningful solely because men have in fact established the conventions for their use' (*ideo valent quia consenserunt in eas—de Doctr. Christ.* II. 24. 37). Augustine nowhere gives any indication that he is aware of the difficulties of this position, oversimplified though it is in comparison with the subtleties of Plato's or the Epicurean treatment. He likes to escape the puzzle as to how, on his view, conventions can have been established in the first place, by invoking the biblical story of the dispersion of tongues at the Tower of Babel and their re-union in the Spirit at Pentecost; and he is, for a man of his insight, astonishingly blind to the extent that communities are created by the language they speak quite as much as they create it: that communities arise where patterns of response are shared, and that possession of a common language at once fosters and is made possible by such sharing of response-patterns. But this further insight would have involved abandoning the strict dichotomy of signs proposed in the *de Doctrina Christiana*.

3. EXPRESSION AND THE WORD

There is no evidence that Augustine in fact abandoned this dichotomy. He never returns to it, but whether the reason for this is that he found it unsatisfactory or that it was merely of

no interest in the many contexts in which he was to speak of
signs throughout his work, it is impossible to say.

Although Augustine never returned to an *ex professo* treatment of signs, there are suggestions of another view of language in some of his remarks about words; and words had
been taken, both in the *de Magistro* and the *de Doctrina
Christiana,* as signs *par excellence*. In the setting of Trinitarian theology, and particularly in the course of his search for
created analogies in human activity and mental functioning
of the ineffable Trinity, Augustine uses the notion of the
'word' as a key-concept.[32] In doing so, he is, of course, drawing on the content of a rich and complex theological tradition
which cannot be outlined here. Whatever may be said about
the debt of this tradition to philosophical sources, some phases
of it bear the unmistakeable stamp of philosophical reflection.
This is true, for instance, of the use made in Christological
thinking from the second century onwards of the Stoic distinction between the λόγος προφορικός and the λόγος ἐνδιάθετος,
a distinction which is found applied in a theological context
as early as Philo. It is often very near the surface in Augustine's theological work. What, he asks, in one of his sermons
on John the Baptist, is the difference between an utterance
(*vox*) and a word (*verbum*)? '. . . A word, if it has no meaning (*rationem significantem*), is not a word. But any utterance, though it be a mere noise sounding without any meaning (*irrationabiliter perstrepat*), like the sound not of speech,
but of a cry, can still be called an utterance though it cannot
be said to be a word. . . . It is a mere crude (*informis*)
sound, which generates or induces a vibration in the ear without conveying a meaning to the understanding. A "word",
however, unless it means something, that is to say unless it
conveys something to the ear and something else to the mind,
is not said to be a word . . .' (*Sermo* 288. 3; cf. *de Trin.*
XIII. 1. 4). 'The word heard sounding outside is the sign of
the word which is luminous within, which is more appropriately called a "word". For what is brought forth by the mouth
of the body is the utterance of the word (*vox verbi*); and
though this, too, is called a "word", it is so only on account of
that which it is being used to manifest externally. . . . That
word . . . is neither brought forth in sound, nor thought in

the likeness of any sound, and need not, therefore, be of any
particular language; it precedes all the signs whereby it is
signified and is begotten by the knowledge (*scientia*) which
remains in the mind, when that knowledge is expressed (*dicitur*) as it is' (*de Trin.* XV. 11. 20). Language like this marks
a profound shift of perspective: words are not now thought
of as signs of things, or as standing for things; the *verbum
quod foris sonat* is the sign of the *verbum quod intus lucet*,
but of this latter Augustine never speaks as a sign; and yet,
this is, in his view, the 'word' most properly so called. Its
relation to 'words' as normally understood, to the significant
sounds uttered when we speak, is left somewhat obscure. Augustine likes to take this relation as an analogy for the union
of the divine Word with his human nature assumed in the
Incarnation: but the analogy is scarcely illuminating, whichever way it is intended to cast its light. In general, he thinks
of the word within as a complete and independent entity or
event, prior to any utterance in language, and embodied in
language solely for the purpose of communication. The medium in which it is embodied is a system of conventional
symbols which signify the unspoken 'word' they contain, but
are otherwise inessential to it.

The distinction between the *verbum quod foris sonat* and
the *verbum quod intus lucet* arises from the looseness of the
relation between saying and meaning. We cannot conceive
of our 'meaning' something without 'saying' something, yet
we know that the two cannot be simply identified, for we
often say what we do not mean. And yet, as Augustine's terminology itself insists, our only way of thinking of the unspoken 'word' is in terms of the ordinary words we speak and
hear. We have to think away, so to speak, what we say and
hear, and think of it sheerly as mean*ing:* we have to think
of a speech-word as it would be if it were not spoken or even
imagined as spoken. Augustine's contention, if this picture of
the movement of his dialectic is correct, is that its being embodied in speech—or any other form of 'language', gesture,
for example—is inessential to what it is, though we cannot
think of it except as a disembodied analogue of its embodiment.

A 'word', in this sense, is essentially meaningful and pre-

sents to the mind what it means, unlike a sign, which is meaningful only to an interpreter who knows the convention of its
use. Its coming into existence is the same as its being known:
'for speaking and seeing, as external, bodily, processes, are
different things; but within the mind, in thinking, the two
things are the same' (*de Trin.* XV. 10. 18). Thus thinking is,
like talking, something we do, and what we can see is what
we can say; but this does not mean, as Augustine insists in
asserting it, that our thoughts are not also a seeing when they
are true, arising from the mind's encounter with what is given
—*exortae de notitiae visionibus* (*ibid.*, 10. 18). The 'word'
which manifests the reality known is here identical with the
achieved knowledge of the reality concerned: any other
'word' would be the manifestation of something else, and no
other 'word' can manifest just this reality. This 'word' is
unique in each instance and has no synonyms. It is the place
of the mind's encounter with the object of its experience: *res
quam videndo intus dicimus* (*ibid.*, 14. 24). Augustine, of
course, with his often tenuous hold on the sense-bound nature
of our minds, did not think of this *verbum cordis* as necessarily some sensuous form or sound—or, we might add, tactual
sensum, bearing in mind Helen Keller's case—created or seen
as significant. He appears, on the whole, to have thought of
it as a purely mental but nevertheless 'solid' product of our
interior activity in thinking, which we could catch ourselves
producing in the process of achieving knowledge. The knowledge achieved is the interior expression of the 'word'; but
spoken utterance is merely 'putting the means furnished by
the voice or by any other corporeal sign at the service of the
word within' (*de Trin.* IX. 7. 12), for purposes of communication. The 'word' itself is independent, not only of sound,
but even of an imagined vocal schema (cf. *ibid.*, XV. 14. 24;
12. 22, etc.).

Augustine's theory of the 'word' approaches language from
the side of the speaker, unlike the sign-theories of the *de
Magistro* and the *de Doctrina Christiana*. The latter are theories of meaning for the spectator and the interpreter, and
prima facie plausible only so long as we keep to that model.
They do not claim to describe what the speaker or thinker is
doing when he is using words or engaging in any other form

of symbolising activity, however rudimentary this may be. When one is using words, images, gestures, etc., in thinking and expressing what one thinks—to oneself or to others—one is not only listening to or looking at them; one is using them precisely to focus, canalise, and give form to one's thinking, often in ways quite startling to oneself. There are not two separate activities here, a process we may call 'creative' and a subsequent one of 'translation', but just one process which we may call 'expressive'. Unlike the sign-theories already discussed, Augustine's theory of the 'word' recognises the 'creative' aspect of symbol making, even though it fixes a gulf between it and its concrete embodiment. The sign-theories, though not dwelt on in this context, do not appear to be superseded, because they can be invoked to account for understanding the sensuous embodiment of the symbol. The reason for Augustine's having two theories of language, one for the *verbum vocis,* approaching it from the hearer's side, and one for the *verbum mentis,* approaching it from the speaker's and thinker's side, is to be sought in his bifurcation of the two *verba.* Had he thought of the *verbum mentis* as a sensuous reality endowed with meaning, or to put this in an equivalent way, of the *verbum vocis* as not a 'mere' symbol correlated with its meaning by conventional rules, then he would have been in a position to close this gap. For as the speaker can also hear the product of his own expressive activity, no special theory is required to account for what the listener does. He does the same thing as the speaker, only where the speaker creates his expressive sensuous form, the hearer has it furnished him by the speaker. It is meaningful or 'language' for him in so far as he can re-enact with its help the speaker's expressive activity embodied in it. Understanding language— if one may use this word in so wide a sense as to include all forms of expressive activity from gesture to art—is no more a matter of interpreting to oneself noises heard or shapes seen than speaking is a matter of translating into a 'language' for the benefit of others what, for oneself, has a prior non-linguistic existence.

To give anything like an adequate account of the *verbum mentis* would take us too far afield into Augustine's profoundly interesting trinitarian psychology. Such a task is still further complicated by the fact that, in his account, a 'word' is begotten by the knower from the known at every level where we can speak of 'knowledge' in any sense. Thus in tracing a trinity in the *homo exterior,* he will detect a 'word' begotten in the encounter of sense-organ and sensum (cf. *de Trin.* XI. 2. 2–3; IX. 11. 16); again, in the generation of a *species* in the mind (*memoria*) derived from that in sense, when it attends to the latter (*ibid.,* XI. 8. 13–15); and, finally, in the generation of a *species* in *contuitu cogitantis,* in the explicit and occurrent awareness of a thing remembered in the act of thinking (*ibid.,* XI. 9. 16). At each stage of this progression inwards a 'word' is begotten in the encounter of the 'faculty of knowledge' concerned with the *species* of its object, the encounter resulting from the will's application of the activity to its object.[33]

The *verbum* 'expressed' by the mind from the *species* of the object known contained in the *memoria* and 'impressed' on this by the object—to follow Augustine's most usual way of speaking[34]—is 'true' in so far as it is a recreation in the mind's actual awareness of the *species* known in the object (cf. *ibid.,* XV. 10. 17; XV. 15. 24). The question—to be asked time and again by Augustine's readers who confront him with an Aristotelian terminology—whether he was thinking of the process of conceiving or of judging as giving rise to the *verbum,* whether, that is to say, this is the expression of a concept or of a true judgement, does not seem to have arisen for Augustine. At the lower end of the scale, *verbum* seems to be something very like the expression of a concept; but the further we penetrate into the mind, the more we find the rôle of judgement predominant in Augustine's account. But it would be mistaken to identify the Aristotelian notion of judgement with the Augustinian *desuper judicium veritatis* (*ibid.,* IX. 6. 10; cf. VIII. 6. 9), in the light of which images and concepts in the mind become material for its judgement. Whereas the former is essentially a logician's or epistemologist's notion, the latter is persistently close to an eschatological perspective. It is often spoken of in a way which suggests that judging involves a judgement of the mind on itself *in specie sempiternae rationis* (*ibid.,* X. 2. 4), on its implication with and submersion among the objects of its daily occupations—since the mind gives to its concepts and images *quiddam substantiae suae* (*ibid.*, X. 5. 7). The mind's judging manifests a dimension of freedom it has over its self-identification with the material images which solicit its care and threaten to engulf it. Judgement is the mind's return to itself from such 'estrangement'[35] incurred by its captivity to the sphere of its practical engagements, to the things to which 'it is stuck by the glue of its attachments' (*curae glutino inhaeserit—de Trin.* X. 5. 7–8. 11; cf. *de Vera Rel.* 29. 52–31. 58). Since, for Augustine, truth is ultimately attainable only *in ratione sempiternae veritatis* and by means of its illumination of the mind, the *verbum mentis* is above all a product of the judgement on the material presented by sense, imagination and memory in its light. 'In this eternal truth, which is the origin of all temporal things, we behold by a perception of the mind (*visu mentis*) the pattern which governs our being and our activities, whether within ourselves or in regard to other things, according to the rule of truth and of right reason; and from it we derive a true knowledge of things which we possess, as it were, in the form of a word conceived by an interior utterance . . .' (*de Trin.* IX. 7. 12).

A great distance separates this from the superficially very similar teaching of the *de Magistro*. There, words were treated as signs, that is, as sensuous things or events endowed with meaning. The rôle assigned to the Interior Teacher was to decipher the signs which, without the light derived from this source, would remain a mere *res*, meaningless and opaque. In the *de Trinitate*, however, the *verbum mentis* is not a sign, because it is not a sensuous reality, and Augustine does not appear to have revised his definition of signs which requires that they be perceived by sense.[36] Here the light of the eternal truth dwelling in the mind does not shine upon the 'word' as upon something opaque and meaningless without its illumination. The 'word', in so far as it is anything at all, is meaningful; this illumination is required not to confer upon the 'word' its meaning, but rather to generate a *verbum* of a thing in so far as it is discerned and evaluated in this light. The light is, so to speak, constitutive of the *verbum* begotten in it, whereas the work of the Interior Teacher is confined to interpreting words already constituted, independently of his activity. Where the Teacher interprets the meaning of signs, illumination as here conceived creates the significance with which it endows its objects. Augustine would probably not have seen in his abandoning his earlier mode of speaking a change of view. No conviction had for him a compelling force comparable to that of his vision of the truth known to him as being imparted to him by God, speaking through his Scriptures or his creatures from without, and through his own mind from within. In Augustine's contemplation of this mystery, words and thoughts were bound to converge in pointing towards the one ineffable source of light: what mattered to him is what they were pointing at, even if they happened to be pointing there from many different places and directions. He is much more concerned with the Interior Teacher dwelling in the mind and teaching within than with the external signs which he deciphers for us; and he is much more interested in his identity with the Word 'whose participation is our illumination, the Word who is the life which is the light of men' (*de Trin.* IV. 2. 4), than he is in the difference between the signs and words interpreted by the one and the 'words' begotten in the light of the other.

APPENDIX: NOTE ON TERMINOLOGY

The correlations of terminology noted here are given merely to avoid some of the opportunities for misunderstanding. No adequate correlation can be provided without at least some account of the theories of meaning of which the terminology forms a part.

1. *Sign* (*Representamen*)—*Object*—*Subject* (*Interpretant*): This is Peirce's terminology, and it coincides closely with Augustine's. Peirce's definition of 'sign' is equally close to that given by Augustine: 'A sign or representamen is something which stands to somebody for something in some respect or capacity' (Buchler, *The Philosophy of Peirce,* London, 1940, p. 99). Modern definitions known to me are all variants of this.

2. *Symbol:* Peirce distinguishes, in the second of his three trichotomies of signs ('according as the relation of the sign to its object consists in the sign having some character in itself, or in some existential relation to its object, or in its relation to an interpretant'—*loc. cit.,* p. 101) what he calls Icons, Indexes, and Symbols. A 'symbol' in his terminology denotes roughly the same sort of sign as Augustine's *signa data:* 'A symbol is a sign which refers to an object that it denotes by virtue of a law, usually an association of general ideas, which operates to cause the symbol to be interpreted as referring to that object' (*loc. cit.* p. 102). Similar, though more narrowly restricted, is the sense given to 'symbol' by Collingwood; on the other hand, he regards symbolism as only one element in expressive language, one which arises as a result of its progressive 'intellectualisation' (Cf. *The Principles of Art,* Oxford, 1938, Chapter XI). A still more restricted sense is assigned to 'symbol' by Professor Ryle such that signs like ⊃ for 'implies', √ for 'square root of', etc., are typical examples of symbols (Cf. the symposium on *Thinking and Language, Arist. Soc. Suppl.* XXV. 1951, pp. 71–72). Professor Price distinguishes from this restricted sense of 'symbol' an extended sense which he allows as legitimate. This latter includes words, phrases, sentences, gestures, diagrams, etc. (*Thinking and Experience,* London, 1953, pp. 143–47). A symbol is defined in a similar sense by Susan Stebbing as 'a sign consciously designed to stand for something' (*A Modern Introduction to Logic,* London, 1930, p. 11). Her further division of these into 'natural' and 'conventional' does not concern us, except to note that the former do not correspond to Augustine's *signa naturalia,* but would be a sub-class of his *signa data.* The distinction has been severely, and I think rightly criticised by

Price (*op. cit.*, Chap. VI). For Mrs. Langer, a 'symbol' includes all the wider meaning which, following Collingwood, I have sometimes spoken of as 'expressive' form. ('Symbols are not proxy for their objects, but are vehicles for the conception of objects'— *Philosophy in a New Key*, 2nd ed., Oxford, 1951, pp. 60–61.) Augustine's definition of *signa data* seems to be intended for 'symbols' in this wide sense; but his account of meaning by convention seems in effect to restrict them to the kinds of sign referred to as 'symbols' by Ryle and Collingwood, and distinguished as 'symbols' in a narrower sense by Price. Masure notes the fluidity of meaning and overtones associated with the words 'sign' and 'symbol' (*op. cit.*, p. 18).

3. *Symptom*: this corresponds fairly accurately to Peirce's 'Index', which he defines as a sign 'which refers to the object it denotes by virtue of being really affected by that object' (*loc. cit.*, p. 102). This is the sense which Price gives to 'sign', which he contrasts with 'symbol' (*op. cit.*, chapters IV–V). This is also equivalent to Mrs. Langer's usage of 'sign' (*op. cit.*, p. 57), though, following a usage of Charles Morris, she suggests in her Preface to the second edition 'signal' as an alternative, precisely with the intention to leave 'sign' free to mean, as in Augustine's and Peirce's terminology, 'any vehicle of meaning, signal or symbol . . .' (*op. cit.*, p. viii). She restricts 'symptom' to mean a sign (signal) which is part of the total condition which it signifies (*op. cit.* p. 57, n. 4).

4. An 'Icon', for Peirce, 'is a sign which refers to the object that it denotes merely by virtue of characters of its own . . .' (*loc. cit.* p. 102). A good case could, I think, be made out in favour of Augustine's dichotomy as against Peirce's trichotomy; but we must merely note here that for Augustine any sign must have *similitudo* in some sense to its object; but as the *similitudo* required is so vague and of such diverse types, it is not, as he notes, sufficient to constitute a foundation for a sign-relation, but requires, in addition, one or other of the relations to object or subject for 'significance' (cf. *de Doctr. Christ.* II. 25. 38). It should be noted, however, that for Peirce, too, some sort of Icon is involved in every Index and some sort of Index in every Symbol.

A *similitudo* of special importance for Augustine may be noted here, which he calls *imago* (and *vestigium*: how these two are distinguished is not relevant here—cf. *de Trin.* VI. 10. 11; IX. 11. 16; XI. 1. 1). This is a *similitudo* which, in addition to likeness, involves some form of existential dependence on an original. Thus, for instance, the reflection of a face in a mirror is an *imago* of the face, but not *vice versa*, although the likeness holds both ways (*de div. quaest. LXXXIII.*, Q. 74). This relation of dependence would make *imago* and *vestigium* classifiable under the heading of *signa naturalia*.

1. H.-M. Féret, O.P., has, I think, established that it was from this field that Augustine came to see the possibilities of a sacramental theology formulated in terms of *signum*. Cf. Res *dans la langue théologique de saint Augustin*, in *Rev. des sciences phil. et théol.*, 29. 1940. pp. 218–43.

2. Cf. H.-I. Marrou, *Saint Augustin et la fin de la culture antique*, Paris, 1938.

3. For a general account, cf. P. H. and E. A. de Lacy, *Philodemus: on methods of inference*, Philadelphia, 1941, especially pp. 157–78; E. A. de Lacy, *Meaning and methodology in Hellenistic philosophy*, in *Phil. Rev.* 47. 1938, pp. 390–409; and P. H. de Lacy, *The Epicurean analysis of language*, in *American Journal of Philology*, 60, 1939, pp. 85–92.

4. Cf. P. H. and E. A. de Lacy, *Philodemus . . .* , p. 133.

5. Cf. Sext. Emp. *adv. Math.* viii. 145–47 and 316–24; Philod. *de Signis*, frag. 4.

6. A sign has the form 'If *p* then *q*'; cf. Sext. Emp. *adv. Math.* viii. 276.

7. Cf. Sext. Emp. *Pyrrh. Hyp.* B. 111–13.

8. Philodemus criticises an ambiguity in the Stoics' usage of 'sign', which, he says, they use to mean the appearance from which an inference is made as well as to mean the inference itself (*de Signis* col. 36). It is easy to see how the Stoic location of the sign-signified relation on the conceptual level could lead to this ambiguity.

9. Cf. Diog. Laert. x. 75–76; Lucret. *de Rer. Nat.* v. 1028 ff.

10. Which ἄντικρυς ἐκ τῆς ἰδίας φύσεως καὶ κατασκευῆς μόνον οὐχὶ φωνὴν ἀφιὲν λέγεται [by the Stoics] σημαίνειν τὸ οὗ ἐστὶν ἐνδεικτικόν. *ibid.*, 154.

11. For this discussion, cf. *adv. Math.*, viii. 145–58.

12. Cf. above, p. 62.

13. On Cicero's attitude to the Epicurean Philodemus, cf. J. F. d'Alton, *Roman literary theory*, London, 1931, p. 160.

14. Cf. Cicero, *de Div., passim.;* (the reference in I. 3. 6 to Zeno's lost work περὶ Σημείων may be either to a work on divination or to a logical treatise.); Stob. *Ecl.* II. 122, 238; Macrob. *Comm. in Somn.* I. xxix. 27 & *Saturn.* xvii. 3; Plotinus, *Enn.* II. 3. 3, 10; II. 9. 13; III. 1. 5; III. 3. 1. etc.

15. Cf. I Clem. 12. 7; *Did.* 16. 6; Clem. Al. *Strom.* 8. 6, *PG.* 9. 585C; Basil, *Ep.* 260, 8, *PG.* 32. 965B, etc.

16. For a discussion of the terminology of typology, cf. J.-P. Brisson's introduction to his edition of the *Tractatus Mysteriorum* attributed to St Hilary, in *Sources Chrétiennes,* Paris, 1947.

17. We shall have to return to a discussion of language in pre-Augustinian writers in another context; cf. below, p. 77.

18. Cf. P. Henry, S.J., *Plotin et l'Occident,* Paris, 1934, pp. 55, 228–29; although there appear to be no direct allusions to this treatise in Augustine, it was well known to Victorinus.

19. *Conf.* IX. 6. 14.

20. The date of the conversation appears to be about a year after their conversion, so Adeodatus must have been about sixteen at the time. *Horrori mihi erat illud ingenium*—Augustine exclaims in the *Confessions,* writing of Adeodatus's precocious intellectual power; and indeed, it is difficult, in reading the record of this conversation, not to take Adeodatus's side time and again in his refusal to acquiesce in some of his father's more palpable sophistries.

21. *ea quae signis significari possunt et signa non sunt . . . ibid.,* IV. 8.

22. *Introduction à l'étude de Saint Augustin,* Paris, 1929, p. 93.

23. Written in 397 as far as III. 25.35, though the present text may be a revision carried out by Augustine in 427, when the rest of Book III and Book IV were added.

24. Cf. above, n. 21.

25. This paraphrase displays the substantial identity of Augustine's with some modern definitions. Cf. Appendix: Note on terminology, below, pp. 86–88.

26. Cf. above, p. 62.

27. Cf. Appendix.

28. Cf. Appendix.

29. This position is argued at length by Canon E. Masure in *Le signe—passage du visible à l'invisible,* Paris, 1954, a work which is truly Augustinian at least in the scope it ascribes to the notion of 'sign'. On the emergence of deliberate from instinctively meaningful activity, cf. particularly Chapters 5–9. It is instructive to re-read Augustine's account of the process of learning to speak in Book I of the *Confessions,* in the light of Masure's suggestions.

30. This statement needs qualification: the *Cratylus* is concerned with the relation of language to thought, and in asking whether words are related to their objects φύσει or κατὰ συνθήκην, Plato raises a metaphysical question. Epicurus, however, traces two chronologically distinct stages in the emergence of language (Diog. Laert. X. 75–76): in the more primitive stage, utterance is the natural response to πάθη and φαντάσματα impinging on awareness; from this, the need for inter-tribal communication led

to the emergence of conventional language. Lucretius stresses the first stage of this process almost exclusively, though his interest is also in the continuity of significance φύσει and θέσει (cf. *de Rer. Nat.* v. 1028 ff). Bailey traces the history of Epicurean thought on this topic and indicates the existence of divergence on both sides of the central Epicurean position. Cf. *The Greek atomists and Epicurus,* Oxford, 1928, p. 382. On the different perspectives of the Platonic and Epicurean discussions, Cf. C. Giussani, *La questione del linguaggio secondo Platone e secondo Epicuro,* in *Mem. R. Ist. Lombardo di Scienze e Lettere, Cl. di Lettere, Scienze storiche e morali,* 20. 1899. 3rd Ser. 11, pp. 103–41.

31.   Cf. Cicero's discussion whether words mean *natura* or *tractatione, Part. Or.* V. 16–17; summary accounts of the debate are also given in Clem. Al. *Strom.* I. 143. 6; Origen, *c.Cels.* I. 24 and V. 45. The commonplace nature of the discussion is strongly implied in Aulus Gellius, *Noct. Att.* X. 24.

32.   Its use, however, is not exclusively confined to such discussions: cf. *Sermo* 288, 3–4; *in Joann. Ev. Tract.* I. 8 and *de Cat. Rud.* 2. 3.

33.   Cf. *ibid.,* XI. 8. 14–15 and XI. 3. 6–4. 7; *acies cogitantis* as Gilson notes, seems almost to amount to a 'faculty' for Augustine. Cf. *op. cit.,* p. 277, n. 2.

34.   Cf. *ibid.,* IX. 10. 15–11. 16; XI. 2. 3; XI. 4. 7; XI. 8. 13.

35.   On this *alienatio,* cf. *de Trin.* XI. 5. 9 and *Retract.* II. 15. 2.

36.   *de Doct. Christ.* II. 1. 1; cf. above, p. 73.

4

The Theory of Signs in St. Augustine's
De Doctrina Christiana

B. DARRELL JACKSON

Augustine describes the subject matter of Books Two and
Three of *De doctrina christiana* by the phrases *'doctrina
signorum'* and *'de signis'*.[1] In these two books he is concerned with the second part of the principles for understanding Scripture (I. I, 1, 2). The first part, which comprises Book
One of the treatise, he calls *'de rebus'* (I. II. 2, 17). There Augustine summarizes the main doctrines of the faith and concludes that the primary principle by which interpretation of
Scripture should be guided is the building of love of God
and neighbor.[2] In Books Two and Three he moves on from
this general principle to more specific advice for handling the
difficulties encountered in Scriptural exegesis. But before taking up these difficulties he states, in a few short paragraphs
(II. I. 1–IV. 5), a theory of signs. Although this theory was
proposed for a definite use and not for its own sake, it is
nevertheless intrinsically interesting. Moreover, Augustine's
use of this theory can be fully appreciated only if the theory
itself is clearly understood. In this article I shall, therefore,
interpret the theory of signs in *De doctrina* II. 1–5 apart from
Augustine's application of it.

First, I shall carefully analyze the text. For clarification
and amplification of certain difficult and important points I
shall refer to other parts of *De doctrina,* some of Augustine's
other writings, and selected Latin writers. Two of Augustine's

Revue des études augustiniennes, 15 (1969), pp. 9–49. Reprinted, with
slight alterations, by permission of the author and Father G. Follet,
editor.

early works will be most important—*De dialectica,* written in
Milan while he was awaiting baptism in 387,[3] and *De magistro,* written two years later. Of his later writings, *De Trinitate* will be useful. On the basis of this textual analysis I shall
formulate Augustine's theory of signs.

Then I shall move to a wider context. First, the possible
background for Augustine's theory will be considered. The
conclusion will be that only in logic were signs treated in the
manner of Augustine's treatment. To establish the extent of
Augustine's contact with the logical tradition I shall, in the
second place, examine what he knows and professes to know
about logic. With this as a basis I shall then compare Augustine's theory of signs with the semantics of the two great logical systems of antiquity—the Aristotelian and the Stoic. My
aim is not just to establish possible sources, but primarily
to clarify Augustine's position.

Several scholars have dealt with the issues which I shall be
considering. R. A. Markus[4] and K. Kuypers[5] have examined
Augustine's theory of signs. H. I. Marrou has looked at Augustine's logic.[6] Several writers have studied Augustine's relation to Stoic logic, especially with reference to *De dialectica.*[7]
I find myself in only partial agreement with most of these
authors. At some points their analysis of Augustine's logic
and of Stoic logic lacks both historical accuracy and technical precision.

A.—THE THEORY OF SIGNS IN *De doctrina christiana* II.
I. 1–IV. 5.

1. *The definition of 'signum'* (I. II. 2 and II. I. 1)

   Augustine twice defines *'signum'* in *De doctrina:*
   Definition 1—"Signs are things which are used to signify
      something (. . . *signa, res . . . quae ad significandum
      aliquid adhibentur.* I. II. 2, 11 f.)."
   Definition 2—"A sign is a thing which causes us to think
      of something beyond the impression the thing itself
      makes upon the senses (*Signum est enim res praeter
      speciem, quam ingerit sensibus, aliud aliquid ex se
      faciens in cogitationem uenire,* . . . II. I. 1, 5–7)".[8]

Both definitions are general. The second is more elaborate
than the first. Both say (a) that a sign is a *res* and (b) that
it bears a certain relation to something else (*aliud aliquid*).
I shall consider each of these points.

A sign is a *res*. In Book One Augustine gives two meanings
to the term '*res*'. First, it refers properly to that which is not
used to signify something else (*quae non ad significandum
aliquid adhibentur*, I. II. 2, 2 f.), such as wood, stone, cattle,
and so on. Second, it refers improperly to anything whatsoever that is (I infer this from '*quod enim nulla res est, om-
nino nihil est*', 13f.).[9] Anything not a *res* in the improper
sense is nothing at all. In this latter sense '*res*' may be applied
to such things as words and the stone which Jacob slept on,
which in addition to *being* something also *signify* something
(4–10). Clearly a sign, like everything else that exists, is a *res*
in this second and improper sense, for it must be if it is to
signify. But a sign is a *res* only in the improper sense, for in
addition to existing it signifies.

A sign is a *res* or thing which bears a certain relation to
other things. Augustine says that things are learned by signs
(*res per signa discuntur*, I. II. 2, 1 f.). It would appear that
his term for the relation of signs to things is 'signify'. So we
have:

(1) things learned by signs, and

(2) signs signifying things.

The second relation must, however, be inferred, for in the
two defining chapters Augustine never says that signs signify
res. Rather he uses the vague terms '*aliquid*' and '*aliud aliquid*'.
In this he is similar to Cicero, who uses '*quiddam*' in his definition.[10] Quintilian, on the other hand, does speak of *alia res*
which are understood by signs.[11] The reason the second relation can be inferred with *res* as the second term is that what
is signified, the 'something else', must be a *res* in at least the
improper sense if it is to be anything at all. In *De doctrina*
Augustine does not investigate further the logical qualities of
this relation. In *De magistro* he had established that the relation of signifying can be reciprocal and reflexive, but it need
not be.[12]

No more can be said about the something signified from
these two chapters (I. II and II. I. 1), except that all the ex-

amples given are of the signification of rather concrete things: an animal by a track, a fire by smoke, emotion by a voice, advance or retreat by a trumpet (II. I. 1, 7–11). More can be said, however, about the relation of signifying itself. Definition 2 includes specification of the mechanism of signifying. Although it does not use the word *'significare'*, it follows immediately upon Augustine's statement that he will now consider signs not as they are but as they signify (I. 1, 3–5).

This mechanism has two stages: (1) the sign is known as an impression upon the senses, and (2) causes something else to come into thinking. These two stages or aspects are duplicated by the definition given in *De dialectica:*

> A sign is something that is (1) itself sensed and which (2) indicates something beyond itself to the mind (*Signum est et quod se ipsum sensui, et praeter se aliquid animo ostendit.* v. 9–10).[13]

The only difference is a trivial one. In *De dialectica* Augustine names the mind, whereas in *De doctrina* he names what the mind does, namely, thinking (*cogitatio*). Quintilian speaks in the latter way when he says that a σημεῖον is that by which another thing is understood (*intelligitur*, V. IX. 9). Cicero's definition, on the other hand, is less anthropological in reference to the second stage, but is the same as Augustine's in the first.

> A sign is something (1) apprehended by one of the senses which (2) signifies something that is seen to follow from it. (*Signum est quod sub sensum aliquem cadit et quiddam significat quod ex ipso profectum uidetur, . . . De inu.* I. XXX. 48).[14]

Because of the generality of all of these definitions, I hesitate to call them 'anthropological'. Indeed Augustine even speaks of the apprehension of signs by animals. (II. II. 3, 9 ff.) Terms like *'cogitatio'* and *'animus'* are, nevertheless, primarily anthropological terms. This should be expected, for Augustine's topic in Books Two and Three is a certain kind of signs in so far as *men* are concerned with it (II. 3, 6–7). In any case, in addition to (1) the sign and (2) what is signified by

it, Augustine's definition of *'signum'* includes within the signifying situation (3) the subject to whom the sign indicates
something. Thus Markus concludes that for Augustine the
relation of signifying is triadic.[15]

2. *'Signa naturalia et data'* (II. i. 2–ii. 3).

After giving this very general description of signs, Augustine divides signs into two kinds, *signa naturalia* and *signa
data*. The former are those which

> without any intention or desire of signifying, make us aware
> of something beyond themselves, as smoke signifies fire. It
> does this without any will to signify (. . . *sine uoluntate
> atque ullo appetitu significandi . . . . Non . . . uolens sig-
> nificare* . . . . ii. 2, 12–15).[16]

Other examples of *signa naturalia* are the track of an animal
and the facial expressions of an angry or sad person. Augustine says he will not discuss this kind of sign further (22–24).

Because it includes the divinely given signs contained in
the Holy Scriptures, the other class is more important (ii. 3,
7–8). *Signa data* are

> . . . those which living creatures show to one another for
> the purpose of conveying, in so far as they are able, the mo-
> tions of their spirits or something which they have sensed or
> understood. Nor is there any other reason for signifying, that
> is, for giving signs (*significandi, id est signi dandi*), except for
> bringing forth and transferring to another mind (*animum*)
> what is conceived in the mind of the person who gives the
> sign (ii. 3, 1–6).[17]

Here the situation is more complex than in the definitions of
'sign'. Now two subjects are involved, the sign-giver and the
one to whom the sign is given. This much is clear. But there
is disagreement in the secondary literature on the precise
nature of *signa data*.

This disagreement focuses on the question of translation.
There is no problem with *signa naturalia*. They may be named
'natural signs'. Most translators call *signa data* 'conventional

signs'.[18] In a short but well documented article J. Engels has argued against this.[19] He correctly points out that what distinguishes these two kinds of signs is the presence or absence of will, intention.[20] Natural signs are those which occur without intention of signifying (*sine uoluntate significandi,* II. 3, 14f.). They merely happen. *Signa data*, on the other hand, are given. They occur because some one wills that they occur. Engels, therefore, prefers a literal translation of '*signa data*' as 'given (donnés) signs'[21] or even 'intentionally given signs'.[22]

Markus suggests an interesting way of looking at the contrast between natural and given signs. They are distinguished ". . . according to whether the relation of dependence is between the sign and the object, or between the sign and the subject".[23] Smoke is a sign of fire and depends upon fire since the latter causes it.[24] Markus goes beyond Augustine, however, when he says that *signa data* depend upon the will of the sign-giver for their significance.[25] At least he goes beyond these early chapters of Book Two. For all that Augustine says here is that *signa data* depend upon the will of the sign-giver for their *occurrence,* not for their *meaning*.

Augustine does comment in other places on the place of will in meaning. In the etymological debates of antiquity the extreme positions were, on the one hand, that words are *naturally* suited to the things they signify and, on the other hand, that words are imposed arbitrarily, that is, by *convention*.[26] When he wrote *De dialectica* Augustine took a middle position, regarding some words as having a natural rationale but consciously diverging from the Stoic view that all words have a natural origin (VI. 3–5, 39–41, and 113–16). In his later writings he seems to move even farther away from the Stoic position. Of particular interest is a chapter in *De doctrina* II where Augustine says that certain letters and sounds mean one thing to the Latins, another to the Greeks, not because of nature but because each society has its own agreement and consent as to their significance (*non natura, sed placito et consensione significandi,* II. XXIV. 37, 10–12 and ff.).[27] Thus in *De doctrina,* at least, Augustine holds that an important class of signs (letters and sounds) has significance by convention. Although he does not here speak of the will, he obviously presupposes its presence in the agreement made within a society.

We can say, therefore, that Augustine speaks of will with respect to both the occurrence and the significance of signs.

	Not willed	Willed
1) Occurrence (II. i. 2–ii. 3)	*naturalia*	*data*
2) Significance (II. xxiv. 37)	*natura*	*placitum et consensio*

Although will operates in both *signa data* and in *consensio*, it operates for different ends in each, namely, for occurrence and for significance. To translate '*data*' by 'conventional' is to confuse these ends. In the early chapters of Book Two now under consideration, Augustine is concerned only with occurrence. As Engels has noted, Augustine does not relate intentional giving and conventional significance.[28] A relation can, however, be inferred from *De doctrina*. The most important type of signs given intentionally are words (III. 4, 10f. and 14–16). Now words and their constituent parts have their significance by convention (II. xxiv. 37). Most intentionally given signs, therefore, are significant by convention.

3. '*Signa data*'—*the full scheme* (II. ii. 3)

> Data uero signa sunt, quae sibi quaeque uiuentia inuicem dant ad demonstrandos, quantum possunt, motus animi sui uel sensa aut intellecta quaelibet. Nec ulla causa est nobis significandi, id est signi dandi, nisi ad depromendum et traiciendum in alterius animum id, quod animo gerit, qui signum dat (II. ii. 3, 1–6).[29]

I have already noted that the definition of '*signa data*' is more complex than the definition of '*signum*'. The added complexity comes first in there being both a sign-giver and a sign-receiver instead of just the latter. This indicates that in *signa data* Augustine takes up the topic of communication (*communicant*, III. 4, 2). Whereas the starting point in the definition of 'sign' is the sign, the starting point in the defini-

tion of 'given signs' is something which a living being wishes
to show to another living being. In the movement from this
something to its being shown Augustine sees several elements.
But because he does not specify or elaborate on the nature of
these elements, considerable use of other passages in *De doctrina* and in some of Augustine's other writings will be required for their interpretation. In particular I shall try to show
that several passages summarized in the table below contain
notions similar to and sometimes identical with those in *De
doctrina*'s description of *signa data*. The key elements of the
latter description (row b) as well as those of the definition
of 'sign' (row a) are included for convenient reference. The
other passages include an analogy for the manifestation in
flesh of the Word (row c), the semantic scheme of *De dialectica* (row d), and an analogy for the Incarnation from *De
trinitate* (row e). The justification for using the latter passage,
which was written nearly twenty years after *De doctrina* II,
is twofold. First, its notions and some of its terms are similar
to the notions and terms of *De doctrina*. Second, the theme
in *De trinitate* XV. x–xi is the likeness of our words to *the*
Word. The same theme is found in *De doctrina* itself (c) and
even earlier (*De fide et symbolo* III. 3–4).

Before turning to the texts I would make a general observation about them. All contain two kinds of notions. In the first
place, each contains something *psychological*. Augustine talks
about the mind, sensation, knowledge, thought, etc. In the
second place, each contains something *semantic*. Augustine
deals with signs, words, signifying, etc. The psychology and
the semantics cannot be separated, although in *De dialectica*
V semantics dominates and in *De trinitate* XV psychology
dominates. In *De doctrina* II. i–iv they are more evenly balanced. Yet the psychology appears in order that a complete
account may be given of signification by living beings, especially by men. The rubric of this book is '*de signis*' and the
application of these early chapters to Scriptural hermeneutics
makes use primarily of the properly semantic notions (*signum, res, significatio*).[30] Hence I shall call the theory in II.
i–iv 'semantics'[31] even though Augustine is concerned as well
with what goes on in the mind of the sign-giver and sign-
receiver.

TABLE – *Signa data*

		(1)	(2)
(a)	*De doctr.* II. I. 1 (Defn. of 'signum')	*signum* (a *res*)	*species, quam ingerit sensibus*
(b)	*De doctr.* II. II. 3 (Defn. of 'signa data')		*motus animi sui uel sensa aut intellecta quaelibet*
(c)	*De doctr.* I. XIII. 12		
(d)	*De dial.* V	*uerbum*	*animus sentit; quod in uerbo intelligitur*
(e)	*De trin.* XV.		*scientia (ab ea re quam scimus)*

(3)	(4)	(5)
cogitatio of *aliud aliquid*		
id, quod animo gerit, qui signum dat	*significandi i. e. signi dandi*	*alterius animum*
cogitatio; id quod animo gerimus; uerbum quod corde gestamus	*uoces; locutio; sonum*	*in audientis animum*
ipso animo tenetur; in animo continetur (*dicibile*)	*uerbum procedit... propter aliud aliquod significandum* (*dictio*)	
cogitatio; uerbum in corde; uerbum quod mente gerimus	*uerbum quod sonat; signum rerum quas cogitamus*	

(1) and (2)[32]
Things and their apprehension

Now I shall take up each of the elements mentioned in the description of *signa data*. Communication starts with things which one living being wishes to show to another. I have placed this starting point—*motus animi sui uel sensa aut intellecta*—in the second column. Because *'sensa aut intellecta'* seems less ambiguous in meaning than *'motus animi'*, I shall consider it first. In *De doctrina* and other writings Augustine uses variations of this pair of terms to designate two classes of objects according to the ways in which they are apprehended. This is implicit in two passages in *De doctrina*. Once Augustine speaks of the diverse goods which move men. Some pertain to the bodily senses, some to the understanding of the mind (. . . *ad corporis sensum . . . ad animi intellegentiam pertinent*, I. VII. 7, 4–6). He gives examples only of the former—sky, sun, earth, body. Then later, in Book Two, Augustine makes a similar division of divinely instituted *doctrinae in gentilibus* into those which pertain to the *sensus corporis*, such as history and astronomy, and those which pertain to the *ratio animi*, such as logic and arithmetic (II. XXVII. 41, 4–5 and XXVIII–XXXVIII).

The same distinction of objects according to mode of apprehension is found in other writings as well. In *De dialectica* a *res*, which is what a sign designates, is said to be whatever is the object of understanding or sense perception or even of ignorance (*Res est quidquid intelligitur uel sentitur uel latet* (V. 2–3). In *De magistro* Augustine makes a universal statement: *All* things which we perceive we perceive either by a sense of the body or by the mind. The former are called *'sensibilia'*, the latter *'intelligibilia'* (XII. 39). Earlier in the book he gives examples of these two kinds of *res*. Romulus, Rome, and a river are instances of *sensibilia;* virtue is an instance of *intelligibilia* (IV. 8 *ad fin*). Later (around 415) in the twelfth book of *De Genesi ad litteram* Augustine expanded this twofold scheme into a threefold scheme—bodily, spiritual, and intellectual vision (XII. VI. 15–VII. 16).[33] The expansion comes in the addition of spiritual vision which is the visualiza-

tion of an absent body. In *De doctrina,* however, the more
normal twofold scheme is found. In *De Genesi* Augustine
gives several more examples of objects seen by intellectual
vision: the mind itself, love, joy, peace, God (XII. xxiv. 50).

Thus the *'sensa aut intellecta'* of *De doctrina* II. ii. 3 (row
b) seems to refer to things which are sensed and understood.
The definition of 'sign' in II. i. 1 (a) furnishes an example of
this. First, the sign (or any other sensible or intelligible thing)
has a being of its own. Then it is apprehended by the senses
(or by the mind in the case of an intelligible thing). The
analysis of *'sensa aut intellecta'* allows us therefore, to say
something about both columns (1) and (2). In column (1)
we have objects or, in Augustine's language, *res;* in column
(2) we have the reception or apprehension of those objects in
two ways. In *De trinitate* XV (e) Augustine calls this reception *'scientia',* which comes about when we know a *res* (*res
quam scimus,* x. 19). He does not use *'scientia'* in *De doctrina*
II. i–iv, but it is interesting that he considers the study of
Scripture to be at the level of *scientia,* and this latter is knowledge of various *res* (II. vii. 10, 13–30).

The phrase *'motus animi'* does not fit into this scheme
easily. It can be interpreted in at least two ways on the basis
of its use in *De doctrina.* First, it refers to emotion, or perhaps
attitude. Augustine uses it of wrath and sadness (II. i. 2, 20),
of that which is expressed by untranslatable interjections (x.
16, 15), and of charity and cupidity (III. x. 16, 32–35). In
this usage he follows Varro, who calls fear 'a certain motion
of the mind'.[34] Taken in this sense *'motus animi'* belongs in
column (2), although in a peculiar way. It is not the apprehension of an external thing (hence it does not belong in
column 1), but originates in the mind. Yet it is similar to
this apprehension in that it may be a kind of raw datum—
something immediately known and as yet unreflected upon.

A second way of interpreting *'motus animi'* has less obvious grounding in Augustine but presents an interesting possibility. In the discussion of the role of consent in language,
Augustine says that the same sound moves men's minds di-
versely (*animos mouent . . . diuerse*), for they understand
it in accordance with the convention of their own society
(II. xxiv. 37, 15–20). Although the association with under-

standing (*intellegit*) might lead us to place this movement
of the mind in column (2), a passage in Seneca suggests that
'*motus animi*' may also belong in column (3). Seneca uses
'*motus animorum*' to explicate the Stoic doctrine of the
λεκτόν.[35] He says there are bodies which we see and sounds
which we speak. In addition there are certain motions of
minds which declare or mean something about bodies (*cor-
porum; de corpore*). I do not wish to discuss the *lekton* at the
moment. It is sufficient to note that it involves more than
apprehension. There is a certain reflection, an attending to
what has been apprehended, and this, as will be seen, belongs
at the next stage (column 3) in Augustine's scheme.

(3)

Conception

Moving to that next stage, there may be some question
whether it is really distinguishable in *De doctrina* II. ii. 3. I
have isolated '*id, quod animo gerit*'. This, Augustine says, is
brought forth and transferred to another mind by giving
signs (4–6). But nothing in the passage distinguishes it from
the things which living creatures show by signs—the motion
of the mind or things which are sensed or understood. On
the basis of the passages in *De doctrina* cited in rows (a)
and (c) it can, however, be set apart from these apprehended
things. In I. xiii. 12 Augustine uses the same phrase, changing
only the person and number of the verb—'*id quod animo
gerimus*' (2 f.). He names this begetting or conceiving in the
mind '*cogitatio*'. Now '*cogitatio*' occurs in II. i. 1 as the name
for a stage distinct from the apprehension of *species* via the
senses. In this stage the mind recognizes that the sign whose
species is apprehended signifies something else. It is conception distinct from reception. 'That which the sign-giver
conceives in his mind' must refer to this conception and is,
therefore, distinct from the apprehension of sensibles and intelligibles (1 and 2).

To explicate '*cogitatio*' requires examination of both earlier and later texts, namely, *De dialectica* and *De trinitate*.
Both will help fill out the scheme in terms of the two kinds
of objects known. In *De trinitate* XV (row c) Augustine re-

tains several of the terms of *De doctrina* I. XIII—'*cogita-tio* . . . , *uerbum est quod in corde dicimus*' (x. 19). This word which is spoken in the heart in conception is begotten of knowledge (*gignitur de scientia*, XI. 20), which I have placed in column (2). Doubtless Augustine achieved greater clarity and depth in the psychology of *De trinitate* than in the psychology of *De doctrina*. But the use of the same terms, for the same reason (to illustrate the Incarnation), and in the same sequence (reception then conception) justifies cautious reference to the later work for illumination of the earlier. Reference to *De dialectica*, because it is an earlier work and is explicitly semantic in content, requires less caution.

In *De trinitate* XI. III. 6 Augustine states what he means by '*cogitatio*'. It consists in the union of memory, internal vision, and will. This trinity of the inner man is suggested to Augustine by a trinity of the outer man—the union of the *res* which is seen, the eye, and the attention of the mind (*animi intentio*) which holds the eye upon the thing which is seen (*De trin.* XI. II. 2).[36] The difference between outer and inner vision lies in what each sees. The eye of the body sees the *species* of a body which is outside it; the eye of the mind sees the *species* which by the medium of the bodily eye has been impressed upon memory. In all of this Augustine distinguishes four *species* which are born step by step in knowing and conceiving. From the *species* of the body comes one in the sense (eye). From this latter comes the *species* in the memory. And when the mind's eye is turned on this *species* by the will, there is born a fourth *species* in the one who conceives (*cogitantis*, XI. IX. 16). These four might be called in turn 'outward appearance of a body', 'impression on the eye', 'received or retained image', and 'the image attended to'. The *species* named in *De doctrina* II. I. 1 (a) would seem to be the second. The important thing to note is that it and the *species* of *De trinitate* both have their origin from a body, an object which is apprehended by the senses. Hence we have an account of the *cogitatio* of *sensa*.

For an account of the *cogitatio* of *intellecta* I shall turn to *De dialectica* (row c). It considers only one sort of intelligible and one that is apprehended in connection with a sensible, namely, a word. But this makes it especially relevant to *De doctrina christiana,* where Augustine concentrates on the words of Scripture. Indeed, the question of the *cogitatio* of *intellecta* is central to *De doctrina* II and III, where Augustine gives precepts for the understanding (*intellegere*) of Scripture.

In the fifth chapter of *De dialectica* Augustine formulates a fourfold semantic scheme. He defines and discusses the *uerbum,* the *res,* the *dicibile,* and the *dictio.* A *res,* as we have already seen, is something which may be sensed, or understood (v. 2–3). A *uerbum* is a sign of a *res,* and when spoken it can be understood by the hearer (. . . *ab audiente possit intellegi, a loquente prolatum,* v. 1–2). Hence a word would seem to be a *res* which is both sensed (heard) and understood. As *res* it belongs in column (1); as sensed and understood, in column (2). With the *dicibile* Augustine moves to the next stage:

> What the mind rather than the ear gains from the word and is contained in the mind itself is called the *'dicibile'.* . . . What I have called *'dicibile'* is, in a sense, the word, yet it is not the uttered or written word but what is understood in the word and held in the mind (v. 50–52, 60–62).[37]

When he speaks of what is understood in the word, Augustine seems to be at the step which I have called 'reception' or 'apprehension', for it is a matter of understanding the meaning of the word. But when he says that the *dicibile* is held or contained in the mind, he seems to be referring to conception. This is not immediately clear from the material just quoted, which concerns the reception of a word. In a passage concerning the speaking of a word, however, Augustine says that words in the mind before utterance (*ante uocem*) are *dicibilia* (v. 73f.). Then when uttered (*proruperunt in uocem*) they are *dictiones* (v. 74–76). This contrast between inner word and outer word corresponds to the contrast between the conceived word and the word which sounds in *De doctrina* I (c) and *De trinitate* XV (e). Hence it seems appropriate to place the *dicibile* at the stage of *cogitatio.* And because in hearing a word the *dicibile* arises after the word is understood, it also seems correct to say that the *dicibile* received in communication is one instance of the conceiving of *intellecta*. The *dicibile* is somehow the content of *cogitatio*. It is not merely psychological; it is not one of the things external to the mind which are sensed or understood. It seems to be an intermediate entity which is central to communication. Why it is central will be seen in the discussion of signifying, the next stage in Augustine's scheme for *signa data*.

(4)
Signifying

There can be no doubt that signifying is explicitly mentioned in *De doctrina* II. ɪɪ. 3. Augustine makes it equivalent to giving signs (*significandi, id est signi dandi,* 4) and says that signs are given only in order to communicate. He probably presents this activity more explicitly than apprehension and conception because he intends to make frequent use of the notion of signification in the rest of Books Two and Three. In any case, whatever his intention, he does in fact apply the properly semantic notions of sign, thing, and signification to hermeneutics; of the psychological notions, on the other hand, he retains only understanding. I do not mean to imply that signifying is non-psychological, for, as we have seen in the previous section, the distinctive feature of *signa data* is the presence of will. Nevertheless, throughout Books Two and Three, Augustine almost always talks about signification (*significatio,* II. xɪɪ. 18, 34, III. xxv. 36, 24 and 34), rather than the more personal signify*ing* (*significandi*). This may be because in those books he is considering the signs of Scripture, which confront us apart from any speaker.

When approached with the sign as starting point, signification is usually seen as a two-termed relation between a sign and what it designates. In *De dialectica* Augustine says that a word is a sign of a thing (*rei signum,* V. ɪ). In *De doctrina* he is more indefinite, replacing '*res*' by '*aliquid*' in his definitions of 'sign'.[38] Later in Book Two, however, he will use '*res*' again as the designatum of a sign (II. x. 15). One writer has said that Augustine's semantics does not go beyond this dyadic scheme of *signum* and *res*.[39] On the basis of my analysis of the texts in this section, I maintain instead

that Augustine has a threefold semantic scheme. Thus I agree
with Markus, as far as he goes.[40] He sees the third element
as the sign-giver or receiver, and it is something connected
with each. It has appeared in the discussion of *cogitatio*.

Augustine says that what is transferred from one mind to
another is that which is conceived in the mind of the sign-
giver. From parallels with other passages (c and e) I have
concluded that this latter is *cogitatio*. In *De trinitate* Augustine
says that words are signs of the things which we conceive
(*uoces in sermone nostro earum quas cogitamus signa sint
rerum*, XV. x. 19 *ad fin*). And in *De dialectica*, even though
he gives the dyadic relation (*uerbum* as *rei signum*), he also
develops the notion of the *dictio*. This latter is a word which
is spoken not for its own sake but in order to signify something else (. . . *propter aliud aliquod significandum*, v. 52–
54). An apparently equivalent way of stating this is to say that
the *dictio* is a union of *uerbum* and *dicibile* (v. 62–64). These
texts suggest that in some sense a sign signifies a *dicibile*. It
may be better, however, to say that a sign *expresses* a *dicibile*.
This way of putting it fits the context of communicating better.

Earlier I noted that the *dicibile* is one sort of content of
cogitatio, but is neither *cogitatio* itself nor some external *res*.[41]
Now the importance of this can be seen. Only something of
this sort could be truly communicated by signs. Obviously the
thing designated is not transferred to the other mind, for the
sign-giver usually does not have it in him to transfer. Nor is
the conceiving transferred, for it is a property of the mind
of the sign-giver, unique to him. It is not thinking that is
transferred, but the thinking *of something*. This something
would seem to be the *dicibile*, which may now be translated
as 'that which is meant' or simply 'meaning'.[42]

Although consistent with what Augustine says, this last
paragraph does go beyond the texts I have examined. But
these texts do suggest that within the signifying situation
Augustine sees not only the sign and the thing signified but
also the meaning conceived by the sign-giver and expressed
in the sign. Still it is not at all clear how meaning thus described fits into the semantic scheme. This can be somewhat
clarified by turning to the final phase of communicating, the
completion of the transfer to the other mind.

(5)

The other mind

De doctrina II. II. 3 (row b) represents this stage only briefly by the phrase *'traiciendum in alterius animum'* (4f.). In I. XIII. 12 (c) Augustine expands it to include the means by which the transfer of what we bear in the mind occurs. It reaches the mind of the listener through his ears (*in audientis animum per aures carneas inlabatur,* (3), that is, by means of one of the senses. Now this sequence of sign and the perceiving of the sign by a sense of the body is the same sequence as is found in the basic definition of 'sign' in II. I. 1 (a). Hence the giving of a sign to another person begins anew the process we have described under columns (1)–(3). A thing is apprehended and cogitated by one mind. Then by the giving of a sign of the thing, the same thing may be apprehended and cogitated by another mind. In effect, then, columns (4) and (5) may be explicated by columns (1)–(3).

The first stage in the transfer to another mind is the reception of the given sign by a bodily sense. In *De trinitate* XV (e) Augustine calls this stage 'knowledge of the thing'. Now the thing we are considering is also a sign. I have found two passages where Augustine clearly states what it is to know a sign. In *De magistro* he says that we do not have knowledge of a sign so long as we do not know of what it is a sign (. . . *signi . . . notitiam, qua caremus profecto, quamdiu cuius signum est ignoramus,* x. 34). Again in *De trinitate* he says that no sign is known perfectly unless it is known of what thing it is the sign (*Neque ullum perfecte signum noscitur, nisi cuius rei signum sit cognoscatur.* X. I. 2 *ad init.*). Hence a sign is not known just by sensing it; it must also be understood (*intellegam, intellegere,* X. I. 2 *ad fin.*). And this occurs when the thing which the sign signifies is known and attended to apart from the sign in *cogitatio.* This stage is reached with certainty when, upon perceiving a sign, say a word, we know what the writer meant by it (. . . *uspiam forte id* [*sc.* a word] *legam, et quid scriptor senserit, nesciam. loc. cit.*). The sign-receiver then has in mind what the sign-

giver had in mind to express by the sign. He knows both what
the sign expresses and what it designates.[43]

Thus that which the sign expresses (meaning, *dicibile*)
would seem to aid the sign-receiver in knowing what the sign
designates (object, *res*). Unfortunately Augustine did not complete enough of *De dialectica* to get to a fuller discussion
of the *dicibile*. And in the semantics of *De doctrina* he does
not discuss anything like it. There he merely mentions the
activity (*cogitatio*) by which meaning is conceived. In the
application to hermeneutics he does occasionally refer to the
meaning conceived by a writer (*sensu scriptoris*, II. XII. 18,
35 and *sensu auctoris*, XIII. 19, 4) and often to the meaning
expressed linguistically, that is, the meaning of a sentence
or word (*sententiam de illis uerbis*, II. XXVII. 38, 8).[44] But
he does not specify how this functions in understanding what
thing a sign designates. His applied semantics is really concerned only with the sign-designatum relation, for in interpreting Scripture the important thing is to move from the sign
to the thing which it designates. Thus while Augustine's semantics involves a triadic relation between sign, meaning, and
thing, only the dyadic relation between sign and thing seems
to have ever been worked out.

We may conjecture, however, that Augustine would have
been sympathetic with some such account as this: The meaning conceived by the sign-giver determines the choice of signs
by which to designate what is being attended to in the sign-
giver's knowledge. That is, the way in which we conceive that
object which we know, determines the way in which we will
try to call it to the attention of another. (Some such relation
between what is conceived and what is expressed is suggested
by Augustine's use of '*uerbum*' to designate both).[45] This is
seen most clearly when we designate the same thing in different ways. To take a modern example, the same point in
space would be designated by the expressions 'the point of
the intersection of a and b' and 'the point of the intersection
of b and c' where a, b, and c are straight lines which connect
the corners of a triangle with the midpoints of the opposite
sides.[46] Each expression designates the same thing, but in a
different way. The same point is thought of, but in a different
way. And the way it is thought of determines the way in

which it is designated, that is, which signs are chosen to designate it. By attending to these signs as signs the reader or hearer understands what the writer or speaker is thinking of. If the point thought of is expressed by the first expression, the hearer reaches it in his thought by thinking of lines a and b as described. If the second expression is used, then a different set of lines guides the hearer to the same point. Hence the way in which the point is conceived determines the way in which it is designated and known.

In the example a knowledge of English and of elementary plane geometry would enable the reader to understand what either sign designates. Normally, however, what we conceive cannot be so unambiguously expressed as in geometry. So it is often more difficult to choose signs which designate what we intend to designate. Augustine deals with this problem, without making these distinctions, in Books Two and Three of *De doctrina christiana*. He talks about what the author means (*quid senserit ille, qui scripsit*) and the meaning of the words (*sententiam de illis uerbis*) and how these may differ, especially in the case of ambiguous words (III. XXVII. 38). Augustine's solution to this problem goes beyond semantic analysis. In particular it relies heavily on the dogmas of faith and the precepts of love set forth in Book One.

Before summarizing the scheme for *signa data* it is necessary to consider two further refinements which Augustine makes in chapters III and IV of Book Two.

4. *The signs peculiar to each of the human senses* (II. III. 4)

Moving to the next chapter, we find Augustine continuing his division of the class of signs. The signs which men give to each other pertain to each of the senses. Although most are given to sight and hearing, Augustine gives examples for each of the five senses.

1) Sight—a nod, gestures, military banners and standards (3–10).
2) Smell—the odor of the ointment with which our Lord's feet were anointed (16f).
3) Taste—the taste of the sacrament of His body and blood (17f).

4) Touch—the woman's touching of the hem of His garment (18–20).

5) Hearing—words, sounds made by musical instruments (10–13).

More signs are given to the ears than to the other senses and most of the signs heard are words. This is the first mention of *uerba* in Book Two. In Book One they were said to be things whose only use is for signifying (I. II. 2, 8–11). Now Augustine, from among all the signs given by men, chooses to concentrate on words. He gives two reasons for this choice. First, as a matter of fact words have become the most important way in which men signify for the purpose of communicating what they conceive in their mind (14–16). Secondly, words are intrinsically superior to other kinds of signs, for by means of words any other sign can be explicated (*enuntiare*) but not vice versa (22–23). A third reason, not given by Augustine, is that in Books Two and Three he will be dealing with the words (actually signs of words) of Scripture.

Hence Augustine's theory of signs is mainly a theory of the meaning of words. It focuses on linguistic signs. It is not applied exclusively in linguistic contexts, however, for in one of the most concentrated uses of the theory of signs Augustine sets forth the proper religious attitude toward the ritual observances of the Jews, the idols of the pagans, and the Christian sacraments (III. v. 9–IX. 13). His theory is sufficiently comprehensive for such wide application.

5. *Letters and the diversity of languages* (II. IV. 5)

In the final chapter on the theory of signs Augustine further specifies the signs which he will for the most part treat, and he begins to examine the problematic with which hermeneutics must deal.

Because sound passes away quickly, men have supplemented spoken words with signs of a more enduring nature. These are letters, which are signs of words (*per litteras signa uerborum*, 2f.). This brings about a change in the sense which receives words. Now the eyes not the ears receive words, or rather receive signs which stand for them (3–4). Augustine had already worked this out in greater detail in *De dialectica* v. 17–31, and he makes no changes in the earlier view. Moreover, he retains the same view later in *De trinitate* (XV. x. 19 *ad fin.*). The important thing to notice here is that, according to Augustine, in the case of a large class of linguistic signs, namely, written words, there are two stages of signifying: (1) written 'words' signify spoken words, and (2) spoken words signify things.

The second thing which this short chapter establishes is that the diversity in words used among the various peoples is the result of sin (4–6). This sin is pride and the tower of Babel is a sign of it (*superbiae signum,* 6–8). Ulrich Duchrow has shown that in some early writings Augustine went even further.[47] In *De Genesi contra Manichaeos* II, 5 he says that the fall made necessary signs themselves, not just the diversity of signs. Prior to the fall men knew God inwardly. After the fall man had to be revived by external means, including words. In *De musica* VI. 41 Augustine further states that God has limited the domination of one man by another by allowing only indirect communication between men, that is, communication through signs. But in *De doctrina christiana* Augustine attributes to sin only the diversity of languages, not language as such. This diversity is, however, enough of a problem. It, along with other problems confronted in interpreting signs, is examined in the greater part of Book Two and in Book Three.

6. *Summary*

In the first four chapters of *De doctrina christiana* II Augustine defines, classifies, and mentions all sorts of signs. He ranges from the track of an animal to the letters of the alphabet. Hence his theory of signs is general. But he is particularly interested in those signs whose occurrence involves the presence of volition. Within this class of signs he has two emphases which indicate the intended field of application of his theory. The first emphasis is anthropological. He says that he will discuss intentionally given signs in so far as men are con-

cerned with them. Even the psychology of the more general
definition of 'sign' (II. I. 1) is an anthropological psychology.
The second emphasis is linguistic. The most important signs
used by men are spoken and written words. Clearly Augustine has suited his theory to the consideration of Holy Scripture. For the signs of Scripture are intentionally *given* by
God, presented to us by *men* (II. 3, 7–9), and set forth in
language (*ab una lingua profecta,* v. 6, 2f.).

Because Augustine eventually states his anthropological and
linguistic interests, I have treated his more abstract description of *signa data* largely in terms of these interests. In that
description I have distinguished the following elements, some
properly psychological, others properly semantic.

(1) Things or objects—These are called 'things' in the
widest use of that term in Book One. The class of things includes everything whatsoever that is, including signs. And it
may be exhaustively divided into those things which are
sensibles, and those which are intelligibles.

(2) Apprehension of things—For men this occurs in two
ways, by sense and by understanding. Sensible things may
be apprehended by any of the five senses. There does not
seem to be a corresponding multiplicity in the apprehension
of intelligibles. When things are apprehended in either of
these two ways they are said to be known.

(3) Conception—Here there is an attending to what is
known. In the case of sensibles, this attention gives rise to a
species or image. In the case of intelligibles, I have singled
out a type especially relevant to Augustine's linguistic focus.
Here attention gives rise to a *dicibile* or meaning when a
word is understood.

(4) Signifying—Just as the will contributes to the conception of a meaning by holding the mind's attention upon what
it knows, so it contributes to signifying by deciding that signs
should be given. The signs thus occurring designate things
which are known by the sign-giver and express what he has
conceived about those things. Here the major semantic notions are involved, but they are separable from psychological
notions only by abstraction.

(5) Communication to another mind—This begins another
cycle of knowing and conceiving with signs as the objects of

apprehension both by sense and intellect. Ideally both the meaning expressed and the object designated are made known to the sign-receiver by means of the sign. But this does not always occur. It is crucial in trying to understand words which designate ambiguously. Although Augustine does not say so, obviously the interpreter of Scripture stands at this fifth stage. He reads the signs in Scripture, attempting to learn what things they refer to. It is not always enough to know what the words usually designate, so some way of determining what their author meant for them to designate must be found. Book One has already given the primary method for determining this: All writers of Scripture conceive of God in a certain way, that is, as the one object to be loved for its own sake (I. xxxv–xl). In Books Two and Three Augustine will devise other means, for example, examination of context.

B.—THE BACKGROUND OF AUGUSTINE'S THEORY OF SIGNS

Already several Latin authors have been found useful in interpreting the theory of signs in *De doctrina christiana*. These come from different fields. Cicero and Quintilian represent rhetoric, at least in the works of theirs cited. Varro, although a man of wide learning, writes as a grammarian in *De lingua Latina,* one of his two surviving works. And Seneca is a philosopher. In this section I shall make a brief inquiry into the place of signs in rhetoric, grammar, and logic, as well as in Christian writings. I shall argue that logic is the only field in which signs were part of a linguistic theory of meaning.[48]

1. *Scripture and Christian authors*

The Greek word for 'sign', σημεῖον, occurs often in the Septuagint and the New Testament. It seems to have been consistently rendered *'signum'* in the Old Latin translations. For example, circumcision is a *signum testamenti inter me et uos* (Gen. 17:11)[49] and Jesus speaks of the *signum Ionae* to those who seek a sign (Luke 11:29–30).[50] By the time

he wrote *De doctrina* Augustine was aware of these occurrences. He quotes Genesis 17:11 in *Contra Adimantum* 16,
which was written before *De doctrina*. Scriptural usage of
'signum' does not, however, seem to provide a basis for regarding its own *words* as signs. It utilizes the term in basically two other ways: (1) of distinguishing marks or indications such as circumcision (Gen. 17:11) and swaddling
clothes (Luke 2:12), and (2) of miracles or wonders such
as the Egyptian plagues (Ex. 7:3) and healing (Acts 4:16).

Ecclesiastical writers earlier than Augustine continued to
use 'sign' principally of non-linguistic entities.[51] In his commentary on John, Origen applies σημεῖον to the star in the
east,[52] to the descent of the Spirit upon Jesus,[53] to Jesus'
good cheer,[54] and to the works of Jesus.[55] In his commentary
on Matthew, he uses the Scriptural phrase σημεῖα καὶ
τέρατα.[56] Similar usage is found in Latin authors. Commenting on Isaiah 7:14, Tertullian says that a sign would not
be from God unless it were a novel and prodigious thing
(. . . *nisi nouitas aliqua monstruosa, iam signum non fuis-
set*).[57] Here he is using 'sign' in the second of the Scriptural
senses. In another passage he uses it in the first Scriptural
sense of the flowering of trees as a *signum* of summer and of
wars as *signa* of the coming of the Kingdom of God.[58] Frequently 'sign' was used of an Old Testament event as a figure
or type of a New Testament event, as in Ambrose and Tyconius.[59] The latter also speaks of Esau and Jacob as signs,
and of numbers as well.[60] I have found only one instance
of 'sign' applied to a linguistic entity in a Church author prior
to Augustine. Origen says that Jesus' having said 'Take these
things hence', when he purged the temple, is a σημεῖον
βαθύτερον.[61] There may be similar passages elsewhere in
Origen and others, but a linguistic application of sign-
language would seem to be the exception in ecclesiastical
writers.

2. *Rhetoric*

In rhetoric signs were a class of argument. Aristotle is
basic here.

. . . the materials of Enthymemes are Probabilities and Signs
(εἰκότων καὶ σημείων), which we can see must correspond
respectively with the propositions that are generally and those
that are necessarily true. A Probability is a thing that usually
happens. . . .[62]

He goes on to distinguish between fallible and infallible signs
(τεκμηρία) both in his *Rhetoric* and in the *Prior Analytics*.[63]
In fact a σημεῖον is probable; only a τεκμήριον is irrefuta-
ble. An example of the former is the argument that a man
has fever because he is breathing hard. An example of the
latter is the argument that a man is ill because he has fever.[64]
Aristotle's relating of this to his syllogistic[65] need not concern us, since none of his rhetorical successors had his logical acumen or interest. It plainly shows, however, that 'sign'
was used by him in an inferential sense.

Cicero and Quintilian follow Aristotle but place inferential sign theory in a more explicitly forensic context.[66] Quintilian gives an example of such a sign and how it should be
treated. Bloodstains on clothing may lead us to infer that the
one who wore them has committed a murder. But since he
may have just had a bleeding nose, further evidence (*testi-
monium*), such as being the enemy of the victim or having
threatened him, is required for what is suspected to be made
certain.[67]

In all of these definitions and examples there is no concern
with words. The meaning of events and how these events can
be used to establish a point are the concerns. Yet rhetoric
cultivated words and their proper and ornate use. So a focus
on language was quite in character for a rhetor such as Augustine. Indeed if rhetors had followed the best of Cicero, as
Augustine does in *De doctrina* IV, instead of the worst
(namely, *De inuentione*), they would have found that the
man of perfect eloquence should study, along with other logical topics, the force of words (*uis uerborum*), that is, their
ability to signify.[68] Thus Cicero recommends semantic study,
but not under the rubric 'signs'.

3. *Grammar*

Perhaps even more than rhetors, the *grammatici* concentrated on words. But so far as I can determine, they did not call them 'signs'. In the basic and influential handbooks of Dionysius Thrax and Aelius Donatus the term 'sign' does not even occur.[69] Nevertheless, in both of them the language of signifying is used in the process of defining various grammatical terms. Dionysius, for example, defines a proper noun as a noun which signifies a particular substance (τὸ τὴν ἰδίαν οὐσίαν σημαῖνον).[70] And Donatus says that a noun is a part of speech which signifies (*significans*) with the case a person or a thing specifically or generally.[71] Neither of these grammarians reflect upon this signifying.

Varro, who is far from being merely a *grammaticus,* not only uses the language of signifying in his grammatical work, *De lingua Latina,*[72] but also reflects theoretically, though briefly, upon signification. In an argument against etymological regularity he says,

> . . . I ask whether by a 'word' they mean the spoken word (*uocem*) which consists of syllables, that word which we hear, or that which the spoken word indicates, which we understand (*quod ea significat, quam intellegimus*), or both.[73]

Moreover, he gives an etymology of '*signum*'. He says that signs are so called because they indicate something (*aliquid significent*).[74] But this etymology occurs in the context of a discussion of the signs of the zodiac. Only in this sense and in the sense of 'symptoms' observed by physicians does Varro use '*signum*' in what survives of *De lingua Latina.*[75]

Hence it would seem that grammarians did not have a linguistic theory of signs.[76] Their work presupposed semantics but only occasionally were semantical issues dealt with. The well educated non-specialist such as Aulus Gellius, reflecting a grammatical and a rhetorical education, might ask often about the *uis* or *significatio* of words[77] but rarely if ever about *significatio* itself.

4. *Logic*

Of the disciplines concerned with words only logic or, as it was usually named in Latin, *dialectica* remains to be examined. And it is in logic that a linguistic theory of signs is found. In both of the major logical systems of antiquity, the Peripatetic and the Stoic, 'sign' occurs in semantic contexts. Aristotle gives his explicit semantic scheme in the opening chapters of *De interpretatione*.[78] There τὸ σημεῖον, σημαίνει, and σημαντική are used in connection with words. As to Stoic semantics there are two primary accounts which give us our best, albeit secondhand, knowledge of Stoic logic. In Diogenes Laertius' *Lives and Opinions of Eminent Philosophers* and Sextus Empiricus' *Against the Mathematicians* we find accounts of Stoic semantics and theory of language. The former does not use 'sign' but the latter does in connection with the same doctrines. In part D of this article I shall examine both Aristotle and the Stoics and compare them with Augustine on the theory of signs.

But first we must ask: What connection did Augustine have with the logical tradition? He received the traditional grammatical and rhetorical education and was a teacher of rhetoric until his conversion. This literary education found little place for logic, which was the concern of the philosophical few.[79] Only grammar and rhetoric were really studied in the schools of the empire.[80] And the rhetors did not follow the recommendation of the orator *par excellence* that they learn either the logic of Aristotle or of Chrysippus.[81] In the following section I shall show that Augustine, unlike most rhetors, may have taken Cicero seriously. If he did, there is good reason to compare his semantics with those of Aristotle and Chrysippus.

C.—AUGUSTINE'S KNOWLEDGE OF LOGIC

The most comprehensive attempt at judging the character and extent of Augustine's knowledge of logic has been made by Marrou. He shows that Augustine turned to logic only after his formal education was completed and under the influence of his newfound philosophical vocation.[82] This was part of his study of all of the liberal arts (*Conf.* IV. XVI). Apparently it consisted mainly of a reading of Varro's *Disciplinarum libri,*[83] which included a *De dialectica.* Augustine took this program of self-education seriously.[84] Soon after his conversion he prescribed a study of all of the seven liberal arts as part of the way to attain happiness through wisdom.[85] But what Augustine himself achieved was another matter. According to Marrou only in *dialectica* did Augustine make significant advance[86] and even then his logic remains elementary, non-technical, eristic, and lacking in rigor.[87] This judgment of Marrou's is based, however, on only part of the relevant evidence. He does not consider, for example, the semantics of *De doctrina christiana* and the discussion of the *disputationis disciplina* found in Book Two of the same treatise. In what follows I shall examine, in the order of their writing, the main passages in which Augustine talks about logic explicitly. I shall seek to establish how much and what kind (Peripatetic or Stoic) of logic he professes to know.

Confessiones IV. XVI. 28 (Written A.D. 399–400 but concerning events ca. 374)

Augustine's first contact with technical logic was his reading of Aristotle's *Categories* (*Aristotelica . . . decem categorias*).[88] He read it on his own when he was twenty years old in, it is generally agreed, the translation of Marius Victorinus.[89] This translation must have had fairly wide circulation, since Augustine's former rhetoric teacher and others in Carthage often discussed the *Categories*. It is the only logic book[90] mentioned by title in the writings of Augustine which I have surveyed. He gives an accurate account of the ten categories here. Later he would put his knowledge of them to good use in Book Five of *De trinitate.*[91] In the *Confessions* he only lamented the futility of his newfound knowledge because he did not then know whence came what was true and certain in it (IV. XVI. 30).

Contra Academicos III. XIII. 29 (A.D. 386)

Arguing against Academic scepticism Augustine uses true things which he says he learned from *dialectica*. Indeed, in this first treatise written after his conversion he could say that he knew more about dialectic than about any other part of philosophy (namely, physics or ethics, III. x. 23 and XII. 27).[92] When asked in the dialogue to enumerate some of the truths of dialectic Augustine shows some knowledge of propositional, that is to say Stoic, logic.[93]

First, he lists several *propositiones* which are true. All have the form which the Stoics called 'non-simple propositions'.[94] In modern terminology these are 'molecular propositions'; in traditional terminology, 'hypothetical propositions'. The three basic connectives are represented.

1) *Implication.* The Stoic συνημμένον. 'If there are four elements in the world, there are not five'. (*Si* . . . , *non* . . . .) $(p \supset \sim q)$.

2) *Conjunction.* The Stoic συμπεπλεγμένον. 'The same soul cannot both die and be immortal'. (*Non* . . . *et* . . . *et* . . . .) $\sim (p \ \& \ q)$.

3) *Disjunction.* The Stoic διεζευγμένον, exclusive disjunction. (a) 'We are now either awake or asleep'. (*Aut* . . . *aut* . . .) $(p \lor q)$, and another, (b) 'What I seem to see is either body or not body'. A better one of this form is in X. 23: 'There is one world or not one'. (*Aut* . . . *aut non* . . . .) $(p \lor \sim p)$.

Augustine knows the technical terms for statements containing these connectives. He does not name the second, but he calls the first 'propositions *per conexionem*' and the third 'propositions *per disiunctionem*'. At III. x. 23 the latter are '*disiuncta*' and '*disiunctiones*'. These were apparently the standard translations of the Stoic συνημμένον and διεζευγμένον.[95] Of all the propositions given by Augustine here, only the two in (3) (b) are true by formal necessity. Augustine probably thought all were formally necessary, for he regards them all as equally true. They could easily be given formal necessity (for instance, in the conjunctive statement by changing 'be immortal' to 'not die').

Then Augustine indicates knowledge of two of the five
Stoic undemonstrated arguments.[96] He gives them in the
form of metalogical statements. This is one of the three ways
in which the Stoics presented them, the other two being as
arguments (λόγοι) with actual propositions and as moods
(τρόποι, σχήματα) with ordinal numerals standing as propositional variables.[97] Here are Augustine's statements with
parallels from Sextus Empiricus and Cicero.

Type 1 undemonstrated argument (p ⊃ q; p; ∴ q)   U1

> Augustine: 'If, of any of the conditional statements which
> I have just mentioned, the antecedent be assumed, it neces-
> sarily involves the truth of the dependent part' (*si . . . quae
> per conexionem . . . pars antecedens assumpta fuerit, trahere
> necessario id, quod annexum est*).
> Sextus: 'A type 1 undemonstrated argument is that which is
> made up of a conditional and its antecedent, and which has
> the consequent of the conditional for a conclusion'.[98]
> Cicero: 'The first form of conclusion is when assuming the
> first, that which is connected with it follows'. (*cum primum
> assumpseris, consequitur id quod annexum est primum con-
> clusionis modum . . . .*)[99]

Type 5 undemonstrated argument (p V q; ∼ p; ∴ q)   U5

> Augustine: 'The propositions involving contrariety or disjunc-
> tion (*repugnantiam uel disiunctionem* [apparently p V ∼ p
> and p V q]) . . . are of this nature. When either one or many
> parts are taken away, there remains something which is made
> certain by the removal (. . . *cum auferuntur cetera, siue
> unum siue plura sint, restet aliquid, quod eorum ablatione
> firmetur*).

Augustine's metalogical statement of U5 is not as technical as
his statement of U1, for the latter contains the technical terms
'*conexio*', '*antecedens*', '*assumpta*', and '*annexum*'. The statement of U5 does, however, have the added touch of allowing
for more than two disjuncts.

De ordine II. xiii. 38 (386)

Placed in the course of studies for the attainment of wisdom, *dialectica* is here given high praise as the *disciplina disciplinarum*, but is given little technical content. Augustine praises it because it is reason's classification, noting, and arranging of its own resources. It guards against error, teaches how to teach and learn (*docere . . . discere*), and knows what it is to know (*scit scire*). The only technical functions indicated for *dialectica* here are definition, division, and synthesis (*definiendo, distribuendo, colligendo*). Under the name of *disciplina disputandi* it is for similar functions called not just 'true' but 'truth' in the *Soliloquies* (II, xi. 21).

De dialectica (386–7)

Scholars disagree on the quality of the logic found in this work. Marrou says it is *banal* and elementary.[100] Duchrow disagrees with him.[101] But there is wide agreement that, whatever its quality, it is deeply influenced by Stoic logic. I shall examine *De dialectica* on four matters: (1) its notion of dialectic, (2) its classification of words, (3) its scope, and (4) its doctrine of words.

The treatise begins, '*Dialectica est bene disputandi scientia*' (i. 1). The first thing to note is that Augustine chooses the Stoic name for formal logic, '*dialectica*'.[102] For Aristotle dialectic was merely a special kind of reasoning, namely, that based on generally accepted premisses.[103] It was probably not Augustine himself, however, who made the choice between Aristotle and the Stoics. '*Dialectica*' was already the name used by Cicero[104] and Varro.[105] His definition appears to be a combination of the Stoic definitions of rhetoric and dialectic. Rhetoric is the science of speaking well (ἐπιστήμην . . . εὖ λέγειν) and dialectic that of discussing correctly (ὀρθῶς διαλέγεσθαι).[106] Augustine's '*scientia*' corresponds to ἐπιστήμη, his '*disputandi*' to διαλέγεσθαι, and his '*bene*', corresponding to εὖ in the definition of rhetoric, replaces ὀρθῶς in the definition of dialectic. Again he is following earlier writers, although apparently none of the latter had used precisely Augustine's terms.[107] The second thing to note is that dialectic is concerned with disputing. This notion of disputation was important in the early dialogues[108] and continued to be Augustine's basic way of thinking of logic. Marrou thinks that this represents a truncation of dialectic.[109] But it is faithful to Stoic definitions. Moreover, as will be seen, it does not limit logic to a theory of debate. *De dialectica* gives dialectic a far larger scope than that.

Immediately following his definition Augustine says that we dispute with words. He then classifies words:

1) Simple—occur alone and signify one thing, e. g., 'man' (I).
2) Conjoint—two or more words occurring together.
   a) Not a sentence, e. g., 'with haste the man toward the mountain' (II).
   b) Sentences
      I) Express intention of the the will—wishes, commands, curses.
      II) True or false
         α) - Simple, e. g., 'Every man walks' (III).
         β) - Complex, e. g., 'If he walks, he moves'.

Duchrow sees in this the Stoic classification of λεκτά.[110] There are striking similarities,[111] but there is one important difference. Augustine is classifying *uerba* (Stoic φώναι) not *dicibilia* (Stoic λεκτά). This is a subtle difference, since it is words that express meanings. In this respect Augustine's classification is closer to Aristotle than to the Stoics.[112] Another divergence from the Stoics is the inclusion of the Aristotelian universal affirmative proposition (II, α). The Stoics apparently took no account of such propositions.[113]

This classification of words gives Augustine the scope of dialectic (IV). A section called '*de loquendo*' deals with simple words. *De eloquendo* treats of non-truth-claiming sentences. *De proloquendo* treats of simple truth-claiming sentences. And *de proloquiorum summa* deals with complex truth-claiming sentences, especially with reasoning from them (he gives two U1 arguments as examples, III. 8–21). This is a comprehensive scheme, capable of covering most of the

topics of ancient formal logic. It does not limit dialectic to a
theory of debate. Martianus Capella, probably a younger contemporary of Augustine, adopted the same scheme for his *De
dialectica*.[114] Capella treated these issues in a basic if elementary fashion. For example, under the fourth rubric he
gives both Aristotle's basic syllogistic and the Stoic undemonstrated arguments.[115] Augustine did not get past *de loquendo*
in his treatise, but from what we learn in other of his works,
it would not seem that he quit because of lack of knowledge.

Under *de loquendo* Augustine did develop a semantic
scheme (ch. v), as we have seen. He also took up etymology
(vi) in a non-Stoic spirit,[116] considered the way words move
men to apprehend things (vii), and the impediments to this
—obscurity and ambiguity (viii–x). Chapters vi–x are more
relevant to the remainder of Books Two and Three of *De
doctrina* than to the theory of signs as such. Hence I shall
not discuss them here.

De doctrina christiana II. XXXI. 48–XXXIX. 59 (396–97)

So far I have considered, with one exception, works written
by Augustine as a new convert to Christianity. And the exception, *Confessions* IV. xvi, although written later, concerns
a period prior to Augustine's conversion. But the author of
De doctrina had been a priest for six years and had recently
been made bishop of Hippo. Moreover, his task in *De doctrina* was to formulate a Scriptural hermeneutics. Precisely
in this context, however, is to be found Augustine's most
sophisticated account of deductive logic. The *disputationis disciplina* finds a prominent place among the divinely instituted
doctrinae in gentilibus which Augustine recommends to the
use of the exegete. By calling this discipline 'divinely instituted' Augustine means that its doctrines are discovered by
men, not instituted by them. He thus believes that logic deals
with notions intrinsic to reality rather than with merely conventional or arbitrary notions. He mentions the following
points.

He distinguishes clearly between truth and validity, *ueritas
sententiarum* and *ueritas conexionum* (49, 20f.; 50, 24–26;
52, 1–2). An inference may be validly carried out upon true

or false propositions (49, 33–35). Hence the rules of validity may be learned in schools outside the Church, but the truth of propositions is to be discovered in the holy books of the Church (36–38).

He gives the Stoic type 2 undemonstrated argument in two forms. First, metalogically, "When a consequent is false, it is necessary that the antecedent upon which it is based be false also (*Cum falsum est, quod consequitur, necesse est, ut falsum sit, quod praecedit.* 50, 9–10)."[117] The Stoics did not usually use 'true' or 'false' in their metalogical statements of the undemonstrateds, but occasionally they did (Sextus, VIII. 228). Second, Augustine gives two actual arguments (50, 20–22 and 51, 4–7):

1) 'If there is no resurrection of the dead, neither was
      Christ resurrected. $\sim p \supset \sim q$
      Christ was resurrected.   q
      Therefore, there is a resurrection
      of the dead'.   p

2) 'If a snail is an animal, it has a voice. $p \supset q$
      A snail has no voice. $\sim q$
      Therefore, a snail is not an animal'. $\sim p$

I give both because only the second is an instance of the simple undemonstrated. The first is really a non-simple argument which requires analysis, that is, some additional steps, to reduce it to proof by the simple undemonstrateds.[118] It is doubtful that Augustine recognized any difference between (1) and (2), since he states this rule (*regula,* 50, 12 and 24) in terms of falsity, not negation. In addition to this valid argument form he gives as an invalid form of inference denying the ancedent ($p \supset q$, $\sim p$, no conclusion) (51, 14–25). All examples of arguments in these chapters involve the Stoic conditional propositions.

Other logical doctrines in these chapters: Propositions of unknown truth value can be regarded as true if they are deducible by valid methods from propositions known to be true (52, 8–9). There are two kinds of falsehood: (1) the false that is impossible ($\sim p \& \sim \diamond p$), and (2) the false that is possible ($\sim p \& \diamond p$, 53, 14–16). Logic includes the science of definition, division, and partition (53, 1f.).

Contra Cresconium grammaticum partis Donati I (406)

In this work Augustine elaborates upon *dialectica* as skill in disputing (XIII. 16, XIV. 17), by which he means distinguishing the true from the false (*uerum discernit a falso*, xv. 19; xx. 25 and II. II. 3). The chief importance of this work for our purposes is twofold. First, Augustine says that the Stoics and especially Chrysippus (the greatest Stoic logician) excell all others in dialectic, and he mentions *libri Stoicorum* which teach how to dispute dialectically (XIX. 24). Second, Augustine defends himself against the charge of Cresconius that he is a *homo dialecticus* (XIII. 16), not by denying it but by establishing the legitimacy of dialectic for the Christian. He does this first by showing that dialectic may be applied to true or to false propositions and hence is neutral. More important, he argues that both Paul and Christ were *dialectici*, because they disputed skillfully with Stoics, Epicureans, and Jews (XIV. 17, XVII. 21–22).

Summary

Judging from these texts, we can say that Augustine had more than a passing acquaintance with logic. It was certainly not a major concern of his, for these few texts contain most of the discussions of formal logic to be found in Augustine's vast writings. Yet at some time in his career he must have read, in addition to Aristotle's *Categories*, some of the *libri Stoicorum* which he mentions, for he usually gives propositions in the Stoic rather than the Aristotelian form and his theory of deduction is exclusively Stoic. In addition, his classification of words and delineation of a semantic schema show marked Stoic influence. Because no Stoic logical writings survive, a judgment as to what Augustine read can only be conjectured. There were numerous Stoic handbooks (εἰσαγωγαί)[119] and Augustine may have read one or more, such as the *Commentarium de proloquiis* of L. Aelius Stilo.[120] As to the five undemonstrated arguments, they were well known in antiquity.[121] Augustine could have learned them from Cicero.[122]

In the light of the Stoic character of his logic it is at first
glance puzzling why in *De ciuitate Dei* VIII. 7 Augustine
says that he prefers Platonic to Stoic logic. He may be mistaken about which logic is whose. Indeed, in VIII. 4 he mis-
takenly attributes to Plato the Stoic division of philosophy
into logic, physics, and ethics.[123] A more likely explanation
is that in this passage (VIII. 7) Augustine is using '*dialectica*'
in reference not to logic but to what is more accurately
termed 'epistemology' (he mentions the Stoic epistemological
doctrine that the mind gets its notions, ἔννοιαι, through
the senses), and Augustine was assuredly a Platonist on
epistemology.

D.—COMPARISON OF AUGUSTINE'S THEORY OF SIGNS WITH ARISTOTELIAN AND STOIC SEMANTICS

In this final section I shall continue the examination of
Augustine's theory of signs in the context of ancient thought.
I have argued that the theory which I have explicated in section A has its major background in the logical writings of
Aristotle and the Stoics. That this background is a direct
source of Augustine's theory is made plausible by the evidence
that he had studied both Aristotle and some Stoic books of
logic. There is no evidence on what he might have read of
Stoic logic, but his knowledge of the latter is extensive enough
to allow the conjecture that he did have contact with Stoic
logic. In this section the question of sources will be raised.
Mainly, however, I wish to compare Augustine's theory of signs
with the work of the two great schools of ancient logic.

1. ARISTOTLE

Categories

Augustine read the *Categories* in a translation by Marius
Victorinus, as noted earlier.[124] Victorinus was a Neoplatonist and his interest in the *Categories* reflects this, for Porphyry
had made it *the* logic textbook for Neoplatonism by his im-
mensely influential Εἰσαγωγή to and commentary on it. Victorinus also translated Porphyry's *Eisagoge*, but Augustine

does not seem to have read it.[125] Although none of Victorinus' translations survive (he also did Aristotle's *De interpretatione*[126]), we can have some idea of the language he used; for he is apparently the source of the fixed terminology of Latin Aristotelian logic which is found in Martianus Capella and Boethius.[127] Since Boethius knew Victorinus' translations,[128] his own translations may be regarded as something of a witness to Victorinus' language. This must be qualified, however, by the fact that Boethius frequently criticizes the choice of words Victorinus makes.[129]

The *Categories* contains little of semantic interest. There are two things to note. First, in chapter 1 Aristotle gives definitions of 'univocal' and 'equivocal', which Augustine follows early. According to Aristotle things are univocally named when they have the same name used with the same definition; things are equivocally named when a common name is used with different definitions. According to Augustine, "Those things with a common name and definition are univocally named. Those things with a common name but requiring different definitions are equivocally named" (*De dial.* IX. 49–51). In *De doctrina*, however, Augustine uses neither 'univocal' nor 'equivocal'. Second, in the important passage introducing the ten categories Aristotle says that each uncombined expression *signifies* either a substance or quantity or etc. (τῶν κατὰ μηδεμίαν συμπλοκὴν λεγομένων ἕκαστον ἤτοι οὐσίαν σημαίνει ἢ ποσὸν ἢ . . . 4 1ᵇ 25–28). This only presupposes semantics, but Boethius, who translates σημαίνει as *'significat'*,[130] reflects in his commentary that the *Categories* treats names of first imposition (those that signify *res*), rather than names of second imposition (those that signify other *nomina*).[131] Although Augustine developed a similar distinction in *De magistro* (VII. 19–20), it is unlikely that the *Categories* stimulated him to do this. In the *Confessions* IV. XVI 28 summary of the *Categories* passage just cited he does not use *'significare'* at all.

De interpretatione

Victorinus translated *De interpretatione* and at least two scholars have said that Augustine read it.[132] Although the

evidence they cite for this has rightly been disputed,[133] the
theory of signs in Augustine's *De doctrina christiana* does
bear striking similarity to the semantic scheme in the first
chapter of Aristotle's *De interpretatione*.[134]

> Spoken words are the symbols of experiences of the soul and
> written words are the symbols of spoken words (. . . τὰ ἐν
> τῇ φωνῇ τῶν ἐν τῇ ψυχῇ παθημάτων σύμβολα, καὶ τὰ γραφόμενα
> τῶν ἐν τῇ φωνῇ). Just as all men do not have the same writ-
> ten words, so they do not have the same spoken words. But
> the experiences of the soul of which the latter are the signs
> (σημεῖα) are the same for all, as are the objects (πράγματα)
> of which the experiences of the soul are likenesses (1 16ᵃ
> 4–8).

The following shows the terminological similarity of Augustine's scheme to Aristotle's:

Aristotle

γράμματα ⟶ φωναί ⟶ ἐν τῇ ψυχῇ ⟶ πράγματα
(σύμβολα) (σύμβολα, παθημάτων
σημεῖα) (ὁμοιώματα)

Boethius[135]
litterae ⟶ uoces ⟶ in anima passionum ⟶ res
(notae) (notae) (similitudines)

Augustine
litterae ⟶ uoces, uerba ⟶ motus animi etc.
(signa) (demonstrare)
↙
(signa) res

At the first stage there is complete agreement. Written
words or letters are signs or symbols of spoken words. Both
are symbols of something else for Aristotle. He apparently
uses σύμβολον and σημεῖον synonymously, since spoken
words are called by both terms. Boethius has translated both
as 'nota', which is good Latin usage for the idea expressed
by σύμβολον.[136] He continues this throughout his translation
of *De interpretatione* whenever σύμβολον and σημεῖον are

used semantically rather than in the sense of 'proof' or 'evidence'.[137] Thus if Augustine had read the work in a similar translation, he might not have picked up a linguistic usage of *'signum'* from it. Yet for Augustine the thing is more important than the word chosen to designate it;[138] moreover, there is some indication that he regarded *'nota'* and *'signum'* as synonymous.[139]

From this point the similarity requires greater qualification. First, Augustine does not say explicitly that words are signs of movements of the soul. Rather he says they are used by living beings to indicate or *express,* among other things, movements of the mind. Second, he does not see a relation of likeness between the mind and things as does Aristotle. Rather he says men seek likeness between *signs* and things (II. xxv. 38, 15–19). And since there are all sorts of similarity, consent among men is required even for such signs. Third, because Augustine does not see a likeness between *res* and the mind, he does not see the designation of *res* by signs as taking place through the natural mediation of the mind, though he does see it in unity with the mind (the *dictio* as a union of *uerbum* and *dicibile*). This is not, however, a great difference, and when Boethius comments on this passage in *De interpretatione* he develops notions similar to Augustine's. He regards the *animae passio* as understanding and says the spoken word signifies both the understanding of the thing and the thing itself.[140] This is close to Augustine's language about the expression of a *dicibile* and the designation of a *res*. Whatever the textual relation between *De doctrina* and *De interpretatione* it seems safe to say that both authors were thinking in very similar ways about the problem of signification.

It should be noted finally that Aristotle continues to use σημεῖον and σύμβολον as well as σημαίνειν and σημαντική in *De interpretatione*. They are applied to the definition of 'noun', 'verb', and 'sentence', that is to say, linguistically (2–4). On the other hand, the anthropological focus, which we have seen in Augustine, is not as pronounced in *De interpretatione*.

2. STOICS

There is a twofold textual problem involved in studying the relation of Augustine to Stoic semantics. In the first place, only secondhand accounts of the Stoic logicians—Zeno, Cleanthes, and the great Chrysippus—have come down to us. Notions of immense subtlety, such as the doctrine of the *lekton,* can be known only through the often confused[141] and sometimes dishonest[142] accounts of others. The later Stoa is much better known, but it had little interest in logic. In the second place, there are no surviving Latin discussions or translations of Stoic logical writings comparable to Boethius' discussions and translations of Aristotle's logical works. At least there are none for Stoic semantics. Although the Stoic propositional calculus was relatively well known, only scattered passages in Varro and Seneca are helpful for determining the Latin vocabulary of Stoic semantics. Pinborg has taken Augustine's *De dialectica* as a prime witness to this vocabulary. Since I intend to compare Augustine to the Stoics, this course is not open to me. I shall have to rely mainly on the Greek accounts of Diogenes Laertius and Sextus Empiricus.

Diogenes Laertius, *Lives VII*

In his life of Zeno, Diogenes gives a general account of all Stoic doctrines (VII. 38). The paragraphs on logic include results of his own research (41–48) as well as a quotation verbatim of Diocles Magnes (49–83), a scholar of the first century B.C.[143] The term 'sign', either as τὸ σημεῖον or τὸ σημαῖνον, does not occur here. But notions are explained which, according to Sextus, do involve sign-language.

The first thing I wish to call attention to in Diogenes is the division of logic (41–43).

$$\tau \grave{o} \ \lambda o \gamma \iota \kappa \acute{o} \nu$$
$$\swarrow \qquad \searrow$$
$$\delta \iota \alpha \lambda \epsilon \kappa \tau \iota \kappa \acute{\eta} \qquad \rho \eta \tau o \rho \iota \kappa \acute{\eta}$$
$$\swarrow \qquad \searrow$$
$$\pi \epsilon \rho \grave{\iota} \ \tau \mathitalic{\tilde{\eta}} s \ \varphi \omega \nu \mathitalic{\tilde{\eta}} s \qquad \pi \epsilon \rho \grave{\iota} \ \tau \mathitalic{\tilde{\omega}} \nu \ \sigma \eta \mu \alpha \iota \nu o \mu \acute{\epsilon} \nu \omega \nu$$

Seneca gives exactly the same division.[144]

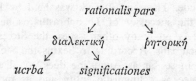

$$
\begin{array}{c}
\textit{rationalis pars} \\
\swarrow \qquad \searrow \\
\delta\iota\alpha\lambda\epsilon\kappa\tau\iota\kappa\acute{\eta} \qquad \rho\eta\tau\sigma\rho\iota\kappa\acute{\eta} \\
\swarrow \qquad \searrow \\
\textit{ucrba} \qquad \textit{significationes}
\end{array}
$$

The important thing here is that the notion of meaning is central to the Stoic conception of logic. Chrysippus apparently stated the φωνή-σημαινομένον division even more 'semantically'. He said that the subjects of dialectic are things signifying and things signified (περὶ σημαίνοντα καὶ σημαινόμενα, VII. 62). By the latter Chrysippus meant λεκτά. I shall consider the doctrine of the *lekton* in connection with Sextus' account.

Under the rubric of 'things signifying' the Stoics considered grammatical subjects. Here they presuppose a theory of meaning in the same manner as the grammarians discussed earlier;[145] they defined parts of speech by what they signify. A common noun (προσηγορία), for instance, is a part of a sentence signifying a common quality (σημαῖνον κοινὴν ποιότητα, VII. 58). Proper nouns and verbs (ὄνομα, ῥῆμα) are defined in a similar way. Although Augustine uses terms that could and sometimes do correspond to ὄνομα, προσηγορία, and ῥῆμα,[146] he appears to have adopted as a technical term only the Stoic λόγος (sentence or statement) as λέξις σημαντική (significant utterance) (VII. 57). This he called by the name *'dictio'*, the word which proceeds in order to signify something.[147]

Sextus Empiricus, *Aduersus Mathematicos VIII*

Sextus gives a brief statement of the Stoic semantic schema in his discussion of where truth and falsity may be located (VIII. 11–13). There are three options: in the thing signified (τῷ σημαινομένῳ), in the sound (τῇ φωνῇ), and in the motion of the mind (τῇ κινήσει τῆς διανοίας). Sextus thinks that the third option is a scholar's invention. He assigns it to no thinker. It apparently is something subjective[148] and thus

is not the *motus animorum* of Seneca, although it could be
Augustine's *motus animi* in so far as the latter is an emotion
or attitude. The second view was held by Epicurus and by
Strato, the successor of Theophrastus as head of Aristotle's
school. As on many other issues, the Stoics disagreed with
the Epicureans. According to Sextus the Stoics take the first
option. In so far as Augustine does not distinguish between
a sentence as a linguistic entity and its meaning, he seems
to agree with the Epicureans and Peripatetics on what it is
that is true or false.[149] However, leaving aside the sign-giver
or receiver, Augustine's semantic schema is (definitely in *De
dialectica* and probably in *De doctrina*) that of the Stoics,
not of the Epicureans, for the Epicureans admit only the
sign and the thing signified.

  According to Sextus this is the Stoic schema:

> The Stoics say that three things are linked together, that
> which is signified, that which signifies, and the object (τό τε
> σημαινόμενον καὶ τὸ σημαῖνον καὶ τὸ τυγχάνον); of these
> that which signifies is speech (φωνήν), as for example, 'Dion',
> that which is signified is the thing itself which is revealed by
> it and which we apprehend as subsisting with our thought
> but the barbarians do not understand, although they hear the
> spoken word, while the object is that which exists outside, as
> for example, Dion himself. Of these, two are corporeal, that
> is, speech and the object, while one is incorporeal, that is,
> the thing which is signified, i.e. the *lekton,* which is true or
> false.[150]

The basic correspondence with Augustine's semantic schema
is of τὸ σημαῖνον with the *signum,* τὸ τυγχάνον with the
res, and τὸ σημαινόμενον or τὸ λεκτόν with the *dicibile*
and notions associated with the latter in *De doctrina christiana.* I shall now say some things about each of these three
pairs.

  The Stoic sign[151] is here plainly a linguistic entity. The
name 'Dion' is given as an example. Augustine's theory is
also linguistic, at least in emphasis. Another emphasis of
Augustine's, the anthropological, is not quite as explicit in
this passage, but it is present in such terms as διανοία and
the discussion of the barbarians' failure to understand.

The Stoic object (τὸ τυγχάνον) is always a body. Augustine uses '*res*' more broadly than this, making it applicable in a wide sense to anything that is. Even when he is thinking of a *res* as what is designated by a sign, he conceives of it as either sensible or intelligible (*De dial.* V. 2f.), that is, as either corporeal or incorporeal. In this Augustine is a Platonist and not a Stoic.

The Stoic *lekton* has several characteristics in common with Augustine's *dicibile:*

1) Both the *lekton* and the *dicibile* are explicated by the notion of understanding. The *lekton* is what the barbarians do not understand (ἐπαΐουσι) when they hear a Greek word. The *dicibile* is what is understood in a word and conceived by the mind.

2) Both the *lekton* and the *dicibile* are made known by signs. The *lekton* is revealed (δηλούμενον) by a sign. Things understood (*intellecta*), among which are *dicibilia,* are shown (*demonstrandos*) by giving signs.

3) Both are explicated by psychological notions. The *lekton* subsists with our thought (διανοία). The *dicibile* is held in the mind (*animus*); it is attended to by thought (*cogitatio*).

4) The only type of sign by which either is expressed is linguistic. The *lekton* is signified by sound (ἡ φωνή). The *dicibile* is understood in a word and comes forth in union with a word as a *dictio.*

The last assertion requires reference to other texts, for the passage in Sextus cited above speaks only of sound and not of language or discourse, even though it gives a proper name as an example of a sound. There are several such texts. Later in the same work Sextus says that the *lekton* is that which subsists in conformity with a rational presentation (λογικὴν φαντασίαν) and such a presentation is one that can be conveyed by discourse (λόγῳ).[152] When one speaks (τὸ λέγειν), we learn from Diogenes, one does more than utter sounds (προφέρονται . . . αἱ φωναί); one expresses λεκτά.[153] And Seneca's explication of the *significationes-uerba* distinction shows awareness of the connection of *lekta* with discourse. He says that there are things which are said and the words in which they are said (*res quae dicuntur et uocabula quibus dicuntur*).[154] In another passage Seneca translates

τὸ λεκτόν by '*dictum*'.[155] In both Greek and Latin, therefore, the choice of technical terms reflects the linguistic focus
of Stoic semantics. Just as λεκτόν seems to be derived from
λέγειν, so '*dictum*' and Augustine's '*dicibile*' and '*dictio*' seem
to be derived from '*dicere*'.

Markus has argued that the originality of Augustine's
theory of signs lies in its use as a theory of *language*.[156] But
the texts which I have been citing show that the Stoics did
speak of signs in their theory of the meaning of linguistic
expressions. Only if one insists that τὸ σημαῖνον does not
denote a sign, can one say that the Stoics did not apply a
theory of signs to language. They used the more common
τὸ σημεῖον non-linguistically in their elaborate theory of inference.[157] It is not clear how these two terms for 'sign' are
related,[158] but Augustine's '*signum*' has something of the
connotation of both. On the one hand, he uses '*signum*' non-
linguistically in his general definition of '*signum*', in the examples which he gives for *signa naturalia*, and in some of the
examples for *signa data*.[159] He even uses one of the stock
examples from Stoic inferential theory—smoke as a sign of
fire.[160] On the other hand, he uses '*signum*' linguistically,
that is, of spoken and written words. Thus, instead of being
novel, Augustine's use of 'sign' seems to be in agreement with
the Stoic tradition.

It might be more correct to say that Augustine is original
among *Latin* authors in calling words 'signs'. Cicero, Varro,
and Quintilian do not seem to use '*signum*' in this way. It is
not used at all in two Latin handbooks of logic which survive from Augustine's period and earlier—Capella's *De dialectica* and the *Peri hermeneias* attributed to Apuleius.[161]

But there would seem to be a more important originality
in Augustine than this. It consists, I suggest, in the application of traditional sign-theory and sign-language to a new
task, the interpretation of Scripture. Briefly Augustine's application consists in using the technical terms of semantics
to make distinctions and definitions which delineate clearly
the problems faced by the interpreter of Scripture.[162] Detailed application of an explicit semantics would seem to be
an innovation in the history of Christian hermeneutics. In
the only hermeneutical treatises prior to *De doctrina* which

survive, *De principiis* IV and *Liber regularum,* Origen and Tyconius use the language of meaning and signifying[163] but neither reflect upon these semantic notions nor make systematic application of them. The clarity and sophistication gained by the use of semantics put Augustine in a better position to provide adequate solutions to the problems of Scriptural interpretation than he might otherwise have been in. Originality of this kind is appropriate to one of the greatest of the synthesizers of Christianity and classical culture. It is an instance of what Augustine so highly recommends in *De doctrina christiana* itself (II. 41–63)—the Christian's retaining of the liberal disciplines, in this case Aristotelian and Stoic logic, to be put to the use of truth (*usui ueritatis,* II. XL. 60, 15), in this case the interpretation of Holy Scripture.

1. *De doctr. chr.* I. II. 2, 1, XL. 44, 15, II. I. 1, 3, and XXXVII. 56, 45. References to *De doctrina* are to book, chapter, paragraph, and line (in that order) of the *Corpus Christianorum* edition of Josef Martin (Series Latina, XXXII, Turnhout: Brepols, 1962). The full reference will not be given when a certain passage is the stated topic of discussion or when the reference would differ only in paragraph and line from one immediately preceding it. I adhere to the following conventions in the use of Latin words:

   a) All Latin words will be italicized.

   b) When *mentioned* in an English sentence, a Latin word or phrase will be enclosed in single quotation marks. E. g., '*Res*' is a difficult term to translate.

   c) When *used* in an English sentence, a Latin word or phrase will not be enclosed in quotation marks. E. g., A *res* can also be a sign.

   d) When a Latin word, phrase, or clause occurs in parentheses to show what I am quoting or paraphrasing, it will be quoted exactly from the text; but when used or mentioned in a sentence, if a noun, the nominative case will be given, if a verb, the present active infinitive will be given.

2. For a sound analysis of Book One see Gilbert Istace, *Le livre 1er du 'De doctrina christiana' de saint Augustin,* in *Ephemerides Theologicae Lovanienses,* XXXII (1956), pp. 289–330.

3. *Retractationes* I. VII (I. VI in Migne; in general references to Augustine's works are to *Corpus Scriptorum Ecclesiasticorum Latinorum* editions. Exceptions will be noted). This work, regarded as spurious by the Benedictine editors of Augustine, is now widely accepted as the *De dialectica* mentioned by Augustine in the *Retr.* For recent discussions of authenticity see H.-I. Marrou, *Saint Augustin et la fin de la Culture Antique,* 4th edition including the *Retractatio* published in 1949 (Paris: Éditions E. de Boccard, 1958), pp. 576–78, and Jan Pinborg, *Das Sprachdenken der Stoa und Augustins Dialektik,* in *Classica et Mediaevalia,* XXIII (1962), pp. 149–51.

4. *St. Augustine on Signs,* in *Phronesis,* II (1957), 60–83 [Reprinted in this volume, Ch. 3].

5. *Der Zeichen- und Wortbegriff im Denken Augustins* (Amsterdam: N. V. Swets & Zeitlinger, 1934).

6. *Saint Augustin,* pp. 240–48.

7. Pinborg *op. cit.;* Georg Pfligersdorffer, *Zu Boethius, De*

Interp. . . . . nebst Beobachtung zur Geschichte der Dialektik bei den Römern, in Wiener Studien, LXVI (1953), 131–54; and Ulrich Duchrow, Sprachverständnis und biblisches Hören bei Augustin (Tübingen: J. C. B. Mohr, 1965), pp. 42–62.

8. From St. Augustine: *On Christian Doctrine*, trans. by D. W. Robertson, Jr., copyright © 1958 by The Liberal Arts Press, Inc. (Indianapolis), reprinted by permission of the Liberal Arts Press Division of The Bobbs-Merrill Company, Inc., p. 34.

9. 'Properly' translates Augustine's *'proprie'* at I. II. 2, 2. He gives no term for 'improperly'. Kuypers, p. 78, calls them 'eine weitere und eine engere Bedeutung', with 'engere' corresponding to 'proper'.

10. *De inuentione* I. xxx. 48.

11. *Institutio Oratoria* V. IX. 9.

12. Reciprocity is illustrated by 'noun' and 'word' which can signify each other, for 'word' is a noun and 'noun' is a word (*De mag.* v. 11). Reflexivity obtains in the case of 'noun' which can refer to itself as well as to other nouns (VI. 18).

13. *De dialectica* will be referred to by chapter and line of chapter of the Benedictine text reprinted in Migne, *Patrologia Latina*, vol. XXXII, columns, 1409–1420 (printed there with the title *'Principia Dialecticae'*). A French translation of this incomplete treatise is found in vol. IV of *Œuvres Complètes de Saint Augustin* (Paris: Libraire de Louis Vivès, 1873), pp. 52–68.

14. For the Latin or Greek text of most classical authors to whom I refer throughout the article I have used the editions in the Loeb Classical Library (London: Wm. Heinemann Ltd., and Cambridge: by permission of Harvard University Press, Cambridge). Exceptions are noted.

15. Markus, pp. 71f. [here, p. 73].

16. Robertson, pp. 34f.

17. *Ibid.*, p. 35, altered.

18. *Ibid.*, p. 34; J. F. Shaw (trans.), *On Christian Doctrine*, in Nicene and Post-Nicene Fathers, First Series, Vol. II (New York: Chas. Scribner's Sons, 1887), p. 536; G. Combès and J. Farges (trans.), *La Doctrine Chrétienne*, in Œuvres de Saint Augustin (Bibliothèque Augustinienne, First Series, XI, Paris: Desclée de Brouwer, 1949), p. 241.

19. *La doctrine du signe chez saint Augustin*, in *Studia Patristica*, vol. VI, ed. F. L. Cross (Berlin: Akademie-Verlag, 1962), pp. 366–73.

20. *Ibid.*, p. 371.

21. *Loc. cit.*

22. *Ibid.*, p. 372.

23. Markus, p. 72 [here, p. 74].

24. *Ibid.*, p. 73 [here, p. 75].

25. *Loc. cit.*

26. See Aulus Gellius, *Noctes Atticae* X. IV, where the contrast is expressed by three sets of terms: *Naturalia-positiua, naturalia-arbitraria,* and φύσει-θέσει.

27. See also *De musica* VI. IX. 24 (Migne, PL 32)—*uocabulis . . . placito enim, non natura imponuntur.*

28. Engels, p. 372.

29. Quoted in translation, above pp. 96f.

30. See, for example, II. x. 15. 3–12—the crucial definitions of *signa propria* and *signa translata,* III. VI. 10–IX. 13—the discussion of various attitudes toward figurative signs, and III. xxv. 34–36— a discussion of the varieties of figurative signification.

31. 'Semantics' may be defined briefly as the analysis of expressions and their signification. See Rudolf Carnap, *Introduction to Semantics* (Cambridge: Harvard University Press, 1942), pp. 9f.

32. These numbers in parentheses correspond to the column numbers in the table.

33. For a full discussion of this see the unpublished Harvard dissertation by Gareth B. Matthews, *An Interpretation and Critique of the Concept of the Inner Man in the Epistemology of St. Augustine,* 1960. I have also made use of a translation of selections from *De Genesi* XII by Gareth and Mary Matthews in mimeograph form (undated) [cf. also Chapter 7 below. Ed.].

34. *De lingua Latina* VI. 48.

35. *Epistulae Morales* 117. 13. For discussions of this passage see William and Martha Kneale, *The Development of Logic* (Oxford: At the Clarendon Press, 1962), p. 141, and Benson Mates, *Stoic Logic* (Berkeley and Los Angeles: University of California Press, 1961; 1st printing, 1953), pp. 11f.

36. For the text of *De trinitate* I have used the edition of Luis Arias, *Obras de San Agustin,* Vol. V (Madrid: Biblioteca de Autores Christianos, 2nd ed., 1956).

37. *Quidquid autem ex uerbo non auris, sed animus sentit, et ipso animo tenetur inclusum, dicibile uocatur . . . . Quod dixi dicibile, uerbum est; nec tamen uerbum, sed quod in uerbo intelligitur et in animo continetur, significat.*

38. See above pp. 93f.

39. Duchrow, *Sprachverständnis,* p. 47 and n. 73. According to Duchrow Augustine is following the common reduction of Stoic semantics from a threefold to a twofold scheme. Duchrow cites Seneca, *Ep. Mor.* 89. 17, as an example of this, but he is

mistaken. For the *uerba-significationes* classification of this passage instead of being a "reduction" of Stoic semantics is good Stoic doctrine. It corresponds to the Stoic division of the subject matter of dialectic into expressions and things signified. The latter are not external *res*, as Duchrow implies, but λεκτά. See Diogenes Laertius, VII, 43 and 63ff., and above, pp. 127f. The Stoics introduced their threefold scheme at another point and Seneca retains it (*Ep. Mor.* 117. 13, discussed above, pp. 103–4).

40. Markus, pp. 71f. [here, p. 73].

41. Above, p. 106.

42. At least two writers think that '*dicibile*' is Augustine's attempt to translate τὸ λεκτόν. Kneale, p. 188, and Duchrow, p. 53. Kneale regards 'what is meant' as the most literal translation of λεκτόν (p. 140).

43. Augustine does not say why this is intellectual knowledge and not sensible knowledge. Two reasons why this is so may be offered. The first is found explicitly in Augustine; the second, as I have put it, is not. (1) In so far as to understand a sign is to know what the sign-giver intended to express by it, it involves the apprehension, through the sign, of the mind of the sign-giver. According to Augustine, mind (*mens*, which is equivalent to '*animus*', *De trin.* XV. I. 1) is an intelligible which may be 'seen' only by intellectual vision. (*De Gen. ad litt.* XII. x. 21 and xxiv. 50). (2) Understanding a sign involves seeing a relation between two things, the sign and the designated object. Even if the object is a body, too (the sign is always corporeal), the relation between the two—signifies—is not a corporeal thing (sensible), and thus is intelligible.

44. See also II. XII. 17, 12, XIII. 19, 1 and 9, XIII, 20, 40, 50 and 58, and xv. 22, 2f. and 26. Augustine does not define '*sensus*' or '*sententia*' anywhere in *De doctrina*.

45. Especially in *De trin.* XV. x–xi (e), but also in *De doctr.* where '*uerbum*' is used once in the inner sense (c) and *passim* in the outer sense.

46. Gottlob Frege, *Ueber Sinn und Bedeutung,* trans. by Herbert Feigl as *On Sense and Nominatum,* in Feigl and Wilfrid Sellars (eds.), *Readings in Philosophical Analysis* (New York: Appleton-Century-Crofts, Inc., 1949), p. 86.

47. '*Signum*' *und* '*superbia*' *beim jungen Augustin* (386–90), in *Revue des Études Augustiniennes,* VII (1961), pp. 369–72.

48. Marrou, p. 16, says that in his reflection on language, signs, and meaning Augustine is mainly a grammarian, though sometimes the logician comes through. Kuypers, on the other hand, states that Augustine learned the meaning of the sign-

142   B. DARRELL JACKSON

significate distinction from the *ars dialectica* not from rhetoric
(p. 13). Markus, pp. 60, 64f. [here, p. 61, 65f.], argues that in
the linguistic application of the notion of sign Augustine went beyond even the logicians. I shall consider his view in part D below.

49. *Vetus Latina,* vol. 2, Genesis, ed. Bonifatius Fischer (Frei-
berg: Herder, 1951–1954), p. 188.

50. *Itala: Das Neue Testament in Altlateinischer Überliefer-
ung,* III. Lucas-Evangelium, ed. Adolf Jülicher (Berlin: Walter
de Gruyter and Co., 1954), p. 134, and B. W. Muncey, *The New
Testament Text of Saint Ambrose* (Cambridge: University Press,
1959), p. 33. For other instances in the New Testament see Jülicher III, pp. 18 and 232; I, p. 112; and IV, pp. 14, 19, and 40.

51. Markus, pp. 63f. [here, p. 64f.].

52. Origenes, *Com. In Iohan. evang.,* I. xxvi, 24. GCS, Bd 4,
Der Johanneskommentar, ed. Erwin Preuschen (Leipzig: J. C.
Hinrichs, 1903), p. 32, line 33.

53. XIII. LIX. 58, p. 290, lines 1–2.

54. X. xiii, 11, p. 183, lines 1–3.

55. X. xlvi. 30, p. 224, lines 1ff.

56. Origenes, *Com. in Math. evang.,* XIII. 22. GCS, Bd 10,
Matthäus-Erklärung, ed. Erich Klosterman (Leipzig: Hinrichs,
1935), p. 240, line 25; XVII. i, p. 577, lines 25 f., and XVII, ii,
p. 612, lines 20f.

57. *Aduersus Marcionem* III. xiii. 4. *Corpus Christianorum,*
Series Latina, I, ed. A. Kroymann (Turnhout: Brepols, 1954).

58. *Adu. Marc.* IV. xxxix. 16. In this passage he also uses *'res'.*

59. Ambrose, *Expositio Euangelii secundam Lucam* VII, 96–
97. Tyconius, *Liber Regularum* IV, ed. F. C. Burkitt in Texts and
Studies, vol. III, no. 1 (Cambridge, 1894), p. 41, line 30.

60. III, p. 29, lines 9f., and V, p. 64, lines 28–30.

61. *Comm. on John* X. xxiv. 6, p. 196, lines 5f.

62. *Rhetorica* I. 2, 1357a 32–35. *The Basic Works of Aristotle,*
ed. Richard McKeon (New York: Random House, 1941), p. 1332.

63. II. xxvii, 70a 2ff.

64. *Rhet.* 1357b 13–20.

65. *An. Pr.* 70a 11–39.

66. *De inu.* I. xxx. 48 and xliii. 81; *Inst. or.* V. ix. 1–16.

67. *Inst. or.* V. ix. 8–11.

68. *Orator* 115.

69. Dionysius Thrax, Τέχνη γραμματική, ed. Gustav Uhlig
(Leipzig: B. G. Teubner, 1884). Donatus, *Ars Minor* and *Ars
Grammatica,* ed. H. Keil in *Grammatici Latini,* vol. IV (Leipzig,
1864. Reprinted by Georg Olms, Hildesheim, 1961), pp. 355–402.
Dionysius is 1st century B.C.; Donatus is 4th century A.D.

70. Τὲχνη ch. 12, Uhlig, p. 36, lines 6–7. Note that he uses the participle τό σημαῖνον, which can sometimes be translated as 'sign'. It does not seem to be appropriate to do so here. The Latin grammarians who followed Dionysius translated it either by the verb *'significat'* or the participle *'significans'* (Uhlig, pp. 24, 34, and 40). It is doubtful that Augustine read any but Latin grammars, although in *De utilitati credendi* VII. 17 he mentions Cornutus, who wrote in Greek, as well as the Latin-writing Asper and Donatus.

71. *Ars minor,* Keil, IV, p. 355, lines 5f.

72. V. 3 and 4; VI. 52; VII. 12, 80, 93, and 107; VIII. 11, 27, and 80.

73. *De ling. Lat.* VIII. 40, trans. by Roland G. Kent in the Loeb Classical Library nos. 333–34 (London and Cambridge, 1938), p. 403. See also IX. 37–*'uox quae significauit'* and *'res quae designetur'*, and V. 2–περὶ σημαινομένων.

74. VII. 14.

75. VII. 50, 73–74; IX. 24; and X. 46.

76. I have not made a thorough search of the grammatical commentaries. A cursory examination of the fourth century commentaries of Donatus on Terence and of Servius on Virgil revealed no linguistic use of *'signum'*.

77. *Noctes Atticae* IV. IX, II. XIX, VI. XVII, X. XXIX, XII. XIV, XIII. III and XVII, and XVII. XIII.

78. I. M. Bochenski, *Ancient Formal Logic* (Amsterdam: North Holland Printing Company, 2nd printing, 1957), p. 29.

79. H.-I. Marrou, *A History of Education in Antiquity,* trans. by G. Lamb (New York: The New American Library, 1964), p. 383.

80. Marrou, *Saint Augustin,* p. 111.

81. *Orator* XXXII. 113–XXXIII. 117.

82. Marrou, *Saint Augustin,* pp. 112–15.

83. *Ibid.,* p. 113.

84. See Aimé Solignac, *Doxographies et manuels dans la formation philosophique de Saint Augustin,* in *Recherches Augustiniennes* I (Paris, 1958), p. 148.

85. *De ordine* II. Marrou, pp. 174–79.

86. Marrou, pp. 237–75.

87. *Ibid.,* pp. 240–48.

88. All statements in part C will be based on the text cited at the beginning (here *Conf.* IV. XVI. 28) unless otherwise indicated.

89. Pierre Courcelle, *Les Lettres Grecques en Occident de Macrobe à Cassiodore* (Paris: Éditions E. de Boccard, 1943), p. 156.

90.   It is mainly metaphysical, but was regarded as logical by
the editors of Aristotle and subsequently in antiquity and the
middle ages. Kneale, p. 25.

91.   Discussed by Paul Henry, *Saint Augustine on Personality*
(New York: Macmillan, 1960), pp. 9f. [Cf. A. C. Lloyd, below,
Ch. 8].

92.   For *Contra Academicos* and *De ordine* (which is considered next) I have used the edition of William M. Green (Stromata
Patristica et Mediaevalia, 2nd fasc., Antwerp: Spectrum, 1956).

93.   Aristotelian logic, on the other hand, is a logic of classes.
Mates, pp. 2f. In my remarks about Stoic logic I shall often refer
to the excellent accounts of Mates and Kneale as well as to some
of the primary sources. I have used a standard notation for propositional logic to represent the various statements and arguments
in symbolic form. Mates, pp. 78 and 101f., and Bochenski, p. 98,
use similar notations in their expositions of Stoic logic. The symbol for implication requires special comment. Stoic logicians interpreted "if . . . then . . ." statements in a variety of ways, including material implication and strict implication. On this see
Mates, pp. 42–51. Since, however, material implication is sufficient for the validity of the undemonstrated arguments, and since
Augustine does not say how he regarded this connective (though
he probably inclined towards viewing it as strict implication if we
may judge from his examples), I use the material implication
symbol "⊃" for "if . . . then . . ." statements in Augustine.

94.   The primary sources for our knowledge of these are
Diogenes Laertius, *Lives* VII. 71–74 and *Sextus Empiricus,
Aduersus Mathematicos* VIII. 108ff. See Mates, pp. 32f. and
Kneale, pp. 147f.

95.   Aulus Gellius, *Noct. Att.* XVI. VIII. 9 and 12.

96.   See Mates, pp. 67–74. On p. 68 he gives a list of the many
sources for our knowledge of these arguments. Diogenes Laertius
lists all five (VII. 80–81). The undemonstrated arguments func-
tioned as axioms in the Stoics' system of deduction.

97.   See Sextus, *AM* VIII. 224 and 227 for all three ways.

98.   *Adu. Math.* VIII. 224. Trans. by Mates, p. 99.

99.   *Topica* XIII. 54.

100.   Marrou, p. 578.

101.   Duchrow, *Sprachverständnis,* p. 42.

102.   Diogenes Laertius, *Lives* VII. 41.

103.   *Topica* I. 1.

104.   Cicero, *Topica* XII. 53, *Or.* XXXII. 113.

105.   Pfligersdorffer, p. 137.

106.   Diogenes Laertius, VII. 42.

107. Quintilian calls rhetoric '*bene dicendi scientia*'. (*Inst. or.* II. xv. 34) Cicero calls dialectic '*ars bene disserendi*'. (*De or.* II. xxxviii. 157).

108. *Contra Ac.* I. i. 4, III. xiii. 29 and x. 44.

109. Marrou, p. 111 n. 3.

110. Duchrow, p. 43.

111. Sextus Empiricus, VIII. 70–74, 93 and Diogenes Laertius, VII. 63–75. See Mates, p. 16, for a summary statement of the Stoic classification of λεκτά.

112. Aristotle, *De interp.* ii–v, where Aristotle speaks of nouns, verbs, and simple and complex sentences. See Bochenski, pp. 28 and 85, on both the Aristotelian and the Stoic scheme. It is probable that the Stoics are dependent upon Aristotle at this point.

113. Mates, p. 32, and Kneale, p. 146.

114. Book IV of *De Nuptiis Philologiae et Mercurii*. This parallel with Capella, who, acknowledges the importance of Varro for dialectic (335 in the ed. by Adolf Dick, Leipzig, Teubner, 1925), has been seen as proof of Augustine's dependence upon Varro's *De dialectica* (Duchrow, p. 42, n. 47). Pfligersdorffer, on the contrary, says the scheme comes from a post-Varronian Stoic school tradition (p. 144). Such issues seem to me quite impossible to decide because of the loss of (a) Varro's *De dial.* and (b) virtually all Stoic logical writings.

115. Dick, 406–20.

116. See Duchrow, p. 56.

117. Robertson, p. 68.

118. See Kneale, pp. 163–76, and Mates, pp. 77–82. Most of the theorems used by the Stoics for analysis have been lost. Kneale gives a highly plausible reconstruction of this aspect of Stoic deduction theory. The first argument above could be proved by U2 with the assumption of the equivalence $p \equiv \sim \cdot \sim p$. See Kneale, p. 168, for the latter.

119. Aulus Gellius, *Noct. Att.* XVI. viii. 1; Mates, p. 8.

120. *Noct. Att.* XVI. viii. 2.

121. See above, n. 96.

122. *Topica* XII. 52–XIII. 57.

123. Augustine was not alone in making such errors. See, for example, Cicero's assignment of Stoic doctrines to Aristotle and Theophrastus (*De inu.* I. xxxv. 61).

124. See above, p. 120.

125. Courcelle, pp. 163–76, does not mention it among the several works of Porphyry which Augustine did read. Nor does Augustine appear to have read Plotinus' Περὶ διαλεκτικῆς. *Enneads* I. 3. Paul Henry, *Plotin et l'Occident*, (Louvain: Spicile-

gium, 1934), pp. 224f., does not list it among the quotations, para-
phrases, or allusions to Plotinus in Augustine. Plotinus regards
dialectic as the way of ascent to the Good. He expresses disdain
for the concerns of formal logic. The only technical content of
his dialectic is Platonic διαίρεσις.

126. Kneale, p. 187.

127. Pfligersdorffer, pp. 133–35.

128. He wrote a commentary on Porphyry's *Eisagoge* based
on Victorinus' translation of the latter. This is in Migne, PL 64,
cols. 9–70.

129. See Courcelle, pp. 264f., for specific instances.

130. PL 64, col. 180A.

131. PL 64, 159C.

132. Gustave Combès, *Saint Augustin et la culture classique*
(Paris: Librarie Plon, 1927), pp. 14f., cites *De ciu. Dei* VIII. 12
and IX. 4 as evidence. P. Alfaric, *L'évolution intellectuelle de Saint
Augustin* (Paris, 1918), p. 232, cites only *Conf.* IV. XVI.

133. Courcelle, p. 156, n. 7, and Marrou, p. 34, n. 7.

134. According to Bochenski, p. 29, Aristotle has a far more
complex semantics than the one in *De interp.*, but it is scattered
throughout the *Physics* and *Metaphysics* and is involved in Aristotle's ontology and epistemology. It does not seem appropriate to
investigate it in this study.

135. PL 64, col. 297A.

136. Cicero, *Topica* VIII. 35.

137. 2, 16ᵃ 28 at PL 64, 303C; 3, 16ᵇ 11 at 306B; but *'signum'*
for 'proof' 1, 16ᵃ 17 at 300D.

138. See, for example, *Contra Ac.* II. XI. 25 where Licentius
says to Augustine, "I have indeed often heard you say that it is a
disgrace for disputants to haggle about words when no difference
about the subject matter remains. . . ." Trans. by J. J. O'Meara,
in *Ancient Christian Writers*, no. 12 (Westminster: The Newman
Press, 1950), p. 91. See Marrou, pp. 243, n. 2 and 349, n. 3 for
other similar passages in Augustine.

139. *De doctr. chr.* uses the former at II. XX. 30, 11, and the
latter at XXII. 33, 31 of the same things but not of words.

140. *Vox enim etiam intellectum rei significat, et ipsam rem,*
PL 64, 297B.

141. See Mates, pp. 12f.

142. See Kneale, p. 142.

143. Mates, p. 9.

144. *Ep. Mor.* 89. 17.

145. Dionysius Thrax is said to have been influenced by the
Stoics. Kneale, p. 143.

146. '*Nomen*' for the first, '*uocabulum*' for the second, and '*uerbum*' for the third; see *De dial.* I. 14f. and 22–24, VI. 17 and 31, VII. 33, and *De mag.* V. 16.

147. *De dial.* V. 52–54 and 62–64.

148. See the refutation of the view at VIII. 137–39.

149. *De dial.* II. 12–18.

150. VIII. 11–12. Trans. by Kneale, p. 140, quoted by permission of the Clarendon Press, Oxford. Actually, only a part of the class of *lekta,* namely, the ἀξιώματα, are true or false.

151. I believe that τὸ σημαῖνον has almost lost its participial flavor and has here become a nominal technical term, unlike the usage in Dionysius Thrax. See above n. 70.

152. VIII. 70. See Mates, pp. 15f.

153. *Lives* VII. 57.

154. *Ep. Mor.* 89. 17.

155. 117. 13; Kneale, p. 141.

156. Markus, pp. 60–65 [here, pp. 61–66].

157. *Adu. Math.* VIII. 140ff.

158. See Kneale, pp. 141f., and Mates, pp. 13f.

159. *De doctr.* II. ɪ. 1–2 and ɪɪɪ. 4.

160. *De doctr.* II. ɪ. 1, 8 and 2, 14f. See *Adu. Math.* VIII. 152. Also compare II. ɪ. 2, 18–22 with *AM* VIII. 173.

161. Apuleius, *Opera Omnia,* vol. 2, ed. G. F. Hildebrand (Leipzig, 1842), 265ff. This second century A.D. work contains no semantics. Capella does have some semantics, but he uses '*nomen*' and '*res*' not '*signum*' (Dick, 355–58).

162. This is done in Books Two and Three of *De doctrina.*

163. Origen, *De principiis* IV. 2–3 and Tyconius, *Liber regularum* IV (Burkitt, p. 36, lines 12f., p. 37, line 11, p. 53, line 8), V (p. 59, line 23), and VII (p. 71, line 7).

MIND AND KNOWLEDGE

5

Si Fallor, Sum

GARETH B. MATTHEWS

As several of Descartes's contemporaries were quick to point out, and as Augustinian and Cartesian scholars have often noted, a number of passages in the writings of St. Augustine seem to anticipate Descartes's *cogito*.[1] (Perhaps it would be fairer to say that Descartes's *cogito* seems to echo a number of passages in Augustine.) Just exactly how close the Augustinian parallels are to Descartes has been a matter of dispute.

I hope that what I have to say in this paper will make a contribution toward settling that dispute. But my primary aim will be to achieve a better understanding of exactly what Augustine is up to in those *cogito*-like passages. My procedure will be to take the single passage in Augustine that is most like Descartes and try to formalize its central argument. The frustrations that face that endeavor will help us, I think, both to recognize and to appreciate the argument's true nature. Having recognized its nature we shall then be in position to make instructive comparisons between it and Descartes's *cogito* argument.

I

Among the five or six passages in Augustine commonly cited as anticipations of the Cartesian *cogito,* the one most often referred to, and the one which I shall concentrate on, is

This paper was written especially for this volume.

the famous *si fallor, sum* ("If I am mistaken, I am") passage
from Book XI of *The City of God;* it follows.

> For we are, and we know that we are, and we love to be
> and to know that we are. Moreover, in the three things I
> have said there is no falsity resembling truth to trouble us.
> For we do not take hold of these things with any bodily
> sense, as we do what is outside us. Thus we perceive colors
> by seeing, sounds by hearing, odors by smelling, flavors by
> tasting, hard and soft things by touching; and in thought we
> turn over incorporeal images that resemble these sensible
> things and we hold them in the memory and by their means
> we are aroused to desire the sensible things themselves. But
> without any teasing imagination of appearances or illusions,
> it is most certain to me that I am, that I know it, and that I
> love it.
>
> Concerning these truths I fear no arguments of the
> Academics in which they say, "What if you should be mis-
> taken?" For if I am mistaken, I am. For one who does not
> exist cannot be mistaken either. And so I am, if I am mis-
> taken. Because therefore I am, if I am mistaken, how am I
> mistaken about my existence when it is certain that I am if
> I am mistaken? Because therefore I, who would be the one
> mistaken, would have to exist to be mistaken, there is no
> doubt I am not mistaken in knowing that I am.
>
> Moreover, it follows that I should not be mistaken even
> in knowing that I know. For just as I know that I am, so also
> I know that I know it.
>
> And when I love these two things, I also add to the things
> I know a third and no less valuable something, this very
> love.[2]

A natural first stab at formalizing the central argument
in this passage (I say this is a natural first stab because it is
the way I first thought the argument went) would be to render it as the following dilemma:

Argument A

(A1)   If I am mistaken, I am.

(A2)   If I am not mistaken, I am.

(A3)   Either I am mistaken or I am not mistaken.

Therefore   (A4)   I am.[3]

This argument is interesting in a number of ways. For one thing, it seems to have the same form as the following argument (which is inspired by Hobbes's and Gassendi's objections to Descartes[4]):

Argument B
(B1) If I walk, I am.
(B2) If I do not walk, I am.
(B3) Either I walk or I do not walk.
Therefore (B4) I am.

Yet Argument A is open to a very natural reading that would make it rather different from Argument B. Premise (A2), "If I am not mistaken, I am," is naturally read as elliptical for "If I am not mistaken *in thinking that I am,* I am"—i.e., as equivalent to "If I am *right* in thinking that I am, I am." And there is no analogous way of taking (B2), "If I do not walk, I am." And so there is no way of supporting (B2) analogous to the obvious and unproblematic way of supporting (A2) that this elliptical reading of it invites. (I do not, of course, mean to suggest that (B2) is without support.)

Before committing ourselves to a full assessment of Argument A and its plausibility, however, we should perhaps ask ourselves how closely it fits the text. What we have to answer is, I think, that Argument A fits the text very, very badly. To be sure, (A1) is stated and argued for. Augustine argues for it by maintaining that "one who does not exist cannot be mistaken either." Augustine does not mean, of course, that non-existent people are infallible. He means something more like this: necessarily, if one does not exist, one is not mistaken. Or this: it cannot be that both x fails to exist and also x is mistaken. (Therefore, necessarily, if I am mistaken, I am.)

So (A1) is both stated and argued for. But neither (A2) nor (A3) is even stated, let alone argued for. If Augustine had stated one of them, it might have been reasonable to construe his argument as an enthymematic stab at Argument A. But with both unstated, there is no reason to say he had a dilemma in mind; so we ought to look for another reconstruction of his reasoning.

II

Here is a rather different approach.

In the passage we have been discussing Augustine claims to know that he exists (and to know that he knows, and to know that he loves to be and to know[5]—but let us continue to ignore the additional knowledge claims). Now the skeptic says, "What if you should be mistaken?"

Augustine's response can perhaps be understood in this way. One decides to be perfectly accommodating to the skeptic. One simply modifies one's claim in such a way as to incorporate in the claim itself the very possibility that so much worries the skeptic. Thus we begin with some claim, φ. When the skeptic points out that one may after all be mistaken, one obligingly agrees, but still insists, ⌜Unless I am mistaken, φ.⌝

The skeptic has been accommodated. One has taken the possibility he is so much concerned about into full consideration; one has given it its due. One has replaced the original claim, φ, with its "AS Transform," as I shall call it (for "Anti-skeptical Transformation").

Now the main moral of the Augustinian passage seems to come into view. In at least one case, viz., the case where φ is "I am," full accommodation to the skeptic turns out to mean no erosion in what is claimed or asserted. For in that case the AS Transform of φ, if supplemented by the unimpeachable premise, *si fallor, sum,* yields the original φ. The argument to show this follows.

Argument C

	(C1)	Unless I am mistaken, I am.
Thus[6]	(C2)	Either I am mistaken or I am.
But	(C3)	If I am mistaken, I am. (*Si fallor, sum.*)
So	(C4)	Either I am or I am.
Therefore	(C5)	I am.

One feature of Argument C that recommends it as an interpretation of the *si fallor, sum* passage is that it makes essential use of the fact that Augustine is directing his argument at skeptics. Incidentally, the reason why "If I walk, I am" is not as good as "If I am mistaken, I am" for Augustine's purposes is that no serious skeptic will meet a claim to know that one exists with the rejoinder, "But what if you should be walking?"

It might be worth pausing here to consider whether there are other interesting arguments of similar form based on AS Transforms. That is, is there some other statement, φ, such that one could accede to the skeptic and substitute the AS Transform of φ for φ — and then go on to argue in similar fashion for φ itself?

I think there are others. I want to say something about two of them.

Argument D

	(D1)	Unless I am mistaken, I am awake.
Thus	(D2)	Either I am mistaken or I am awake.
But	(D3)	If I am mistaken, I am awake.
So	(D4)	Either I am awake or I am awake.
Therefore	(D5)	I am awake.

Argument E

	(E1)	Unless I am mistaken, I am here.
Thus	(E2)	Either I am mistaken or I am here.
But	(E3)	If I am mistaken, I am here.
So	(E4)	Either I am here or I am here.
Therefore	(E5)	I am here.

How would (D3) be supported? Presumably by arguing that

(a) Whoever is mistaken is awake.

Although many philosophers, including Augustine[7] and Descartes,[8] have rejected (a), a case might be made out for it. One might try arguing along these lines: To be mistaken is to think that p when it is not the case that p; but the most one could do when asleep is to *dream* that one thinks that p; and dreaming one thinks that p (when not p) no more counts

as making a mistake than dreaming one has seduced a prin-
cess (without her consent) counts as committing rape.[9]

What about (E3)? This time the support called for will be
very different. Certainly we don't want to have to appeal to
this:

(b) Whoever is mistaken is here.

The plausibility of Argument E doesn't rest upon a connection between being mistaken and being here (or upon a connection between being mistaken and being wherever the person who enunciates the alleged connection is). Rather it rests
upon a connection between *using* the indexical "I" and *using*
the indexical "here." One wants to say that the rules for using
indexicals are such that "I am here" has to be true.[10]

Argument C is two-faced. It can be taken in such a way
that it is more like Argument D; or it can be taken in such a
way that it is more like Argument E. Which way one takes
it depends on how (C3) is to be supported. If it is to be supported by appeal to a connection between being mistaken and
existing, the argument will be like Argument D (which appeals to a connection between being mistaken and being
awake). But if it is supported by appeal to a connection between *using* the indexical "I" and existing, the argument will
be more like Argument E (which appeals to a connection
between using "I" and using "here").

If we grant that Augustine in the *City of God* passage we
have been discussing is actually offering Argument C, or a
very close relative of it, then we have to say, I think, that he
gives it a D-like face, rather than an E-like face. That is, he
supports (C3) by making a connection between being mistaken and existing rather than by making a connection between using the pronoun "I" and reporting that one exists.
If he had said, as Descartes does in the "Second Meditation,"
"'I am' is necessarily true as often as it is uttered or conceived," we should have a glimmer of the E-like face. Instead
he merely says, "For one who does not exist cannot be mistaken either." And that reasoning supports "If Bildad is mistaken, then Bildad exists" just as well as it supports "If I am
mistaken, I am." The point about using the first-person pronoun "I" does not figure in Augustine's argument.

I think that Argument C is indeed much closer to the *si*

fallor, sum passage we are discussing than Argument A is. However, it has a fatal flaw, a flaw that it shares, incidentally, with Argument A. The flaw is that, whereas both these arguments yield the conclusion, "I am," Augustine's answer to the Academic skeptics is supposed to vouchsafe "I know that I am."[11]

Could one use the same form of argument to support "I know that I am"? No, for the premise parallel to "If I am mistaken, I am" would have to be "If I am mistaken, I know that I am." And that premise has nothing to recommend it.

We must try a different approach.

III

The *si fallor, sum* passage from the *City of God* that we have been discussing and the several other *cogito*-like passages in Augustine belong to a rather large family of passages in which Augustine is occupied with answering skeptics. His earliest extant dialogue, *Contra academicos* ("Against the Academics," or "Skeptics"), is devoted almost solely to this project. *Contra academicos* does not, in fact, contain any *cogito*-like passages. Instead of trying to vouchsafe knowledge of his own existence, Augustine is there chiefly concerned to vindicate knowledge of mathematics and knowledge of how things seem in sense perception (see *Contra academicos* II. 11. 25–26). Still, Augustine does exhibit in that work his interest in reasoning *contra academicos*.

Descartes, too, wanted to put down the arguments of skeptics. But that aim was subsidiary to his major purpose of providing a rational reconstruction of our knowledge. Descartes's major purpose has been so common to modern philosophy that we naturally read it back into Augustine. And perhaps that is the trouble with our efforts so far to interpret the passage from the *City of God*. We have assumed that Augustine is out to establish an elementary truth such as "I exist" or "I know that I exist." But perhaps that isn't his project at all. Perhaps his purpose is rather to put down the arguments of skeptics, to reason, not constructively, but destructively—*contra academicos*. To do that satisfactorily may not involve establishing any such conclusion as "I exist" or "I know that I exist."

How does one answer a skeptic? It depends, of course, on what the skeptic says. Sometimes the skeptic will argue that one can't know that p because p is not something anyone could possibly be in a position to know. (A Humean argument that we don't know whether the Principle of Induction holds may go that way.) But a more common skeptical move is to remind us that we have often been mistaken in the past and therefore might be mistaken again this time. Schematically the exchange goes this way:

Knowledge claimant: I know that p.
Skeptic: (1) You have often been mistaken in the past.
Therefore (2), You might be mistaken about whether p.
Therefore (3), You can't be certain that p.
Therefore (4), You don't know that p.

Each of the steps in this argument deserves scrutiny. Each step has a certain plausibility; yet each step relies for its plausibility upon a suppressed premise that ought to be questioned. It is enough for our present purposes, however, to identify (2) as the step that Augustine concentrates on.

The point Augustine tries to make is that the reasoning to "You might be mistaken about whether p" breaks down in at least one case. Specifically, it fails where "I am" is substituted for "p" in the knowledge claim. Suppose the exchange begins this way:

Knowledge claimant: I know that I am.
Skeptic: But you have often been mistaken in the past.
Therefore, you might be mistaken about whether you are . . .

It is this move that Augustine denies the skeptic. Here again are Augustine's words:

. . . I fear no arguments of the Academics in which they say, "What if you should be mistaken?" For if I am mistaken, I am. For one who does not exist cannot be mistaken either. And so I am, if I am mistaken. Because therefore I

am, if I am mistaken, how am I mistaken about my existence
when it is certain that I am if I am mistaken?

The skeptic's taunt ("What if you should be mistaken?") is
meant to conjure up a possibility that will undermine the
knowledge claim. But, in this context anyway, the taunt turns
out to be vain and hollow. The possibility it would conjure
up (viz., the possibility that I am mistaken about whether I
am) is no possibility at all. About my own existence it cannot
be that I am mistaken. Skeptic dismissed.

But if Augustine's reasoning in this passage is purely *contra
academicos*, how does Augustine support his claim to know
that he exists? More specifically, what is the argument summarized in this line:

> Because therefore I, who would be the one mistaken, would
> have to exist to be mistaken, undoubtedly I am not mistaken
> in knowing that I am.

The answer is, I think, that this is not the summary of an
argument which yields (or is meant to yield) the conclusion,
"I know that I am." What it summarizes instead is Augustine's rebuff to the skeptic's question, "What if you should
be mistaken?"

To put the point in a different way, there are other conceivable threats to a claim to know that p besides the threat
that one might be mistaken. Perhaps the most important kind
of threat concerns the reasons one has for thinking that p.
Thus, even though I am not mistaken about what I claim to
know, I may have insufficient reason or evidence to be justified in making a knowledge claim. Augustine's skeptic is
innocent of worry over this threat (indeed, he is innocent of
worry over all other conceivable threats besides the threat
that one might be mistaken). So, in putting down his skeptic,
Augustine does something different from (something less
than, if you prefer[12]) providing a justification for a claim to
know that one exists.

Nor is this an oversight on Augustine's part. He considers
knowledge of his own existence direct and immediate and
therefore as something neither capable of justification by ap-

peal to something more basic, nor, of course, requiring any such justification. ". . . What is so present to the mind," he asks rhetorically in the *De trinitate*, "as the mind itself" (X. 7. 10). "But when it is said to the mind," he goes on a little later, "'Know yourself!' it knows itself the moment it understands what is said: 'yourself'; nor does it know itself for any reason other than that it is present to itself" (X. 9. 12).

In fact Augustine introduces the *si fallor, sum* passage we have been discussing by insisting on the immediacy of one's knowledge of oneself. Here again is what he says:

> For we are, and we know that we are, and we love to be and to know that we are. Moreover, in the three things I have said there is no falsity resembling truth to trouble us. For we do not take hold of these things with any bodily sense, as we do what is outside us. Thus we perceive colors by seeing, sounds by hearing, odors by smelling, flavors by tasting, hard and soft things by touching; and in thought we turn over incorporeal images that resemble these sensible things and we hold them in the memory, and by their means we are aroused to desire the sensible things themselves. But without any teasing imagination of appearances or illusions, it is most certain to me that I am, that I know it, and that I love it.

Two points I wish to emphasize are these: (i) Self-knowledge, unlike knowledge of "what is outside us," does not require the instrumentality of the bodily senses. (ii) Self-knowledge, unlike memory of sensible things and reflection upon them, does not require the mediation of mental images. In both these respects, then, self-knowledge (according to Augustine) is direct and immediate.

Still, the skeptic ought to be answered. And Augustine answers him. But what is required is not an argument to support the conclusion that I exist, or that I know I exist. It will be sufficient to show that the skeptic's taunt ("But what if you are mistaken?") is vain. And that is what Augustine shows.

IV

Augustine's *si fallor, sum* is thus not an argument, or part of an argument, intended to establish that one exists.[13] Since Descartes's *cogito, ergo sum* is such an argument (or perhaps the union of two such arguments), Augustine's reasoning is basically, and not just incidentally, different from Descartes's.

Perhaps the best way to clarify this difference is to state it with respect to what Jaakko Hintikka says about Augustine in his splendid article on Descartes, *"Cogito, ergo sum:* Inference or Performance?"[14] Here is Hintikka's verdict on the matter of whether Augustine had anticipated Descartes's *cogito:*

> In so far as I know, there is no indication that Augustine was ever alive to the possibility of interpreting his version of the *Cogito* as a performance rather than as an inference or as a factual observation. As far as Augustine is concerned, it would be quite difficult to disprove a "logical" interpretation such as Gassendi and others have given of the Cartesian *cogito* argument. What he dwells on is merely the "impossibility of thinking without existing." I do not see any way in which Augustine could have denied that *ambulo, ergo sum* or *video, ergo sum* are as good inferences as *cogito, ergo sum* and that the sole difference between them lies in the different degree of certainty of their premises (p. 130).

Hintikka is right, I think, in doubting that Augustine was ever "alive to the possibility" of supposing that "I exist" verifies itself whenever it is uttered or conceived.[15] And since Hintikka argues persuasively that Descartes was alive to precisely this possibility, here is one very interesting and important respect in which Augustine's argument is not like Descartes's.

Hintikka maintains that Descartes's *cogito* is part inference, part performance.[16] Having concluded that Augustine's argument is not even part performance, Hintikka seems to assume that it is therefore an inference ("or a factual observation" he adds—but he doesn't do anything with that possibility); indeed he assumes that Augustine's argument is an inference that parallels this Cartesian argument:

Si cogito, sum.	If I think, I am.
Cogito.	I think.
Ergo sum.[17]	Therefore, I am.

Hintikka concedes that this argument falls victim to such Gassendian and Hobbesian parallels as

Si ambulo, sum	If I walk, I am.
Ambulo.	I walk.
Ergo sum.	Therefore, I am.

All one can say in its defense, he thinks, is that the second premise, *Cogito*, has a degree of certainty greater than the parallel *Ambulo*.

But what does Hintikka suppose the parallel Augustinian argument might be? He doesn't say. Could it be that he has this in mind?

Si fallor, sum.	If I am mistaken, I am.
Fallor.	I am mistaken.
Ergo sum.	Therefore, I am.

Presumably not. The mistake relevant to "If I am mistaken, I am" is surely the mistake of thinking that I am. Certainly Augustine does not suppose that one is in position to assert that one is mistaken in thinking that one exists (!) and to conclude that therefore one exists! It is more like this— Suppose I were mistaken in thinking that I am. Then, insofar as *what* I think (viz., that I am) is a mistake, it follows that I am not. But, insofar as I *do* anything (including make a mistake), it follows that I am. Therefore from "I am mistaken in thinking that I am" it follows both that I am not and that I am. Therefore it can't be that I am mistaken in thinking that I am.

Perhaps Hintikka had some other passage from Augustine in mind. Though he cites no passages, he does refer to Augustine's *De trinitate*. Here is the main *cogito*-like passage from that book:

> It is an inner knowledge by which we know that we live, where not even the Academic can say, "Perhaps you are sleeping, and you do not know, and you see in dreams."

For who does not know that things seen by those who are asleep are very similar to things seen by those who are awake. But he who is certain about the knowledge of his own life does not say in it, "I know that I am awake," but "I know that I live." Whether he, therefore, sleeps or whether he is awake, he lives. He cannot be mistaken in his knowledge of this even by dreams, because to sleep and to see in dreams is characteristic of one who lives.

Nor can the Academic argue as follows against this knowledge: "Perhaps you are insane . . ." [B]ut he who is insane lives; nor does he make this retort to the Academics: "I know that I am not insane" but "I know that I live." He can never, therefore, be deceived nor lie who says that he knows that he lives (*De trinitate* XV. 12. 21).[18]

There are several interesting and important differences between this passage and the one from the *City of God*. For one thing, Augustine here seeks to answer *specific* skeptical suggestions ("Perhaps you are asleep . . ." "Perhaps you are insane . . .") rather than, as in the *City of God* passage, to answer merely the general skeptical move, "Perhaps you are mistaken." For another thing, Augustine is here interested in the knowledge that he *lives* rather than in the knowledge that he *exists*. The soul (*anima*) is what animates or vivifies a body. And I suspect that Augustine's talk of knowing that he lives has something to do with his effort in Book VIII of the same work to say how he knows that there are other souls or minds (animators or vivifiers). He seems there to present an early statement of the argument from analogy for the existence of other minds (or souls).

But whatever the differences between this passage and the one from the *City of God*, it seems incontestable that here, too, Augustine is arguing *contra academicos* rather than using *modus ponens* to establish the conclusion that he exists.

Hintikka says that Augustine dwells on "the impossibility of thinking without existing." If he did, we should have a basis for constructing an Augustinian argument to parallel the *cogito* inference. But I know of no passage in which he does this. What he insists on instead is the impossibility of being mistaken without existing. (To the *City of God* and *De trinitate* passages already cited we could add this sentence

from the very early work, *De libero arbitrio:* "For if you did
not exist it would be impossible for you to be mistaken"
[II. 3. 7].)

Pointing out the impossibility of being mistaken without
existing (or living) does not establish my existence. But it
does turn aside a familiar skeptical thrust; and so (according
to Augustine) it safeguards my direct and immediate knowledge that I exist, and that I live.

1. Cf. Étienne Gilson, *Études sur le rôle de la pensée médiévale dans la formation du système cartésien* (Paris: Vrin, 1951), *"Le cogito et la tradition augustinienne,"* pp. 191–201.

2. *De civitate dei* XI. 26; author's translation.

3. Compare the following argument, which Jaakko Hintikka says Descartes "could have resorted to" (he doesn't say that Descartes did resort to it): "If I am right in thinking that I exist, then of course I exist. If I err in thinking that I exist or if I as much as doubt whether I exist, then I must likewise exist, for no one can err or doubt without existing. In any case I must therefore exist: *ergo sum.*" (*"Cogito, Ergo Sum:* Inference or Performance," reprinted in *Descartes: A Collection of Critical Essays,* Willis Doney, ed. (New York: Doubleday, 1967), p. 114.

4. *The Philosophical Works of Descartes,* Haldane & Ross, trans., Vol. II (New York: Dover, 1955), pp. 62 and 137.

5. The passage as a whole makes clear that Augustine arrives at the figure of three, rather than four, things "in which there is no falsity" by counting as one the last two things he claims to know. Thus he claims to know (1) that he is, (2) that he knows he is, and (3) that he loves to be and to know that he is.

6. I am proceeding here as if "Unless I am mistaken, . . ." had the force of "~ (I am mistaken) ⊃ . . . ." In fact I think it does not. A man who said, "Unless I am mistaken, that's a Picasso", would be making a poor joke if, upon discovering that the painting was a Braque, he said, "You see, what I said was right —I said that if it weren't a Picasso I would be mistaken; it wasn't and I *was* mistaken, so what I said was right." However, I shall soon reject this line of reasoning as an interpretation of Augustine anyway. So, in the meantime, the reasoning here is offered *e concessis.*

7. Cf., e.g., *De Genesi ad litteram* XII. 2. 3. In this particular passage Augustine gives a somewhat amusing account of trying to persuade someone in a dream that they are (both) in a dream.

8. ". . . On many occasions I have in sleep been deceived . . ." *Meditation* I, Haldane & Ross, Vol. I, p. 146.

9. Cf. Norman Malcolm, *Dreaming* (London: Routledge & Kegan Paul, 1959), p. 112: ". . . one who is asleep cannot make judgments and therefore not erroneous judgments. The worst that can happen to him in this line is to dream that he is deceived, and that is not so bad."

10. There may be some interesting complications. In his "In-

dicators and Quasi-Indicators" (*American Philosophical Quarterly*, April 1967), Hector-Neri Castañeda seems to make a contrast between liability to error in the case of "I" and liability in the case of "here." He says this:

> A correct use of "I" cannot fail to refer to the entity it purports to refer [to]; moreover, a correct use of "I" cannot fail to pick up the category of the entity to which it is meant to refer. The first-person pronoun, without predicating selfhood, purports to pick out a self *qua* self, and when it is correctly tendered it invariably succeeds. . . . ["Now" and "here"] succeed in always picking out a time or a place, although they may in principle fail to pick out the category of physical or external time and space as in a dream (pp. 86–87).

Castañeda's idea seems to be that "here" purports to pick out a physical or external place (and "now" a physical or external time); but when "here" is used in a dream, it does not succeed. The suggestion is not just that "here" as uttered in a dream would pick out a "non-physical" or "internal" place, but rather that, purporting to pick out a physical or external one, it would—now what? Mislead? Have one uttering a falsehood? Lead one to make a mistake?

I am not at all clear that Castañeda wants to say that "I am here," as uttered in a dream, would be false. But whatever Castañeda's views on this matter are, what he says at least suggests that someone might want to deny what I have asserted above, viz., that "I am here" has to be true.

11. Thus his retort to the Academics culminates in this line: "Because therefore I, who would be the one mistaken, would have to exist to be mistaken, there is no doubt that I am not mistaken in knowing that I am."

12. If you prefer to say "something less than" you will suppose that the project of offering a justification of a claim to know that one exists is a reasonable project; as I try to bring out in the next paragraph, Augustine does not agree.

13. Or that one knows that one exists.

14. In *Descartes: A Collection of Critical Essays,* Willis Doney, ed. (New York: Doubleday, 1967), pp. 108–39.

15. See Hintikka's article (especially pp. 116–21) for a clear discussion of existentially inconsistent and existentially self-verifying sentences and statements.

16. That is, part of the time Descartes seems to be offering us an inference with true premises to support the conclusion, "I exist." And part of the time Descartes seems to be pointing out

something peculiar about the "performance" of uttering or conceiving "I exist"—viz., that the utterance or conception of "I exist" is self-verifying.

17. Hintikka's discussion (pp. 111–12) suggests that he would formalize the Cartesian argument this way:

1) $B(a) \supset (\exists x)(x = a)$
2) $B(a)$
∴ 3) $(\exists x)(x = a)$

But there are reasons to be unhappy with such a formalization. Hintikka writes:

[I]s not
$B(a) \supset (\exists x)(x = a \& B(x))$
a provable formula in our lower functional calculi? And does not this formula entail (1) in virtue of completely unproblematic principles? (p. 112).

But what underlies the provability of (1), as Hintikka himself is careful to point out (p. 113), is rather different from anything Descartes might have offered as support for *Si cogito, sum*. For the latter one would expect either something turning on the *use* of the indexical "I," or (much more likely) something about the connection between thinking and existing, such as "It is impossible to think without existing." But what underlies the provability of (1) is what Hintikka calls "existential presuppositions," which, as Hintikka puts it, "make more or less tacit use of the assumption that all the singular terms with which we have to deal really refer to [designate] some actually existing individual" (p. 113). Such "existential presuppositions" have nothing to do with the connection between thinking and existing and not much, really, to do with the use of indexicals.

Moreover, not only is (1) a "provable formula in our lower functional calculi," so is (3), quite without appeal to (2). So conceiving *Si cogito, sum* as the provable theorem, (1), has us conceiving *Sum* as (iii) and therefore the *modus-ponens* argument, (1)–(2)–(3), as rather silly. (I owe this last point to Wiley Gillmor.)

18. Taken, with minor alterations, from the translation by Stephen McKenna in *The Fathers of the Church*, Vol. 45, *The Trinity* (Washington: Catholic University, 1963), p. 481.

6

Augustine on Speaking from Memory

GARETH B. MATTHEWS

In the twelfth chapter of his little dialogue,[1] *De Magistro*,
Augustine makes a most peculiar claim regarding memory:

> When a question arises not about what we sense before us,
> but about what we have sensed in the past, then we do not
> speak of the things themselves, but of images impressed from
> them on the mind and committed to memory.[2]

Augustine seems to be saying that whenever we are asked
about familiar, but absent, sensible things we respond by
changing the subject, that is, by talking of our memory images instead. Now it is certainly true that we sometimes do
this sort of thing. When asked to describe something from
memory I may plead that I have only the haziest (mental)
picture of that particular thing. I may offer this as a reason
for not trying to answer the question itself. Or, again, I may
preface my answer to the question with the claim that I have
an especially clear (mental) picture of the object enquired
about. I may use such a prefatory claim to give authority to
my report and elicit credence in it. But these two responses
would lose their point if we were never able to describe the
absent things themselves. For admission that one has only
the haziest recollection of something would not really count
as a reason for not trying to describe that thing unless we
were sometimes able to succeed in such descriptions. And

Reprinted, by permission of the author, editor, and the publisher, from
American Philosophical Quarterly Vol. 2, No. 2, April 1965, pp. 1–4.

claiming to have a very good recollection of something gives weight to one's words simply because a good recollection affords a good basis for making assertions about the things themselves.

Augustine might more plausibly have said that we speak from memory of sensible things *according to* our memory images. But he did not. What he did say is so peculiar that one cannot help wondering whether he really meant it.

I

We might hope to eliminate or at least mitigate the paradox by finding a better translation for Augustine's Latin. Perhaps *"loquimur"* in the context *"non iam res ipsas, sed imagines . . . loquimur"* should not be rendered "speak of," as I have rendered it, but in some quite different way.

I have checked a half dozen standard translations of this passage. Two of these do seem to relieve the paradox. This is one of them:

> . . . ce ne sont plus les choses elles-mêmes que nos paroles indiquent, mais les images. . . .[3]

The doctrine expressed here is that some of our words point to (or indicate) things which are present, whereas others point to (or indicate, or perhaps are signs of) our memory images rather than the things themselves. Unfortunately this translator pays a very high price for his version; he has to change the subject from "we" to "our words." The result is more of a gloss than a translation.

The other divergent translation is this one:

> But when a question is asked not regarding things which we perceive while they are present, but regarding things of which we had sense knowledge in the past, then we express in speech, not the realities themselves, but the images impressed by them on the mind and committed to memory.[4]

This translator uses "express in speech" for *"loquor"*; he reserves "speak about" for *"dico."* And he renders *"res"* as "reality," reserving "thing" or "things" for appropriate Latin pronouns (e.g., he translates *"de his, quae . . . sentimus"* as "of things which we perceive").

The force of this translation is to suggest that, according to Augustine, we can do something called "expressing realities in speech" and something called "expressing in speech images impressed by realities on the mind and committed to memory" and that these activities are distinguishable from merely speaking about things and speaking about the images of things. Such a suggestion is welcome, insofar as it gives us hope that Augustine is not after all denying what seems so obviously true, viz., that we do sometimes speak of sensible things from memory.

But what are we to make of the suggestion? Just what is it to express realities in speech? And how does this differ from speaking of (or about) things? I would not know how to explain, let alone defend, such a distinction, either in itself, or as an interpretation of Augustine. The translator provides no explanatory footnote. In the absence of satisfactory clarification, I conclude that the relief from paradox which this second translation promises is delusory.

Moreover, I have no helpful alternative translation to offer. This leads me to take seriously the possibility that Augustine in fact said what I have translated him as saying. Does the surrounding discussion in *De Magistro* make it plausible for one to conclude that Augustine really did say this and mean what he said?

II

I think it does.

Augustine's main concern in *De Magistro* is to say how it is we succeed in learning things.[5] But in the course of the discussion he takes up several subsidiary matters, including a worry about how one person can succeed in answering another's question. "If you had entertained that very first question of mine solely according to the sound of its syllables," says Augustine to his interlocutor, Adeodatus, "you would have given me no answer, for I should have seemed to you to ask nothing." To this Adeodatus replies, "I agree with you that we cannot converse at all unless upon hearing words our mind is led to the things of which the words are signs."[6] That is, one man cannot succeed in responding to another man's speech unless the mind of the second man is led to the things signified by the words of the first man.

Of course Adeodatus' comment engenders its own puzzlement. How can one man's mind be led to the things signified by the words of another man? The *De Magistro* answer to this last question is that the first man's words prompt the second man to look at the things signified.[7] Without pushing the regress of puzzlement further, let us consider the significance of this last Augustinian doctrine.

For a person to be able to look at the things which certain words signify, those things must be available to him for inspection. According to Augustine "intellectual things" (*intelligibilia*) are available to every man according to his inner light.[8] But "sensible things" (*sensibilia*) are directly available only to one who happens to be located in their immediate vicinity. So when talk turns to familiar, but absent, sensible things, it cannot be the things themselves one's mind is prompted to look at; it must be images of them "impressed on the mind and committed to memory."

If we grant Augustine the natural supplementary principle that that which a man's words signify is what he speaks of, we arrive at the paradox with which we began, viz.:

> When a question arises, not about what we sense before us, but about what we have sensed in the past, then we do not speak of the things themselves, but of images impressed from them on the mind and committed to memory. Indeed I do not know how we come to call (the things we speak of) real, since what we look at are counterfeits (i.e., images), unless it is because we explain, not that we see and sense them, but that we have seen and have sensed them. Thus we carry these images in the recesses of the memory as proofs (*documenta*) of things sensed before. Contemplating them in the mind we tell no falsehood when we speak in good conscience, but indeed they are for us proofs (*documenta*).[9]

Augustine is maintaining that memory claims of a certain sort are (so to speak) ellipses. Questioned about what color my neighbor's house is I answer from memory, "The house is brown." But according to Augustine such a response is (as we might say) elliptical. To express myself completely I should have to say, "I have the impression that the house is brown," or "It is my recollection that the house is brown."

Augustine's talk of memory images as "proofs" (*documenta*)[10] of things sensed before might suggest that he considers memory images an infallible guide to the truth about absent sensible things. However, the explicit assurance that he gives us is this: "Contemplating (these images) in the mind we tell no falsehood when we speak in good conscience. . . ." Augustine does not say that when we speak in good conscience we *make no mistake* about the absent things; he says only that *we tell no falsehood* (*non mentimur*). I take it that what Augustine has in mind here is the fact that a person cannot be mistaken about his own impressions in the straightforward way he can be mistaken about sensible things themselves. Of course one may lie about one's impressions. Or by slip of the tongue or through ignorance of the language one may misdescribe them. But the impressions, unlike the things themselves, simply are what they seem to be.

As we noted earlier, Augustine seems to suppose that a person trying to answer a question is limited to reporting on what he can in some way perceive. Thus a person "looking at" memory images, rather than at things themselves, is limited to reporting on those images. If then images simply are what they seem to be, memory images do "prove" or establish the answers offered by a candid and conscientious respondent.

The moral of all this seems to be that when answering questions about sensible things from memory we need worry only about the conscientiousness of our report; we are unable to give the kind of answer that could be honestly mistaken (i.e., the kind of answer that would be about the things themselves rather than about the respondent's own impressions).

III

What of it? Suppose Augustine did say and mean to say
that when we answer questions about sensible things from
memory we really speak, not of the things themselves, but
of our memory images. Why is this significant?

I have suggested that Augustine is led to make this paradoxical claim upon considering how we manage to answer
questions in general and, in particular, how we can succeed
in answering questions about sensible things from memory.
Augustine decides that we are able to do the latter by looking
at memory images the questioner's words remind us of.
And that leads him to suppose that, in making such answers,
we speak of the images we look at rather than of the things
themselves (which, of course, we can no longer see). But
we are asked about sensible things and we answer by speaking of our images of them. So we change the subject. Indeed, Augustine seems to think we have to change the subject. Thus, after beginning with a worry about how it is we
succeed in answering questions about sensible things from
memory, Augustine ends with the unwelcome assurance that
in fact we do not succeed.

In this way Augustine's analysis miscarries. The analysis
seems called for by the puzzling character of a common accomplishment. But from the analysis it follows that there
really is no such accomplishment. So what we are left with
is, at best, an explanation of how it is that we seem to be
able to do something we really cannot do.

I suggest that the reason the analysis miscarries is that
Augustine is overly restrictive in construing the puzzle he is
dealing with. "How can we answer questions about sensible
things from memory?" can be taken in at least two rather
different ways, and these ways ought to be distinguished.
Taken in one way, the question means: (1) What mental
mechanism makes it possible for us to speak of things from
memory? Taken in another way, it means: (2) How does one
make a response count as answering a question about absent
sensible things? Augustine worries about (1) to the neglect

of (2); and for this reason his analysis of speaking from memory miscarries.

Augustine's supposal that we answer questions about sensible things from memory by looking at our memory images is certainly an appropriate approach to (1). It may or may not be true that some (or all) people need to "look at" their memory images to be able to answer such questions. But, true or not, there is at least nothing paradoxical or unreasonable about supposing this to be the case.

Question (2), however, requires a different approach. It will not be satisfactory to say that a response based upon a look at one's memory images automatically counts as answering a question about absent sensible things. What the respondent says must be made liable to confirmation and disconfirmation by evidence other than the "proof" of his own memory images if it is to count as an answer to a question about absent sensible things (and not merely as a report of the respondent's own impressions). In fact, an answer considered confirmable by the evidence of other people's memory reports (*inter alia*) is by that very fact not about impressions but about the things themselves, whatever the mechanism of each individual's recall may be. And this is the beginning of a proper answer to (2).

The miscarriage of Augustine's analysis and the paradox in which it results are instructive because they point up the danger in worrying about the mechanism of question answering to the neglect of the logic of enquiry. Augustine is right in thinking that there is no mental mechanism which can give us direct access to absent sensible things. But he is wrong in concluding from this that, when talk turns to such things, we are therefore limited to giving introspective reports on our mental images. In fact the situation is quite otherwise. By making our statements liable to correction from other sources we overcome the imagined limits of mental mechanism and manage to answer questions about the absent things themselves. We need not change the subject unless we want to.

NOTES

1. Sometimes Augustine uses *"memoria"* very broadly to include not only memory but also imagination and conception generally (cf. especially Book X of the *Confessions*). The vast Augustinian secondary literature includes many good discussions of this concept of *memoria* (e.g., Étienne Gilson, *The Christian Philosophy of St. Augustine* [New York, 1960], especially pp. 75 and 100–4). My subject here is something more limited. I mean to be talking about what we, as well as Augustine, would call memory claims. So far as I can tell, what Augustine says specifically about these has been neglected in the secondary literature.

2. "Cum vero non de his, quae coram sentimus, sed de his, quae aliquando sensimus, quaeritur, non iam res ipsas, sed imagines ab eis impressas memoriaeque mandatas loquimur" (*De Magistro* 12. 39). I follow the critical edition of *De Magistro* (*Corpus Scriptorum Ecclesiasticorum Latinorum*, Vol. 77, sect. 6, pars. 4 [Vienna, 1961], p. 48). However, the standard Maurist or Benedictine edition (J. P. Migne, *Patrologia Latina*, Vol. 32 [Paris, 1845], col. 1216) differs here only inessentially in punctuation and in pronominal usage.

3. *Oeuvres de Saint Augustin* (Paris, Desclée de Brouwer et Cie, 1941), Vol. VI, p. 105. The translation is by F. J. Thonnard.

4. *The Greatness of the Soul* (and) *The Teacher* (Westminster, Md., Newman, 1950), pp. 178–79. The translation is by Joseph M. Colleran.

5. See especially *De Magistro* 11. 36–38 and 14. 45–46.

6. *Ibid.*, 8. 22.

7. *Ibid.*, 8. 23, 10. 33–35, 11. 36.

8. *Ibid.*, 12. 40.

9. *Ibid.*, 12. 39.

10. *"Documentum"* from *"docere,"* to teach, also carries the suggestion of instruction. This connotation, though important for the context in which the passage quoted above appears, is inessential to the quotation itself.

7

The Inner Man

GARETH B. MATTHEWS

> . . . There is someone within who can see through the eyes.
> So when sometimes you think within you—the inhabitant
> having turned inwardly aside—you do not see what is before
> your eyes. For the windows are open in vain when he who
> gives heed through them is absent. It is therefore not the eyes
> which see, but someone who sees through the eyes. Awake
> him, arouse him![1]

Of all philosophers, St. Augustine is perhaps the most
enamored of talking about the mind as a man inside. Perhaps
one reason for this is that the expression *"homo interior"*
has for him a certain theological sanction; St. Paul uses its
Greek equivalent (ὁ ἔσω ἄνθρωπος) in three of his epistles.[2] But perhaps just as influential on Augustine's thinking,
and philosophically rather more interesting, are two inner-
man ways of speaking characteristic of biblical writers generally, viz., (1) the personification of parts of the body ("The
eye of the adulterer also waits for the twilight, saying, 'No
eye will see me'"—Job 24:15; "The ear of the wise seeks
knowledge"—Proverbs 18:15) and (2) the report of what a
man thinks, hopes, fears, and desires as what he says or does
in his heart ("Then I said in my heart, 'What befalls the fool
will befall me also . . .'"—Ecclesiastes 2:15; "You have
heard that it was said, 'You shall not commit adultery.' But
I say to you that everyone who looks at a woman lustfully

Reprinted, by permission of the author, editor, and the publisher, from
American Philosophical Quarterly, Vol. 4, No. 2, April 1967, pp. 1–7.

has already committed adultery with her in his heart."—Matthew 5:27–28).

By supposing that the inner man may be said to have eyes, ears, a mouth, etc.,[3] and by supposing that whatever a man says or does in his heart is done "inside," by the inner man,[4] Augustine links these two biblical ways of speaking to the general notion that the mind is a little man inside.

Typically Augustine speaks of remembering, imagining, visualizing, conceiving, and understanding as cases of seeing something with the inner eye.[5] He describes what a man is thinking on a particular occasion, as well as the intention he forms to do something, as the speech of an inner voice, or, equivalently, as what a man says in his heart.[6] He conceives the desire to do something as doing it already in one's heart.[7] And he distinguishes the man who acts with a pure motive from his Pharasaical neighbor by saying that, though both, for example, give alms outwardly, only the man of pure motive also gives alms inwardly.[8] In short, the family of inner-man locutions provides for Augustine a connected way of conceiving mental functions and narrating psychological episodes.

I

Augustine's conception of the function of words like "inner," "inwardly," and "in the heart" is simple and direct. He expresses it here:

> . . . a man is not just a body, or just a soul, but a being made up of both body and soul. . . . The soul is not the whole man, but the better part of a man; the body is not the whole, but the inferior part of a man. *When both are joined together they have the name "man," which, however, they do not either one lose when we speak of them singly.* For who is prohibited from saying, in ordinary language, "That man is dead and is now in peace or in torment," though this can be said only of the soul; or "That man is buried in that place or in that," though this cannot be understood except as referring to the body alone? Will they say that Holy Scripture

follows no such usage? On the contrary it so thoroughly
adopts it, that even when a man is alive, and his body and
soul are joined together, it calls each of them singly by the
name "man," speaking of the soul as the "inner man" and
the body as the "outer man," as if there were two men, although both together are one man. (*De civitate dei* XIII. 24.
2; my italics.)

Augustine's idea is that the function of "inner" in the expression "inner man" is to make specific what otherwise
would have to be surmised from the context, viz., that on
this occasion one is using "man" to refer to only that part
of a man which is separable from the body at death, viz.,
his mind or soul.[9] And the function of "outer" in the expression "outer man" is correspondingly to make explicit a
reference to the body alone. In view of the fact that Augustine treats inner-man locutions in a connected way this means,
first of all, that on his view inner seeing, inner speaking,
inner smiling, inner giving, etc.—since they are all activities
of the inner man—should be considered activities of an entity
distinct and separable from the body. It means, secondly, that
whenever a man is said to do or say something inwardly (or
in his heart), this, too, should be thought of as the action of
an entity distinct and separable from the body.

If Augustine were right about all this, then only a metaphysical dualist could allow himself the use of inner-man
locutions without being inconsistent. For to say of someone
that he wept inwardly, or that he could see his old sweet-
heart in his mind's eye, would be to say something that entails
metaphysical dualism. What reason is there for thinking that
this is so?

II

When the outer man has been deserted by its inhabitant,
Augustine tells us, "there is no one to move the steps to
walk, the hands to work, the senses to perceive" (*Sermo*
173. 3. 3). What has left the body is something that, when
present, "rules the body, moves the limbs, guides the senses,

prepares thoughts, puts forth actions and obtains images of innumerable things" (*Enarrationes in psalmos* 145. 4).

With this causal picture of the relation between mind and body in view, one might expect that the locutions of inner seeing, inner speaking, inner smiling (etc.) would offer a basis for causal explanation of certain abilities that human beings have. Indeed Augustine does seem to suppose that the explanation of our ability to visualize the face of an absent friend rests on the fact that we have a mental picture on file that we can take a look at from time to time.[10] And one might say that the reason I can, in general, be expected to know what I am thinking, is that my inner ear is in very close proximity to my inner mouth, out of which come my thoughts.

In reality this inner-man talk provides no help toward causal explanations. For the would-be cause (inner picture of such and such a character under such and such conditions of observation, etc.; or inner speech of this or that quality under these or those acoustical conditions) is not identifiable apart from the would-be effect (successful visualization, or knowledge of what one is thinking). And unless causes are identifiable apart from their alleged effects we have no basis for a causal explanation.[11]

If this problem about identifying the would-be cause as distinct from the alleged effect is common to inner-man analogies generally (and I believe it is, though I shall not try to establish that here), we cannot say that inner-man analogies offer a basis for explaining our characteristically psychological abilities. And therefore we cannot say that the idioms of our language that express inner-man analogies commit us to dualism by laying bare the causes of our abilities to behave as we do.

Closely connected with the worry about how it is we know what we are thinking and what we intend to do is another line of argument worth mentioning here. Since a man can know what his inner voice is saying without knowing anything about his physiological states, since he can know what he says in his heart without even knowing what the physiological function of the heart is, it must be that a man who is reporting his thoughts and intentions is reporting on some-

thing completely non-physiological. Augustine presents the
materials for this line of argument in this passage:

> For although we are said to think in the heart and we may
> know what we think without anyone else's knowing it, yet
> we do not know in what part of our body we have that heart
> where we (are said to) think, unless we learn it from some-
> one else, who does not know what we are thinking.[12]

One thing to concern oneself with here is precisely the
respects in which a report on a man's "outer" speaking can
be properly considered a report on something physiological,
or even something physical. (There is, for example, no way
to record in ordinary German script the use of a uvular, as
opposed to a lingual 'r', though they differ markedly in sound
and certainly in the physiological mechanism used to produce
them.) It may be that the inner-outer dichotomy encourages
a rather oversimplified contrast between the physical (or
physiological) and the non-physical (or non-physiological).

Anyway I shall not discuss this line of argument, not because it is unimportant, but because it rests fundamentally
upon the very difficult matter of understanding avowals of
one's own thinking, one's own intentions, etc.—whether or
not these avowals are couched in the idioms of the inner
man.[13] If they can be understood satisfactorily when purged
of inner-man locutions, then surely to re-express them in
terms of the inner man will not commit anyone to dualism.

I think the most interesting way in which inner-man locutions might commit us to dualism is through committing us
to the contingency of the connection between the mind, its
states and actions, and the body, and its states and actions.
That is, if the contrast we draw through inner-man locutions
between what a man does inwardly and what he does outwardly is such as to entail that the relation between mind
and body is purely contingent, then inner-man locutions do
entail dualism.

Before trying to decide whether or not they do, I should
like to follow now in some detail what Augustine understands
to be the nature of one important inner-outer contrast, viz.,
that between inner and outer speaking.

III

Thinking is inner speaking. Augustine mentions at least three different considerations that make this analogy appropriate. One thing is that we can, and often do, entertain verbal imagery. "The words of all audible languages," he reminds us, "are also thought in silence." The "rhythm of syllables" and the "tunes of songs . . . are present by means of their incorporeal images to those who think and turn over such things in silence" (*De trinitate* XV. 11. 20).

A second consideration is that we can and do use locutions like "said in his heart" and "said to himself" to report a man's thinking. Commenting on the biblical locutions "they said, thinking" and "they thought, saying" Augustine says that both expressions mean "that they spoke within themselves, and in their heart, i.e., spoke by thinking" (*De trinitate* XV. 10. 17).

The third consideration arises from a certain picture of the mind or soul as something that gets the body to perform certain functions upon command. Thus "no one does anything willingly that he has not first said in his heart" (*De trinitate* IX. 7. 12).

I say Augustine mentions these three different considerations that make plausible the notion that thinking is inner speaking. But when he gets down to the business of telling us exactly what a true inner word is, it becomes clear that none of these three considerations makes plausible the notion that thinking is the utterance of such words as these. The true inner word of thought, he says, "is neither Greek nor Latin, nor of any other tongue." Ordinary "outer" words, even when they are entertained in verbal imagery, are but the "garment" of a thought. The true inner word is "couched in the heart, nude to the thinker, till it is clothed by the utterance of the speaker that it may proceed forth" (*Sermo* 187. 3. 3). Metaphysics imposes modesty; the word of thought cannot escape unclothed; but the clothing should never be confused with what it clothes.

Chief among the several reasons Augustine offers for insisting that the true inner word of thought is quite unlike any outer word, even one entertained in imagery, are these:

(1) One may have a thought before one has decided how to express it in "outer" words.[14]

(2) The same thought may be expressed by different "outer" words.[15]

(3) One may be able to pronounce "outer" words one does not understand, make slips of the tongue, babble, recite words by rote, etc.[16]

Suppose we concentrate on (3). Thinking, Augustine supposes, "underlies" meaningful speaking.[17] The speaking may, of course, go on without the thinking, or the speaking and the thinking may just fail to correspond. In the former case a man may be babbling or saying something by rote; in the latter case he may be dissembling, or using an expression he fails to understand, or making a slip of the tongue. Now if we suppose that thinking is inner speaking, we invite further regress. For the inner speaking, to be meaningful, would need to be backed by inner-inner speaking, etc., indefinitely.[18]

To stop the regress Augustine must say that there cannot possibly be such a thing as inner mouthing of inner words, inner speaking without comprehension, inner slips of the tongue, etc. (Hence the denial that a true inner word of thought can be identified with any verbal image; for a verbal image may be entertained without comprehension, etc.)[19] But with such possibilities ruled out completely, inner speech becomes unintelligible *as speech*. For a word is precisely the sort of thing that may be mouthed, pronounced mechanically, mistaken for another word, etc.

The notion that the true word of thought is itself outwardly unpronounceable undermines the three considerations listed above that make initially attractive the notion that thinking is inner speaking. First, the fact that we can and do entertain verbal imagery is no longer relevant. For a word of thought is not an ordinary word, or set of words, entertained in imagery.

Secondly, the fact that we can and do report a man's thinking as what he says to himself, in his heart, is no longer relevant either. For it is not as though what we so report could ever be a direct quotation. And to think of it as a translation, much as the Soviet Ambassador's remarks in Russian might be reported in English, perhaps within quotation marks, will not do either. For at least the Soviet newspapers may give the Ambassador's remarks in the original. But it is inconceivable that anyone should ever report a word of thought "in the original."

Thirdly, the picture of the mind or soul as something that gets the body to perform certain actions upon command becomes unintelligible once we realize that the mind is supposed to speak a metaphysically private mumbo-jumbo.

What Augustine is on to with his inner-speech analogy is the intimate relation between speaking and thinking; but he misconceives it. He wants us to view inner speaking (thinking) and outer speaking as species of a common genus—one an activity of the mind or inner man, and the other a corresponding activity of the body or outer man. But this will not do.

A man's thinking is what is expressed by what the man says when he says what is on his mind, or else by what the man *would* say if he *were* to say what is on his mind. The reference to speech in this formula (to either what a man says or what he would say if he were to speak his mind) may appear inessential. For the formula seems to come to this: a man's thinking is what is expressed by what expresses or would express his thinking; that is, a man's thinking is a man's thinking.

But the reference to speech is not eliminable in this way. Suppose a man says, ". . ." If he is awake, attending to business, has a command of the language, has not made a slip of the tongue, is sincere and candid, then these words express his thinking. It is not that when he succeeds in speaking his mind what he and we know to be expressed by these words matches the thought inside him. Or better, for what is expressed by his words to "match" the thinking "inside him" is just, in this simple case, for him to say what he says sincerely, with comprehension, etc.

A central role of the inner-speech metaphor is to help us relate a variety of situations to certain model cases. We relate situations in which one keeps one's thoughts to oneself, cases in which one is deceitful, cases in which one misspeaks, etc., to the model case of completely candid and successful speech. The inner-speech metaphor also helps us to relate to one another speeches in two different idioms (or in two different languages) as expressing the same thought. For the claim that somebody is thinking such and such can be understood as the claim that it is in certain respects *as if* he had said just that (sincerely, with comprehension, etc.), though perhaps actually he said something quite different or indeed nothing at all.

Thinking is not really a *kind* of speaking. But it is, if you like, *as-it-were* speaking.[20] That is, when a man is said to be thinking such and such, it is in certain respects (roughly specifiable in the context) *as if* he were saying just that.

IV

What I said in the last section about the functions of the inner-speech analogy will apply quite generally to a whole class of inner-outer contrasts. The class is made up of contrasts in those activities whose outer performance may be said, on occasion, to *express* a corresponding inner performance. A simple example is the inner smile. A man who is amused, say, by the lisps of a child and bites his lip to hide his amusement, may be said to smile inwardly. A mechanical smile, on the other hand, may be described as an outer smile with no corresponding inner smile. It is the man who smiles naturally and spontaneously who backs his outer smile with a corresponding inner one. And in his case the outer smile may be said to express his amusement (i.e., the inner smile).

This is a perfectly general approach to certain mental functions and psychological episodes. In the model case (the sincere speech uttered with comprehension, etc., or the natural and spontaneous smile) we speak of an inner act or activity corresponding to (and therefore expressed by) an outer act or activity. The locutions of inner-outer contrast are then a way of relating other situations to the model case.

It may be helpful to remind philosophers, preoccupied as they are with the mind-body problem, that the use of an inner-outer contrast sometimes has very little to do with whether there is anything mental "underlying" the physical. Augustine's contrast, mentioned earlier, between giving alms outwardly and giving alms inwardly is a case in point. Here the model case is the case of someone whose gift is a direct and uncalculating response to need. A penniless widow may be said to give inwardly, though she lacks the means to give outwardly. And the Pharisee, wanting to be admired, may give outwardly on a lavish scale without giving inwardly at all. Yet it is not that the Pharisee's giving is merely outward because it is mechanical and unthinking. The trouble is that it is wrongly motivated.

It is natural to ask whether the idioms of our language that express inner-man analogies could not be eliminated without loss to anyone but a rhetorician—whether the philosopher who concerns himself with expressions like "he said in his heart" and "he smiled inwardly" is not concerning himself with something that had best be left to philologists. A beginning reply would be "Yes, certainly they could be eliminated; 'he said to himself' can be replaced by 'he thought' and 'he smiled inwardly' by 'he was mildly amused without showing it.'"

Yet to handle the question this way is to miss the importance of these analogies. I am inclined to say that the concept of being amused is, in part anyway, an analogical extension of the notions of smiling and laughing and that the concept of thinking is, in part anyway,[21] an analogical extension of the concept of speaking. If I am right in saying this, then the fact that we can replace talk of inner smiles and inner speech with talk of amusement and thinking is rather uninteresting. The point is that our conception of what it is to be amused is built up from model cases of smiling, and our concept of thinking is built up from model cases of speaking. Being amused and thinking are, in this respect anyway, analogical concepts. And so also, in a similar way, are other concepts that are closely linked with inner-man locutions.

V

Augustine supposes that what we say about the inner man we say about an entity that animates the body for a time and leaves it at death. If he is right, then our very use of inner-man locutions such as "said in the heart" and "smiled inwardly" commits us to mind-body (or soul-body) dualism.

In Section III we followed Augustine's attempt to take seriously the dualism he believes to be inherent in one inner-man locution, "said in the heart," and its equivalents. We said that Augustine takes inner speaking to be something that animates outer speaking in such a way that when a stretch of inner speaking "underlies" a properly corresponding stretch of outer speaking, the result is that a person may be said to understand what he is saying, to be sincere in saying this, etc.—otherwise not. Augustine's development of the notion of inner speaking is a failure because inner speaking either itself needs special "backing" to be sincere, uttered with comprehension, etc., or else it must be thought to be automatically sincere, uttered with automatic comprehension, etc.; but in the latter case it is unintelligible as speech.

We could generalize our conclusion by saying that any attempt to understand inner x-ing as psychical "backing" for a purely physical operation (outer x-ing) will either invite further regress or else make inner x-ing unintelligible as x-ing.

In Sections III and IV, I suggested an alternative approach to inner-man locutions. I suggested that they be interpreted as calling our attention to certain model cases of human behavior in such a way that when one is said to do something inwardly, it is in certain respects as if one had done this in conformity to the model case. And when one is said to do something merely outwardly, one's action fails to fit the model case in important respects, though it resembles it in a superficial way.

So the inner-outer contrast cannot be understood satisfactorily in the dualistic way Augustine would have us understand it. And it can be understood satisfactorily in quite another way. The question now remains, why should we have thought originally—not only that inner-man locutions might be *open* to dualistic interpretation—but that using them perhaps *commits* us to Augustinian dualism?

I think the answer is very simple. The contrast we draw between what a man does inwardly and what he does outwardly is such that there is a merely contingent relation between the inner and the outer man. That is, there will be, in general, no contradiction in ascribing one state or action to the inner man and a completely different, even opposite, state or action to the corresponding outer man. The inner man may smile while the outer man frowns or weeps. A person may be inwardly terrified, though outwardly calm and poised. The outer man may say, "What a charming evening!" while the inner man says, "A dreadful bore."

The contingency of this relation between what one may be said to do inwardly and what one may be said to do outwardly insinuates mind-body dualism. But we must be wary. Inner-outer contingency entails Augustinian mind-body independence only if we can identify the inner man with what Augustine takes to be the mind and the outer man with what he takes to be the body.

Let us remind ourselves what Augustine takes a mind to be (in this life, anyway). It is an entity whose activities underlie the being and behavior of the body in such a way as to make the difference between merely physical activity and the conscious, animated, meaningful, purposive behavior characteristic of living human beings. But what we have said about the locutions of inner *x*-ing means that the attempt to interpret them as reporting on the activities of what Augustine takes to be the mind is a failure. Yet the locutions have a perfectly good use in our language. And that use can be given a satisfactory alternative analysis. We must conclude that what Augustine takes to be a mind cannot be identified with something we are thought to report on when we speak of inner *x*-ing.

Nor can we identify what Augustine takes to be the body with the subject of the locutions of outer *x*-ing. Let us remind ourselves what an Augustinian body is. It is the "part" of a man that is buried at death. It has physical characteristics and may be moved in various ways. But no psychological predicates may be applied to it, or to its behavior.

Consider now an inner-outer contrast. Suppose we report that the outer man says, "What a charming evening!" while the inner man says, "A dreadful bore." What we are reporting is a case of dissembling. A person says one thing and thinks something quite different. But it is not true that the outer man's speech on this occasion is merely an unconscious physical movement, something completely "unbacked" by anything mental or psychical. What we have here is a case of dissembling. And the outer words, though insincere, are chosen, understood, and used quite purposefully. Otherwise they could not be said to be insincere. And so the subject of the outer speech is not an Augustinian body, but a dissembling person.

Take another example. A mother who is terrified of electrical storms is eager to prevent her children from developing the same phobia. When the children call her to their bedside during a storm she reassures them. She is outwardly calm, relaxed, and confident. But inwardly she quakes. Who or what is the subject of this outer calm? Not an unthinking physical object, but a mother who is really frightened but determined to behave in such a way as to hide her fear. Her outward calm is not a physical shell that conceals her feelings; it is a deliberate and self-conscious pattern of behavior that is meant to reassure her children.

One might have expected that "inner man," "outer man," and the whole family of inner-outer locutions would be technical terms in Augustine and that he would therefore not be bound to use them in conformity with our ordinary ways of talking. But it is quite clear, as I suggested at the beginning, that Augustine draws these locutions from the Bible, where they are certainly not used as technical terms. It is equally clear that Augustine means what he has to say about the inner man to be, among other things, an interpretation of these biblical locutions. Moreover, the question before us is whether inner-man locutions, as we all use them (no doubt partly through the influence of the Bible), commit us to Augustine's dualism. And the answer to that question is clearly *No*.

NOTES

1. Augustine, *Sermo* 126. 2. 3. (Translations from Augustine in this paper are my own, though I have freely consulted existing translations.)

2. "For I delight in the law of God in my *inner man,* but I see in my members another law at war with the law of my *mind* and making me captive to the law of sin which dwells in my members." (Romans 7:22–3; emphasis mine.) Other occurrences of the expression are to be found at 2 Corinthians 4:16 and Ephesians 3:16. For an example of Augustine's concern with what "inner man" means in the Pauline epistles see Augustine's *Contra Faustum manichaeum* XXIV:2. (Quotations from the Bible in this paper follow the Revised Standard Version, with occasional alterations.)

3. ". . . Our very own mind, that is, the inner man, to whose uniform knowing diverse things are announced through the five, as it were, messengers of the body . . . sees the light . . . hears the word . . . catches the scent . . . drinks of the fountain. . . . and enjoys the feel. . . . Nor are these different things, but one understanding that is expressed by the names of so many senses" (*In Ioannis evangelium* 99. 4).

4. "The inner man has an inner mouth . . . [and] the things that proceed from this mouth come from the heart" (*De continentia* 2. 4).

5. See especially *De Genesi ad litteram*, Bk. XII, on the "three kinds of vision."

6. See, e.g., *Sermo* 187, 225 and 288 and *De trinitate* VII. 7. 12.

7. See, e.g., *Sermo* 179. 7. 7.

8. See, e.g., *De sermone domini in monte* II. 2. 9.

9. Augustine identifies the inner man indifferently as a man's soul (*anima*), his rational soul (*animus*), and his mind (*mens*). The quotation above contains an example of the first identification. Examples of the second and third can be found at *Confessiones* X. 6. 9 and *In Ioannis evangelium* 99. 4 respectively.

10. See, e.g., *De trinitate* XI. 3. 6.

11. One must be careful here. Peter Geach suggested to me, for purposes of comparison, the causal statement, "Smith craves to take cocaine because of taking cocaine." The concept *taking cocaine* is logically linked to the concept *craving to take cocaine.* And for this reason identifying the cause and identifying the effect cannot be completely independent of one another. Yet there is no conceptual reason to suppose that, on a specific occasion, we

shall be unable to identify an instance of the cause, Smith's taking cocaine, as distinct from and independent of the effect, Smith's craving to take cocaine. ("Funny thing," Smith might honestly say, "I took my usual cocaine this morning and now I simply don't want any more of the stuff.") So my point is not just that the concept of a mental picture is logically linked to the concept of visualization; it is that on a given occasion the "presence" of a certain mental picture under good conditions of "mental observation" is not identifiable apart from the "resultant" visualization itself.

12.   *De anima et ejus origine* (IV. 6. 7).

13.   Thus Augustine presents a similar line of argument stripped of reference to the inner man in this passage: ". . . when the mind knows itself, it knows its own substance; and when it is certain about itself, it is certain about its own substance. . . . Yet it is not at all certain whether it is air, or fire, or some body, or something bodily. Therefore it is not any of these." (*De trinitate* X. 10. 16). Cf. Descartes, *Meditation* II.

14.   See, e.g., *In Ioannis evangelium* 14. 7.

15.   See, e.g., *Sermo* 288. 3.

16.   See, e.g., *De trinitate* XIII. 20. 26.

17.   Cf. Wittgenstein, *The Blue Book* (Oxford, Blackwell, 1958), pp. 34 ff.

18.   Cf. Gilbert Ryle, *The Concept of Mind* (London, Hutchinson, 1949), p. 296.

19.   When I speak here of stopping a further regress I am going beyond what Augustine actually says. What Augustine says is, e.g., that one who memorizes a string of Greek words without knowing what they mean remembers only what pertains to the outer man, i.e., he does not retain the thought that is expressed by these words (*De trinitate* XIII. 20. 26). I mean for my talk of regress to be a way of stating in summary fashion Augustine's concern with the various differences there are between a thought and its expression and his insistence that "inner expressions" are, in these respects, like thoughts rather than expressions.

20.   Cf. Peter Geach, *Mental Acts* (London, Routledge and Kegan Paul, 1957), p. 75, where "the concept *judging* is viewed as an analogical extension of the concept *saying*." See also Wilfred Sellars, "Empiricism and the Philosophy of Mind," *Minnesota Studies in the Philosophy of Science*, Vol. 1, ed. by H. Feigl and M. Scriven (Minneapolis, University of Minnesota Press, 1956), pp. 253–329, especially pp. 307–11, 317–21.

21.   I think there is more to these concepts than this. But I cannot hope to unravel the other strands here.

8

On Augustine's Concept of a Person

A. C. LLOYD

In *De Trinitate*, Augustine presents a theory about the difference between being a person and not, say, a machine. The theory depends on his account of the mind's knowledge of itself and is expressed in X. 10. 13 as a refutation of the hypothesis that the mind could know itself to be fire or anything else material. But it results only indirectly from the intention of the book, which is to explain, so far as it can be explained, the doctrine of three persons in one substance. The nature of a human person is relevant only as an image or incomplete analogy of the divine trinity. Consequently the claim to find such a philosophical theory in the book is likely to be exaggerated and in need of qualifications.[1] The purpose of what follows is to suggest these qualifications. It is confined to the *De Trinitate*. But if we abstract the elements of homily and of Scripture which pervade the analogies and take only the philosophical concept of a person this concept is a formal one. So for the greater part I shall be concerned with Augustine's treatment of the Aristotelian categories of relation and substance: this occurs chiefly in the first or theological half of the *De Trinitate*, but it is the logic not the theology, of course, which matters here. To understand his use of the *Categories,* it is best to start by presenting the gist of his argument in more explicitly Aristotelian terms. He understood them but took more for granted by his readers than (may one say?) he could have done today. An incidental

This paper was written especially for this volume.

result may be to make it clearer how much of the theory depends on Neoplatonic rather than Aristotelian notions.

Suppose that "A" and "B" are proper names or descriptions, never mind what of, and that it is the case that A is paternal and B filial. (Augustine will commonly write, "paternal is said of A," where "paternal" is a predicate in a proposition, but not a predicate-expression in a sentence; it is an Aristotelian *term* which I will represent by italics, because putting "paternal" in quotation marks or merely abstaining from quotation marks would be equally wrong by the conventions of modern logic.) If *paternal* and *filial* are said in the category of substance they are either differentiae or propria. The substance of something is *what* it is in the sense of answering the question "quid est?" as distinct (so Aristotle believes) from the question "quale est?" It is the most determinate species to which the subject belongs, and this can always be expanded into, is equivalent to, a genus with a differentia ("Socrates is a rational animal"). Terms which, being deducible from it, belong necessarily and only to that species are "per se accidents," more conveniently called propria. Genus, differentia, and proprium are substantial properties, that is to say technically "are said in the category of substance"; all others belong to an accidental, i.e., non-substantial, category, such as quality, relation, place. In the present discussion there is no question of *paternal* and *filial* being genera: but the possibility, which is ignored or insufficiently distinguished by Augustine, of their being propria is important. If they are propria, the conclusion required for the argument will not follow without some further premises. To be capable of laughter is not the same as to be capable of grammar, but both (which are propria) are said of the same substance. (Indeed if they were not *Wisdom* would present the same problem as *Son*.) To rule them out as propria Augustine and his opponents must be assuming that they are not deducible from the defining characteristic of God, that they are data only of Scripture. But as we shall see he is unclear about this.

If then, the argument now assumes, they are in the category of substance they are differentiae. But they cannot be differentiae. For whatever *x* is, in neither "*x* is paternal" nor "*x* is filial" is *paternal* or *filial* said of *x* per se. (Augustine uses the translation, "*ad se*," which is contrasted of course with "*ad aliquid*" not "*ad aliud*.") A differentia is in the category of substance because it signifies the most determinate kind of thing some individual is—in other words, what some substance is or what the substance *of* some individual is. This means what it is in itself or by itself (the Platonic characterization of the substantial, or truly existent, will be recognized) or *per se*. Only a per se term can therefore signify a substance (or the substance of something); and in this context a per se term or expression is one which does not logically imply the existence of something other than what it refers to. This is what rules relations out of the category of substance. "The third largest island" refers uniquely to Borneo: but it does not describe the substance of Borneo, for it entails the existence of two other islands. Again every human may be causally dependent on the existence of another human, but every uncle or father is logically dependent on the existence of another human, standing, moreover, in a special relation to him: it is what is "said," i.e. "meant," by "uncle" or "father."

Therefore being neither propria nor differentiae (nor genera) *paternal* and *filial* are not said substantially (in the category of substance). Therefore it does not follow that A and B are different substances. Augustine says (V. 5. 6) that therefore they are not different substances—which he has not of course shown: but the point is unimportant because it is clear both to himself and to the reader. He goes on (V. 6. 7) to argue that his thesis applies equally if we replace *filial* and *paternal* by *begotten* and *unbegotten*, although when he departs from the purely logical argument to use a favorite premise from Scripture, his own logic goes astray. For he correctly points out that while the Son is equal to the Father, this cannot be in respect of his relation, viz. his sonhood, since the Father has no sonhood, and invalidly infers that it must be in respect of his substance.

More important to the structure and to the intention of his opponents' case is the objection that according to logic, that is, Aristotelian logic, what is not a substantial property of something is an accidental property of it—whereas God

has no accidental properties. "Accidental" can be taken here
as equivalent to "non-necessary" or "contingent." To this,
too, he has a philosophical as well as a scriptural or ad
hominem reply. What is said to be accident, he argues (V.
4. 5 ff.), is said to be so only because the subject of the accident (*cui accidit*) is capable of change. For even the so-
called inseparable accidents imply the capacity for change in
the matter or substrate of the property in question. ("Inseparable accidents" were a post-Aristotelian invention, made
familiar by Porphyry's *Isagoge*. They were accidents because
predicated primarily of individuals, and because their subjects
were conceivable without them—but at the same time their
subjects "would not exist" without them.[2]) For example, the
crow cannot lose the black color of its feathers as long as its
feathers are there, but it loses it when they or the bird itself
ceases to be. (This is of course a ruinous piece of logic on
Augustine's part, for a moment's reflection shows that it
would remove the possibility of substantial attributes as well:
e.g., *winged* as a differentia of *bird*. . . . But better logicians
than he were probably floored by inseparable accidents.)
Similarly it is the immutability of God which entails the absence of accidents in him. But the relative and therefore non-
substantial terms which are attributed (truly or scripturally)
to God, including *father* and *son*, belong to him eternally
and therefore immutably, so that they do not imply the mutability of their subject; we can therefore have a case of attributes which are neither accidental (or contingent), which
would have made it impossible for them to belong to God, nor
substantial, which would have made more than one god by
making more than one substance out of God.

The next stage introduces the concept of a person. It is
defined negatively, so far as it is defined at all; and this is un-
objectionable. What I want to emphasize is that it is a formal
concept: its only properties, whether or not they are compatible, are those which belong to Aristotelian logic. Augustine says (V. 8. 9) that the per se or substantial attributes of
God belong to each person of the Trinity singly, but to God
as a trinity. If this were not so there would be three gods
(genus), or three great beings (proprium). For to be, in the
case of God, is to be great. This is given a standard Platonic

or Neoplatonic proof by Augustine which would have been quite unacceptable to Aristotle: God is great by being identical with greatness; if he were not, there would be something, viz. true greatness, greater than God, which would be a contradiction (V. 10. 11). He concludes that there is one substance and three persons, *"Ego et Pater unum sumus,"* not *"unum est."* But if we ask, "Three *what?*," human speech is at a loss, and if we say, "Three persons," it is not so much to say that as to avoid saying nothing (V. 9. 10). In short, the meaning of a "person" of the Trinity is for Augustine something which is a relation without being in an accidental category, or (for those who like a doctrine about predicables distinguished from a doctrine about categories) a relation which is not attributed accidentally.

The way in which such relative though non-accidental attributes are properly applied to God, he continues (V. 11. 12), is not the way in which the substantial attributes are properly applied to God. "Son" cannot be said of the Trinity at all, and "Father" only in a more or less analogical way by reference to God's adoption of his creatures.

He has not managed to make this last—and no doubt theologically essential—claim consistent with his starting point in the earlier chapters. In fact it entails a contradiction. Not only can *God* be said of the Son but the Son is identical with God; for according to Augustine himself, diversity of substance implies plurality of gods; from this it follows that singleness of gods implies sameness of substance; singleness of gods is also, according to Augustine, a necessary fact, so that God is at the least (i.e., if he is not a species) member of a necessarily one-member class; and whatever has the same substance as such an object must be identical with that object. Since therefore God is identical with the Son, a fortiori, *Son* can be said of *God*.[3] The attempt to have three persons and one substance entails a non-symmetric identity.

Has not Augustine already conceded that the Trinity is a mystery? Certainly. But what is philosophically misleading and mistaken on his part is what I think is suggested by the whole scheme of the *De Trinitate*, and some readers have thought it the explicit and philosophically valuable message of the work. This is the suggestion that the mysteriousness lies, or partly lies, in the concept of what is now and by us, but not then and by Augustine, called the concept of a person—as though the paradox will be lessened as a result of introspecting the depths of our personality.

This must not be misunderstood. There is no philosophical reason why someone should not hold that the biblical descriptions of the so-called persons of the Trinity do not describe ideal properties of the so-called persons that Smith and Jones are but Smith's and Jones's cats and chairs are not. Since these descriptions are concerned with concrete and empirical, psychological concepts such as loving, an understanding of the ideal properties may entail or at least be improved by observation and introspection. Secondly, it would not follow from the fact that φ is an ideal property of x that it is not part of the concept of x. We say as an idiom that ideally a cat is a good mouser when we mean that a cat ought to be a good mouser but is not necessarily a good mouser. But the fact—supposing it is one—that a cat necessarily has whiskers does not exclude having whiskers from the list of properties possessed by an ideal cat. Indeed it entails its inclusion. But clearly it does not follow from the fact that φ is an ideal property of x that it *is* part of the concept of x. This conclusion requires further and usually independent evidence. Anyone who tried to show that the so-called persons of the Trinity, or more precisely certain biblical descriptions, were relevant to the concept of a person in the ordinary sense could only do so by also showing that knowledge of those descriptions was unnecessary to the understanding of the concept. For this understanding would be presupposed by any argument to the effect that the descriptions were descriptions (i.e., true and not merely purported descriptions) of the concept. In short, the problem would be to know which of the properties in a description of the ideal person were both necessary and ideal properties. Nor is it soluble by self-observation. Good mousers that went on that principle would make bad zoologists. Certainly the analogies between the persons of the Trinity and constituent parts of the human mind which make up a large proportion of the *De Trinitate* are a mixture of Neoplatonic metaphysics and a sort of self-observation: but that does not look appropriate to the problem either.

It must be stressed that the *De Trinitate* in no way—certainly in no logical way—depends on using the same *word* for the theological job and for the everyday description of people. The divine term of the analogy is given a technical name like "essentia" while the human term of the analogy is introduced as "homo" (IX. 2, 2 *in.*), although it is also said that "persona" can be applied to man as well as God (VII. 4, 7 *fin*).

The personality which is possessed by a human being is examined because man is an image of God, and therefore it will indirectly reveal the personality which is possessed by the components of the Trinity. This is taken to be a matter, not of observing people, but of self-observation. He proceeds immediately to talk in the first person singular; and (if we omit the Neoplatonic metaphysics) this is taken to be a matter of reporting only my interior feelings, thoughts, and so on, and not any external behavior. These feelings, thoughts, and so on, or else the subject which has them, are identified with mind and not merely in the abstract but in the particular case of "I love." He simply says, "Let us rule out of consideration the numerous other things of which man is composed; and so that we can have as far as possible an uninterrupted search for what we are at present seeking, let us treat mind alone" (X. 2. 2). The reasons for both these familiar Augustinian moves need not be discussed here. But the combination of moves suggests serious qualifications for the concept of a human person such as it is to be found in the *De Trinitate*. Suppose that Smith is a person. Propositions containing a third-person pronoun can refer to Smith and be replaced synonymously by the name "Smith." Examining them and comparing them with propositions containing other pronouns will cast light on what is involved in being a person. But it is far from clear that a proposition whose grammatical subject is a first person pronoun can be replaced synonymously by the name of a person. It may well be possible to meet the objection. One might be able to argue, for example, that if φ is a necessary predicate (or alternatively a meaningful predicate) of "I," then it is a necessary (or alternatively a meaningful) predicate of "he" and that its meaning is the same with both types of subject. But more generally this Augustinian concept of *a man* or *a person* is as it stands the concept of *one's own mind*.

"The concept of a person" no doubt conceals a number of philosophical questions. The question what "I" refers to is connected with the problem of the identity of a self: what is it for it to be the same self that my first person singular statements are about if they are made yesterday and today? But one might reasonably suggest that this whole group of questions is openly denied a place in the *De Trinitate*. For at any rate the last book emphasizes one respect in which specifically personal activities, if we may call them that, of God and of a man fail to be analogous. In the one case they are identical with their "subject," in the other they are not. There is not a father *who* loves or a son *who* understands: but if I love or understand there is an I which is distinct from the loving or understanding (XV. 22. 42–23. 43). Nothing is said about the logical status of this "I" to correspond with the description of a person in the Trinity. Nor is there any discussion of its relation to the mind, whose identity with it seems to have been taken for granted in the earlier books.

It might now be asked whether the scheme of the work really envisages a contribution to the subject of human personality at all. But it must do because we are to find a likeness of the Trinity in ourselves, and likeness is a symmetric relation.[4] In Augustine the biblical claim that man was made in God's image always goes hand in hand with the Platonic duty for man of assimilation to God. In fact we find him claiming not merely that the Father, the Son, and the Holy Spirit are persons, but that God is a person. For my purpose I took his argument in two stages. The first purported to show the logical status of properties such as being a son and being a father; the second used that to introduce the formal, or logical, concept of a person as distinct from a substance.

It is now necessary to look at a third stage, in which Augustine says that, in God, to be is to be a person. "Person" has of course the abstract meaning which it had in the second stage. But this stage is to my mind more obviously suggestive for the problem of a more concrete concept of human personality. This is not so much because it is God as such who is virtually made a person—although that is not without im-

portance—as because the argument has to develop a notion
of hypostatized relations. And that a person, in the everyday
sense, has more to do with relation than with substance seems
to me (though I leave the matter till later) to be a point of
departure toward a type of theory which is in sharp and welcome contrast with the main tradition. It is only a point of
departure and Augustine is no more than suggestive. As we
shall see, he does not even accept the suggestion. In this stage
I am again allowing myself to look at the logic of the position
he is in, for his concept of a person is still formal.

In Book VII, Chapter 6, Augustine appears to contradict
what he had said about the proper applications of the terms,
Father, Son, and *Holy Spirit*. In God, he now says, to be is
to be a person, although "to be" is said per se and "to be a
person" is said relatively. The Trinity, which is one God, consists of the three persons. It is impossible for any other person
to exist from that same substance in the way that more than
three statues can be made from gold or more than three men
from the same "nature."

Certainly this can be regarded as simply spelling out the
theory of the first stage that the persons, while relations, were
non-accidental. But to express it by requiring us to call God
a person brings to a head, as he intends it to, the problem of
what it is *to be* a person. For he knows quite well that in
Aristotelian logic what is called the "substance" of x is the
same thing as what it is to be x. (His use of the term "essentia" at this stage means "being" and is meant to recognize
the Aristotelian standpoint; it marks no departure from the
standpoint of the earlier stages, as some anachronistic translations would imply.) But the trouble now is this. The conjunction of *Father, Son,* and *Holy Spirit*, which is all that
can be attributed to God as a person according to the
second stage of Augustine's argument, belongs to the category
of relation, according to the third stage, as much as *Father*
does. But so long as we remember that being a person is a
relative attribute, it does not matter what it amounts to: let us
call it "P." Then although wisdom, for example, is a substantial attribute, to be God is to be wise, and to be God is to
be P, so that to be wise ought to be to be P. But this seems
impossible. For "x is wise" would have to imply "x is P"; but

since P is a relation, "x is P" implies the existence of a y
which is not identical with x; and from this it would follow
that "x is wise" implies a y which is not identical with x, so
that wisdom, contrary to the hypothesis, would be a relation.

The upshot is that there is now a powerful motive for making the relative or personal attributes substantial. In the
earlier stages the point was to make them relative, which
seemed to imply not being substantial, though still necessary.
Now the price of their being necessary has to be paid, and
this seems to imply their being substantial. I think that making relations substantial, which means turning them into non-
relational properties, has not always been distinguished from
just hypostatizing them, making them say *ante rem* universals.
In logic, if we can quantify over one-place predicates, there
is no reason why we should not quantify over two-place
predicates: it is another matter altogether to analyze a two-
place predicate as a one-place predicate. We can understand
the second task as one of making the relation independent
of its correlate. Does Augustine try to do this? It looks very
much like it when he interprets the third of the persons of
the Trinity. (The historical antecedents of his interpretation
are not relevant.) The Holy Spirit is taken as the love which
is *common to* the Father and the Son (XV. 19. 36). This
suggests a conflation of two different distinctions, the distinction between the general and the particular (or specific), and
the distinction between the substantial, or per se, and the
relative. Where the relation is a *symmetric* one this looks
plausible. If A is to the left of B (non-symmetric relation),
it is not the case that A and B are to the left; nothing can be
inferred about them as a pair, but only as an ordered pair.
If A is beside B (symmetric relation), A and B are side by
side. And since this is implied by "A is to the left of B" and
also by "A is to the right of B," while neither of these propositions is implied by "A is beside B" (or by its logical equivalent, "B is beside A"), it follows that the symmetric relation
side by side can be called a genus of which the non-symmetric
relations, *to the left* and *to the right*, are species. What, however, does not follow is that the genus is not just as much a
relation as the species. If it does not look like one, that is
because it is said per se of both its terms, and this is confused

with something which would make it per se or substantial, but which is not the case, namely being said per se of each of its terms. Being side by side, neighbors or cousins, is said of the pair (as the grammatical requirement of the plural shows); being to the left or father is not said in ordinary English of a pair, but it is reducible in logic to an *ordered pair*. In short, both are two-place predicates, and are therefore excluded from the Aristotelian category of substance. For "A and B are side by side" is short for "A is beside B and B is beside A."

Many Neoplatonists, and particularly Plotinus, criticized the Aristotelian logic for failing to recognize a per se, or substantial, property or activity that, they believed, was involved in every relation. Perhaps the simplest way to convey the model which they had in mind is like this: every transitive verb, like "hitting" or "loving," entails an intransitive verb having the same subject, as though one had to do some hitting or do some loving in order to hit or love someone and it was logically possible to do the first without the second, as a fire might be thought to be hot, i.e., heating, without heating anything. It will not do. But it is not altogether an implausible picture; and one, though not the only, ground for it is the confusion that we have just been looking at, of a symmetric or generic relational property with a non-relational property. People who are hitting or loving each other are sometimes said to fight or to be in love.

Is Augustine guilty of this confusion? An unqualified answer is not possible. For the most part, his treatment of the Trinity shows no signs of it. Father and Son are persons, and if fatherhood and sonhood cannot be made substantial because their non-symmetricality makes them obviously relative, then so much the better because we shall have to look elsewhere, namely to the one God, for their substance. But the Holy Spirit, which never could have looked like the same kind of affair, is treated much more like a quality of the other two persons because it is a symmetric relation. It is true that at the point where this is hypostatized, as it is, so that we expect Augustine to have betrayed himself into giving us the *substance* of a person, he tells us that this love is nothing but God or the Trinity (XV. 19. 37). Thus the formal position of all three persons seems to be identical. But it is not, for unlike, say, wisdom, love is not a quality but a relation. Whatever St. John said, it is appropriate in Augustine's theory to define a person and not a substance. But if Augustine had in mind the Plotinian notion of per se activities involved in relations, and what I have suggested is a fallacious ground for doing so, it is easy to understand how the objection should have escaped him.[5] Logically absurd though it is, the theory seems to be explicit in Boethius: "God's production of a son is substantial, but the attribution to him of *father* is relative" (*De Trinitate* 5).

The same problem can be seen as the problem of God's simplicity. The second term of the relation love is its correlate, the object of love: if these are identical in God there is no relation, and if there is a relation there is no longer simplicity. Nor is there simplicity if love implies something else, namely knowledge, as Augustine claims it does. Indeed correlation is incompatible with simplicity only because it is such a case of implication. The traditional way (also found in Augustine) of dealing with it was to make out that it was not something *else* which was implied, because the love and the knowledge were self-love and self-knowledge. But for the more general case of implication the only hope was to trust in the Plotinian model—or paradox—of the second hypostasis, Intellect or Being, in which the Ideas are said to be united—literally one—and yet each is itself. It is now familiar to scholars that this was explained by the analogy of a Stoic theory of what we might call chemical mixture, and which was also used, or reported, by Porphyry to explain the union of soul and body.[6] This *unio inconfusa* provided the formula for the so-called Athanasian creed. Augustine certainly had it in mind when he was faced by the problem of the personal attributes and their mutual implication. For, though later on and not in the theological section that we have mostly been concerned with, he himself proposes the standard Stoic analogy of wine mixed with water and honey.[7] Of course this is another way of describing the paradox, not a solution of it, and I mention it partly to emphasize the fact. The Neoplatonic borrowing of a formula from Stoic physics has sometimes been claimed as an advance made in philosophy. Much more generally, essential features of what I have proposed as implicit or perhaps as only suggested in Augustine can be recognized as explicit in Thomas Aquinas. Aquinas has a plurality of ideas in God's mind which are yet not plural (*S.T.* I. 15. 2), and in thoroughly Neoplatonic fashion seems to think that the relations expressed by the "procession of the Word" and "the procession of love" cease to be relations if they are "interior" (*ibid.* 27. 5; 28. 4).

Considered as a contribution to the philosophical topic of human personality, the *De Trinitate* was bound to be significantly defective. A person was first assumed to be a mind, then identified with an unexplained ego which (in contrast with God's logical simplicity) is the distinguishable subject of personal attributes. The question of what these attributes are is answered by amalgamating traditional faculty psychology, some Neoplatonic metaphysics, and the biblical descriptions of God. The formal concept of a divine person had to be made a relational concept. This task—or the task of combining it with Aristotle's substance—was unsuccessful. But the implication that for a human being to be a person is for him to stand in certain relations is attractive just because it breaks with the traditional concept of a person as a substance. For *substantial* meant *logically independent*. What is philosophically promising is a move which makes a person not just causally dependent, "for his development," on others but logically dependent for his existence as a person on others or at least one other. Only then can social roles, or functions which are relational because they imply interaction, be recognized as essential attributes. Augustine borrowed from the *Nicomachean Ethics*' examination of friendship for his own account of love.

But he was not tempted to make the move that would break with the tradition.[8] For this there was more than one reason. There were the theological requirements of Christianity, in particular that of individual immortality. There was the influence of Platonism which taught that the real self was to be found within; and for that matter, self-sufficiency was equally the lesson of the Stoics. Thirdly, the program itself of the *De Trinitate* might be thought to dictate a purely internal, insulated personality since it was to be the reflection in us of something definable ex hypothesi in terms of God by himself.[9] But one may remark that it was Augustine who chose the program. Anyway, he did not accept the opportunity of making an analogy between the interior relationships of the Trinity and *exterior* or mutual relationships of human persons. The only object to which these persons have a necessary relation is God himself, who is of course to be found within us. Consequently the love, the understanding, the knowledge that chiefly interest Augustine are each man's self-love, self-understanding, and self-knowledge.

NOTES

1. A surprising but extreme instance of such exaggeration is P. Henry's *Saint Augustine on Personality*, "The Saint Augustine Lecture 1959" (New York, 1960).

2. Porphyry, *Isagoge*, ed. Busse (*C.A.G.* IV, 1) p. 22, l. 1.

3. Cf. VII. 3. 4.

4. Augustine's awareness of philosophical as well as theological problems raised by this fact is brought out by R. A. Markus, "'Imago' and 'similitudo' in Augustine," *R. des ét. august.* X (1964), pp. 125–43.

5. He seems implicitly to be juggling with "the Word," which has to be the word *of* something (VII. 2. 3), in the same way as with "love."

6. H. Dörrie, *Porphyrios' "Symmikta zetemata,"* "Zetemata" 20, Munich, 1959; R. A. Markus in *Cambridge History of Later Greek and Early Medieval Philosophy*, Cambridge, England, 1967, pp. 357–58. For Plotinus, *Enn.* V. 9[5], 6.

7. IX. 4. 7. In the summary provided by IX. 5. 8 we have another of the formulas, *"nulla commixtione confunditur."*

8. Pp. 23–24 of Henry, *op. cit.*, which say the opposite, seem to me a long way from Augustine or the fifth century.

9. *Bonum diffusivum sui* is quite another matter.

GOD AND FREE WILL

9

Augustine on Foreknowledge and Free Will

WILLIAM L. ROWE

The problem with which this paper is concerned is raised in the following passage in Book III of St. Augustine's treatise *On Free Will*:

> ii, 4. (Evodius) . . . I have a deep desire to know how it can be that God knows all things beforehand and that, nevertheless, we do not sin by necessity. . . . Since God knew that man would sin, that which God foreknew must necessarily come to pass. How then is the will free when there is apparently this unavoidable necessity?
>
> iii. 6 (Augustine) Your trouble is this. You wonder how it can be that these two propositions are not contradictory and incompatible, namely that God has foreknowledge of all future events, and that we sin voluntarily and not by necessity. For if, you say, God foreknew that a man will sin, he must necessarily sin. But if there is necessity there is no voluntary choice in sinning, but rather fixed and unavoidable necessity. You are afraid that by that reasoning the conclusion may be reached either that God's foreknowledge of all future events must be impiously denied, or, if that cannot be denied, that sin is committed not voluntarily but by necessity. Isn't that your difficulty? (Evodius) Exactly that.[1]

The problem, as Augustine sees it, is to show how it is possible both that we voluntarily (freely) will to perform certain actions and that God foreknows that we shall will to per-

Reprinted, by permission of the author and the publisher, from *Review of Metaphysics* 18 (1964), pp. 356–63. Copyright by the *Review of Metaphysics*.

form these actions. The argument which gives rise to this problem may be expressed as follows:

(1) God has foreknowledge of all future events.

(2) Hence, if a man is going to sin, God foreknows that he will sin.

(3) Whatever God foreknows must necessarily happen.

(4) Hence, if God foreknows that a man will sin, he must necessarily sin.

(5) But if such a man must necessarily sin, there is no voluntary choice in his sinning.

(6) Therefore, such a man does not have free will.

I shall begin by examining Augustine's solution to this problem.

Augustine, if I understand him correctly, proposes to solve the problem by denying premiss (5). That is, he denies that if a man must necessarily sin, there is no voluntary choice in his sinning. Suppose that a man is going to sin and, hence, is going to will or choose to sin.[2] Given that God foreknows that a man is going to will to sin, it appears to follow from premiss (3) that it is necessary that the man is going to will or choose to sin. But if a man must necessarily will or choose to sin, how can we claim that he, nevertheless, voluntarily or freely wills to sin? It is this question that Augustine sets himself to answer.

Augustine's answer to the question just raised is that even though a man *necessarily* wills to sin he, nevertheless, freely wills to sin. The reason this is so is that the will is something that is always in our power, and whatever is in our power is *free*. The important passages in which he explains and argues this point are the following:

> But if he (a denier of free will) . . . says that, because he must necessarily so will, his will is not in his own power, he can be countered by the answer you gave me when I asked whether you could become happy against your will. You replied that you would be happy now if the matter were in your power; for you willed to be happy but could not achieve it . . . we cannot say we do not have the power unless we do not have what we will. If we do not have the will, we may think we will but in fact we do not. If we cannot will without willing those who will have will, and all that is in our

power we have by willing. Our will would not be will unless it were in our power. Because it is in our power, it is free. We have nothing that is free which is not in our power, and if we have something it cannot be nothing. Hence it is not necessary to deny that God has foreknowledge of all things, while at the same time our wills are our own. God has foreknowledge of our will, so that of which he has foreknowledge must come to pass. In other words, we shall exercise our wills in the future because he has foreknowledge that we shall do so; and there can be no will or voluntary action unless it be in our power.[3]

. . . there is nothing so much in our power as is the will itself. For as soon as we will (*volumus*) immediately will (*voluntas*) is there. We can say rightly that we do not grow old voluntarily but necessarily, or that we do not die voluntarily but from necessity, and so with other similar things. But who but a raving fool would say that it is not voluntarily that we will? Therefore though God knows how we are going to will in the future, it is not proved that we do not voluntarily will anything.[4]

For if that is to be called *our necessity* which is not in our power, but even though we be unwilling effects what it can effect—as, for instance, the necessity of death—it is manifest that our wills by which we live uprightly or wickedly are not under such a necessity; for we do many things which, if we were not willing, we should certainly not do. This is primarily true of the act of willing itself—for if we will, it *is;* if we will not, it *is* not—for we should not will if we were unwilling. But if we define necessity to be that according to which we say that it is necessary that anything be of such a nature, or be done in such and such a manner, I know not why we should have any dread of that necessity taking away the freedom of our will.[5]

Augustine's proposed solution, I believe, proceeds as follows. Granted that a man necessarily wills to sin, it does not follow that his will is not in his power, that he does not freely will to sin. To see that this is so we must first see what it means to say of something that it is not in a man's power. Augustine's view is that to say that *x* is not in a man's power is to say (roughly) that the presence or absence of *x* is not a result of the man's will. That is, *x* is not in a man's power if and only if either (1) *x* fails to occur even though the man wills to do x—for example, running a mile in four minutes is not in my power because the feat fails to be accomplished even though I will to accomplish it—or (2) x occurs even though the man does not will to do x—for example, my growing old is not in my power because it occurs even though I do not will it to occur. Thus where x is something that occurs, the question whether x is in our power reduces to the question whether x would occur even though we do not will it. This much granted, Augustine argues as follows. Even though a man necessarily wills to sin, we cannot say that this sinful act of will is not in the man's power. For clearly the act of will would not occur if the man did not will. To say that the man's willing to sin is not in his power is to say that the man wills to sin even though he does not will to sin—and this is impossible. Thus Augustine seems to hold that it is a necessary truth that the will is in our power and, therefore, free. As he puts it, "Our will would not be will unless it were in our power. Because it is in our power it is free." The fact that a man necessarily wills to sin does not conflict with his freely willing to sin because his willing to sin (although necessary) is still in his power—for it would not occur were he not to will to sin. In this way Augustine is led to reject premiss (5) in the argument under consideration. That is, he rejects the claim that if a man must necessarily sin, there is no voluntary choice in his sinning.

There is, I believe, a mistake in Augustine's reasoning in support of the claim that even though a sinful act of will is necessary it is, nevertheless, in one's power. His analysis of "x is not in our power" is, in part, "x occurs even though we do not will x." Thus my growing old is not in my power because I grow old even though I do not will to grow old. He argues, as we saw, that to say my willing to sin is not in my power is to say that I will to sin even though I do not will to sin—which, of course, is impossible. But surely there is a mistake here. If the case of my willing to sin is to parallel the case of my growing old then to say that my willing to sin is not in my power is not to say that I will to sin even though I do not will to sin; rather, it is to say that I will to sin even though I do not will to will to sin. The point I am making can be expressed just as well by taking as an example an act of will that does not occur—say, the act of willing to refrain from sinning. This act of will which does not occur corresponds to my act of running a mile in four minutes, which does not occur either. Now on Augustine's analysis of "x is not in our power" it follows that x is not in my power if I fail to do x even though I will to do x. Thus it follows that running a mile in four minutes is not in my power if I fail to run such a mile even though I will to run a mile in four minutes. Consider now the case of my willing to refrain from sinning. Parallel to the case of running a four-minute mile, the proper analysis of "willing to refrain from sinning is not in my power" should be, on Augustine's view, the following:

    (a)   I fail to will to refrain from sinning even though I will to will to refrain from sinning

rather than,

    (b)   I fail to will to refrain from sinning even though I will to refrain from sinning.

(a) and (b) are not the same. (b) seems to express an impossibility—hence Augustine's conviction that the will would not be will unless it were in our power. About (a) I wish to make two comments. First it is not clear that the phrase "I will to will to refrain from sinning" makes any sense at all. G. E. Moore suggested that there is such a thing as ". . . making an effort to induce ourselves to *choose* a particular course."[6] If there is such a thing as Moore suggested and if we take the phrase in question as expressing that thing, then perhaps we can interpret (a) in such a way that it expresses an intelligible proposition—namely, that I fail to will to refrain from sinning even though I make an effort to will or choose to refrain from sinning. The second comment is that if we so interpret (a) then it seems clear that (a) may be true and, consequently, we cannot conclude, in the simple way Augustine does, that it is in a man's power to will to refrain from sinning, that the will is something that is always in our power. Therefore, I conclude that Augustine has not made good his claim that, even though a man necessarily wills to sin, his willing or choosing to sin is voluntary or free. If this is so, it follows that Augustine has not succeeded in showing that premiss (5) is not true, and, therefore, has not

214   WILLIAM L. ROWE

succeeded in solving Evodius' problem of how God's foreknowledge is compatible with the freedom of the will.

Returning to the argument that Augustine wishes to refute,
it would seem that there is a logical mistake either in the
drawing of (4) from (3) *or* in the interpretation of (3). Let's
look at (3) for a moment. Let "*p*" pick out some event. We
must distinguish between interpreting (3) as (3a) "It is necessary that if God foreknows *p*, *p* will happen"—here the
necessity applies to the *conditional* "If God foreknows *p*, *p*
will happen"; and (3b) "If God foreknows *p*, *p* will happen
necessarily"—here the necessity applies not to the conditional
but to its consequent "*p* will happen." Since (4) is drawn
from (3), and since (5) presupposes that (4) is an instance
of (3b) rather than of (3a)—otherwise we have no reason
for supposing in the antecedent of (5) that the man in question must *necessarily* sin—it is clear that the inference from
(3) to (4) is valid only if (3) is interpreted as (3b) rather
than (3a). But, although (3a) is accepted as true within the
context of classical theology, classical theology need not—
and to my knowledge does not—hold (3b) to be true.[7] Hence,
either the inference from (3) to (4) is valid but (3) (interpreted as (3b)) is not true *or* (3) (interpreted as (3a)) is
true but the inference from (3) to (4) is invalid. On either
account, we have sufficient grounds for rejecting the argument Augustine presents.[8]

In this paper I have (1) explained and criticized what I
take to be Augustine's main reason for rejecting Evodius' argument that God's foreknowledge is incompatible with free
will, and (2) suggested another way of rejecting the argument. Augustine does make, however, one further point
which merits attention. He points out that the line of argument Evodius has taken implies not simply that *God's* foreknowledge is incompatible with free will but that anyone's
foreknowledge is incompatible with free will. For he shows
that on Evodius' reasoning it is foreknowledge generally and
not God's foreknowledge specially that causes the events fore-
known to happen by necessity. This creates a difficulty for
Evodius since he believes that *we* sometimes foreknow the
decisions and actions of men without thereby rendering those
decisions and actions *involuntary*.

The importance of this *ad hominem* argument against Evodius must not be overlooked. For if we claim that there is a *special* problem for the theologian who believes in divine foreknowledge and human freedom then the reasons we give in support of that claim must at some point concern *God's* foreknowledge, rather than foreknowledge generally. Otherwise, the theologian is involved in no more or less a difficulty than anyone who believes that *we* sometimes foreknow the free decisions and actions of men.

NOTES

1. *On Free Will*, trans. by John H. S. Burleigh, in *Augustine: Earlier Writings*, The Library of Christian Classics, Vol. VI (Philadelphia, 1953), pp. 172–73.

2. On Augustine's theory the essential element in every sinful act is "a movement of the will away from unchangeable good to mutable good." (*Ibid*. (III. 1. 1), p. 170.)

3. *Ibid*., (III. 3. 8), pp. 175–76.

4. *Ibid*., (III. 3. 7), pp. 174–75.

5. Augustine, *The City of God*, Bk. V. Ch. X, trans. by J. J. Smith, in *Basic Writings of St. Augustine*, Vol. II (New York, 1948), p. 68.

6. *Ethics* (London, 1912), pp. 135–36.

7. Both Boethius (see *The Consolation of Philosophy*, Book V, 6) and Aquinas are clear on this point. In considering a proposition similar to (3), Aquinas distinguishes between taking it as (3a) and as (3b). He then claims, in effect, that (3a) is true but (3b) is false. Thus he says: "Hence also this proposition, *Everything known by God must necessarily be,* is usually distinguished, for it may refer to the thing or to the saying. If it refers to the thing, it is divided and false; for the sense is, *Everything which God knows is necessary.* If understood of the saying, it is composite and true, for the sense is, *This proposition, 'that which is known by God is' is necessary"* (*Summa Theologiae,* I, 14, 13, ad 3). Thus, no problem arises in classical theology in connection with (3b)— for that proposition is rejected as false. However, a problem does arise out of accepting (3a) and claiming, in addition, that the *antecedent* of (3a) is itself necessary. Thus in discussing the necessarily true conditional statement "If God knew that this thing will be, it will be" Aquinas explicitly points out concerning the antecedent "God knew this contingent to be future" that "it must be said that this antecedent is absolutely necessary" (*ST.,* I, 14, 13, ad 2). In order to avoid the conclusion that no future event is contingent, Aquinas distinguishes between things as they exist in the knower (God) and as they exist in themselves. His suggestion is that in saying that "this thing will be" is absolutely necessary we are speaking of it only as it exists in God, and not as it exists in itself. As it exists in itself it is *contingent,* as it exists in God it is *absolutely necessary.* It is interesting to note that this difficulty does not arise in Aquinas' discussion of the divine *will.* ". . . But the divine knowledge has a necessary relation to the thing known; not the divine will to the thing willed. The reason for this is that knowl-

edge is of things as they exist in the knower; but the will is directed to things as they exist in themselves. Since then all other things have necessary existence inasmuch as they exist in God; but no absolute necessity so as to be necessary in themselves, insofar as they exist in themselves; it follows that God knows necessarily whatever He knows, but does not will necessarily whatever He wills" (*ST.*, I, 19, 3, ad 6; Cf. *Summa contra Gentiles*, I, 81). Having admitted that God's willing *p* is not necessary, Aquinas is free to assert that *p* need not happen by necessity. He points out, of course, that the conditional proposition "If God wills *p*, *p* will happen" is necessary, but denies that any necessity need attach to the consequent "*p* will happen" (*CG.*, I, 85). Thus he is able to say, "Although the non-existence of an effect of the divine will is incompatible with the divine will, the possibility that the effect should be lacking is given simultaneously with the divine will. God's willing someone to be saved and the possibility that that person be damned are not incompatible; but God's willing him to be saved and his actually being damned are incompatible" (*De Veritate*, 23, 5, ad 3).

8.   This way of rejecting Augustine's argument was argued in some detail by C. E. Caton and myself in a joint paper, "Divine Foreknowledge and Contingent Events," presented at the meeting of the Western Division of the American Philosophical Association, May 1961.

10

Augustine on Free Will and Predestination

JOHN M. RIST

There is still no consensus of opinion on Augustine's view of each man's responsibility for his moral behaviour. No one questions that Augustine held that every man is responsible, but judgements diverge radically on the implications to be drawn from this responsibility. There are those who attribute to Augustine the full-blown Calvinist position that each man has no say in his ultimate destiny, since that destiny is predetermined before the creation of the world: some are predestined to salvation, others to damnation. Other interpreters reject this view in varying degrees. They will not hold that for Augustine man's will is enslaved, or they would dispute about the sense in which it is enslaved and the sense in which it is free. Among the educated public, rather than among professional philosophers or psychologists, the very word 'freedom', or the phrase 'freedom of the will', is held to denote something desirable; hence if Augustine can be shown to hold that the will is free, he can be hailed as a philosopher of freedom.

It is not in the least surprising that an examination of Augustine's theories of the will, freedom, and grace is still of great contemporary interest. Most of Augustine's philosophical theories of man depend on his psychological insights, in particular into his own behaviour, and the accuracy and therefore the wide applicability of these insights and observations have made his *Confessions* in particular a work of universal

Reprinted from *Journal of Theological Studies*, N.S. 20 (1969), pp. 420–47, by permission of the author and the Clarendon Press, Oxford.

interest. Interpretation of Augustine is not therefore merely the concern of the professional theologian, nor, as far as we can tell, would Augustine have intended it to be, for some of his greatest writings are dedicated to pagans as well as to Christians. Furthermore it must still be emphasized that for Augustine it is impossible to demarcate the boundary between philosophy and theology. Hence it becomes impossible to discuss 'philosophical' questions, like that of the freedom of the will, without recourse to theological problems like the operations of grace. It is unfortunate that many interpreters have implicitly or explicitly tried to make such distinctions and to impose them on Augustine's recalcitrant writings. Hence recently R. A. Markus, writing on 'Human Action: Will and Virtue', has tried to determine Augustine's view of freedom while ruling out discussion of predestination, grace, and justification.[1] Even Gilson finds himself obliged to plead lack of theological competence as a way out of more detailed examination of the relationship of grace and free choice,[2] and that in spite of the fact that he has given us a fruitful primary examination of these views himself.

Those who plead theological incompetence or attempt to separate theological issues from issues of philosophy are letting the matter go by default. Theologians have never been hesitant about operating outside the bounds of Augustinian 'theology' and discussing problems of his 'philosophy' and psychology, and there is no reason why they should. In fact from his own age, from the *Defence of St. Augustine* of Prosper of Aquitaine through the writings of Calvin to Jansen's *Augustinus* and the orthodox replies, right down to recent successive numbers of the *Revue des études augustiniennes* and other modern journals, the struggle to determine Augustine's view of free will and grace has continued with unabated vigour and often unabated ferocity. Yet despite all that has been said, it may still be claimed that many expositions are as biased as ever and that the texts are not presented without much 'bad faith'. The body of Augustine's writings is very large, and it is easy to pull contrary opinions out of them. Yet at this stage of scholarly exegesis the mere presentation of a thesis which could be correct but which does not rule out the possibility of contrary theses is inadequate. Although in the study that is to follow I have not listed every available text on every matter of controversy under discussion, although I have not listed every interpreter by name nor examined every thesis in detail, it is my contention that the synthesis I shall attempt to present, if correct, negates other syntheses, and that all Augustinian texts which are relevant to the subject matter are in harmony with it. I have attempted to indicate the areas where evidence is weak in order not to conceal the fact that Augustine had not necessarily asked all the questions about his synthesis which we in later years have been able to ask. Finally, I have tried to avoid giving a misleading impression of Augustine's thought such as can be produced by those who are willing to hide behind the ambiguities of words like 'freedom' and 'grace'. 'Freedom' in particular is now almost a meaningless term. It was not meaningless for Augustine, though it did not carry the same emotional overtones as those with which we are familiar.

Let us begin with the fact that the word *voluntas*, which we are in the habit of translating as will, does not denote for Augustine a part of the human psyche; rather it is the human *psyche* in its role as a moral agent. As in Seneca, the word *voluntas* is in Augustine almost to be translated as 'moral self' or 'moral personality'. Quoting Luke 2:14, Augustine will describe the good as men 'of good will' (*bonae voluntatis*),[3] where it is clear that the goodness of the 'will' is the indication of the goodness of the man. Thus *voluntas* is not a decision-making faculty of the individual, as subsequent philosophy might lead us to suppose, but the individual himself. Hence it can be good or bad. Furthermore it is the basic core of the human person. It makes no sense, Augustine argues against Evodius in the *De Libero Arbitrio*,[4] to ask what is the cause of the will. Man is born with a *voluntas*, but since he is himself *voluntas* he cannot disclaim responsibility for his actions on the ground that he did not 'will' them. For Augustine, if a man does something, he 'wills' it. To ask of a man, 'Why does he will this?' cannot be to suggest that he is not responsible for his acts. A man wills what is good, says Augustine, because he is good; he wills what is bad because he is bad. Good deserves praise, bad deserves

blame. It makes no sense, Augustine will argue, to say that
a man is 'compelled to will' (*cogi velle*).[5] If a man is compelled, he claims, he does not will, though he may later come
to will what he is now compelled to do. Evidently this analysis
only recognizes external compulsion as compulsion. What we
should call psychological compulsions are not compulsions
for Augustine. They are simply the individual working out
his own nature. Thus in Augustine's view all action is done
willingly or unwillingly, and all unwilling action is done after
a conscious struggle in which the individual is overborne by
external pressure. Thus in the moral area sins committed
through an unthinking acceptance of the norms of one's up-
bringing or environment are always deserving of punishment.
If we sin 'automatically', we sin willingly.

From this doctrine of the nature of the human 'will' it is
easy to move towards Augustine's theory of free choice. Each
human being can make decisions by virtue of what Augustine
calls his free choice (*liberum arbitrium*). Consistently
through the whole range of his writings Augustine is insistent
that everyone has this power of free choice, but in view of
our understanding of his concept of the will (*voluntas*),
which he also holds to be free,[6] we should be careful in our
interpretation of 'free choice'. We make choices, clearly
enough, under the sway of certain kinds of motivation. If
we have formed good habits and delight in the good in a certain area of human activity, then we shall make good choices
'freely' in that area; if, however, our habits are bad, then
our choices in that area are bad. Yet although they are bad,
they are still for Augustine free choices for which we are
individually responsible. Our habits are like a weight around
our necks, and they reflect, or rather they are identical with,
our likes and dislikes. Hence Augustine will equate a man's
delight (*delectatio*) with his love: *non enim amatur, nisi quod
delectat.*[7] And his love is a weight (*pondus*) which drives
him to good and evil, or rather is his good and evil will.[8]
By love I am carried wherever I am carried, says Augustine
in the *Confessions.*[9] It is clear that this 'weight' which Augustine envisages, this 'delight' which marks his will and impels
him to act will be operative upon his choices. But still Augustine will say that his choices are free. In the *Confessions*

Augustine points out continually that he was plagued by lust. Like St. Paul he recognizes a conflict between his will and his 'members'. Elsewhere he observes that swearing, once become habitual, is beyond our control to restrain.[10] These deeply ingrown habits represent a living death for the individual. The soul is like Lazarus in the tomb,[11] bound by its evil habits. And yet through all these and many similar passages there is no suggestion that man is not able to exercise 'free' choice, no suggestion that he is not responsible for what he does. The power and incisiveness of Augustine's psychological insights serve to highlight the insistence that man's choices are still free, that our will is free and that our moral helplessness is still our moral guilt. *Trahat sua quemque voluptas;* Augustine quotes this Virgilian phrase with approval.[12] We recall the equally notorious Stoic tag, *Fata volentem ducunt sed nolentem trahunt.* It is not surprising that if the *voluptas* is provided by divine grace, people have been tempted to say that for Augustine this grace is irresistible. Leaving Jansen for a modern scholar, we may observe that Peter Brown has recently committed himself to saying that according to Augustine 'a man is capable of allowing himself to be "drawn" to act by the sheer irresistible pleasure of the object of his love.'[13] But Augustine never uses the word 'irresistible' in this sort of context, and we must remember that 'to be compelled to will' in his view makes no sense. In other words for all that Augustine says about habit, man's choices are still 'free'.

At this point we should recall that we are discussing Augustine's view of humanity after the Fall. It is true that he would say that Adam was free and that we ourselves are free, but there is no reason to assume that we are free in the same sense as Adam before the Fall. Indeed we are free in a quite different sense. But for the time being we must leave Adam aside and concentrate on Augustine's theory of the freedom of our choices in our 'fallen' state. In brief, when Augustine says that our choices are free, he does not mean that we are autonomous beings, able to weigh up good and evil courses of action and decide upon the one or the other. Unless he is helped by God's grace, fallen man's freedom of choice is only the freedom to sin. We are free and able to do evil of our

own accord, but we are unable to choose the good freely. Of
ourselves we are free from virtues,[14] and free to do evil.[15]
Our free choice is sufficient for evil (*liberum arbitrium ad
malum sufficit*).[16] In short, when Augustine says that fallen
man is free and has free choices, he means that he is free
from virtue and the slave of vice, free from one kind of love,
that is, devoid of *caritas*, but the servant of its opposite,
namely *cupiditas*. Man belongs to one of two camps and obeys
one of two rulers. *Regnat carnalis cupiditas ubi non est Dei
caritas*.[17] Since *caritas*, which brings the soul joy and love
for the right, is the gift of God, the fallen soul, unless helped
out of its miseries, is a slave and captive to evil.[18] Hence
we come to the familiar Augustinian paradox: fallen man
has free choices, always of evil, but does not enjoy *freedom*
(*libertas*). Freedom is obedience to God, the choice and performance of good works under the guidance of God's grace.
It is freedom from the necessity of sin.[19] Thus we are brought
to the view that, although our 'wills' and our 'choices' are
free, in the sense that we alone are responsible for them,
yet without the intervention of God we are bound to an evil
which we cannot escape.[20] As Augustine is fond of repeating to the Pelagians, the free will we dispose of is nothing
to boast about.[21] If, therefore, we wish to inquire whether
we have any freedom whatsoever, in the sense of any ability
to break out of the web of evil-doing in which we are en-
meshed by the Fall, we shall have to consider whether we
have any autonomy whatsoever in our relations with God.
The fear would seem to be that once caught up in sin, as all
of us are, we can only escape by being completely impassive
and by being moulded willy-nilly in accordance with God's
purposes. This would make us little more than living puppets.
But before we inquire further into Augustine's thought in
this area, we shall have to consider his theory of the divine
will and of the sin of Adam and of the fallen angels. For an
understanding of man's uncorrupted nature and the uncorrupted natures of the angels before they fell may help us to
grasp Augustine's psychological and theological analyses of
our present conditions.

We have seen that, although our wills and choices are
free, we still need freeing from sin. Although we are *liberi*,

we are not *liberati*. And if we are *liberati*, that is, if we enjoy freedom, we are *servi Dei*. But just as 'free' must be understood as 'free from', as in 'free from sin', 'free from virtue', so 'freed' must be understood as 'freed by God'. Although, therefore, we are 'free' agents in the sense that we are responsible for our acts, we are unfree, until God intervenes, in that we are in bondage to sin. Hence it is more accurate to say that *liber* in the phrases *libera voluntas, liberum arbitrium* means 'responsible', and it will often be translated that way in the remainder of this discussion. But if we are responsible beings, in the sense of beings held responsible for our acts by God, the problem of God's justice arises. How can we be held responsible for our sins if we are slaves of sin and have no freedom whatsoever in the sense of autonomy, no ability to act of our own accord in the direction of escaping from the necessity of being evil? These questions must be considered; they will involve a discussion of Augustine's theory of the solidarity of the human race in Adam as well as an examination of whether salvation and damnation, moral life or sin, is as arbitrary a matter of God's *fiat* as Calvin found Augustine to have proposed. We shall have to ask ourselves whether Augustine held that the responsibility of the individual has no necessary connection with that individual's personal behaviour; for that would be the case if our 'responsible choice' is an act whose moral flavour is irrevocably fixed by our mere membership in the human race.

Even if Augustine was not clear on the matter when he wrote *De Libero Arbitrio*—and he denies this in the *Retractationes*—he is certainly consistent in his later works in holding that all good acts which we perform, all acts, that is, which spring from a will which has been freed from sin, require the 'assistance' (*adiutorium*) of God. And this assistance is not merely the co-operation of God with a weak desire of the will for moral behaviour and salvation. God's assistance is required if fallen man is ever even to want to reform his life. Hence again and again Augustine will quote the text of Proverbs 8:35: *voluntas praeparatur a Deo*.[22] What Augustine wishes to make plain beyond any possibility of doubt is that, unless our 'will' is so prepared, we shall always be slaves to evil. At the time of preparation we have done nothing

which we could claim God is rewarding. God's action pre-
dates our 'merits'; it occurs *sine ullis praecedentibus meritis*.[23]
But when Augustine asserts repeatedly that God's grace is no
kind of reward for merits, he understands by 'merits' good
deeds done or foreseen. God does not prepare a man's will
because he sees he will achieve a degree of goodness, but
in order that he may achieve a degree of goodness. And because a man is able to perform some acts well—because his
will has been prepared—it does not follow that he will continue to act well; he may have received grace, but not the
grace of perseverance. Indeed we must notice a very important feature of Augustine's doctrine of the freeing of the will
by God. Unless the infusion of grace is continued, the will
will revert to type, that is, it will be only adequate for evil.
Augustine holds very firmly that it is impossible to attain perfection, that is, a state in which relapse into sin is impossible,
during this life. He imagines the relationship between grace
and the soul in the same way as that in which Aristotle
imagined the relationship between force and a moving object.
Unless the object is kept in motion by the continued pressure
of the mover, it will come to a halt. Similarly unless the sinner is kept on the straight and narrow path by the continual
pressure of grace, he will fall back into his evil habits. Augustine pointed out to Julian of Eclanum that it had come to
his notice that an eighty-four-year-old man, who had lived
in continence for twenty-five years, had just taken a concu-
bine.[24] For some reason persevering grace had not been
given him, or at least not received.

Thus for Augustine no one can know that he is saved
and even those who are saved do not lead perfect lives. Not
only do they need continual help, for without this help they
would be utterly unable to act for good, but even when in
receipt of help their evil and corrupted natures are continually struggling to reassert themselves. Augustine seems to
have been worried that if he allowed anyone, even with God's
help, to reach a state of achieved perfection in this life, the
help would become unnecessary. And he is convinced by
the Bible that its consistent message is that God's help is always necessary. So insistent is Augustine on this point that
even in the case of Mary he is very careful in his remarks

about her being without sin. The Pelagians had claimed that various Old Testament worthies had lived sinless lives. Augustine ridicules the idea. What do you suppose these men would say if we asked them whether they lived without sin?, he asks Pelagius. As for Mary, says Augustine, I do not wish to query Pelagius' claim that she was sinless 'out of honour to the Lord'. When discussing her further he is careful to point out that for this sinlessness to be attained, grace for overcoming sin had to be given 'in every particular' (*omni ex parte*).[25] It is important to observe that what Augustine says is not that she could not sin, but that grace was given to her in every particular of life so that the ever-present possibility of sin was overcome. It appears that Augustine's view of the grace accorded to her should be compared with his view of the situation of Adam, which we shall consider at a later stage. For the present it is sufficient to observe that both Adam and Mary seem, for Augustine, to have had the possibility of sinning (*posse peccare*) but that Mary was given the grace which prevented that possibility from becoming actualized.

Mary, in Augustine's view, is a special case. In general he seems to have held that good men, even those who enjoy the grace of perseverance to the end, are liable to failure in particular actions. As a result of the permanent weakness of fallen man, a weakness which is not removed by baptism, the life even of the saint is a series of failures and successes.[26] Not only is the saint able to sin, but he actually sins. Only after death is the stage reached in which sin is impossible (*non posse peccare*) and freedom (*libertas*) is attained.

We have now reached the point at which it becomes imperative to consider whether in Augustine's view predestination is twofold: some are predestined to salvation, others to damnation. In the *De Dono Perseverantiae* predestination is defined as a foreknowledge and 'preparation' by God of those acts of kindness (*beneficia*) by which those who are saved are saved. What this seems to mean is that all those who are saved are saved by God's acts of kindness. It does not follow from Augustine's *definition* of predestination that all those who are offered such acts of kindness are in fact saved. And for the moment we may leave aside the problem of how

many God wishes to save. In the *De Dono Perseverantiae*
Augustine argues that those who are not saved are left in
the *massa damnata*;[27] that is, in the case of those who are
not saved there is no positive impulsion to damnation originating from God. Since damnation is the reward of sin, it therefore follows that Bavaud is right in remarking that 'Saint
Augustin refuse toujours de dire que Dieu meut positivement
sa créature au péché'.[28] As Augustine himself would put it,
God does not wish (= cause) the damnation of any man, but
in another sense he wishes it, that is, he is willing to let it
happen in certain circumstances. What these circumstances
are can be examined later. For the present we can affirm that
Augustine was conscious of the distinction between positively
willing something and being willing to let something happen.
*Non ergo fieri aliquid nisi omnipotens fieri velit, vel sinendo
ut fiat, vel ipse faciendo.*[29]

There are a number of passages in Augustine's writings in
which the formal definition of predestination given in *De
Dono Perseverantiae* does not seem to cover his position. In
the *De Dono Perseverantiae* predestination is a matter not
merely of foreknowing the destiny of each individual, but
of preparing the acts of kindness by which the saved are
saved. Predestination, therefore, in so far as it involves God's
action rather than merely his foreknowledge, is concerned
with salvation. Thus there would be predestination to salvation and lack of predestination leading to damnation. But
in *De Anima et eius Origine* Augustine speaks of predestination to death,[30] a phrase which *De Dono Perseverantiae*
would have to reject. However, the difference between the
two works is here merely verbal. 'Predestination to death', as
Bavaud says, does not imply a positive impulsion to evil by
God and is thus not predestination in the same sense as predestination to salvation; for predestination to salvation involves positive good acts by God. In the *De Anima* God
punishes those 'predestined to death' because they are sinners,
but he does not help them to sin in order to punish them.
Similarly in *De Gratia et Libero Arbitrio* grace is offered to
some who accept it,[31] but in the case of those whom he
'hardens' God allows them to be deceived and hardened. 'God
hardened Pharaoh's heart' means that God allowed Pharaoh's

heart to be hardened. We have not, of course, yet faced the question of whether or not the grace which saves is 'irresistible'. If it is, it would follow that such grace is not offered to anyone who is allowed to be hardened. But for the moment we are working with Augustine's formal definition of predestination, that it is a preparation of God's acts of kindness. The passage from *De Gratia et Libero Arbitrio* is not opposed to this. But we are beginning to disentangle two quite distinct questions. Is grace irresistible to those to whom it is offered? So far we have found no decisive reason to answer this question in the affirmative. All we know is that all those who are saved are saved by grace, not that all those to whom saving grace is offered are saved. The second question, which, as we shall see, must be kept distinct from the first, is: Is grace even offered to all?

The passage from *De Gratia et Libero Arbitrio* is paralleled by very similar language in the *Encheiridion*.[32] Here Augustine speaks of those 'predestined to punishment'. Augustine argues that in the case of angels and of men who have sinned, God makes good use of the evil of sin in that his 'predestination to punishment' is righteous. But again, although clearly God foreknew the sins of such people, Augustine does not say that he impelled them. Predestination to punishment therefore means the foreknowledge and acceptance by God of the fact of calamitous sin. Such sin is turned to serve the purpose of a demonstration of justice. The guilty are punished, but they are really guilty. They choose to be guilty.

There are then two possible ways in which a man can be reprobate. He can reject the saving grace which is offered to him, or he may not be offered saving grace at all. We may defer the latter question until later in the discussion, since it is clear that those to whom no grace is offered are bound to fall into sin. This question is, in Augustine, irrelevant to the problem with which our discussion began, namely, in what sense can we be said to have a 'free' will and to make free choices. We can be sure that for Augustine those who are not offered grace will not be able to make free choices, except of inevitable evil. Far more interesting and important philosophically is whether those who *are* offered the grace

of baptism and the grace of perseverance are bound to accept them, whether in fact any vestige of Adam's original
freedom is left to them, whether in the case of the 'elect'
grace is irresistible and the individual has no choice but to be
'free' to act rightly in all matters of ultimate significance for
his soul. In brief, does Augustine teach moral determinism
for the elect? Is it in fact the case that at least as far as fatal
sins are concerned *non posse peccare,* inability to sin, is *in
practice* the rule even in this life, since on every occasion of
sin God will present circumstances in such a way that the
'will' will certainly choose the correct course of action. This
at least seems to be the opinion of Gilson, who writes as
follows: 'When God wants to save a soul, to have it consent
to His saving grace, He has but to choose either some external
circumstances with which the soul is to find itself surrounded,
or graces to which its will is to find itself submissive.'[33] As
Gilson rightly points out, on this theory Augustine's doctrine
would be that grace is irresistible without being constraining.
It is not constraining in that, as we have seen, anything which
the 'will' chooses is a free choice of the will. In this sense man
is not constrained, but if Gilson's view is a correct interpretation of the theory of Augustine, fallen man, even he who
is elect, is no more than an animated puppet. The problem
is: Does Augustine think that God offers grace to certain
individuals in such a way that he knows they will be unable
to reject it? Are the elect simply responding to the appropriate stimulus from God in the same inevitable fashion as
iron is drawn to a magnet?

In order to grasp more clearly the nature of man after the
Fall, it is necessary to understand what he was like before
the sin of Adam. And the sin of Adam can only be understood in relation to the sin of Satan. We are faced in fact
with the problem of the nature of spiritual beings before they
are affected by sin. On the matters relevant to our present
inquiry we are fortunate enough to dispose of a fairly considerable amount of evidence. Just as Satan was originally
endowed with the greatest potentialities for good, so, according to Augustine, Adam was endowed with every possibility
of goodness. He was physically healthy and of enormous
intellectual power.[34] His soul was completely at peace; he

was untroubled by excessive fears or desires. His mind and body worked together in perfect harmony. His wisdom is evidenced by his ability to name the different animals. God could have made him incapable of sin, but chose not to do so.[35] Instead he bestowed upon Adam the genuine power of free choice. Adam received an *adiutorium sine quo non*, a degree of assistance which enabled him to choose the good if he wished.[36] Adam was already the recipient of three valuable opportunities. If he so chose, he could be free from sin, free from death, and free to persevere in the good or not to desert the good. Hence when Adam sinned, he sinned with full knowledge.[37]

Adam knew what was required for the maintenance of his paradisal state, just as Satan had known it. He had only to rely on God and his well-being was assured.[38] It is important to observe that Adam did not need to be 'prepared' to rely on God by God himself; he himself could take the initiative. That he failed to do this was the mark not of a failure of God's grace but of an inexplicable submission to pride. Adam's enormous sin is thus beyond the range and beyond the imagination of contemporary sinners;[39] and its consequences are disastrous to a proportionate degree. As a result of Adam's sin comes sin, death, and a general desertion of the good by mankind. All the descendants of Adam are scarred by 'concupiscence', and by what Augustine calls 'ignorance' and 'difficulty', the sheer inability to carry out what we know to be right. The human race has been corrupted by Adam, because all men are in some sense 'in Adam'. Augustine repeatedly misquotes St. Paul to the effect that we all sinned in Adam (*in quo omnes peccaverunt*),[40] where the Greek text reads ἐφ' ᾧ (Rom. 5:12), but although this text supports Augustine's position it does not dictate it.

All men, Augustine argues, are identical with Adam. All men sinned in Adam on that occasion, he writes, since all were already identical with him in that nature of his which was endowed with the capacity to generate them.[41] Again in *De Nuptiis et Concupiscentia* we read that through Adam's sin all men are sinners, since all are that one man;[42] and in the *City of God* the same argument occurs.[43] We all existed in that one man (*omnes fuimus in illo uno*). The specific form by which we were to live had not yet been created, but our 'nature' was present in the seed from which we were to be born. It seems to be Augustine's view that Adam's semen, which was, with his other parts, corrupted by sin, in some sense is the seed of the whole human race. In some sense our 'nature' existed in that semen; hence we are in fact Adam; hence the sin which Adam committed is our sin. All men who are thus born by the ordinary processes of deposition of semen in the vagina are a tainted growth. Adam's tainted seed is thus in a sense the 'nature' of every man, and every man who generates by sexual means thus produces more tainted offspring. The seed is not merely the bearer of weakness and potentiality of sin; it also is the bearer of actual sin. All seed is Adam; hence all those who grow from seed are Adams, and thus guilty of the original sin of Adam.[44] Augustine is therefore in no doubt of our solidarity with Adam. We share in his sin; we share in his guilt and in the weakness which he has to endure in his fallen state. In a sense we are Adam. The solidarity with Adam and the resultant misery of our lot is vividly portrayed by the phrases in which Augustine describes fallen humanity. The evidence has never been better summarized than by Rottmanner: we are a *massa luti, peccati, peccatorum, iniquitatis, irae, mortis, perditionis, damnationis, offensionis, originis vitiatae atque damnatae;* we are a *massa tota vitiata, damnabilis, damnata.*[45] *Massa peccati* is perhaps the most normal description Augustine gives of fallen humanity. It seems likely that Augustine's concept of the oneness of man in Adam is influenced by the Stoic and Neoplatonic doctrine of σπερματικοὶ λόγοι, which are themselves all contained within the Divine Logos of the world. In Neoplatonic theory each of the λόγοι σπερματικοί, the 'natures' of particular things in the world, can be said to be identical with, and at the same time independent of, the Logos of the whole.

The Fall of man therefore means that human nature is disastrously damaged and in urgent need of a physician.[46] Augustine is fond of comparing Christ to a healing doctor who tends the sicknesses of humanity. The problem which concerns us, however, is the degree of damage done to Adam's original nature. Is the corruption total? Although there are a very few passages in which Augustine says that as a result of the Fall our nature is 'dead',[47] these must be regarded as hyperbolical expressions of the view that Adam's sin has inflicted so grave a wound on human nature that it cannot heal up of its own accord. The help of God is essential if we are not to be the slaves of sin, for our nature is corrupted, wounded, weakened, vitiated.[48] In a sense Augustine does not step beyond the bounds of his opinion when he says that this nature is dead, for even if not quite dead it needs a life-giving act of grace to revive it. But Augustine's normal opinion seems to be clear when he expresses himself to the effect that the last vestiges (*extrema vestigia*) of our nature have escaped destruction, and that some sort of spark of reason, still recalling the creation of man in the image of God, has not yet been extinguished.[49] This is in fact the only logical view Augustine could have taken. Clearly our *voluntas*, our moral personality, survives; if it did not survive it would not be 'sufficient for evil', as it is as a result of the Fall. Rather the *nature* which we have received is damaged but still existent. What we therefore need to inquire is whether Augustine saw any connection between the fact that some vestiges of reason and of our likeness to God still remain in us and the problem of our relationship with God if we are in fact numbered among the elect. In other words do the *vestigia* of our original nature have anything to do with the process of our possible salvation? If they do, then grace may not in fact be irresistible, and although our *voluntas*, our moral will, is 'prepared' by God, yet we may not be simply puppets accepting (without question) that preparation.

Before continuing further, however, we must revert to Augustine's accounts of the nature of predestination. There is no need to argue that it is Augustine's view that God's grace precedes human merits, that no merit is possible without God's prevenient action, and that God does not bestow grace on those whom he foreknows will be naturally meritorious. However, the view still appears to be current that grace may be withheld by God from those whom he foresees will sin frequently. Hence Bavaud writes: 'Dieu ne réfuse la grâce de la persévérance finale qu'après la prévision de nombreux démérites.'[50] This view, which seems to date back to Prosper of Aquitaine,[51] is specifically ruled out by Augustine himself. Speaking in the *Encheiridion* of the famous text 'Jacob I have loved but Esau I have hated', Augustine observes that if God had wished us to understand that predestination is governed by the future good works of the one or the future evil works of the other, he would not have spoken as he did.[52]

We have already noticed that both Satan and Adam are free of all moral evil before they fall. They have the choice and the power to avoid sin. Their weakness, therefore, the weakness by which they choose death rather than life, sin rather than God, can only be explained metaphysically. God could have created beings incapable of sin.[53] Even though all beings are *ex nihilo*, that does not entail their necessary sinfulness.[54] However, it appears to be Augustine's view that the free choice given to Adam and to Satan is incompatible with the impossibility of sinning except in the case of God himself. All created beings which are endowed with the power of choice will be liable to sin, and therefore it is likely that some of them will sin in fact. Such sins, it must be repeated, are not the result of the *moral* weakness of the individual, nor of a conflict between concupiscence and moral knowledge, for such a struggle exists only in fallen humanity; rather they spring from a metaphysical weakness endemic in all creatures that are at the same time endowed with a genuine power of choosing. In his last work, the *Opus Imperfectum contra Julianum*, Augustine observes that if the angels were left to their own free will, unsupported by God's help, they might fall as Satan fell, and become a new race of devils.[55] The whole theory is admirably summed up in the *City of God*.[56] Augustine has been explaining Adam's sin as that of disobedience promoted by pride. He continues as follows: 'Such worsening (sc. of the will) by reason of a defect is possible only in a nature that has been created out of nothing. In a word, a nature is a nature because it is something made by God, but a nature falls away from That Which Is because a nature was made from nothing. Yet man did not so fall away from Being as to be absolutely *nothing*, but in so far as he turned himself toward himself, he became less than he was when he was adhering to Him who is supreme Being.'

We can summarize the unfallen condition of man as follows. He is free from moral evil, though necessarily possessed of the ontological weakness that is the lot of all that is both free and created. After the fall of man some 'spark' of his original nature survives. We may assume therefore that when human beings are reborn in Christ, something of their original character would again become visible. Now before he fell Adam was able not to sin (*posse non peccare*); in the case of those who are the elect, after they have attained their final perseverance they will be unable to sin (*non posse peccare*), a greater boon in the eyes of Augustine. However, the attainment of this perfection does not occur in this life. Even the elect are not perfect; hence even the elect are *liable* to sin. Our problem is why they are so able. Is it because they are restored by grace to a state resembling that of Adam? The answer to this must be No, for if they were restored to this state, any sin which they committed would be a sin laden with the monstrous consequences of Adam's original sin. Their individual sins must therefore be occasions when God's grace in Christ does not support them in every particular minor circumstance of the moral life. As we have already observed, it is only Mary who is so supported.

Thus we can see that if any vestige of Adam's original free choice remains even for the elect, that vestige is not shown in the moral acts of the elect individual. Nor in fact is it shown in his acts of intention or acts of will, for *voluntas praeparatur a Deo*. There is only one area in which any vestige of 'free choice' can possibly be left to the individual member of the elect. The problem can be stated as follows: When God offers grace to the man he wills to save, is it possible for this grace to be rejected? If rejection were possible, acceptance would also be possible, and those to whom salvation is offered would at least enjoy a vestige of the free choice with which the human race was originally endowed. As for those who are left in the *massa damnata*, they would be of two classes: those whom God has not willed to save, and those who rejected the saving grace offered to them by the exercise of their vestige of man's original free will. We should observe that, whereas for Adam perfection would be the result of a positive act of initiative by which man chose to rely on God, for the saved among fallen humanity it would be merely the passive acceptance of a salvation offered by God.

Gilson's version of the salvation of those who are saved is as follows:[57] 'When God wants to save a soul, to have it consent to His saving grace He has but to choose either some external circumstances with which the soul is to find itself surrounded, or graces to which its will is to find itself submissive. . . . Thus in Augustine, grace can be irresistible without being constraining.' In other words the wills of the elect are only free in the sense we discussed at the beginning of this paper. They not only cannot act without God's help, or will without God's help, but even the acceptance or rejection of help is dictated to them. No vestige of Adam's free choice thus remains. Though Gilson does not say it, his Augustine is a moral determinist: fallen men are puppets.

Gilson asserts that God's grace is in some sense 'irresistible,' but he does not understand 'irresistible' in the Jansenist sense. Man is not 'compelled' to be saved, because, as we have seen, the will by which he is enabled to act rightly is not 'compelled to will.' *Cogi velle*, as we saw, is in Augustine's view a contradiction in terms. One either wills one thing or another. Whatever one wills one wills freely. Hence for the saved grace is not irresistible in the sense of compelling. The will, which is transformed and which, as we have seen, is always responsible, can thus be called free. But though Jansenist determinism is thus avoided, the puppet nature of fallen man, his servitude to another version of determinism, is maintained.

Augustine regularly maintains that God did not desert man till man had deserted him.[58] That is a fair account if all men are one in Adam. Does even a watered-down version of this apply to the individual fallen man? Does God offer anyone the chance to desert him even by a non-acceptance of grace? Certainly by the time he wrote the *Retractations* Augustine was sure that faith was a gift of God; he withdraws an earlier statement to the contrary.[59] Nor is the situation changed by such texts as that which asserts that it is the part of our personal will (*propriae voluntatis*) to agree to God's call,[60] for this will is itself 'prepared' by God. The crux of the matter in fact is to be seen in the problem of the word *praeparatur* in the famous text *voluntas praeparatur a Deo*. Does *praeparatur* imply that God enables us to will, or that he arranges so that we should in fact will (freely)? The problem can only be solved by an examination of a number of passages which describe the operations of God's mercy and God's grace.

The *De Correptione et Gratia* provides the most notorious passage which has been interpreted to mean that God's grace moulds the human will to its own purposes, without any vestige of self-determination remaining for man: *'Subventum est igitur infirmitati voluntatis humanae, ut divina gratia indeclinabiliter et insuperabiliter ageretur.*[61] The crux of the problem lies in the meaning of the two adverbs. It has been suggested that they indicate that God's grace is irresistible. But the meaning does not seem to be quite clear. It may be that Augustine says that grace is transforming. Or he may be saying that the human will is influenced by an influence which operates in a specific way, that is, *indeclinabiliter et insuperabiliter*. That is, according to this passage, Augustine may be arguing not that grace is irresistible or transforming, but that it is unswerving and all-conquering. The emphasis is not on grace's effects on the soul but on its nature. Perhaps Augustine does not mean that its dominion is absolutely guaranteed in every case, but that it is by nature sovereign; theoretically it cannot be overcome.

As Augustine continues the *De Correptione,* this interpretation still seems possible. God helps the weak, says Augustine, so that they may have an unconquerable will to good (*ut ipso donante invictissime quod bonum est vellent et hoc deserere invictissime nollent*). It is just possible that Augustine means that the weak may (or may not) have such an unconquerable will, the matter being dependent on man's acceptance of grace. In other words the whole passage may possibly be open to the explanation that grace enables man to persevere in the good, while still leaving open the chance that he may of his own volition choose, like Adam, not to do so. Augustine does not use the word 'irresistible', and this word is too tainted with subsequent discussion to be helpful; in any case we have argued above that *cogi velle* is meaningless in Augustine's context. So the passage from *De Correptione et Gratia* may be taken to say either that grace transforms the will so that we will 'freely' (i.e. from ourselves) whatever God leads us to will, or that it merely enables the will to accept or reject an offer of salvation. Accepting this offer would entail accepting obedience to God as the absolute and certain road to freedom and salvation.

That grace is transforming and that the elect cannot but be saved if such is God's will—will being understood as intention—is, however, made finally certain by Chapter 13 of the reply to the second question of Simplicianus. The argument runs as follows. We are all familiar with the biblical text 'many are called, but few are chosen'. This implies, says Augustine, that calling does not produce the good will (*effectrix bonae voluntatis*) by which we can live a good life. If our salvation were merely a question of obedience to the call of God, then it would not be entirely God's work. Indeed, according to Augustine, it would be man's work. Perhaps, Augustine continues, some of those who are called but do not respond would be able to accommodate their will to faith if they were called otherwise. Is it the case that only those who are found 'suitable' obey? But this argument seems unsatisfactory because it would seem to suggest that the suitability rests somewhere in man's nature, rather than in God's grace. In fact Augustine rules out the possibility which his metaphysical theories of man's nature and fall have made available to him, namely, that perhaps the *vestigia rationis* which are not destroyed by the Fall could at least acquiesce when saving grace is offered. But even this vestige of freedom is apparently to be rejected. Augustine now takes the view that God does not pity 'in vain'. The effectiveness of God's mercy cannot be subject to any power of man. If God so wills, out of his pity for the elect, that they be saved, he will arrange the circumstances of their lives in such a way that they will in fact choose the right. God calls many but pities few. Those whom he pities are saved. When God pities a man, he calls him in such a way as he knows to be suited to his character, with the result that he will not reject the call (*cuius autem miseretur sic eum vocat, quomodo scit ei congruere ut vocantem non respuat*). Once again we are back to the basic Augustinian alternative: man is a slave either of God or of evil, either of *caritas* or of *cupiditas*. And those who are the slaves of *caritas* are made so by God. When discussing salvation Augustine seems to forget the doctrine which we found him expounding earlier, the doctrine that God's *voluntas* can be shown either in doing something (*faciendo*) or in allowing something to happen (*sinendo*).[62] Although he is certainly prepared to use this idea—and it seems to be the way in which he avoids attributing to God the positive desire to condemn the reprobate to eternal punishment—he does not use it to preserve even a vestige of Adam's free choice for fallen humanity.

Augustine's determination that God's will should in this matter be treated as a positive force is brought home to us by his insistence on perverting the obvious meaning of the text 'God wishes all men to be saved' (1 Tim. 2:4). We know, argues Augustine, that all are not in fact saved; in fact the greater number are lost. When we ask how this happens, the usual answer is that men do not wish to accept salvation.[63] But this cannot be the case with infants; they are capable of neither assent nor refusal. Hence, Augustine argues, salvation is independent of man's fallen will; it is a matter of God's omnipotence. God has mercy on those whom he will. When God wills that a man be saved, the matter is settled. The man is saved; his evil will is turned to good. The text 'God wishes all men to be saved' must be interpreted to mean that all those who are saved are saved by God's will. If God wishes a man's salvation, salvation follows of *necessity*.[64] The last phrase is particularly important as an emphasis on the puppet-like status of fallen man. Accordingly when elsewhere Augustine says that a true answer to the question, Why is a man, even when assisted by grace, unable to live without sin? is that he does not want to,[65] we are to understand that God has allowed him not to want to. In the case of such sins God has not so arranged the circumstances of a man's life that he will freely, but still of necessity, choose the good.

Augustine's perverse reading of the text 'God wills all men to be saved' is not limited to the *Encheiridion* and thus cannot be explained away as a slip. On the contrary, as we have seen, it accords with some of his most deeply held views. Elsewhere he will suggest that in the scriptural text 'all men' means only 'all the elect,' or that it means 'men of every kind.'[66] The most pathetic passage on this subject is from the *De Correptione et Gratia*.[67] God, argues Augustine, makes us (that is, those who preach his Gospel) wish all men to be saved. The only conclusion from this extraordinary passage is that the Christian preacher is made by God to be more merciful than God himself. Presumably Augustine found the readiness to accept the condemnation of others which he felt drawn to attribute to God too unpleasant to accept for himself.

We must conclude this part of our discussion therefore by asserting that at least from the time of Augustine's reply to the questions of Simplicianus, and quite probably before that also, fallen man is totally subject to the acts of God. We suggested that the passage about grace acting *indeclinabiliter et insuperabiliter* might possibly mean that God enabled man to choose the right if he wished. We must now conclude, however, that such an interpretation is almost certainly incorrect and that in the *De Correptione*, as in all others of Augustine's later works, man is not even able to accept or reject whatever graces may or may not be offered to him. But he is still free.

Furthermore we should observe that the fact that Augustine holds that foreknowledge is in a sense prior to predestination does not affect his doctrine at this point.[68] Certainly Augustine holds that God's knowledge of what he will do is in a sense prior to his decision to act, but this priority is simply on the analogy of the temporal priority of a thought that such and such will happen to a decision to make it happen now. Obviously, as Augustine says, foreknowledge is possible without predestination, but not vice versa. In this sense too foreknowledge is prior. But it is vain to argue from this kind of priority that the salvation of any individual fallen man is any less totally the act of God's will and God's will alone. Romeyer is right that Augustine did not change his views about the relationship of foreknowledge and predestination after his reply to Simplicianus,[69] but that means that the doctrine of total dependence, already explicit in this reply, is maintained consistently until the end of his life.

It is clearly to be regarded as no more than special pleading when Sage tries to deny the obvious reading of Augustine's comments on 'God wishes all men to be saved.'[70] According to Sage the 'volonté salvifique universelle' is not really denied by Augustine. Augustine must be read in context. He makes exaggerated statements on this subject because he is overconcerned to reject the Pelagian overemphasis on the unaided power of man. But this explanation, despite its form-critical and contemporary ring, will not do. The essence of Augustine's position is presented in an unmistakable way in the reply to Simplicianus (A.D. 396) at a time when the Pelagian problem had not yet appeared. In his work *De Praedestinatione Sanctorum* Augustine confesses to having been in error at a very early stage of his writings on the subject of faith.[71] Faith, he had thought, was not preceded by grace. Yet he does not mention the other possibility, namely that grace *enables* man to accept or reject faith. Perhaps Augustine thought this would involve an infinite regress. At any rate, although, by his teaching that even after the Fall a spark of man's original nature remained, Augustine had opened the door to such a possibility, he does not seem to have made any use of it.

According to Augustine there are two groups among fallen humanity: the saved who exemplify God's mercy and the damned who exemplify God's justice. It is not helpful to discuss these groups in terms of a *wish* of God for two cities, one of good and one of evil—a wish predating the creation of the world.[72] Augustine does not talk about two cities in this kind of context. The difficulty into which Augustine is led, however, lies in his concept of divine justice. When God refuses to show mercy to those whom he declines to save, he is acting justly, according to Augustine, because all men deserve condemnation as partakers in sin. Hence if all were condemned, God would be just, and if (as is the case) some are left unsaved, he is equally just. When faced with the question, Why does God save this particular group?, Augustine has no direct answer. God's judgement is the key to salvation and this judgement is just. At the resurrection we shall recognize this justice, even though we cannot do so now.[73] God's justice is so far beyond our understanding that it cannot be recognized by human standards of measurement.[74] Augustine takes refuge behind the Pauline *O altitudo* and the other scriptural texts which indicate that God's ways are past finding out. But his attempt to escape the difficulties in which he is involved is unsatisfactory. Normally Augustine is ready to apply the human reason to the most opaque areas of theological inquiry with hardly a second thought. The man who will speculate endlessly on the theology of the Trinity is hardly to be allowed to rely on the weakness of our minds to comprehend the relation of human justice to divine justice,[75] unless he can establish the absolute necessity of an appeal to the Pauline *O altitudo*. But in fact Augustine has got himself into the difficulties about justice through an unwillingness to take scriptural texts about the desire for universal salvation seriously. Because he has been unable to relate these texts to a theory about the divine 'will', he is prepared to abandon the texts. And abandoning the texts leads to his problems about justice. Yet for Augustine the Platonist, who thinks of human justice as an image of divine justice, it is quite impossible to posit such total incomprehension by man of that divine justice. For if we are quite as unable to grasp divine justice, we can hardly know anything about human justice either. Yet while saying all this, we are still no nearer an acceptance of the position that God founded two cities, one of which was designed to show his mercy, and the other his justice. The showing of God's justice is rather an act of God bringing good out of evil, a display of justice out of the evil of the fall of Satan, Adam, and the descendants of Adam.

It seems, therefore, that there is material in Augustine's thought from which he could have developed a theory that, although grace precedes works and 'prepares' the will of fallen man, yet man could still accept or reject it. However, he chose not to develop this possibility and man is a puppet, free in the sense only of being arranged to act in a way which is not subject to external pressures. All men are thus 'free'; the elect are free from serious sins, the damned are free from virtue. The elect are slaves of *caritas;* the damned are slaves of *cupiditas*.

There is a final point which should be mentioned briefly. It is the consistent view of Augustine that the souls of all created beings, both men and angels, have an inherent weakness. This weakness is *superbia*.[76] Pride, arising from the non-existence from which souls are called by God, consists in deserting God and pleasing oneself. The idea is pre-Augustinian. It occurs in Plotinus and before Plotinus. We read at the opening of *Ennead* 5. 1. 1 the following lines: 'What can it be that has brought the souls to forget the father, God, and, though members of the Divine and entirely of that world, to ignore at once themselves and it? The evil that has overtaken them has its source in self-will, in the entry into the sphere of process, and in the primal differentiation with the desire for self-ownership' (trans. MacKenna–Page). Plotinus does not talk of *superbia,* but of τόλμα and of τὸ βουληθῆναι δὲ ἑαυτῶν εἶναι. Sin for individual souls consists of a desire to be an independent being, to be, in effect, like God. The difference from Augustine is not very great. Burnaby has argued, indeed, that in another passage (*Enn.* 1. 8. 3) Plotinus rejects a theory very similar to that of Augustine, that is, a theory that moral evil is a privation of good in the soul itself.[77] Plotinus' position, however, is not quite as Burnaby suggests: it seems to be his view that a soul which is apart from matter, that is, the World Soul, has only the unactualized possibility of wrongdoing, but that individual souls, because of their role as direct causes of matter are different.[78] Hence the origin of sin for the individual soul in Plotinus can reside in its τόλμα—a position not too distinct from that of Augustine. The difference between the two would seem to lie in the fact that Plotinus is still dualist enough to associate the weakness of the individual soul not with its material element viewed strictly as an element of non-being, but viewed as material. Thus Augustine, who recognizes that the weakness in created things lies in the fact that they are *ex nihilo,* pushes Plotinus' position to its logical conclusion. For Plotinus, sin which is τόλμα arises for the soul because it is associated with matter (ultimately equal to non-being) as its cause; for Augustine sin, which is *superbia,* may arise for the soul because it is *ex nihilo.*

In concluding this study there is a basic question which cannot be evaded. Augustine seems to hold that the lot of the elect, even in this life, is superior to that of Adam before the Fall. It is superior in that the elect are maintained on the path of *libertas,* the good life, by God. In other words for Augustine living the good life, even as a kind of puppet, is superior to being in the position where one is also living the good life but has the option of deserting it. Augustine prefers to live a good life without option to a good life with the choice of rejection. Why should this be? Perhaps because God himself is not free from virtues. God's own life is a life of the good only with no opportunity to choose the bad. But if this is Augustine's reason for his preference, it should be observed that the parallel between man and God is not exact. God is by his own nature bound to be good; man's nature, the nature of a created being, is not of this kind. Man can only be bound to the good by a new act of God. And this act of God can only occur at the sacrifice of one of the greatest gifts given to Adam, namely his ultimate autonomy on the matter of moral choice. This autonomy was not a Pelagian 'indifference of the will', a situation where the will can choose in total 'freedom' between good and evil; it was a state of love for God made the greater for the possibility of rejection.[79] Perhaps Augustine was too concerned at the fact that under the first creation men and angels could and did sin unaccountably. Their sin was due to their existence *ex nihilo,* and thus they would sin for reasons which are basically unintelligible. Rather than face this ultimate uncertainty as the best state possible for a creature, Augustine preferred to place the possibility of salvation entirely under God's control, a control which he believed to be both rational and just. The alternatives facing Augustine were either indeterminacy (nonbeing) or God as the basic 'cause' of salvation. As he saw it, even Adam had no real choice; the elements of nothingness in his nature made his fall an inexplicable and (for him and all others who would fall similarly) irresistible phenomenon. Better God's *fiat* than such an uncertainty. Even while believing that Augustine has sacrificed something of the original excellence of man to this fear of uncertainty, we can more readily sympathize with his position if these indeed are among his motives for adopting it.

AN APPENDIX ON PERSECUTION

Augustine's theories about the freedom of the will and predestination are linked in an interesting way with his attitude

towards the use of persecution to secure the unity of the
Catholic Church and to compel outsiders to come in. As we
know, Augustine was never liberal in his attitude towards the
use of force.[80] Few, if any, Christians of his age would have
been. Even the Donatists, who attempted to show themselves
as the Church not of the persecutors but of the persecuted,[81]
the Church, that is, of the martyrs, were only proponents of
this position when they themselves were unable to use force.[82]
If they had the chance to use force, to boycott a Catholic
community, to beat and maim priests who had gone over to
the Catholics, they were frequently prepared to do so. As
Augustine put it in his letter to Vincentius, a bishop of a
Donatist splinter group noted for the non-violence of its methods, peaceful methods were adopted when fiercer ones were
unavailable.[83] Moderation for the Donatists was a choice of
impotence, not of strength. And this must be held to be true
even though Augustine exaggerates the brutalities of the Cir-
cumcellions for polemical purposes and admits that only a
limited number of the Donatists supported their extremism.[84]

Coercion then was an accepted part of religious life
throughout Augustine's career. We hear no complaints by
Christian contemporaries about Ambrose's attitude to the
Jews over the synagogue at Callinicum, and it has often been
pointed out, from the time of Gibbon on, that although the
emperors passed the edicts against paganism at the end of
the fourth century, it was the bishops, the leaders of the Christian communities on the spot, men like Theophilus at Alexandria and Aurelius at Carthage, who were responsible for
the violent overthrow of the ancient temples and the destruction of the ancient cults.[85] Augustine himself, though claiming to be only concerned with the well-being of his own flock
and for the recovery of deserters from the fold during the
period between 393 and 399,[86] is already in 394 describing
a Donatist church as a *basilica haereticorum*.[87] And heretics
were already liable to punishment under the penal laws of
the Empire.

As has often been noticed, two things only held Augustine
back from taking a tough line in the 390s: simple inability
to do so at a time when the militant wing of the Donatists
under Optatus of Timgad was all-powerful in North Africa,

under the patronage of the local dynast and later rebel against imperial power, Gildo. But apart from this kind of political problem Augustine was also afraid—and this was a fear which partly outlived Gildo and Optatus—that a policy of rigour would bring into the Church a large number of nominal Christians, *ficti*, who would dilute the quality of the pure sheep of Christ.[88]

In terms of Augustine's personal spiritual growth, the latter argument was something which came to be outgrown. In the earlier days of his life as a Catholic he had subscribed to the view that those who had come into the Church of their own volition would be in a state of holiness. Hence the contrast between such pure souls and the crowd of near-pagans, near-Donatists who would mingle with them as the result of forcible conversion, would be considerable. But as Augustine came increasingly to the conclusion that living a Christian life is a daily struggle in which God helps his own in ways which pass our understanding, the important point became only to get people into the Church—the one place which God had ordained would be the source of their salvation. Baptism is normally essential for salvation. It brings a man within the area of grace. Once inside God will act as he wishes. Augustine thus seems to have come to conceive one of his main functions as bishop and as servant of God as being the bringing of men into the physical Church. In so doing he is God's agent of predestination, and as an agent he is responsible for his flock. It is noteworthy how frequently Augustine insists that he is as bishop accountable for the sins and omissions of his flock.[89] It is a terrible responsibility which Augustine faces with fear and trembling.

We cannot be sure when Augustine worked out the major lines of his doctrine of the elect, but, as we have seen, the doctrine is already present in the reply to the second question of Simplicianus. In other words by the time the opportunity to persecute arrived, first with the closing of pagan temples in 399, a theory to avoid the difficulties caused by the presence in Church of feigned Christians was at hand. Conversion, Augustine came to believe, is totally dependent on an act of God's grace; and Christians, in particular bishops and priests, are the instruments of that grace. The problem then is how can the bishop most effectively act as God's instrument. And from his reading of the scriptures Augustine came to an answer to that question. God, he read, has always chastised the true Israel, both in Old Testament times and under the new dispensation.[90] God brought force to bear on Paul as he travelled along the road to Damascus. God urged that those outside should be compelled to come in.[91] Suffering is necessary to break the numbing force of bad habits.[92] Unless external pressures are brought to bear on the individual, he will be in the grip of long-standing habits and will never want to change his mind. Man's freedom is not impinged upon by such methods,[93] for in Augustine's view, as we have seen, if a man wants to do something he does it freely. External constraint leads to the birth of a 'good' will inside us.[94]

In his role as corrector of heretics the bishop is like a father or a schoolteacher or a doctor.[95] In all these respects he is also like God who is the Father, the teacher, and the doctor of fallen men. Augustine feels the weight of being in such a position of authority. He comments to Paulinus on the darkness which overwhelms the mind when it reflects on how to correct without injury.[96] He is himself always concerned lest punishment and the use of force should become a substitute for instruction. What he wishes is that force be used to soften up the heretic so that instruction is possible. What the modern man misses, in reading such passages of Augustine, is any recognition of the effect that the use of such methods may have on the character of those who employ them. Clearly it would have been useless to tell Augustine that the methods of coercion which he advocated were cruel. He would have replied that he was being cruel to be kind. Error, he thinks, has no rights.[97] The necessity of toughness is emphasized in the well-known reply of Augustine to Dulcitius in 420.[98] Dulcitius, an Imperial agent acting against Donatism in Africa, was defied by Gaudentius of Timgad. Rather than hand over his church, said Gaudentius, he would barricade himself and his congregation inside. Rather than submit, he would burn himself and his congregation. The threat does not worry Augustine. He is inured to Donatist violence and suicides. Since, according to pre-

destination, some will be punished in Hell, argues Augustine,
it is good to save those we can. If a few Donatists burn themselves to death, that is a small price to pay for the large number who have been brought within the orthodox fold by a
policy of persecution. As has been pointed out, Augustine
and his fellow bishops thought that they were the agents of
God in an important stage of cosmic history. It never occurred to them that the methods with which they were pro-
moting the Christianization of North Africa were other than
salutary in the long run. Like all others who are convinced
that they have a monopoly of the truth, and that it is their
duty to spread it, Augustine cannot conceive that his methods could be injurious to anyone. And no one could have
convinced him that he was not bringing people into the
Church; clearly he was doing that. But it did not occur to
Augustine to wonder whether the use of force, even when
accompanied by instruction, could be dangerous to the character of those who use it. Augustine appeals to the use of
force by God to secure the conversion of Paul. He then puts
himself in God's place. It is not he who uses force, but
through him God works out the salvation of his elect. He is
free of personal responsibility; he speaks with the voice of
the Church.[99]

This is the context in which we can best understand the
notorious *dilige et quod vis fac*. Behind this tag, used to justify persecution of the Donatists, lies a great deal of thought
on the correct attitudes to be adopted by a father who has
to punish.[100] But Augustine did not notice that only God
can love fully, and hence, presumably, that only God would
be justified in using force as a means of conversion. Or perhaps he did recognize this but was so certain that he was
doing God's will that he thought that his own love was simply
the working out of God's love—a pathetic situation if correctly described.

Augustine's view that force may be the means God has
chosen to wake up some of his elect and that the human soul,
buried in its vicious and long-standing habits, can only be
aroused by 'inconveniences' (*molestiae*) should predispose us
to think that his use of force was not an isolated incident but
represents a general theory. Some have tried to argue that,

although Augustine came to recognize the utility of force in dealing with the Donatists, he would not have regarded it as a regular theological weapon. There is no substance in that view. Other heresies too can be the result of bad habits. A salutary shock may have to be administered to others besides the *pars Donati*, for some of these others may be recalled by God *per molestias*. In fact Augustine advocates a similar tough policy against the Pelagians, and for the same reasons.[101] In any case, as Augustine had argued long before, it is the heretic who is the *real* persecutor; he is the persecutor of Mother Church.

For the majority of men, Augustine came to believe, fear is the means by which the disastrous pressures of evil habit can be overcome.[102] There are very few, he holds, who have come to God without the pressure of fear.[103] That fear is not only the fear of infernal punishments, which often seem rather remote even to the believer. Under the Christian Roman Empire a readier means is at hand. We can see why Augustine is not too fussy about the means he employs when he believes such gains to be at stake. He consistently opposed the death penalty for heretics,[104] both for fear lest they should gain the reputation of martyrs and because the opportunity of correction is lost. He rejected the notion of using *agents provocateurs* to detect the secret heretic.[105] He preferred the use of fines and social pressures to actual force. Yet he had nothing to say about many of the violent punishments meted out by the Imperial laws to which he appealed. He rejects the punishment of maiming,[106] but apparently accepts any kind of flogging, including the use of lead whips, without a murmur.[107] Nor does he object to the illegal imprisonment imposed on his Donatist rival by the Catholic bishop of Hippo Diarrhytos.[108] Nevertheless these abuses were probably accepted by Augustine more out of weakness than as matters of policy.[109] His theory at least is consistent, provided the all-important premisses are accepted. The premisses are that the bishop, in encouraging the use of force, is merely and wholly the instrument of God's love in saving his elect, and that no one harms himself by the systematic use of coercion on other people's consciences.

NOTES

1. R. A. Markus in *The Cambridge History of Later Greek and Early Medieval Philosophy* (Cambridge, 1967) p. 381.

2. E. Gilson, *The Christian Philosophy of Saint Augustine* (New York, 1967), p. 320, n. 66.

3. *De Gratia et Libero Arbitrio* II. 4.

4. *De Libero Arbitrio* III. 50.

5. *Contra Jul. Op. Imp.* I. 101.

6. *De Grat. et Lib. Arb.* 15. 31; *Op. Imp.* I. 82.

7. *Serm.* 159. 3. 3.

8. *De Trin.* XIV. 6; *De Grat. et Lib. Arb.* 17. 33. For *consuetudo, Conf.* VIII. 9. 21, etc.

9. *Conf.* XIII. 9. 10. Cf. Gilson, op. cit., p. 310, n. 29.

10. *Contra Fort.* 22.

11. *De Serm. Dom. in monte* I. 12. 35.

12. *Tract. in Joh.* 26. 4.

13. P. R. L. Brown, *Augustine of Hippo* (London, 1967), p. 374.

14. Cf. *Op. Imp.* I. 109. It is misleading to speak without qualification of fallen man being capable of some good (as is done by J. Chéné, *La Théologie de Saint Augustin: Grâce et Prédestination* (Le Puy, Lyons, 1961), p. 41, and C. Boyer, 'L'adiutorium sine quo non', *Doctor Communis*, xiii (1960), p. 8). All good done by fallen man is with God's help, though this help is not necessarily sufficient to salvation.

15. *Op. Imp.* I. 94; *De Nupt.* I. 30–31; *De Corr. et Grat.* 1. 2; 12. 35; 13. 42; *Contra II Litt.* I. 2. 5.

16. *De Corr. et Grat.* 11. 31.

17. *Ench.* 31. 117.

18. *Ep.* 217. 3; *Contra Jul.* II. 8. 23.

19. *De Nat. et Grat.* 66. 79.

20. For further discussion of 'freedom' (*libertas*), sometimes called true or real (*vera*) freedom, see Gilson, op. cit., pp. 323–24.

21. *Contra II Litt.* II. 19.

22. For about fifty references to this text see A. Sage, 'Praeparatur voluntas a Deo', *Revue des études augustiniennes*, x (1964), pp. 19–20.

23. As Sage points out ('Faut-il anathématiser la doctrine augustinienne de la prédestination?', *R.E.A.* viii [1962], p. 240), Augustine does not say *ante praevisa merita*.

24. *Contra Jul.* III. 10. 22.

25. *De Nat. et Grat.* 36. 42. For the universality of sin see *De Pecc. Mer.* II. 7. 8.

26. *Contra Il Litt.* III. 5; cf. *De Pecc. Mer.* II. 17–18.

27. *De Dono Pers.* 35.

28. G. Bavaud, 'La doctrine de la prédestination et de la réprobation d'après S. Augustin et Calvin', *R.E.A.* v (1959), p. 433.

29. *Ench.* 24. 95.

30. *De An. et eius Orig.* 4. 16.

31. *De Grat. et Lib. Arb.* 23. 45.

32. *Ench.* 26. 100.

33. Gilson, op. cit., p. 155.

34. *Op. Imp.* V. 1; *De Gen. ad Litt.* VIII. 25; *C.D.* XIV. 26.

35. *De Cont.* 6. 16.

36. *De Corr. et Grat.* 32–33.

37. *C.D.* XIV. 11.

38. *C.D.* XIV. 27.

39. *Op. Imp.* IV. 104; *Contra Jul.* I. 7. 33.

40. *De Nupt.* I. 3. 8; II. 5. 15; *Contra Jul.* I. 3. 8; *De Corr. et Grat.* 6. 9, etc.

41. *De Pecc. Mer.* III. 14.

42. *De Nupt.* II. 15.

43. *C.D.* XIII. 14.

44. Augustine frequently appeals to the authority of Ambrose to help his demonstration that all born of sexual intercourse are, by that fact, in receipt of the taint of original guilt. *De Nupt.* I. 35. 40; II. 5. 15; *Contra Jul.* I. 3. 10; I. 4. 11, etc.

45. O. Rottmanner, 'Der Augustinismus' (1892), translated into French by J. Liébaert, 'L'Augustinisme', *Mél. de science religieuse*, vi (1949), pp. 33–34.

46. For the medical analogy see *De Pecc. Mer.* III. 12. 21; *De Nat. et Grat.* 27. 31; *De Corr. et Grat.* 5. 7.

47. *Natura mortua, Op. Imp.* V. 23; *Ench.* 30.

48. *De Lib. Arb.* III. 13; *De Nat. et Grat.* 19. 21, etc.

49. *C.D.* XXII. 24. 1–2; XIX. 13. 2.

50. Bavaud, *op. cit.*, p. 431.

51. Prosper, *P.L.* 45, col. 1834. Cf. Portalié, *D.T.C.* i. 2391.

52. *Ench.* 25. 98; cf. *De Div. Quaest. ad Simp.* I. 2. 8.

53. *De Cont.* VI. 16.

54. *Op. Imp.* V. 39.

55. *Op. Imp.* V. 57.

56. *C.D.* XIV. 13; cf. *De Spir. et Litt.* 28. 48.

57. Gilson, *op cit.*, p. 155.

58. *De Corr. et Grat.* 11. 31.

59. *Retract.* I. 23.

60. *De Spir. et Litt.* 34. 60.

61. *De Corr. et Grat.* 12. 38.

62. *Ench.* 24. 95.

63. *Ench.* 24. 97.

64. *Ench.* 27. 103 (*quia necesse est fieri si voluerit*).

65. e.g. *De Pecc. Mer.* II. 17. 26.

66. Cf. *De Corr. et Grat.* 15. 44; *C.D.* XXII. 1. 2; *Contra Jul.* IV. 8. 44.

67. *De Corr. et Grat.* 15. 47.

68. *De Praed. Sanct.* 10.

69. B. Romeyer, 'Trois Problèmes de Phil.', *Arch. de Phil.* 7. 2 (1930), pp. 234–43. Cf. Chéné, *La Théologie,* p. 40. But Chéné is again misled into over-estimating the strength of man in the process of salvation. It is true that men are impelled to *act* by God, but they are impelled without alternative. For Augustine that means that they are free agents.

70. A. Sage, 'La Prédestination chez S. Augustin d'après une thèse récente', *R.E.A.* vi (1960), p. 37, n. 12. Cf. Sage, 'Les Deux Temps de Grâce', *R.E.A.* vii (1961), p. 229. A similar attempt to deny the obvious meaning of Augustine's words is made by F. J. Thonnard, 'La Prédestination augustinienne: sa place en philosophie augustinienne', *R.E.A.* x (1964), p. 123. Again the argument is supported by wishful thinking, not by evidence.

71. *De Praed. Sanct.* 3. 7; cf. *Retract.* I. 1. 23. 2–4.

72. For a rejection of the Two Cities thesis see Sage, 'La Prédestination', pp. 31–40.

73. *Ench.* 24. 95; *De Grat. et Lib. Arb.* 23. 45.

74. *De Div. Quaest. ad Simp.* I. 2. 16. Cf. *De Dono Pers.* 8. 18; 14. 35; *De Praed. Sanct.* 8. 14; *De Pecc. Mer.* 21. 29.

75. Cf. *Op. Imp.* III. 24.

76. *De Lib. Arb.* III. 76; *C.D.* XIV. 13. 1.

77. J. Burnaby, *Amor Dei* (London, 1938), p. 149, n. 6.

78. J. M. Rist, *Plotinus: The Road to Reality* (Cambridge, 1967), p. 128.

79. Cf. Boyer, 'L'adiutorium', p. 10.

80. Cf. Brown, *op. cit.,* pp. 233–34.

81. *Coll. Carthag.* 3. 258; *Contra Litt. Petil.* II. 23. 214.

82. R. Joly, 'S. Augustin et l'intolérance religieuse', *Rev. Belge de Phil. et d'Histoire,* xxxiii (1955), p. 274, seems to imply that toleration was a principle of Donatism; but though it is certainly true that the Donatists frequently appealed for toleration, their own practice, when they had the chance to be intolerant, was hardly better than that of the Catholics. Cf. the Maximianist schism of 394–95.

83. *Ep.* 93. 11.

84. *De Haer.* 69.

85. Cf. especially P. R. L. Brown, 'Religious Coercion in the Later Roman Empire: The Case of N. Africa', *History,* xlviii (1963), pp. 301–2.

86. *Enarr. in Ps.* 21. 31.

87. *Ep.* 29. 11.

88. *Ep.* 93. 17.

89. Cf. *Ep.* 23. 3 and 6.

90. Cf. Brown, *Augustine,* pp. 237–38, where many references are given.

91. Cf. (e.g.) *Ep.* 93; 185. 22, etc.; Joly, *op. cit.,* p. 276.

92. *Conf.* I. 14. 23; *Ep.* 89. 7; cf. P. R. L. Brown, 'St. Augustine's Attitude to Religious Coercion', *J.R.S.* liv (1964), p. 112.

93. *Contra Litt. Petil.* II. 83. 185.

94. *Serm.* 112. 8; cf. Joly, *op. cit.,* p. 286.

95. *Epp.* 93. 7; 185. 7, etc.

96. *Ep.* 95. 3.

97. Joly, op. cit., p. 275; cf. *Ep.* 185. 24: 'You compel to evil, we to good.'

98. *Ep.* 204.

99. *Serm.* 129. 4.

100. Cf. J. Gallay, 'Dilige et quod vis fac', *Recherches de science religieuse,* xliii (1955), pp. 545–55.

101. Brown, *Augustine,* pp. 361–63. The Pelagians offered many of the same texts in favour of their view of free will as the Donatists; cf. Brown, *op. cit.,* p. 236.

102. Brown, *Augustine,* pp. 237, 249–50.

103. *De Cat. Rud.* 5. 9.

104. *Ep.* 133. 2; 139. 2.

105. *Contra Mend.* 6. 11.

106. *Ep.* 134.

107. *Cod. Theod.* 16. 5. 37, etc. Cf. W. H. C. Frend, *The Donatist Church* (Oxford, 1952), p. 263.

108. *Coll. Carthag.* 1. 142.

109. Cf. Augustine's inability to act firmly *against* the secular authorities in the case of Marcellinus (*Ep.* 151).

TIME

11

Time and Contingency in St. Augustine

ROBERT JORDAN

As a text for my remarks[1] I shall choose the following lines, which are found not in the famous eleventh Book of the *Confessions* but in the twelfth Book of the *De civitate Dei:* "For since God is the supreme existence, that is to say, supremely is, and is therefore unchangeable, the things that He made He empowered to be, but not to be supremely like Himself. To some He communicated a more ample, to others a more limited existence, and thus arranged the natures of beings in ranks."[2] This passage fails to mention time, let alone tell us what it is, but, when its implications are drawn, it tells us something much more important, namely, why the whole question of time is worth considering at all. The question "What?" is undoubtedly important but undoubtedly less important (if we had to make a choice, which, of course, we do not) than the question "What of it?"

St. Augustine's understanding of time is such that it makes time a problem not of physics nor of cosmology, although there are cosmological implications too, but of moral philosophy. And since moral philosophy, for Augustine, is inseparable from the problem of the ultimate destiny of the soul, his conception of time is a part of his conception of the religious life of man. Accordingly, I propose to summarize Augustine's theory of the nature of time in the first part of the paper, treating it, so far as possible, as a separate topic of a

Reprinted from *Review of Metaphysics* Vol. 8 (1954–55), pp. 394–417, by permission of the author and the publisher. Copyright 1955 by the *Review of Metaphysics*.

theoretical nature. However, since the whole problem is a practical one in the Platonic sense, I propose, in the second part of the paper, to interpret this theory in Augustinian terms in an effort to show the significance of the whole question of time and eternity and limited being for Augustine's theory of man. This is an immense subject. Consequently, in order to impose some boundary upon it, I have restricted myself to the contrast of "the Unlimited" and "the Limited," "the Unchangeable" and "the Changeable" as a means of giving the interpretation a single accent.

Augustine's investigation of time is a study in contingency, finiteness, creatureliness, dependency, incompleteness, imperfection—a study of the limitation of being that characterizes *any* finite entity, that entity which *is,* but which is not He Who Is. Time exists because there are existent things in the universe which are just so much reality, but no more. The existence of only one of these things is of genuinely intimate concern to man—himself. And, of course, this suggests subjectivity. Augustine's view of time is habitually described as a subjective view or a psychological view. The designation is misleading and the language unfortunate. I shall try to suggest why the subjectivism, if it does exist, is innocuous. In one sense, the obvious one, time could not fail to be a subjective matter since the poignancy of temporality is primarily a human concern, and the moral and spiritual life of man is the immediate context of that concern. But this does not mean, as Mr. Russell, for example, seems to think, that time is necessarily unreal. Russell says, "St. Augustine, whose absorption in the sense of sin led him to excessive subjectivity, was content to substitute subjective time for the time of history and physics. Memory, perception, and expectation, according to him, made up all that there is of time. But obviously, this won't do. All his memories and all his expectations occurred at about the time of the fall of Rome, whereas mine occur at about the time of the fall of industrial civilization, which formed no part of the Bishop of Hippo's expectations. Subjective time might suffice for a solipsist of the moment, but not for a man who believes in a real past and future, even if only his own."[3] This quotation would provide a sufficient excuse for the second part of this paper. For, apart from the quite staggering irrelevance in the quotation, Russell seems to think that what makes time important is the fact that in it we confirm or disconfirm a scientific or an historical theory. Augustine, on the other hand, thinks that time is important for quite another reason—it is in time that a soul is saved or lost.

Indeed, it is with this theme that the eleventh Book of the *Confessions* opens. The first six chapters proclaim the creation of the world and the radical difference between the creator and the created, the eternal and the temporal. And we are told what the temporal is, "Behold the heaven and earth are; they proclaim that they were made, for they are changed and varied."[4] More specifically, the creature is a thing of time and change "since in proportion as anything is not what it was, and is what it was not, in that proportion does it die and arise."[5]

Chapters 8 and 9 reaffirm the contrast of the finite with the immutable standard against which the finite is measured, and Chapter 10 contrasts the will of God with that of the creature on the basis of the necessity of recognizing two distinct orders. The distinction is required, for example, by the question: If it was the will of God that the creature should exist, why did the creature not exist from eternity? The answer is elaborated in the next chapters in terms of the nontemporal as contrasted with the temporal, the everpresentness of God's eternity as against the "times which never stand" because "no time is wholly present."[6] The whole section is climaxed in Chapter 13 by the statement that time did not exist before the creation, since that would involve the Creator Himself in time, thus contradicting His everpresentness and eternal unchangeableness. God made time along with creation.[7] All this is by way of prologue.

In Chapter 14, Augustine turns to the question of time itself, but the context from which this problem has emerged has been clearly revealed and it should not be forgotten. It is a moral-religious one. Augustine's perplexity is born of wonder, not of peeping curiosity. We have been given the broad significance of temporality and now we have the question itself: "For what is time?" Yet the question is never divorced from its original context. For time is immediately coupled with non-being or the tendency not to be. ". . . We cannot truly say that time is, unless because it tends not to be."[8] This absolute contingency is a constant theme of Augustine's writings and surely it is the principal statement of the whole time motif in the *Confessions,* the central notion around which all of his remarks are centered. It is the tendency toward non-being that distinguishes the temporal from the eternal because "should the present be always present, and should it not pass into time past, truly it could not be time, but eternity."[9]

In Chapter 15, Augustine shifts from time itself to the experience of time and it is worth noticing that his account of the consciousness of time is a generalized one. He does not discuss his private expectations. Consequently, we may say that his point of departure is certain spiritual facts rather than physical facts and that this is all there is to the subjectivism of his method. His analysis turns up a paradox, the resolution of which is said to constitute Augustine's contribution to the nature of time. The matter may be condensed into something like the following: We speak of long and short times but only in terms of the past or the future. But neither the past nor the future exists. A thing exists only in the present, existence being used here in the full-bodied sense of actuality. Now, the present cannot be long. It is not spatial and cannot be divided, despite our apparently ineradicable tendency to spatialize and divide it. Any selected unit, such as a day or an hour, is subject to continuous abridgment. Hence the present cannot really be long or short. It just *is.*

Our experience, then, would seem to be impossible, which is itself another impossibility. For we certainly do make comparative judgments (Chapter 16). The problem becomes, then: How can we arrive at measures of time, a problem of terrifying proportions because it would seem that we must be measuring the non-existent, which would be absurd. We cannot measure what does not exist. All the same, we do measure; that much is a plain fact.

Augustine proceeds, in Chapters 16 through 19, to argue that times or intervals of time are measured only when they are passing. But it is plain that in order to measure we must perceive (*sentire*) and, again, perception is only of things

present. Therefore, it would seem, further, that we make true
statements about the past and the future only by means of
memory, or by premeditation or anticipation, both based on
what now exists in the present. The important consequence
of these facts is stated in Chapter 20. It is that our customary
language, like so much of our familiar usage in practical discourse, is quite improper in so far as it refers to three times
—past, present, and future. It serves the purpose of ordinary
communication but it is inexact. There are not three times,
strictly speaking, but three modes of present time—a present
of things past, a present of things present, and a present of
things future, each with its corresponding act of the mind—
memory, sight (*contuitus*), and expectation,[10] and each, we
must suppose, though Augustine does not say so directly, with
its reference to a past, a present, and a future state of affairs.
The presence referred to here is presence before the mind.
The mind can hold before it as present what is really not
present in the strict sense.[11] The passage certainly demands
epistemological justification, a service which might have mitigated the subjectivity of the whole account. However, no such
justification is offered and no adequate description is given
here of how the mind performs this trick.[12]

But perplexity is only beginning, because our measures of
time are spatial. If we examine our activity we see that we
measure spaces of time while they are passing. Yet the present, we noticed previously, has no space, which leaves us with
the immodest contention that we measure what is coming
from the non-existent and is going into what does not exist
as yet, *by* what is now but is spaceless and, therefore, not
measurable. At this point Augustine asks for divine illumination, an altogether understandable petition.

Chapter 23 introduces the old notion that time is the motion of the heavenly bodies only to reject the idea on the
ground that any motion would do as well. Even more important than that, Augustine here indicates his interest in time as
it is in itself. "I desire to know the power and nature (*vim
naturamque*) of time, by which we measure the motions of
bodies . . . not . . . what that is which is called a day, but
what time is . . ."[13] His previous references to comparative judgments all indicate that time is relational. This ref-

erence to "time itself" is not, I think, a repudiation of the
relational view, though it does emphasize Augustine's disin-
terest in the physical approach to time. The section concludes
with the initial, rather provisional, statement of the famous
Augustinian definition, "I see that time, then, is a certain
extension" (distention, stretching, *distentio*).[14] And he adds,
"But do I see it, or do I seem to see it?"

Perhaps, after all (Chapter 24), time might better be defined in terms of the motion of a body. Yet, it cannot be
that, because a body stands still in time as clearly as it moves
in time. Besides, there is a perfectly clear distinction between
the motion of a body and that by which we measure the
length of that motion, the latter alone deserving to be called
time. Recalling the psychic fact of measurement by time, Augustine now reaffirms it in the form, "I measure the motion
of a body by time." Now this would be impossible unless it
was also possible to measure the time itself in which the
body moved. Hence, the question is "How do we measure
time itself?"

Augustine had previously suggested that we measure the
long by the short, thus arriving at comparative judgments in
terms, for example, of "double" or "half." But there is no
way of getting any certain measure of time with this method.
Indeed, Augustine has crossed this ground before without
success. Such units are spatial, not temporal, and any selected
unit of passing time such as the short syllable which Augustine uses as an illustration, can easily be reduced in length
or drawn out, thus destroying the usefulness of the unit and
leaving the old question: What is the measure of time? The
only positive result so far is that time is some kind of extension. In fact, it is, as he says, probably an extension of the
mind itself.[15] It is not immediately clear why this must be
the answer. There simply seems to be no other alternative,
since it has already been shown that when a comparative
judgment such as "This is double that" is made, it cannot be
either the past or the future that is measured because they
do not exist; nor can it be the present because the present is
not stretched or extended.

However, Augustine has already made another suggestion
which he takes up again, namely, that we measure "times

passing"—which might answer the question: What do we measure when we measure time? But this will not do either, because we cannot measure a thing unless it has a beginning and an end, and these limits cannot be assigned until the thing to be measured has ended. But when it has ended it has ceased to exist and, by the same token, has ceased to be measurable. The difficulty seems to be that only what is fixed can be measured.

So, Augustine argues (Chapter 27), that if neither past, present, future, nor even passing times can be measured, we simply do not measure times themselves "but something in the memory, which remains fixed. In thee, O my mind, I measure times."[16] The impression (*affectionem*) which things make on the mind and which remains present in the mind even when the things are gone, is what we measure. For this three operations of the mind are required, (1) expectation, (2) consideration (the act of marking attentively), and (3) memory. By a mental act, then, I can relate myself to the past and the future holding them, as it were, in the present and thus measuring them. And this capacity encompasses not merely the act of reciting a psalm (as in Augustine's illustration) but "holds in the longer action, of which that psalm is perchance a portion; the same holds [he goes on] in the whole life of man, of which all the actions of man are parts; the same holds in the whole age of the sons of men, of which all the lives of men are parts."[17]

And then there follows hard upon this sentence—which is really the conclusion of Augustine's discussion in the eleventh Book—the rushing and wonderful passage in Chapter 29. For Augustine ignores the obvious difficulties and perplexities which, I think it must be said, still remain, and carries his reader breathlessly to the true goal of his endeavors, sweeping away times and changes and pressing on to the eternal. It is as though Augustine were saying, "See what this means; see how it works when we have come this far." And the word "distention" is now made to carry the burden of "distraction"—". . . behold my life is but a distraction"—but no longer, for he is to put away distraction, ". . . forgetting the things that are past; and not distracted, but drawn on (*non distentus sed extentus*), not to those things which shall be and shall pass away, but to those things which are before, not distractedly but intently (*non secundum disten-tionem sed secundum intentionem*), I follow on for the prize of my heavenly calling, . . . But I have been divided amid the times, the order of which I know not; and my thoughts, even in the inmost bowels of my soul, are mangled with tumultuous varieties, until I flow together unto Thee, purged and molten in the fire of Thy love."[18]

Turning to the difficulties of which I have just spoken, three, at least, seem to be peculiarly formidable. In the first place, Augustine has not, I think, told us at all clearly what time is in itself, and this, after all, was his announced intention.[19] The reason for this is complex and will be discussed later. In the second place, it would appear that what he has arrived at in Chapter 29 is more correctly designated as "eternity" than as "time." For if we turn back to Chapter 14, we shall recognize this passage, "But should the present be always present, and should it not pass into time past, truly it would not be time but eternity."[20] Now, in Chapter 29, the goal we are seeking is clearly one in which we are to enjoy a kind of ever-presentness whose virtue is that it frees us from distraction. It is to this that we are to "extend" ourselves, this to which we are to be attracted.[21] Two things can be said of it, however, which distinguish it from eternity, so that Augustine may be said to have provided, in advance, something of an answer to the present difficulty. First, he has already said (Chapter 14) that we cannot maintain that time is, unless it tends not to be. That is, unless it tends to flow on into the past. And the presentness before the mind made possible by the mind's "distentio" is, presumably, of this flowing kind, though the notion requires further elaboration. In the second place, Augustine explicitly says in the last two Chapters of Book XI that no times are co-eternal with the Creator, ". . . no times are co-eternal with Thee, nor any creature, even if there be any creature beyond all times."[22] Further, in Chapter 31, he restates the distinction between the two orders, Divine and human, in such a way as to make it impossible legitimately to claim for man the possession of knowledge in the mode of the unchangeably eternal. Nevertheless, the following passage suggests that the "presentness" which is the

goal of human striving is an analogue of the Divine presentness: "Surely, if there be a mind, so greatly abounding in
knowledge and foreknowledge, to which all things past and
future are so known as one psalm is well known to me, that
mind is exceedingly wonderful and very astonishing; because
whatever is so past, and whatever is so to come of after
ages, is no more concealed from Him than was it hidden
from me when singing that psalm, what and how much of it
had been sung from the beginning, what and how much remained unto the end."[23] Of course, while it is quite true
that, for Augustine, the most important thing we can do with
time is transcend it, we still want to know what it is that we
have transcended.

Finally, there is a third difficulty which might be stated
as follows: Augustine has suggested, in his definition of time,
a *relational* conception of time. At least, such is my understanding of him. But a relation must have a foundation, and
we are not told in the eleventh Book of the *Confessions* what
this foundation could be. It will be my contention in what
follows that Augustine does tell us what the foundation is,
over and over again, in everything that he writes concerning
this question, including the *Confessions* and especially the
twelfth Book. But before going on to that question I should
like to insist again that it is unrewarding to interpret the
eleventh Book as introspective psychology. When classical
realism has made an honest woman of phenomenology we
shall be able to use that term, and I even hazard its use now.
It may be difficult for a modern mentality to acknowledge
that Augustine's discussion of time could be objective and
yet an interlude within a prayer. But Augustine finds it altogether natural to treat spiritual or psychic facts as falling
within the sphere of the natural intentionality of the mind.[24]
In this, he was less, not more, subjective than we are, with
our easy but usually unexamined assumption that prayer
is distinctively and essentially subjective and private. I admit
that the bulk of Augustine's evidence is drawn from the examination of consciousness, but I also venture to say that he
discusses what is *given* to that consciousness and that it can,
therefore, qualify as objective evidence. More than that, the
eleventh Book, in point of fact, neither begins nor ends with

the self. It begins, as it ends, with God. It is worth remembering that even consciousness of self, in Augustine, leads to God. Consciousness of self in subjectivism leads to precisely nothing except the act of "cogito."

The twelfth Book of the *Confessions* is a commentary, primarily, on the first chapter of Genesis. Many of its pages are multiply significant, bearing as they do upon Augustine's theory of creation and on his metaphysics in general. One theme is especially relevant to this discussion and has to do with the history of Augustine's ideas about matter and form. He explains that he had the greatest difficulty attaching any meaning to the term "matter," being disposed always to think of it not as unformed—for what could exist between what is really formed and what is nothing at all—but rather, he says, as defective in beauty, that is, comparatively formless. This difficulty led him, he says, to look more deeply into mutability, into that in bodies "by which they cease to be what they had been, and begin to be what they were not; and this same transit (shifting, *transitum*) from form to form I have looked upon to be through some formless condition, not through a very nothing; . . . For the mutability of mutable things is itself capable of all those forms into which mutable things are changed."[25]

He concludes that such processes involve some sort of continuity, a formless matter which is not nothing but almost nothing (*prope nihil*).[26] There is considerable debate as to whether this substratum is Aristotle's prime matter since Augustine seems to have another version of "matter" in the *De Genesi ad litteram* according to which matter is not pure potency but is in some sense actual in itself.[27] At any rate, the latter position is not held in the *Confessions,* although the concluding lines of Book XIII, Chapter 7 might be taken to support it. The debate may be ignored except in one respect. This unformed matter is not in time and is not subject to time. It was created by God out of nothing, of course, but it does not possess the conditions of mutability and, by the same token, it does not possess temporality either. Here is one passage from Chapter 8: "But the earth itself which Thou hadst made was formless matter, because it was invisible and without form, and darkness was upon the deep. Of which invisible and formless earth, of which formlessness, of which almost nothing, Thou mightest make all these things of which this changeable world consists, and yet consisteth not; whose very changeableness appears in this, that times can be observed and numbered in it. Because times are made by the changes of things, while the shapes, whose matter is the invisible earth aforesaid, are varied and turned."[28]

In point of fact, there are two things which are not in time or regulated according to time, unformed matter and the Heaven of Heavens, an "intellectual creature" not co-eternal with God any more than matter is, but a partaker of eternity which "surpasses all the rolling changes of time."[29] The Heaven of Heavens is, in itself, changeable, but is said to "restrain its own mutability" by a perfect contemplation of the unchangeableness of the Creator.[30] I shall return to this question later. Matter, on the other hand, is, in itself, incapable of temporality since "it had not that by which it could be changed from one form into another, either of motion or of repose, whereby it might be subject unto time."[31]

In making these distinctions, Augustine refers repeatedly though often indirectly to time. However, his conception of time here is, clearly, quite different from the conception of Book XI, at least at first sight. Of course, he is not talking about the soul in these passages but about mutability in the broadest sense and, in particular, about two non-changing or non-temporal things. But we learn, by contrast, what the temporal is. "For where there is no shape nor order, nothing either cometh or goeth; and where this is not, there certainly are no days, nor any vicissitudes of spaces of time."[32] Again: "Who would tell me . . . if the formlessness only remain, through which the thing was changed and was turned from one figure (*species*) into another, that that can exhibit the changes of times? For surely it could not be, because without the change of motions times are not, and there is no change where there is no figure."[33] And yet again, speaking of the visible earth, Augustine says that successive changes of times may take place in this world "on account of the appointed changes of motions and of forms."[34]

On further consideration, however, it is more nearly correct to say that these passages present not a different version of time but the that-without-which there could be no time. Or, in other words, they reveal the foundation in reality of what is described in the eleventh Book in psychological or spiritual terms.[35] This is the sense in which Augustine's theory of time may be said to have physical implications. It seems, indeed, much like Aristotle's version simplified, and it seems to me not unfair to say that the two theories are complementary. Augustine does not define time as Aristotle does, because his cosmological interest is indirect. Aristotle brushes the Augustinian problem in passing[36] but does not dwell on it for reasons comparable to those that lead Augustine to treat the physics of time as a subordinate issue, namely, that it *is* subordinate to his main interest.

Before turning to the implications of the passages I have quoted, it should be noticed that not two but three elements, of course, figure in the whole time problem—the temporal, the eternal, and what St. Thomas later called the mean between them, the Augustinian term for which is also the *aevum*.[37] All three figure in Augustine's conception of the significance of the temporal because all three must be considered if we are to understand how Augustine elaborates his concept of the real foundation of temporality and what this means for human existence and human destiny. Time is founded on a mode of being. So is eternity. So is aeviternity. These are diverse modes of existence and there is, consequently, a metaphysical problem which, as Gilson insists, conditions the solution of the problem of time.[38]

Turning now to the question of the unchangeable with which I began, I should like to draw upon a passage from Dom Butler's *Western Mysticism* in which he expresses this great Augustinian theme of the search for the immutable by combining several texts into a single statement. Besides, mysticism is an altogether appropriate context for Augustine's teaching on time. "The intellectual or philosophical conception by which Augustine predominantly thinks of God is as the Being that is not subject to change: 'He truly Is, because He is unchangeable' (*De nat. boni*, 19). It was mainly the intellectual necessity he felt for Something Unchangeable as the basis and background of things changeable, that led him more than anything else, out of Manichaeism into Christianity, and in his search for God he usually represents his mind as passing ever upwards through the grades of things subject to change, till it arrives at that Being 'in Whom there is no variation.' And so his mystical experiences are often expressed in terms of this idea: e.g., as a perception of something unchangeable (*Enar. in Psalm.* XLI. 10); a beholding with the mind's eye something unchangeable (*ibid.*); a learning something divine and unchangeable (*C. Faust.,* XXII. 54). The same fundamental idea runs through the following descriptions of the act of contemplation, as the perception of unchangeable Good (*ibid.,* XXII. 53); as some vision of unchangeable Truth (*De cons. evang.,* I. 8); as the search for some unchangeable Truth (*Enar. in Psalm.* XLI. 7). Or again, the Light unchangeable; as where he says he 'saw with the eye of his soul, above his mind, the Light unchangeable' (*Conf.,* VII. 16); or 'arrived by some kind of spiritual contact at the Light unchangeable' (*Sermon.* LII. 16). These partly Neoplatonic, partly Joannine conceptions of Truth and Light are favorite ideas with Augustine when speaking of contemplation and mystic experience."[39]

Against this is measured the being that tends to non-being, the being that changes. What does it mean to be a creature? It means to be, and it means to have received being, but it means also, and for that very reason, to partake of a double tension—the tendency to be and the tendency not to be. These are correlative terms. For the tendency not to be, which Augustine associates so pointedly with temporality, would, in itself, be meaningless. The tendency toward non-being *per se* would be the tendency toward nothing at all, which is a contradiction.[40] A tendency is a tendency toward *something*. All tendencies are intentional. The tendency to be is prior, ontologically, and the tendency not to be derives from it and has meaning only in relation to it. So Sertillanges says, "The tendency of every creature to persevere in being is a reality, but this tendency does not come from its own power, it comes from the cause from which it derives its being; as, on the other hand, if we say that it tends to non-being, this is not because of its nature but because of its deficiency . . . creatures, as soon as they exist, tend to exist and not to collapse. But first of all they must exist. Now they do not exist of themselves. And thus the power that they need is not one which would prevent them from collapsing when they existed, but one which makes them exist."[41] Mascall puts it this way: "And these two facts—the fact of the distinction and the fact of the relation—are only two aspects of the one fundamental cosmological truth, the truth of finite being, as genuinely existing and yet existing with an existence that is altogether derived."[42]

"Not because of its nature but because of its deficiency." This is the challenge of time for Augustine and without its threatening contingency and overtones of hesitant commitment our response might appropriately be the unruffled Aristotelian one, uninhibited by feelings of awe and directed to settling a piece of business.[43] The difference is one of awareness, an awareness of spiritual dimensions, and it brings with it a hazard. Aristotle can ask himself what we usually mean when we speak of time, noting that since we must speak of it there is really nothing to be gained by speculating about its existence, and can proceed to his definition with the psychological security of the perfectly adjusted philosopher. Of course, he cannot be the philosopher of Augustine's definition—*amator Dei*—but then, he didn't mean to be. But anyone who chooses the Augustinian way will find that it leads through tortuous spiritual thickets in which lurk such threats as the possible conclusion that time is, on the one hand, just one damned thing after another, or perhaps, after all, just some kind of everlasting tea party.

Contingency in the sense of radical dependence in being cannot, therefore, be divorced from the necessary and immutable, and so time cannot be discussed intelligibly or, at any rate, cannot be discussed fruitfully, apart from the eternal. To do so would mean that escape from the *mere* flux of time would have to be conceived negatively. Yet, this is never the way we intend to speak of such deliverance, as a mere dissolution into emptiness. And it is not, of course, the way Augustine speaks of it. His doctrine of illumination in particular, but almost everything he utters on creation and the created, attest to his passionate repudiation of two not unfamiliar views: the modern version of time which, in Brunner's language, is the clock-watching version of the contem-

porary man who is obsessed with time and yet is so busy that
he never has time for anything,[44] and the more ancient
spiritualistic view of the man who always has time but for
whom time is mere appearance and not reality so that, un-
happily, the time he has does not exist.[45]

Now, all writers who discuss the Christian conception of
time naturally appeal to Augustine for his matchless contributions to the content of the phrase "fulness of time." The
reason, apart from the richness of his language, is that Augustine neither trivializes time by reducing it to the number
of motion nor de-existentializes it by reducing it to mere appearance. Time is always a question of spiritual life and
death.[46] The creature is an existence tragically menaced by
the threat of futility at best and by non-existence at worst.
The problem of time is to give to creatures an anchorage in
reality and a place in history, to give to the whole sensible
world meaning and significant being rather than an absurd
existence that gives rise only to nausea.[47] So, in a sense, Augustine uses this very threat of non-existence to mediate between the creature and the genuine fulness of being, making
the most of the limit to reach the Unlimited, turning the
greatest and most pervasive of all threats, non-existence or
bare formless existence, into a way of salvation.[48] For whatever the significance of the fulness of time may be, it is not
an encounter with Nothingness but an encounter with
Being.[49]

The only way in which victory can be claimed for the
temporal nature of man is by affirming that while man is
not everything he is at least something in a positive way[50]
and that, further, as something, he is in relation to the Unlimited which exists as the measure of the limited. If one rejects Pantheism, as Augustine does, there seems to be only
one way of conceiving such a notion, namely, an analogical
way. If this is the case in Augustine's doctrine, we should
expect him to argue that man's escape from temporality or
his victory over it is possible because he is capable of enter-
ing into a relation with the eternal which results in something that is, in one sense, the same as and, in another sense,
different from the eternal, since analogy is the relational sim-

ilarity of different things, a likeness of unlike things. And this, I suggest, is what Augustine does.[51]

The unlikeness is stated unequivocally, in the passages of the *Confessions* already cited and in many others. The created, even if it were created from eternity, is not co-eternal with the Creator.[52] God is He Who Is. In God there is nothing past, nothing future. Whatever is there, simply is.[53] ". . . for anything, whatever in short be its excellence, if it is changeable, does not truly exist; for there is no true existence wherever non-existence has also a place . . . Sift the mutations of things, thou wilt find WAS and WILL BE: think on God, thou wilt find the IS, where WAS and WILL BE cannot exist."[54] So much for the distinction. But the relation, the likeness, is equally clear. Man shall enjoy eternal life which he shall possess at the end of time for ever and ever.[55] He shall be like God; he shall see God face to face.[56] Man frees himself from the subjection of temporality and partakes of eternal life. Yet he does not cease to be a limited being; he does not cease to be mutable. "For in himself man is not, for he is changed and altered if he participate not in Him Who is the same. He is when he seeth God; he is when he seeth Him Who Is; and by seeing Him Who Is he also according to his measure beginneth to be. . . . The fulness of delight and the sufficiency of riches is God Himself, Himself the same. . ."[57] Furthermore, man, in attaining the object of his love, will "stand fast" and will overcome non-being, even while remaining a limited being.[58]

This attainment is fulness of being and fulness of time so far as the limited being is concerned.[59] But, even allowing for the confirming evidence of revelation, there is the additional difficulty of determining whether such fulness of time is merely "more of the same," a kind of endless time or whether it is a participation in the eternal. It is difficult to make any sense of Augustine's position except as reaching the latter of these two conclusions. In the contemplation of God the creature attains a mode of existence which is the perfection of his own limited being but, beyond that, the experience is one which, because of the *object* that terminates it, is qualitatively different from the experience of the mutable.[60]

There is danger in all of this of reading into Augustine the

terminology and meaning of later Thomistic thinking on analogy. All the same, I want to use a suggestion of James Anderson, who seems even more willing to take this risk than I am.
Professor Anderson says, "Now when St. Augustine declares:
"Just as the soul is the life of the body, so God is the blessed
life of man" (*De civ. Dei*, XXI. 26), he is not speaking
metaphorically; he is propounding a strict and proper analogy.
Indeed, since God is the beatifying principle of the soul, which
is itself the principle of life, God is, exactly, the life of our
life. *Vita vitae meae*, Augustine exclaims, (*Conf.*, VII. 1. 2;
Conf., X. 6. 10),"[61] and Anderson goes on to argue that
the great Augustinian saying that God is, in a sense, nearer
to us than we are to ourselves, can be given "a purely metaphysical interpretation and extension . . . universalized and
seen to be true for every being as such."[62] The likeness that
obtains between God and the creature is a likeness in the
order of existence, in the act whereby they exist, "precisely
inasmuch as they both exist, in a mode proportionate to their
natures,"[63] but unlike each other in that God is pure act
without composition or mutability, whereas the creature is a
"mixed" being which exists at all only in so far as it participates in the act whereby God exists.[64] Thus in this likeness
in unlikeness to the Creator lies the opportunity of time, an
opportunity, as Coomaraswamy reminds us, which must be
seized, for if we do not participate in eternity now, the opportunity may be forever lost.[65]

Yet it is not more than a participation, though Augustine
would prefer, no doubt, to say that it is not less. At the same
time, because time has a foundation in reality, this participation is not merely a negative, subjective reaction of with-
drawal. And it is because the finite is ontologically ordered
to the Creator that Augustine's view provides for the qualitative differences that distinguish the creature's temporality from
the same creature's "fulness" of time. The soul is perfected
by its object and it is by changing the object of our attention
that we overcome the flux of time. The creature cannot, because of ontological dependence, become immutable. But
he can, by knowing the object which is unchangeable, "restrain" his own mutability.

Turning back to the three difficulties I mentioned earlier,

something may be said, in conclusion, for each of them in the light of these Augustinian analogies. First of all, the reason that Augustine does not say clearly what time in itself is, is simply that there is no time in itself in an absolute sense. Time, in answer to the third objection that a relation must have a foundation, is a relational entity with a foundation in the limited and mutable being. If we persist in asking the question: What is time as time? or What is time in itself?— really an improper question—the best answer is that it consists in measureable successiveness. In short, Augustine's meaning is quite consonant, it seems to me, with the later Thomistic definition and with the distinction between the material and formal factors in time, the material factor being actual successiveness outside the mind, the formal factor being the "measurement" which is supplied by the intellect.[66] Combining the teaching of the eleventh Book of the *Confessions* with the analogical passages of the twelfth Book and other passages I have cited on successiveness and mutability, the following definition, entirely Augustinian I think, would result: *Time is a relation, with a foundation in successive states of finite or limited being, whose measurement is a cognitive act terminating in the "distentio" of the mind.*

Does time exist without man's measuring glance? Certainly Augustine maintains that the foundation continues to exist. And it might be argued, on his terms, that God's knowledge embraces the whole time span in any case, and is the absolute measure of all times, however variable they may be— for the quite simple reason that God is the absolute measure of everything there is.[67] But the qualitative differences that make time spiritually significant cannot exist, obviously, except through the experience of the limited being for whom they are significant. And in this limited sense, every creature might be said to have its own time, although this exclusiveness, not being of the physical *order,* is not incompatible with a common clocktime. So, while it is true that, as Mascall observes, "St. Augustine tends to look upon time as an impression made by a changing thing upon the mind of an observer, and St. Thomas as a measure inherent in the changing thing itself,"[68] I should insist that nothing but confusion results from taking these differences as signifying incompatibility.

One stresses the formal, the other the material factor, but the *relational structure,* in each case, is identical.

The remaining objection—that Augustine's analysis seems to culminate in the ever-presentness which is the final goal of spiritual striving rather than an awareness of the true nature of temporality—I have already considered. It should be remembered that Augustine seems to have a poignant realization of the inadequacy of language for the description of man's mutable ever-presentness. The creature, being variable and mutable in its very nature, cannot attain to true eternity. True eternity can only be divine eternity. Yet the term "everlastingness" fails by defect as much as the term "eternity" fails by excess. Accordingly, I have tried to emphasize the objectivity of Augustine's view, particularly his insistence on the fact that the creature is perfected by the object of its contemplation and knowledge. Augustine combines the philosophic conception of participation with the linguistic description of mysticism. The difference between divine eternity and human participation in eternity is that while God lacks nothing, either in being or in essence, man can be said to lack nothing only in a limited sense, even when he attains complete self-realization. Fulness of being, for the creature, is fulness only according to the measure of the creature, and is bounded by a no-moreness of being which the creature cannot overcome. But perfection in kind is real perfection.[69] To say what participation in eternity "feels like," so to speak, would seem to require participation in it and, since most of us are disqualified for this task, it would seem proper to pay attention to the deliverances of the mystic on this point, if on no other.

By interpreting Augustine in this way, I have tried to suggest his affinity with the other great writers on time in the classical tradition. In his study of *Four Views of Time in Ancient Philosophy,* Leonard Callahan reaches what seems to me an unnecessarily negative conclusion. He says, "It seems fairly clear that the problem of time is an entirely different problem for each of the four ancient philosophers whom we have been discussing (i.e., Plato, Aristotle, Plotinus, and Augustine). The differences in the nature of the problem arise first of all from the fact that each philosopher is looking for a different kind of being, a kind of being that is in accordance with his view of reality as a whole."[70] But it seems doubtful whether each of these philosophers *is* looking for a different kind of being. The object of the quest in each case is the Unchangeable. And that time is an entirely different problem for each of them is even more doubtful. Only Aristotle's treatment is markedly different from the others, for reasons traceable to the context of his inquiry—time being, primarily, a problem of physics for Aristotle.

Plato's "moving image of eternity" lacks the dimension of lived experience that we should now look for, I suppose, in any adequate treatment of time. But this abstractness is surely mitigated if one reads the *Phaedrus* and the *Symposium* along with the *Timaeus*. Both Plotinus and Augustine object to the Aristotelian treatment of the question because it tends to limit itself to what is for both of them an accidental attribute of time, leaving us to wonder what time is in its essence, and because it fails completely to do justice to the spiritual significance of time for the life and destiny of the human soul.

Nevertheless, in each case, the relational structure which these philosophers are considering, is the same. Therefore, it would seem more just to say that they concentrate their attention on different aspects of the problem of time. Indeed, it is as a consequence of this diverse treatment that the relational nature of time is exhibited. And until time is seen to involve a relational structure there might well be no end to the fruitless search for the essence of time-in-itself. But because time is relational, we are prepared to acknowledge not only the measuring instrument, but the reality it measures, and to give to each of them an appropriate recognition in accordance with the motive and end of any given inquiry about time.

I take it that this is the moral of Augustine's teaching on this subject. Limited being is, from one point of view, of course, a problem of physics, the science that treats of being *qua* changeable. But among these limited beings, arranged in ranks, is man, who is not only changeable, but restless; who not only moves toward an end, but moves toward an end which he can understand. To such a being, time defined as the measure of motion is a truth of limited usefulness and, being isolated from value, is of no spiritual significance at all. It is a mere invitation to engage in calculation. But, for Augustine, time is an invitation to participate in eternity.

NOTES

1. This paper was originally presented before the Southern Society for Philosophy of Religion on March 4, 1954.

2. *De civ. Dei*, XII, 2 (translations, unless otherwise indicated, will be those of *Basic Writings of Saint Augustine*, ed. by Whitney J. Oates, 2 vols. [New York, 1948]).

3. Bertrand Russell, *Human Knowledge: Its Scope and Limits* (New York, 1948), p. 212.

4. *Conf.*, XI. 4.

5. *Conf.*, XI. 7.

6. *Conf.*, XI. 11. Cf. *De Trin.*, I. 1.

7. *Conf.*, XI. 13. Cf. *De civ. Dei*, XI. 6.

8. *Conf.*, XI. 14 ". . . non vere dicamus tempus esse, nisi quia tendit non esse."

9. *Ibid.* Cf. *De beata vita*, 4, 30 and *De civ. Dei*, XIII. 11, ". . . the present occupies no space, but is only the transition of time from the future to the past."

10. *Conf.*, XI. 20.

11. See *De quant. an.*, 33. 71 and *De Trin.*, XV. 7.

12. The mind is illuminated by the apprehension of the form. See *De Trin.*, XV. 15.

13. *Conf.*, XI, 23.

14. *Ibid.*

15. *Conf.*, XI. 26.

16. *Conf.*, XI. 27. Cf. *De musica*, VI. 8. 21.

17. *Conf.*, XI. 28.

18. *Conf.*, XI. 29.

19. *Conf.*, XI. 23.

20. *Conf.*, XI. 14.

21. *Conf.*, XI. 30; XII. 12.

22. *Conf.*, XI. 30.

23. *Conf.*, XI. 31.

24. There are many passages in Augustine on revelation as a "drawing" and on the way in which the will and the reason are "drawn" to act, e.g., *De lib. arb.*, III. 25: "He who wills, wills something (objective), which, unless it is suggested from without by the senses of the body, or, in ways within unknown, comes into the mind, one cannot will" (tr. Tourscher, [New York, 1937], p. 417). Compare the famous ascent of the soul in *De quant. an.*, 33. 70–76 and *In Joan. evang.*, XXVI. 2–5.

25. *Conf.*, XII. 6.

26. *Conf.*, XII. 6; XII. 8.

27. See C. J. O'Toole, *The Philosophy of Creation in the Writings of St. Augustine* (Washington, 1944), p. 27f. St. Thomas interprets Augustine according to Aristotle and, therefore, maintains that Augustine's *materia informis* is the same as prime matter.

28. *Conf.*, XII. 8.

29. *Conf.*, XII. 9.

30. *Conf.*, XII. 9; XII. 12.

31. *Conf.*, XII. 12.

32. *Conf.*, XII. 9. See also *De musica,* VI. 10. 27.

33. *Conf.*, XII. 11.

34. *Conf.*, XII. 12.

35. See *De civ. Dei,* XII. 15 "For where there is no creature whose changing movements admits of succession, there cannot be time at all"; and, speaking of the angels, he says ". . . still their movements, which are the basis of time, do pass from future to past and therefore they cannot be co-eternal with the Creator, in whose movements we cannot say that there has been that which now is not, or shall be that which is not yet." See also *De civ. Dei,* XI. 6 ". . . time does not exist without some movement and transition . . ."

36. *Physics,* IV. 14. 223a, 16–29.

37. *De ordine,* II. 16. Cf. *Summa theol.,* I, q. 10, art. 5.

38. E. Gilson, *Introduction à l'étude de saint Augustin* (Paris, 1949) pp. 249, 255.

39. Dom Cuthbert Butler, *Western Mysticism,* 2nd ed. (London, 1951), p. 35. References are as cited in Butler's notes.

40. *Ep.* XI. 3 (CSEL 34, II. 27).

41. A. D. Sertillanges, *Saint Thomas d'Aquin,* p. 68. Quoted in E. L. Mascall, *Existence and Analogy* (London, 1949), p. 147. See also Augustine, *Solil.,* I. 1. 4; *De beata vita,* 4. 33; *De civ. Dei,* XIII. 17 and 23.

42. E. L. Mascall, *op. cit.,* p. 148.

43. On the Aristotelian *attitude* to the problem of time see H. A. Wolfson, *Cresca's Critique of Aristotle* (Cambridge, 1929), p. 94.

44. See *De civ. Dei,* XIII. 23.

45. See Emil Brunner, "The Christian Sense of Time," *Cross Currents,* I (1950), pp. 29–30.

46. *De Trin.,* II. 9.

47. See the illuminating comments of R. C. Taliafero in his translation of the *De Musica, Fathers of the Church,* Vol. 4, pp. 375–76, note 21, and his remarks on memory as the mediator between time and eternity, pp. 163–64.

48. *De cons. evang.,* I. 35. 53.

49. *De lib. arb.*, III. vii. 21.

50. *De lib. arb.*, III. xxv. 76 (CSEL, 43, III, 58–60).

51. See Lewis M. Hammond, "Theology as Theoretical and Practical Knowledge," in *Christianity and Reason*, ed. by Edward D. Myers (New York, 1951), esp. pp. 91 and 93.

52. *De civ. Dei*, XII. 15, 16; Cf. XI. 6; X. 31; IV. 12. See also *De Gen. ad litt.*, V. 16 (CSEL 28, I. 159–60) and VIII. 26 (CSEL 28, I. 265); *De Trin.*, I. 1.

53. *In Ps.* CII, 27–31, *Nicene and Post Nicene Fathers*, First Series (New York, 1888), Vol. VIII, pp. 501–2. Cf. *De nat. boni*, XXXIX; *De Trin.*, IV. 18 and XV. 5.

54. *In Joan. evang.*, XXXVIII. 10, *Nicene and Post Nicene Fathers*, First Series (New York, 1888), Vol. VII, p. 220; cf. *De Trin.*, IV. 18 and XV. 26.

55. *Ep.* CXCIV. v. 19 (CSEL 57, 4. 190–91).

56. *In Ps.* CV. 3.

57. *In Ps.* CXXI. 5, 6, 8, 12. See also and esp. *De Trin.*, IV. 18.

58. *De lib. arb.*, III. 7. 21. Cf. *De Trin.*, I. 6 and *De ordine*, II. 2. 7, 8; *De civ. Dei*, XII. 8.

59. *De natura et gratia*, LXXXIV; *De spiritu et littera*, LIX.

60. See John Marsh, *The Fulness of Time* (London, 1952), passim, but esp. p. 181. Marsh's conclusions coincide generally with the Platonic-Augustinian view of time and eternity and contrast very sharply with the influential interpretation of Oscar Cullman set forth in his *Christ and Time* (Philadelphia, 1950), esp. pp. 45 and 46.

61. James F. Anderson, *The Cause of Being* (St. Louis, 1952), p. 147. (References as cited by Anderson.)

62. *Ibid.*, p. 148.

63. *Ibid.*, p. 159.

64. *Conf.*, VII. 11: "And I viewed the other things below Thee, and perceived that they neither altogether are nor altogether are not. They are, indeed, because they are from Thee; but are not, because they are not what Thou art. For that truly is which remains immutably. It is good, then, for me to cleave unto God, for if I remain not in Him, neither shall I in myself; but He, remaining in Himself, reneweth all things. And Thou art the Lord my God, since Thou standest not in need of my goodness." See also *Conf.*, XI. 4, and *De Trin.*, IV. 2: ". . . He made us partakers of His divinity."

65. See A. K. Coomaraswamy, *Time and Eternity*, Artibus Asiae (Ascona, Switzerland, 1947), esp. pp. 78 and 130 ff., where this aspect of the problem is effectively developed in connection

with both Eastern and Western theories of time and its relation to eternity.

66. See James F. Anderson, *op. cit.*, p. 53.

67. *De Trin.*, VI. 10 seems to argue against this idea: "nothing passes away or succeeds to the knowledge of God." But compare *De civ. Dei*, XI. 10, where Augustine says that the world "could not have existed unless it had been known to God." Both passages *seem* to be ambiguous because they employ analogous concepts. But on the basis of *De Trin.*, I. 1 God should be able to know succession without suffering succession since God *fashions* the changeable without *being* changeable in Himself. On the whole question of God's creativity and knowledge, see the remarkable article by Josef Pieper, "On the 'Negative' Element in the Philosophy of Thomas Aquinas," in *Cross Currents*, IV (1953), pp. 46–56.

68. E. L. Mascall, *He Who Is* (London, 1945), p. 100, n. 4.

69. *De lib. arb.*, III. 15, "In those things therefore which fail or are deficient because they have been given limited being only, so that all in proper order may complete integral time, no one finds fault or blames defect or failure. Because no one can say (reasonably):—It ought to remain,—while, in fact, it can not pass the proper limits given to it" (tr. Tourscher [New York, 1937], p. 343).

70. Leonard Callahan, *Four Views of Time in Ancient Philosophy* (Cambridge, 1948), p. 188.

12

Empiricism and Augustine's Problems about Time

HUGH M. LACEY

Many recent writers on Augustine's philosophy of time assume that when Augustine expressed bewilderment about what time is, he was looking for a definition of time.[1] They point out that such a quest is misconceived, that it is based on a confusion, and they knowingly point out that Augustine's writings bear witness to this fact. Consequently they feel that all they have to do is to trace the source of Augustine's confusions and no further issues will remain.

Their initial assumption, however, is mistaken. Augustine's worries were not linguistic ones, although to be fair to the recent critics his worries were exacerbated by some linguistic muddles. He knew perfectly well that he had no trouble talking about time. This he accepted as a fact. His problem was that, although he used temporal terms correctly very easily, he did not know to what they referred. He wanted to know whether time is a feature of the objective physical world, or whether time is a subjective phenomenon; whether temporal relations are relations among physical events, or relations among private, mental events. Ordinary usage did not supply answers to these questions. Indeed, correct ordinary usage is compatible with temporal terms sometimes referring to features of the physical world, sometimes to subjective phenomena. He also wanted to know whether temporal discourse requires reference to specifically temporal entities, i.e., entities or moments which exist independently of things, or whether

Reprinted from *Review of Metaphysics* Vol. 22 (1968), pp. 219–45, by permission of the author and the editors.

time is adequately accounted for in terms of the temporal relations among events; whether the measurement of time depends upon the measurement of specifically temporal objects, or whether it is accounted for in terms of features of physical processes. In the course of his inquiry Augustine repeatedly expressed bewilderment. This bewilderment is due not to his being unable to find other words to do the job of "time," but to the fact that the answers do not readily emerge from ordinary ways of talking about "time."

In other words Augustine's problems are problems central to the metaphysics of time. They are the traditional problems: objectivity versus subjectivity; absolute versus relational.

In this paper I propose to demonstrate that Augustine's famous chapter on time in his *Confessions* contains a quite coherent argument for time as subjective (with one important qualification to be introduced). He does not come up with a clear view, however, on the absolute-relational issue, and I will only touch in passing his arguments relating to it. My plan will be as follows: first, I will set out his argument in stark form; secondly, I will examine in detail the content of his conclusion; thirdly, I will discuss the arguments that he gives for his premisses; fourthly, I will discuss which premisses must be given up in order to avoid his conclusion; finally I will show that an argument very similar to Augustine's has led to an important contemporary version of the relational theory of time, viz., Reichenbach's causal theory of time, and that meeting this argument has important consequences regarding the foundations of empiricism.

1. *Augustine's Argument*

The argument draws upon six fundamental premisses:

A. Only the present exists, i.e., only that which is contained in the present exists, or only present things exist, i.e., past and future times, past and future things do not exist.[2]

B. The present has no temporal extension.[3]

C. What does not exist cannot be perceived or measured.[4]

D. What we measure when we purport to measure time is extended.[5]

E. Only past and future times are said to have extension.[6]

F. The present contains memories of the past and expectations of the future.[7]

From A, B and C, he infers:

(a) Only the temporally extensionless present can be measured, (i.e., only that which is contained in the temporally extensionless present can be measured.)

Therefore:

(b) What we measure as time (or what we measure when we purport to measure time) is contained in the temporally extensionless present.

From A, B, and E, he infers:

(c) The only times that are said to have extension are not part of the temporally extensionless present.

From (b) and (c), he infers:

(d) What we measure as time is not the time that is said to have extension.

The argument so far is valid. Noting D, (b), (d), he asks: What is this extended thing that is contained in the extensionless present, which we measure when we purport to be measuring time? Seizing upon F, he proposes:

(e) We measure not past time, nor future time but memories of the past and expectations of the future.

Augustine's exact words are:

> It is in you, my mind, that I measure time. Do not interrupt me, or rather, do not allow yourself to be interrupted by the thronging of your impressions. It is in you, I say, that I measure time. As things pass by they leave an impression in you; this impression remains after the things have gone into the past, and it is this impression which I measure in the present, not the things which, in their passage caused the impression. It is this impression that I measure when I measure time. Therefore, either this itself is time or else I do not measure time at all. . . . it is not the future that is long, for the future does not exist; a long future is a long expectation of the future. Nor is the past long, since it does not exist; a long past is a long memory of the past. (*Confessions*, Bk. XI, Chs. 27, 28.)

Now, this conclusion is not entailed by the conjunction of the stated premisses. Accordingly its status must be viewed as that of an hypothesis which explains what is going on when we purport to measure time, an hypothesis arrived at by eliminating possible alternatives. He defends this hypothesis with the aid of two further premisses:

G. Time is not the motion of any body. When I measure the motion of a body, I do not measure time.[8]

H. The measurement of time requires that there be a fundamental form of measurement in which direct temporal comparisons are made.[9]

Augustine uses G against those who maintain that if measured time is to be identified with anything it is with the motion of a body, and since direct comparisons can only be made among the existing, H does not seem to allow that there might be another alternative to Augustine's hypothesis.

2. *Augustine's Conclusion*

Despite the *prima facie* plausibility of the premisses, despite the validity of the argument right down to the penultimate step, despite the reasonableness of the final step, Augustine's conclusion is difficult to evaluate, for nowhere does he work out in detail its ramifications. So there is no straightforward way in which we can evaluate either its adequacy or even its coherence.

It seems to me that there are two strands to Augustine's philosophy of time, one subjectivist, one objectivist; that neither is developed in any detail; and that he lacked sufficient linguistic equipment to develop the latter.[10] The subjectivist strand relates to the measurement of time, the objectivist to time itself. The conclusion of the argument refers only to the former. Let us see how the latter coheres with it.

It is clear enough, I think, that for Augustine tensed discourse, or, equivalently, discourse employing as primitives "past," "present," and "future," is the foundation of temporal discourse. Furthermore, it is clear that he regards this discourse as thoroughly objective, i.e., it is not to be construed as referring to memories or expectations, but to past and future events. Accordingly he does *not* adhere to the following analysis of the past:

x is past $\equiv$ There is a memory of x.

If Augustine held an analysis like this he would not be able (non-trivially) to say that a memory was caused by a past event. Memory comes into the analysis when we want to measure the past, not when we simply talk about it. Past events are real enough. True, for him, they do not exist, but they once existed and they have causal repercussions now. Some of these causal repercussions relate to the memory; others do not, and the others would exist whether or not objects with memories existed. Furthermore, we can make true statements about the past, even in cases where no memory is involved. Otherwise his own conclusion regarding the nature of time (quoted above) could not be stated, since this conclusion requires the truth of past tense statements such as "things, in their passage, caused the impressions in the memory." And surely we do not remember such things causing such impressions. So past events do have a certain reality for Augustine.

It is here that his linguistic equipment was lacking: existence was not sufficiently comprehensive to incorporate all reality. This comes out more starkly when we recall that Augustine regarded the succession of events as real, yet his self-imposed poverty of language prevented him saying: "There is an objective succession of events."[11] When I say that Augustine regarded the succession of events as real I mean that he held that in such statements as "I predicted x, and then x happened, and afterwards I remembered x," the connectives "and then," "and afterwards" are not themselves to be analyzed in terms of memory, expectations, or any other mental events. In talking about such successions of events, Augustine repeatedly uses the metaphor of temporal "passage," and he seems to be misled by this metaphor into holding that objective successions are described by such sentences as: "x was future, then x was present and then x was past."[12]

But this objective past and this objective future do not exist, and according to the argument they cannot be measured. What we measure as time is a mental impression—past time, a memory; future time, an expectation. Measured time is a thoroughly subjective business. One might wonder where the ordinary topological relations, "before," "after," "simultaneous," fit into Augustine's theory. Augustine himself sheds no direct light on this matter. At first sight, it might appear that their proper place would be in the objective strand, perhaps introduced by way of using such connectives as "and then."[13] But I don't think that such a line would accord with Augustine's whole train of thought. For these are relations between events, and just as non-existent events cannot be perceived, they cannot be related. For this reason I think that the topological properties of time must fall into the same category as the metrical ones, i.e., the topological relations (or some of them) are relations among mental events. If this is so, then there is point in reconstructing our way of talking about these relations, so that these truths are made explicit.

We might reconstruct "before" in something like the following way:

E_1 is before $E_2 \equiv (E_2$ is happening$)$. $(E_1$ is remembered$)$
$\qquad$ or $\qquad (E_1$ is happening$)$. $(E_2$ is expected$)$

But what if E_1 and E_2 are both in the past or both in the future? Then there are two ways that I can think of in which we might recursively extend the explication (e.g., consider them both in the past.)

1. E_1 is before $E_2 \equiv$ It is remembered that E_2's happening was simultaneous with a memory of E_1.

2. E_1 is before $E_2 \equiv$ A memory of the past displacement of E_1 is longer than a memory of the past displacement of E_2.

There is one major difficulty with this kind of explication as it stands, viz., that it does not allow the truth of the proposition: given any ordered pair of point-events, one, and only one, of the relations "before," "after," and "simultaneous" holds on the ordered pair; and this is generally taken to be a necessary truth. For the explication does not allow topological relations among events neither observed, nor remembered, nor predicted by some person. The Augustinian might be content just to accept this consequence, but if not, various ways out suggest themselves. One way out of the difficulty might

be to posit an omnipresent mind, and determine all the topological relations by reference to its observations, memories
and expectations. Another way might be to define all events
that are happening now (whether observed or not) to be
simultaneous. Then the recursive explication might be extended by such moves as:

If E_3 was simultaneous with E_2 and E_2 is before E_1, then
E_3 is before E_1.

Whether or not such ways out could ultimately be adequate does not concern me here. All I want to point out is
that up to this elementary stage there is nothing patently
absurd about the explication. True, it is counter-intuitive and
its full working-out would have to surmount some serious
difficulties, but *prima facie* it is not incoherent. It may be that
an honest following of the argument would lead one to it.

The same point applies when we extend the explication to
simple quantitative comparisons as in the following first steps
of a recursive definition, when A and B are processes:

A is longer than B = A totally overlaps B.
A totally overlaps B = Any part of B that is either observed, remembered, or predicted is
either observed, remembered, or predicted, respectively, as simultaneous
with a part of A.

Incidentally, the fact that there is such a simple extension of
the explication of the topological relations to quantitative
comparisons reinforces my contention that Augustine would
have to see the topological and metrical properties as fitting
into the same strand of his philosophy of time.

This quantitative explication cannot easily be extended to
more interesting cases. On this explication, overlapping processes can be quantitatively compared, but no others, and no
numerical assignments can be made. Recall that it is memories
and expectations—mental impressions—that have a measure.
How then can we quantitatively compare the following processes with respect to the time that they take:

(a)   Minute hand on clock moves from 12 to 1.
(b)   Minute hand on clock moves from 1 to 2.

Both processes, we know, take five minutes. But Augustine
cannot compare them directly, since they don't overlap, nor

are they indirectly comparable unless we assume that some other processes are equal in temporal measure, but such other processes, in turn, are not directly comparable. There seems to be no way out of this impasse—certainly calling upon our experience of duration would not help.

This impasse arises, it seems to me, because it is hard to see what sense can be made of talking of the measure of mental impressions, the measure of memories and expectations. "The memory of a long past," yes; but not "a long memory of the past." Unfortunately Augustine nowhere talks about clocks, and so nowhere does he give us a theory of how mental impressions are to be measured. I doubt that he was aware of the impasse. Nevertheless, he does give a hint. He says: "I measure something in my memory which remains fixed"— thereby suggesting that at any instant the impressions are there in the mind, only awaiting comparison with a standard, just as physical objects are there in the world awaiting comparison with measuring rods. And what constitutes this standard in the case of the mental impressions? Augustine gives no clue. But perhaps it is doing no violence to Augustine's main lines of thought to suggest the following. Consider any ideal periodic process, such as the oscillations of an ideal pendulum. Let us *stipulate* that the memories of any two oscillations are equal in measure, and of measure 1 unit. Then in the normal recursive manner extend the metric to all the required mental impressions, e.g., a memory is of unit 2 if the process of which it is a memory coincides (in the memory) with two consecutive oscillations of the pendulum. If someone objects to this account that mental impressions are not the sort of thing that have measure,[14] then the reply could be made that such a view rests on a prejudiced analysis of the nature of measurement—for look here I have produced a theory of the measurement of mental impressions. Admittedly the account that I have sketched has a number of verbal peculiarities, but it is not necessarily the worse for that. Some writers claim that Augustine has produced a coherent (if false) account of the topological properties of time, but that it lapses into incoherence when applied to the metrical properties.[15] According to the account that I have produced, the analysis of the metrical properties stands or falls with that of the topological properties. And the latter is, I maintain, a coherent analysis, even if adherence to it would significantly narrow the domain of temporal discourse. Such a narrowing would be undesirable, but logic sometimes compels the acceptance of the undesirable. Augustine, at least, has argued to this conclusion; we cannot reject it without showing his argument to be unsound. Some writers have maintained that Augustine's conclusion is paradoxical and that we can infer from this fact that the conjunction of the premisses is false.[16] If I am right, such an argument is unsound. If we want to avoid the conclusion we must find independent grounds for rejecting relevant premisses.

3. *Augustine's Premisses*

I will examine each of the premisses in turn.
A.   Only the present exists.
There are two possible interpretations of this:
  (A$_1$)   "Exists" is taken to be in the present tense. Then the premiss is tautologically true.
  (A$_2$)   "Exists" is taken to be used tenselessly.
Augustine himself did not formulate such a distinction. Wittgenstein suggests that Augustine did not think of (A$_2$) because he was misled by mistaking the metaphor of temporal passage for a literal description.[17] Thus he conceived events to be entities which change and which come in and out of existence, rather than as entities that happen, and as such to be events that exhibit temporal relations with one another in virtue of their succession rather than as a consequence of their simultaneous occurrence. He took tensed discourse to reflect an ontological reality, to reflect the nature of events.
B.   The present has no temporal extension.
Augustine's argument for this may be simply expressed as follows: consider any temporal interval of non-zero measure. If such an interval is divisible, then if one part is present no other part is, since distinct parts of an interval are not simultaneous. Now, since any part of an interval can be present, and temporal intervals are infinitely divisible, i.e., are ultimately composed of extensionless events or moments, it follows that at most one extensionless part of a process can be

present at once. Therefore, no temporal interval of non-zero measure can be wholly present at once.

Several challenges might be made to this argument:

1. It might be denied that being co-present entails being simultaneous.

2. It might be denied that temporal intervals are infinitely divisible.

3. It might be denied that a point-event can be present (except perhaps derivately, in virtue of an interval which contains it being present).[18]

Part of the trouble here is that the word "present" has several different uses. There certainly is a use of "present" according to which "x is present" is equivalent to "x is simultaneous with this utterance."[19] On this usage, the present is extended, and denials (1) and (3) are appropriate. But then the denials would amount to no more than semantic disagreement. Furthermore, if Augustine is right, this extended "present" may in fact *be* partly an extended memory and partly an extended expectation. Unless denials (1) and (3) correspond to something ontological, rather than linguistic, Augustine's argument is not undercut. It is hard to see how they would do this, unless accompanied by denial (2). Denial (2), if substantiated, would suffice to undercut the argument. Such a denial has been made, for example, by Whitehead, who maintained that becoming is discrete.

C. What does not exist cannot be perceived or measured.

Corresponding to (A_1) and (A_2) there are two interpretations (C_1) and (C_2). On (C_1), the premiss is *prima facie* false, since it is very rare indeed that an event or state of affairs that is observed is simultaneous with the event of observation. The nearest approximation is something like: an observed event or state of affairs has effects that are simultaneous with the relevant event of observation. No doubt, in order to counter this point, Augustine would have to claim that it is usually impressions that we observe and measure, *contra* common sense. But surely this is a consequence unforeseen by Augustine who must have thought (along with his contemporaries) that light has an infinite velocity.

On (C_2), the premiss is true; but (C_2) in conjunction with (A_2) produces the same consequences as (C_1).

D is a truism. E and F are taken by Augustine to be facts, even though, I submit, F is not completely uncontroversial.

G. Time is not the motion of any body. When I measure the motion of a body, I do not measure time.

Augustine's argument for this premiss is instructive. It proceeds by way of a series of intermediary conclusions:[20]

(1) Time cannot be defined as the motion of the heavenly bodies, for:

a. The heavenly motions have no priority over other motions.

b. Whether or not the heavens existed, whether or not light came from the heavens, we could still measure other motions, e.g., "the whirlings of a potter's wheel."

c. It is logically possible that the sun complete its trip around the earth in half the usual time, or that the sun stand still for the duration of a battle, during which time goes on.

Therefore, the motion of the heavenly bodies constitutes neither time nor the measure of time.

(2) Time is not definable as the motion of any body.

a. No body is moved except with respect to time; and when a body is moved we measure how long it moves by time.

We cannot measure how long it moved unless we know *when* it started and when it stopped.

Therefore, time is distinct from any motion, since we cannot measure a motion, unless we can first measure time.

b. The passage of time is compatible with any specified body standing still (not necessarily with all bodies standing still)—so, no matter which object we choose, time is not its motion, nor is its measure definable in terms of the object's motion.

It is this strand of thought incidentally that I see as leading to absolute time. Time is distinct from any motion; yet this rests uneasily with his other fundamental thesis (which I do not intend to discuss) that God created time when he created the world, in virtue of his creation of the world.[21] He does not sort out this apparent incompatibility.

Some comments on the argument:[22]

(3)   In 2(a), Augustine states the tautology that we measure how long a motion takes by means of *time*. He omits to mention that, in fact, we make such a measurement by means of a *clock,* i.e., a physical object with a certain kind of motion. No doubt, he would be quick to point out that a clock exhibits periodic motions of equal duration, and that we need to be able to measure time in order to determine that these periods are equal. Now, it is true that if we can make sense of the notion of measuring time without reference to motions, then that is one way of breaking the regress of measuring the duration of motions by reference to the duration of other motions. But it is not a necessary way, for there are alternative ways. The obvious alternative is to stipulate conventionally that certain motions are of equal duration. Say, for simplicity, that the periodic motions of the sun about the earth are stipulated to be of equal duration. But then, won't we fall prey to the argument under (1)? We would indeed be in an odd spot if we stipulated without qualification that all the motions (past, present, and future) of a certain class were equal in duration, for then if the sun did "stand still," our known laws would have to undergo alteration.[23] But we don't need to make such an unqualified stipulation. The context of stipulation allows many liberties, in particular the revision of stipulations, bound of course by the requirement of consistency, and revise them we will if the desire for simplicity of laws requires it. On this account, that two consecutive periods of a good clock's motion are equal in duration is not simply a factual matter—yet facts do have an interplay, in the sense that subsequent factual discoveries may lead to metrical revisions.

(4)   In 2(b), Augustine has argued correctly that the passage of time does not require the motion of any specified body, and *a fortiori* it does not require the existence of a clock contemporaneous with the universe. On the account that I have given in (3), some motion is necessary for the measurement of time, even if it is the motion of different bodies at different times (assuming that no sense can be made of the notion of measuring time without recourse to motions).

In the above argument (1)-(2), Augustine temporarily laid aside the context of his earlier theses. In my refutation (3)-

(4), I have followed suit. Nevertheless, he still has up his sleeve an overarching objection:

(5) Time is not the motion of a body, because I cannot measure motion until it has ceased to exist. So I cannot measure it. So it cannot be the time that I do measure.[24]

H. The measurement of time is dependent upon some direct temporal comparisons being possible.

This is false as I have argued above in (3). No doubt Augustine has in mind length as a paradigmatic case of measurement, where we have standard measuring rods that we can directly compare with any length (at least in principle). But, even here, how do we know that two separated measuring rods remain equal in length: no method of direct comparison is possible, so even here we can't do without convention. Similarly, I have argued that Augustine himself will have to call upon convention or stipulation in order to sustain his own theory of time.

4. Cutting Short Augustine's Argument

We are now in a position to ask: what are the various ways in which Augustine's conclusions might be avoided? What combinations of the premises may we reject? I have just argued that H is false, but also that its falsehood is compatible with Augustine's conclusion. Furthermore, very little in the argument hangs upon it, so that rejecting it will not help us much if we want to avoid the conclusion. I have also argued that there are grounds for asserting the falsity of G, provided that we do not accept A, B and C. Accepting the status that I have already assigned to D, E and F, it follows that A, B and C will be the controversial premises.

As I have already indicated, I believe that (A_2) and (C_1) are false. Let us reject them. Then we are free to say of events, episodes, states of affairs, etc., that they exist (tenseless) if and only if they have happened, are happening or will happen, thus eliminating the highly misleading tensed use of "exists" in connection with events that I have already pointed to in my discussion of A. If we do this, Augustine's overarching argument (5) for G no longer stands. Then I regard my refutation of G as decisive.

If we make these moves—and I have argued that we should —nothing stands any longer in the path of the following conception of time. There is a set of events partially ordered by such physical relations as before, after, simultaneous. We may idealize if we like, since we have not rejected B, and talk of the set of point-events totally ordered by these relations (subject, of course, to the qualifications of the Special Theory of Relativity). The temporal metric is then easily introduced onto either set. The duration of a process is equal to the number (which may be fractional) of periods of a standard clock that totally coincide with it (assuming, for simplicity of discussion, that we take 1 period = 1 unit). How do we determine this? In the simplest and most fundamental case by observing the reading on the clock simultaneous with the beginning of the process and the reading simultaneous with the ending, and subtracting the difference. We do not measure time as it passes, but we do measure the duration of a process as it happens. (Of course, there will be many cases when we have to make indirect calculations, but indirect calculations presuppose the fundamental method.) In short, nothing further in Augustine's argument stands in the path of a thoroughly objectivist account of time.

My conclusion at this point is by no means uncontroversial. Mundle, among others, has argued that Augustine's argument is undercut *only if* B is rejected.[25] A, he says, only gets us into trouble when coupled with B, and he omits to mention that C is a crucial premiss in Augustine's argument. His argument merits discussion for it raises an important issue.

First, however, let me point out that the rejection of B alone, or even accompanied by the rejection of G and H, will not extricate us from Augustine's conclusion. True, we will then have a present with finite (non-zero) extension—still, on Mundle's account, not a very long present. It is a present corresponding to a phenomenal whole, of duration perhaps of the time we take to utter a sentence—long enough, admittedly, to make some temporal measurements. Could we then construct measurements of the past out of temporal measurements made in the past? If we try, we find that all Augustine's problems arise again, for any motion of longer duration than the present can only be measured after it has

ceased to exist, and so on. We might be able to measure the
duration of a past motion, by summing the durations of those
small parts of it which were measured, but still we would be
measuring a memory if we are measuring something that
exists.[26] To avoid a subjective philosophy of time we need
to reject premisses other than B. Do we need to reject B?

Mundle does not directly challenge my conclusion that retention of B is compatible with an objectivist philosophy of
time. His argument is that retention of B is not compatible
with an empiricist philosophy of time, or rather that the retention of B together with empiricist assumptions leaves us
with Augustine's conclusion. He considers (quite appropriately) only such topological relations as "before." He states
that an empiricist requires that such elementary temporal relations be given in observation, i.e., that they be observation
terms, to use the terminology of contemporary logical empiricism. The empiricist, he goes on, also maintains that a
sensation (observational datum) that a person has at an instant must be simultaneous with that instant. However, whatever relations may hold among sensations at a durationless
instant, the relation of "before" cannot be one, for, by definition, the two terms of this relation cannot be simultaneous.
A fortiori, one of them cannot be simultaneous with the instant under consideration. Therefore "before" cannot be an
observation term, for at best it is given experientially as a relation between two sensations, one of which has to be remembered before the determination can be made. Therefore, what
we normally refer to as the observation of a succession of
events is at best a succession of observations of events pieced
together by the memory. The empiricist is thus convicted of
subjectivity (although Mundle does not draw this stark inference).

It is important to note that the above argument relies on
the assumption that it is central to empiricism that a complete
sensation can be present (in Augustine's sense), and thence
durationless. No contemporary version of empiricism holds
to such an assumption. I will now argue that one contemporary version of empiricism runs afoul of an argument closely
related to Augustine's and is convicted of subjectivity, but not
because it upholds B. I will show how one version of em-

piricism has unsuccessfully tried to meet this argument without amending its empiricist assumptions, and then I will sketch an amended version of empiricism that is fully compatible with the conception of time that I have traced above.

5. *Empiricism and the Philosophy of Time*

Logical empiricism requires that the basic temporal terms be observation terms. Otherwise the empirical content of a statement of the form "E_1 is before E_2," where E_1 and E_2 are observable events, would be identical with that of the observation statement "(E_1 occurred) . (E_2 occurred)." The following theses and definitions are typically held by proponents of logical empiricism, although they are not meant to be an exhaustive characterization of logical empiricism.

I.   A *basic observation statement* describes only events or states of affairs having effects simultaneous with the event of observation, *via* which we have grounds for the truth of the statement. (Such an event of observation has finite duration.)

II. A statement is not a basic observation statement if it entails basic observation statements which describe events, each of which can be observationally discerned individually, but which are not simultaneous.

III. An *observation statement* is defined as any statement which is either a basic observation statement, or a compound statement, all of whose components are basic observation statements and all of whose connectives are extensional. Any statement logically equivalent to an observation statement is also an observation statement.

IV. *Observation terms* are the non-logical terms that occur in observation statements.

V.   Only observation terms refer to things, objects, events and relations in the physical world (independently of the presence of observers).[27]

Consider any statement of the form:

$$E_1 \text{ is before } E_2$$

where E_1 and E_2 refer to observable events. (1) is not an observation statement since it entails O_1 . O_2 where $O_1 = E_1$

occurred, and $O_2 = E_2$ occurred, and where, by hypothesis, E_1 is not simultaneous with E_2, thus violating II. (1) must rather be construed as being established by a succession of events of observation, whose outcome is the pair of observation statements joined by the non-extensional connective "and then." Similarly, what we ordinarily refer to as the observation of a movement or the observation of a succession of events is to be construed as a succession of observations of events, pieced together by the memory. Since (1) is of the simplest form that a statement containing "before" can be, it follows that "before" is not an observation term.[28] Therefore, by V, "before" does not refer to an objective relation in the physical world. Rather it must be seen as fundamentally a relation among mental events (e.g., among two observations and verified by recourse to memory). This is Mundle's conclusion, without his basic premiss. Something very like the argument that I put in Augustine's mouth regarding the topological relations has cropped up again.

Is there any way in which the empiricist can avoid this conclusion, and at the same time preserve the above features of the analysis of the observation language? One possibility suggests itself: explicate or *reconstruct* "before" in such a way that (1) becomes equivalent to an observation statement. The general idea behind this suggestion is that there might be a characteristic of some observable events such that if we are comparing two events, one of them having this characteristic may be sufficient for asserting that it is before the other. Another way of putting the general idea is that it might be possible, given descriptions of observable events (omitting any reference to temporal relations among them) to establish what temporal relations do hold among them on the basis of observable characteristics of the events which are referred to in the descriptions. To give the simplest example: suppose that all observable events were marked with a number, and suppose that it just happened that the order of the numbers corresponded to the "observed" temporal order of the events (say, God wanted to help out the empiricist). Then we might reconstruct "before" *via* the equivalence:

E_1 is before $E_2 \equiv O_1$. O_2 . the number of $E_2 >$ the number of E_1.[29]

This illustrates the general idea. A serious attempt to develop it was made by the early proponents of the causal theory of time, especially Reichenbach.

In summary (and without any of the necessary qualifications), Reichenbach's idea was to define the temporal relations by way of Leibniz's recursive schema which begins:

E_1 is before $E_2 \equiv E_1$ is the cause of E_2,

and then to reconstruct "cause" as an observation term. He notes that if E_1 is the cause of E_2, then a small variation (a mark) in E_1 is associated with a small variation in E_2, but a mark on E_2 is not associated with a mark on E_1. So that if the events and markings are repeated a number of times, we should observe the following combinations of events (where an asterisk indicates a marked event):

$$E_1 E_2 \qquad E_1{}^* E_2{}^* \qquad E_1 E_2{}^*$$

and not the combination

$$E_1{}^* E_2.$$

Conversely, if we observe the above three combinations, and not the final one, we may infer that E_1 is the cause of E_2. This inference is the foundation of the reconstruction of "cause" as an observation term. The reconstruction of "before" on the foundation of this reconstruction of "cause" fails, however, because the pairing of events involves temporal presuppositions. Similarly, I have argued elsewhere, all subsequent attempts at a causal reconstruction of the temporal relations have failed.[30]

For a long time, I was very puzzled by some of the philosophical arguments that have been proposed on behalf of the causal theory of time. Such arguments insist that subjectivity can be removed from the foundations of time only if we eschew all recourse to our experience of time in the semantics of time.[31] I believe that the above argument makes explicit the worry that underlay the polemics of Reichenbach against subjectivity. I suggest that Reichenbach must have held a thesis similar to II. Otherwise, why not take "before" as an observation term? He does dwell on the alleged un-

reliability of temporal judgments. Such unreliability could
lead to the demand for clarification of the synthetic connections between cause and time, but hardly to a definitional
connection. To lead to a quest for definition (logical reconstruction) the unreliability must be seen to spring from a
deeper subjectivity. In his major epistemological work, Reichenbach writes: "We have shown that the basis of our knowledge is the world of immediate things appearing at one moment. . . ."[32] (This implies a restriction very close to II.)
He also explicitly includes memory reports in the class of
basic (observation) statements.[33] Statements of the form (1)
do not fit simply into this basic class. How are they to be con-
structed out of the basic class? The most obvious way would
be identical with that which I developed on Augustine's behalf. Simplifying:

E_1 is before $E_2 \equiv (E_2$ is happening$)$. $(E_1$ is remembered$)$,

where each of the conjuncts of the definiens are basic statements. Memories, however, cannot be separated from the
subject having the memory. Such a reconstruction, therefore,
would involve temporal discourse in irremovable subjectivity.
Within the context of the class of basic statements so analyzed,
the causal theory of time is the obvious next recourse.

If the above argument is correct, the desire to construct a
causal definition of time sprang from a concern similar to
Augustine's. Augustine was worried about how we can compare events, some of which do not exist now. The early proponents of the causal theory of time worried about how we
can compare events not given in the same event of observation. The combination of V and II functions very similarly to
the combination of A and C. If I am right that the causal
theory of time fails, then both worries lead to a subjectivism
in the philosophy of time.

The argument just presented shows that a version of empiricism that accepts I–V is incompatible with the objectivity
of time. But where has this left us with regard to Augustine's
premiss B?

Mundle argues that if the empiricist wants to retain the
objectivity of time (in the face of the difficulty which he diagnosed) then he must revise the foundations of empiricism,

and that this revision will bring in premises incompatible with B. My diagnosis of the empiricist's difficulty, as we have seen, is different from Mundle's. Must my remedy also be incompatible with B?

Mundle's revised empiricist position is as follows: deny that an event of observation always occupies the minimum duration for perceptual discernment (i.e., deny II). Such an event is still of short duration—the length of the endurance of the sensation. Then it is true that an observation statement may entail observation statements which describe successive events (at the same place or closely related places), provided that they all have effects simultaneous with (i.e., have simultaneous parts with) each other and the event of observation which leads to the first observation statement (thus retaining I). So we can say that a person can simultaneously observe successive (non-simultaneous) events, *and observe them as successive*. Then the empiricist has retained "before" as an observation term.

Note that so far I have not even had occasion to mention B. Mundle takes it for granted that an event of observation occupies the present. I suspect this is his definition of "present". Thus, for him, the denial of II involves the denial of B. If this interpretation is correct, then in denying B Mundle is merely disagreeing with Augustine about the use of words. There is nothing wrong with Mundle's usage, although in using it, one runs the risk of confusing the phenomenal with the real—worse, of suggesting that we are committed to the discreteness of becoming and that there is no theoretical usage of "present" corresponding to Augustine's usage. At any rate, mere redefinition of words will not enable one to avoid Augustine's conclusion, only the rejection of premises (A_2) and (C_1) will.

Mundle's solution for the empiricist, if he wants to avoid subjectivity, is to deny II but retain I. I will now argue that the retention of I is arbitrary, restrictive, and highly artificial. According to his solution we simultaneously observe non-simultaneous events; not only that but simultaneously with observing these events we observe them *to be* non-simultaneous. Let us say that the duration of an event of observation is t and that the minimum duration for perceptual discernment is t'. Now consider the following situation: there are three lights, L_1, L_2, L_3, close together, close to me, and all within my perceptual field. L_1 is flashed at O; L_2 at t_1; L_3 at t_3. $t' < t_1 < t$; $t' < t_2 - t_1 < t$; $t_2 > t$. The following statements are true:

      (i) L_1 is flashed before L_2.
      (ii) L_2 is flashed before L_3.
      (iii) L_1 is flashed before L_3.

Since the event of observation of L_1's flashing is completed before L_3 begins, by I, (iii) is not an observation statement. But (i) and (ii) are observation statements since the events of observation of L_1's and L_2's flashings, and L_2's and L_3's flashings respectively overlap. Compare (i) and (iii): on Mundle's account, only observation is employed in the establishment of (i), but memory has a role in the establishment of (iii). But is it true that memory is not employed in the establishment of (i)? It is not in virtue of the simultaneity (i.e., overlap) of the events of observing the flashings of L_1 and L_2 that we affirm (i); it is in virtue of the first event beginning before the second event, and enduring for a time (albeit short) non-simultaneously with it, and once the second event has started it is only by way of memory that we can assert this. Appearances can deceive, and they have deceived in this case. There is no essential difference between (i) and (iii) with respect to observational status. Thus retention of I is ungrounded, once II is rejected.[34]

It seems to me that the empiricist will have to be more liberal than Mundle allows. He will have to allow, e.g., that events of observation are not simply isolated; that there is no clear distinction between events of observation and remembering; that any line of demarcation is essentially pragmatic. Roughly speaking, his criterion of the observational will be: an observation statement describes a state of affairs which is the cause of the observer's having the belief described in the statement, provided that the statement is uttered soon after the acquisition of the belief. Then the role of memory in observation can be left to empirical investigation.[35] That memories and temporal relations among mental events are involved in observations of temporal relations does not imply that temporal relations are ontologically dependent upon such mental events. Just the fact that spatial relations among cells in the brain are involved in the observation of spatial relations does not imply that spatial relations are ontologically dependent on those in the brain. Our knowledge and our concepts depend on the existence of such things, but what our concepts refer to does not.

6. *Summary*

To sum up: Augustine's argument fails because A_2 and C_1 are false. Once we have rejected these premisses, nothing further in Augustine's argument, including premiss B, stands in the path of an objectivist philosophy of time. In reply to the suggestion that B coupled with basic empiricist assumptions stands in the path of such a philosophy, it was demonstrated that the assumptions of one version of empiricism (with or without B) leads to subjectivity because of premisses resembling A_2 and C_1. A suggested revised version of empiricism, retaining B, is quite compatible with the objectivist philosophy. In short, only the premisses A_2 and C_1 need to be given up.

APPENDIX

In an early writing, Carnap produces the following "rough explanation" of "observation term":

A predicate 'P' of a language L is called observable for an organism (e.g., a person) N, if, for suitable arguments, e.g., 'b' (where 'b' designates a thing or an event), N is able under suitable circumstances to come to a decision, with the help of few observations, about a full sentence, say 'P(b)', that is, to a confirmation of either 'P(b)' or '~P(b)' of such a high degree that he will either accept or reject 'P(b)'.[36]

In a later writing,[37] he attempts to clarify this "rough explanation" by listing certain conditions that the observation language as a whole must satisfy. One of these conditions, the requirement of extensionality, states: "The language contains only truth-functional connectives, no terms for logical or causal modalities."

It seems to me that on the most straightforward reading this condition excludes "before" and hence all temporal terms from the observation language. Carnap did not draw this conclusion, as is clear from the fact that he frequently cites sentences of the form "P(a) at t" as instances of observation sentences.

Consider a sentence of the form:
$$E_1 \text{ is before } E_2, \ldots \qquad (1),$$
where E_1 and E_2 refer to observable events. (1) is logically equivalent to:
$$O_1 \text{ and then } O_2, \ldots \qquad (2),$$
where $O_1 = E_1$ happens and $O_2 = E_2$ happens. (For simplicity read the "happens" as "tenseless present," although there would be no difficulty in re-expressing (2) as a disjunction of sentences of the above form where the O's were tensed observation sentences.) Let us assume that a sentence logically equivalent to an observation sentence is also an observation sentence. Carnap does not explicitly make this assumption, but it seems a natural one to make. Then if (1) is an observation sentence, so is (2); but, by the requirement of extensionality since "and then" is a non-extensional connective, (2) is not. Therefore, (1) is not an observation sentence.

Perhaps the requirement of extensionality can be dropped? Difficulties would arise if that was done. The condition was devised in order to exclude such features as causation, purpose, and logical necessity from the observation language. Nothing in the "rough explanation" excludes from the observation language such sentences as: "His striking the match caused the flame" and "He went to the table in order that he pick up a glass of beer." Drop the requirement of extensionality, and sentences like these will become observation sentences, and terms like "cause" and "in order that" observation terms. Yet retaining the requirement excludes temporal terms from the domain of observation terms.

Perhaps the assumption introduced above can be dropped? For example, why not accept (1), but not (2) as an observation sentence? This would not suffice to get rid of the troublesome cases in the previous paragraph, for we could simply devise a language in which the content of these sentences was expressed in atomic sentences, like (1).

It might be suggested that a pragmatic, rather than formal ground could be used to include temporal, but not causal and purposive terms. A ground something like: in contexts where Carnap's "rough explanation" applies, temporal judgments are more reliable than causal and purposive ones. So, for practical purposes, include the temporal and exclude the others. The trouble with this sort of line is that the reliability of temporal judgments is constantly under attack. As we have seen, Reichenbach based the need for a definition of time on this alleged unreliability.

I can see no way out of the position that if "before" is accepted as an observation term, then there is no non-arbitrary way of excluding terms like "cause" and "in order that." Carnap excludes the latter. On the same grounds, "before" is excluded. If, however, in the face of this sort of argument, it was proposed that the requirement of extensionality be dropped, then the restrictiveness of empiricist criteria of cognitive meaningfulness would be significantly lessened. Incidentally, I think that this argument shows that my II follows from this Carnapian requirement provided that "basic observation statement" is read as "atomic observation sentence."

This exclusion of "before" from Carnap's observation language has interesting consequences regarding his analysis of the empirical significance of terms. He is not obliged to commit "before" to the limbo of the insignificant, for his criterion allows it to be a significant theoretical term, since from (1) and the correspondence rule, "$(1) \rightarrow O_1$," O_1 can be inferred, but not from the correspondence rule alone. This significance, however, is obtained at a cost, for (1), construed as a theoretical sentence cannot be confirmed observationally, since (1) and "E_2 is before E_1" have identical observational consequences. We thus have empirically significant sentences that cannot be verified under the given restrictions on observation. The criterion, assuming that it is in other respects satisfactory, thus may suffice to formally pick out the meaningful theoretical terms, but it has lost its rationale. No longer is it a verification based criterion of meaning. It has long been suspected that verificationist criteria do not do justice to statements about the past. Perhaps the trouble is more radical: they do not do justice to any temporal statements.

1. By "definition" I mean "nominal definition" not "real defini-tion." R. M. Gale traces the source of Augustine's problems to the fact that time cannot be ostensively defined. This is overly simple as the subsequent exposition will demonstrate.

2. "It is now, however, perfectly clear that neither the future nor the past are in existence, and that it is incorrect to say that there are three times—past, present, and future." Augustine, *Confessions*, trans. by Rex Warner (New York: Mentor Books), Bk. XI, Ch. 20. All quotations from the *Confessions* are from Book XI of this edition. To facilitate checking references, I have cited chapter numbers.

3. "If anything can be meant by a point of time so small that it cannot be divided into even the most minute particles of mo-ments, that is the only time that can be called 'present.' And such a time must fly so rapidly from future to past that it has no dura-tion and no extension. For if it does have any extension, it can be divided into past and future; whereas the present does not take up any space." *ibid.*, Ch. 15.

4. "For it is impossible to measure the past, which is no longer in existence, or the future which is not yet in existence, unless perhaps one is going to be rash enough to maintain that it is pos-sible to measure something which does not exist." *ibid.*, Ch. 16. Augustine also appears to hold a stronger thesis: "how can we say that something that does not exist at all is either long or short?" *ibid.*, Ch. 15.

5. "But how can we measure time except in some sort of ex-tension? . . . In what kind of extension, then do we measure time as it is passing by? . . . We cannot measure something which has no extension." *ibid.*, Ch. 21.

6. "Nevertheless, we say 'a long time' and 'a short time', though we only use these expressions about the past and the fu-ture." *ibid.*, Ch. 15.

7. "When I recollect the image of my boyhood and tell others about it, I am looking at this image in time present, because it still exists in my memory. . . . But I do know this, that we often pre-meditate our future actions, and this premeditation is present while the action which we are premeditating, being in the future, does not yet exist." *ibid.*, Ch. 18.

8. "Time, therefore, is not the motion of a body." *ibid.*, Ch. 24.

9. "I measure the motion of a body in time. Is it the case that I do not measure time itself? But could I measure the motion of a

body—how long it lasts, how long it takes to go from one place to another—if I were not measuring the time in which the motion takes place? How, then, do I measure time itself? Do we measure a longer time by means of a shorter time . . ." *ibid.*, Ch. 26.

10. A number of writers, e.g., R. Suter "Augustine on Time with Some Criticisms from Wittgenstein," *Rev. Int. Phil.* (1962), pp. 378–94, have failed to discuss Augustine's objectivist strand. In line with this, Suter (p. 389) states incorrectly that Augustine overlooked that there are facts about the future and the past. He also maintains incorrectly that, for Augustine, the past and the future exist in the mind (p. 388) whereas Augustine maintains that they do not exist. Memories and expectations exist in the mind, and it is these which we measure when we purport to measure the past and the future. C. W. K. Mundle, "Augustine's Pervasive Error Concerning Time," *Philosophy*, Vol. XLI, No. 156 (April 1966), p. 165, makes the same mistake.

11. Similarly he would regard change as real, but he could not say: "There is change."

12. "But all the time my attention is present and through it what was future passes on its way to become past. And as I proceed further and further with my recitation, so the expectation grows shorter and the memory grows longer, until all the expectation is finished at the point when the whole of this action is over and has passed into the memory." *Confessions*, Ch. 28.

13. Such a program is suggested in W. Sellars, "Time and the World Order," in *Minnesota Studies in the Philosophy of Science*, Vol. III, ed. by H. Feigl and G. Maxwell (Minneapolis, 1962), Section XI.

14. Such an objection is made by Suter (*op. cit.*, pp. 391–92). Suter further objects: "For suppose we agree that we have both an idea of five o'clock and an idea of an hour. Presumably, for him, such ideas need not involve any reference to clocks or to any other instrument which we ordinarily use to measure time." Therefore, he concludes, Augustine's time is not our time. But Suter does not justify his presumption, he merely takes it for granted. This is overhasty as the explication sketched above demonstrates. Suter's complaint, that Augustine owes us a fuller explanation of this theory of time, is, however, justified. I have tried to construct what such a fuller explanation might look like.

15. E.g., Suter, *op. cit.*, p. 392.

16. "In view of their paradoxical implications, Augustine's premisses must surely be rejected," Mundle (*op. cit.*, p. 166).

17. Wittgenstein, *The Blue and Brown Books* (Oxford, 1958), pp. 106 ff.

18. It will be clear from my expression of Augustine's argument why I am unconvinced by Suter's objection (*op. cit.*, pp. 389–90) that Augustine systematically equivocates in using "present." Cf. J. N. Findlay, "Time: A Treatment of Some Puzzles," in *Problems of Space and Time*, ed. by J. J. C. Smart (New York, 1964), p. 346.

19. Mundle (*op. cit.*, p. 167) makes this point.

20. *Confessions*, Chs. 23, 24.

21. "For if eternity and time are rightly distinguished by this, that time does not exist without some movement and transition while in eternity there is no change, who does not see that there could have been no time had not some creature been made, which by some motion would give birth to change . . . and thus, in these shorter or longer intervals of duration, time would begin?" Augustine, *The City of God* (XI. 6), in *The Basic Writings of St. Augustine*, Vol. II, ed. by W. J. Oates (New York, 1948), p. 148.

22. Waismann, *The Principles of Linguistic Philosophy* (New York, 1965) makes similar comments to some of those made below.

23. This sort of situation can always arise, unless we can get a periodic motion of an object not subject to normal physical laws.

24. *Confessions*, Ch. 27.

25. Mundle (*op. cit.*, p. 167). See also Findlay (*op. cit.*, p. 346).

26. This argument suggests that it is incorrect to identify Augustine's problem with Zeno's problem of how happenings that take no time can be combined into a happening of finite, non-zero duration, cf. Findlay (*op. cit.*, p. 345).

27. It is well known that there are heavily qualified versions of this extreme thesis, but they are irrelevant to the present argument. Also the thesis might not be held in such a general form, but only with respect to particular cases. I think that Reichenbach held it with respect to the particular case of time.

28. "Before" is excluded from being an observation term on characterizations of the observation language other than that given above. As far as I can tell, Carnap does not explicitly hold to II. Yet on the most straightforward reading of his account, "before" is excluded. For details, see Appendix at end of this article.

29. Assuming for simplicity the logicist thesis on number.

30. For details, see H. Reichenbach, *The Philosophy of Space and Time* (New York, 1958), pp. 135 ff. Regarding other versions of the causal theory of time, see H. Lacey "The Causal Theory of

Time: A Critique of Grünbaum's Version," *Philosophy of Science,* Vol. XXXIV, No. 4 (December 1968).

31. H. Reichenbach, *The Direction of Time* (Berkeley, 1956), pp. 1–17; A. Grünbaum, *Philosophical Problems of Space and Time* (New York, 1963), p. 192. Other philosophical arguments for the causal theory of time have been examined in Lacey, *op. cit.*

32. H. Reichenbach, *Experience and Prediction* (Chicago, 1938), p. 282.

33. *Ibid.*, pp. 180–82.

34. In the Appendix at end of this article certain consequences of the rejection of II are outlined.

35. Even in the paradigmatic case of an observation report of a static situation, e.g., "The house is red," it is customary to say that a few acts of observation are needed to establish the statement (See Carnap's "rough explanation" in the Appendix). So that it is hard to think of an observational context in which memory is not involved in some way.

36. R. Carnap, "Testability and Meaning" in *Readings in the Philosophy of Science,* ed. by H. Feigl and M. Brodbeck (New York, 1953), p. 63.

37. R. Carnap, "The Methodological Character of Theoretical Terms", in *Minnesota Studies in the Philosophy of Science,* Vol. 1, ed. by H. Feigl and M. Scriven (Minneapolis, 1956), p. 41.

SOCIETY

13

Political Society

P. R. L. BROWN

Isidore of Seville once wrote that if anyone told you he had read all the works of Augustine, he was a liar.[1] From the time of his conversion to Catholic Christianity, in 386, until his death in 430, Augustine wrote some 117 books.[2] Of these books, not a single one is devoted to political theory. Even the title of the book, in which we study his 'political ideas' —'*City of God*', *De civitate Dei*—is misleading, Augustine treated this as a technical term, taken from the Psalms,[3] to express what we might call 'The Communion of Saints'.

The book itself took thirteen years to write, that is, from 413 to 426. Even Augustine thought it a bit too long; and we tend to dismiss it, as Henry James dismissed the Russian novels of the last century, as a 'loose, baggy monster'. Above all, *De civitate Dei* is a book of controversy. It should never be treated as though it were a static, complete photograph of Augustine's thought. It reads like a film of a professional boxing championship: it is all movement, ducking and weaving. Augustine is a really stylish professional: he rarely relies on the knockout; he is out to win the fight on points. It is a fight carried on in twenty-two books against nothing less than the whole of the pagan literary culture available to him.[4] Thus he is reluctant to follow an argument through to its conclusion in one move: instead, he twists a definition here, demolishes another there, proposes one to annoy an opponent,

Reprinted, by permission of the author and the publisher, from *Trends in Medieval Political Thought,* ed. Beryl Smalley (Oxford, Basil Blackwell, 1965). Ch. 1, Saint Augustine, pp. 1–21.

ignores it in the next few chapters, then takes it up again,
no less than seventeen books further on, that is, ten whole
years later.[5] To try to extract from this infinitely flexible book
a rigidly coherent system of political ideas is like trying to
square the circle: it is a problem that has fascinated many
great minds, and baffled all of them.

Yet this book dominated the political thought of the early
middle ages; and Augustine is one of the few thinkers of the
Early Church who can be called 'contemporary' to ourselves.
In this, he is like a planet in opposition: given the vast distance of time and culture that separates him from us, he
has come as close as possible to the preoccupation of our
own age. Why is this so? Perhaps it is because the whole
emphasis on what is fruitful in political theory has shifted.
The texts which the student usually has to study for his ex-
aminations, and especially the works of the 'classical' political
theorists, Hobbes, Locke, and Rousseau, already belong to
the past. But the attitudes of Augustine and of many medieval
theorists, though expressed in a foreign language and forming
part of a framework of ideas to which we are unaccustomed,
somehow remain relevant.

'Classical' political theory, from the seventeenth century
onwards, was based upon a Rational Myth of the State. By
myth I mean the habit of extrapolating certain features of
experience, isolating them, in abstraction or by imagining
an original state in which only those elements were operative,
and using the pellucid myth thus created as a means of explaining what should happen today. The tendency, therefore,
was to extrapolate a rational man; to imagine how reason,
and a necessity assessed by reason, would lead him to found
a state; and to derive from this 'mythical' rational act of
choice a valid, rational reason for obeying, or reforming, the
state as it now is. By contrast, medieval thought, like modern
thought, is neither concerned with a myth of the state, nor
to base the fact of political obedience upon this myth. Both
regard it as impossible to extrapolate and isolate man in such
a way. Political society exists concretely: whether because
of God, or history, does not matter; it is there. Above all, the
link between the individual and the state cannot be limited
to a rational obligation. As it exists, in fact, it is mysterious.

We are linked to political society by something that somehow escapes our immediate consciousness: by a whole tangled skein of pressures and motives, some rational, many more not so. It is the nature of this tangled skein that perplexed medieval, as it now perplexes modern, thinkers. A man just finds himself in a situation in which men, for all the world like himself, are in a position to kill him, or to order him to kill others. Should this be so? Is it worth it? Is it right? In what circumstances may it be resisted? By what means may it be controlled? Thus, Augustine will not give us a fully-worked-out 'myth.' Instead, he will do something more important when dealing with an intractable reality: he will tell us where it is worthwhile looking; and, in so doing, he will direct some very bright beams indeed into crucial areas of the human situation.

For this reason, our paper will not claim to summarize the political ideas of St. Augustine:[6] rather, it will attempt to delineate the distinctive manner in which he thought; to introduce the general reader to Augustine's assumptions, to what problems he thought were important, to the particular viewpoint from which he chose to impose meaning on the 'blooming, buzzing confusion' of human political society. Augustine's spontaneous reactions, therefore, as they appear at random in his sermons and letters, will often provide us with material that throws quite as vivid a light on his basic assumptions as do his professed formulations of political theory. Such a study must also, with regret, leave to one side the problem of the sources of Augustine's ideas, and their destiny throughout the middle ages; it can only claim to be a portrait, not a landscape.

The central problem of Augustine's thought is one which we all have to face: to what extent is it possible to treat man as having a measure of rational control over his political environment? The discovery that the extent of this control is limited has revolutionized political theory. Half the world is committed to some form of Marxist determinism: and the other half, far from rallying to Hobbes, Locke and Rousseau, studies Freud, the social psychologists, and the sociologists. On this point, Augustine is quite explicit: 'For no one is known to another so intimately as he is known to himself, and

yet no one is so well known even to himself that he can be
sure as to his own conduct on the morrow. . . .'[7] This is
the specifically Augustinian contribution to the problem of
free will and determinism: for him, man is so indeterminate,
so discontinuous, so blind in his intentions and haphazard
in his attempts to communicate, that he must be determined
by some forces outside the horizon of his immediate consciousness—for Augustine, of course, by God.

For this reason, one should begin studying Augustine's political theory in Book Ten of his *Confessions*, which he wrote
around 397 or 400, that is, a good thirteen years before he
wrote the *City of God*. Here we have Augustine's man, revealed by meditation on his own 'memory', in fact on his
whole inner world: 'Great is this power of memory . . . a
spreading, limitless room within me. Who can reach its utter-
most depths? Yet it is a faculty of my soul, and belongs to
my nature. In fact, I cannot totally grasp all that I am.'[8]
Above all, man is discontinuous: he is incapable, by himself,
of maintaining a continuous moral intention: 'As for the
allurement of sweet smells, I am not much troubled. . . . At
least, so I seem to myself; perhaps I am deceived. For that
darkness is lamentable in which the possibilities in me are
hidden from myself: so that my mind, questioning itself upon
its own powers, feels that it cannot rightly trust its own report.'[9] And, if man is discontinuous, his communication with
others remains an unfathomable mystery. It is here that we
can see most plainly how Augustine must invoke God to give
meaning to this mystery. Communication is like putting a
trunk-call through a vast telephone exchange: God is the
operator, and it is He, and He only, who puts you through
to what He thinks best: 'For you, O Lord, the most just ruler
of the universe can so act by Your secret influence upon
both those who consult and those who are consulted—neither
of them knowing what they do—that when a man consults he
hears what it behoves him to hear, given the hidden merits
of souls, from the abyss of Your just judgement. Let no man
say to You: What is this? or Why is this? He must not say it,
he must not say it. For he is a man.'[10] Now if man cannot
determine himself entirely in consciousness, in moral intention, in communication, how much less can he claim com-

plete self-determination in politics: how can he presume to
claim to impose an intention planned by his reason on that
scrambling box of human wills, presided over by God. It is
typical of Augustine that he should cite the biblical text which
is central to the Christian idea of kingship throughout the
middle ages and beyond—*cor regis in manu Dei*, 'the heart
of the king is in the hand of God'—but that he should deliberately complete the quotation: '*Just like a running stream,*
so is the heart of the King in the hand of God: He deflects
it wherever He wants.'[11]

It is from this direction that we must approach Augustine's
contribution to the Christian doctrine of passive obedience.
He is a man for whom the delusion of self-determination
appears as far more dangerous than any tyranny: 'Hands off
yourself' he says. 'Try to build up yourself, and you build
a ruin.'[12] It is important to note the way in which this obedience is seen to rest on the individual. Augustine makes frequent use of the crucial passage of the thirteenth chapter of
St. Paul's Epistle to the Romans: *Omnis anima potestatibus*
sublimioribus subdita sit, non enim est potestas nisi a Deo:
quae autem sunt a Deo ordinatae sunt . . . : 'Let every soul
be subject to the governing powers, for there is no power
but from God; these, coming from God, are subject to His
ordering.'[13] This is a free translation, in Augustine's sense.
In it, the weight shifts to the last part—*quae autem sunt a*
Deo ordinatae sunt. This does not mean that the 'powers that
be' are divinely sanctioned in a crude sense: it is more that
they are obeyed for the sort of reasons that would induce
a man to obey any aspect of God's ordering of the world. A
man is humble before his rulers because he is humble before
God. His political obedience is a symptom of his willingness
to accept all processes and forces beyond his immediate control and understanding. Thus, he can even accept the exercise
of power by wicked men. In this, Augustine's view of obedience is strictly analogous to his view of illness, another phenomenon plainly beyond man's control and constantly frustrating his intentions. What does he do, he once wrote to a
friend, when he feels depressed, and cannot preach well?
Flectamur facile ne frangamur—'Let us bend easily, lest we
be broken'. 'No man plans what he should do better than one

who is more prepared not to put into action what is checked
by the divine power, than he is avid to insist on doing what
is thought out by his human calculations. For *many are the
thoughts in the heart of man, but the counsel of the Lord
endureth for ever.*'[14]

Because this obedience is based upon a religious attitude,
it cannot be absolute. After all, the Christian Church had, in
Augustine's opinion, grown because of the *pia libertas*[15]—
the pious independence of the martyrs, who had refused to
obey orders to sacrifice. The cult of the martyrs was the only
form of popular devotion in the Early Church; and, in Africa,
the accounts of how these 'prize fighters of the Lord' had
snubbed raging governors were read from the altar on innumerable anniversaries. But we must remember that these
accounts are all courtroom scenes; and, as in a courtroom,
the individual's heroic gesture is strictly cut off from the outside world. It is framed in a straightforward protocol of correct behaviour. There is no appeal to the outside world—
to political movements, to mobs, to immediate action of any
kind. The martyrs remain, in the minds of late Roman bishops, courageous, but, like themselves, punctilious. Occasions
for disobedience do not worry Augustine: what concerns him
is the correct way to express an overriding love of God. One
incident shows this plainly. That thoroughly un-Augustinian
body of men, Augustine's own congregation at Hippo, had
lynched the commander of the local garrison. Augustine is
profoundly shocked. He agrees entirely that the man was a
very wicked man; that his flock had been victimized by him.
But the true, humble Christian, St. Laurence, on whose
martyrdom he had been preaching, had limited his disobedience to a courteous refusal to sacrifice. Such a Christian would
have nothing to do with an act of arbitrary violence, against
a man set above him by God, for good or ill.[16] Perhaps no
thinker except Confucius has placed so great an emphasis
on obedience as being produced and determined by the need
to maintain an exacting standard of personal integrity and
inner equilibrium; and on the need to avoid 'rancour', whose
ideogram, derived from a 'closed up heart', plays such a part
in the opening columns of the *Classic of Filial Piety*.[17]

An acute sense of the spiritual dangers of excessive claims

to self-determination lies at the root of Augustine's doctrine of passive obedience: and it forms a somewhat oppressive feature of his political activities as a bishop. But it is only the negative facet of a positive doctrine. It is the positive doctrine of *ordo*—of the divine order of the universe—that predominates in the *City of God*. Man cannot claim complete self-determination because of his place in the divine order of things: in that order, he is tuned to one pitch and to one pitch only.[18]

We need only look around us to be surprised by the beauty of this order: '*Omnis ordo a Deo:* All order is from God. We must admit that a weeping man is better than a rejoicing earthworm. But I could still expatiate in praise of the earthworm. Consider his shining complexion, his rotund body, the perfect way in which his top fits his middle, and his middle, his tail end; how, in his humble way, all his parts strive to make up a united whole. There is no single part of him so formed as not to harmonize with the proportions of any other.'[19] But man, unlike the earthworm, is an extremely complicated and notoriously erratic being. Above all, he is capable of a bewildering variety of loves. In his sermons, Augustine's men appear, not as 'dust and ashes', but as sturdy sinners, whose capacity to enjoy what they do strikes him as quite natural. 'The world', he says, 'is a smiling place.'[20] Little wonder, then, that it is enjoyed immoderately. The tenacity of their affections amazes him: think of highwaymen, tortured because they will not reveal the names of their accomplices. 'They could not have done this without a great capacity for love.'[21] Augustine is acutely aware of the juxtaposition of these two elements. On the one hand, there is the self-evidence of a divine order of supreme beauty, to be contemplated in nature and in the absolute certainties of the laws of thought: on the other hand, the fact that, in this beautiful universe, the human soul tends to disperse itself in a baffling multiplicity of intense but partial loves. Such human loves only hint at a lost harmony: and it is the re-establishment of this harmony, by finding man's proper place and rhythm, that constitutes, for Augustine, the sum total of Christian behaviour.

Augustine's moral thought, therefore, is devoted to the re-establishment of a lost harmony. Because of this, human action is judged in terms of its relations. A good action is one that is undertaken in the light of a relation to a wider framework: the word *referre*, 'to refer', or 'relate', is central to Augustine's discussion of human activity; and for Augustine, of course, this human activity, of whatever kind, can only reach fulfilment when it can take its place in a harmonious whole, where everything is in relation to God.[22]

It is from this direction, then, that Augustine approaches problems of political behaviour in a Christian ruler. The exercise of power, the establishment of order, the administration of punishment, and the fighting of wars have their place in the order of human loves and human needs: Augustine is the last man to ignore their existence. Along with art and learning, political activity is among the 'great things' that human beings just do keep on doing with characteristic intensity.[23] In Book Five of the *City of God*, the problem of political activity is dealt with at length in this fashion. To Augustine, his present age of Christian emperors is different from the pagan past, because the Christian emperors are aware of this true harmony, and the pagans were not. In Augustine's treatment of them, the ancient Romans emerge as undeniably heroic figures: Augustine plainly regarded them with the same sort of intense ambivalence as we now regard our own Eminent Victorians. But they were utterly unaware of the true nature of man's harmony. Instead, they set about establishing their own. It was a harmony based upon rigid self-control: they cowed their lesser vices with a stupendous pride and by a love of praise that led to exemplary public conduct.[24] They had their reward. God allowed them to conquer lesser men and to establish a remarkable city; but it was a mere *forma*—a perfect, but dead, shell.[25] God, who laughs the proud to scorn (with a rather bloody-minded humour characteristic of African authors), had used all this feverish activity to spell out words in a language which the old Romans could not have understood; they were to provide stirring examples of fortitude to inspire Christian martyrs and the dispirited members of the 'redeemed family', the Church,[26] 'while they themselves conduct their own cases down below—whether successfully or not, is not at all relevant'.[27] Thus, the pagan empires of the past grew, prospered, and fell for reasons of which the protagonists were entirely unconscious; from the point of view of God they were the incidental by-product of an experiment which, to put it mildly, has little to do with political theory.

With a Christian ruler the picture changes dramatically, to an historian, somewhat unconvincingly. Augustine's summary of the virtues of a Christian prince, and his portraits of Constantine and Theodosius, are, in themselves, some of the most shoddy passages of the *City of God*.[28] But in the framework of Augustine's ideas they are quite explicable. The Christian ruler differs from the pagan, not in the amount of power he wields, nor in the nature of the state which he maintains; he differs only in his awareness of where this power stands in God's order, to what it is related, what ends it may serve.[29] Above all, he will admit no illusion as to the ultimate source of what Augustine would have us regard as the by no means despicable 'consolations'[30] of political success. In Book Five of the *City of God*, Constantine, the first Christian prince, appears very much as he appears on his coins: decked out in the massive finery of his imperial robes, but with his eyes raised to Heaven.[31]

By now it should be plain that what we call Augustine's political thought gravitates around problems of man's behaviour in politics. The Christian subjects to whom he preached, and the Christian officials to whom he wrote advice, were not, for Augustine, 'natural political animals'; they were men faced with a whole range of aims and objects of love, of which those created by living in political society were only some among many others. They reacted to these aims not because they lived in a particular type of state, but because they were particular types of men. Put briefly, Augustine's political theory is based upon the assumption that political activity is merely symptomatic: it is merely one way in which men express orientations that lie far deeper in themselves. The Christian obeys the state because he is the sort of man who would not set himself up against the hidden ways of God, either in politics or in personal distress. The Christian ruler rules as he does because he is humble before God, the source of all benefits.

These remarks on the duties of the subject and the quality
of the Christian ruler were welcome at the time. They showed
that Christian ethics could absorb political life at a moment
when pagans had begun to fear that Christianity had proved
itself incompatible with Roman statecraft. They influenced
the middle ages profoundly, because they provided a totally
Christian criterion of political action in an unquestioningly
Christian society. They do not, however, exhaust Augustine's
thought on the state: they provide no answer to the question
of why this form of political life exists at all. Indeed, in
Augustine's opinion, one swallow did not make a summer.
When he wrote the *City of God,* he was convinced of the
collective damnation of the human race, with the exception
of a small few, predestined to be 'snatched' from that 'damned
lump.' The symptoms, therefore, which tend to predominate
in his description of human political activity can only be
thought of as symptoms of a disease. The roots of this disease
go very deep indeed: it is first diagnosed, not even in Adam,
but in the Fall of the Angels. The most blatant symptom of
this Fall is the inversion of the harmonious order established
by God.[32]

It is characteristic of Augustine that he should regard the
most basic relationship in the divine order as one of dependence,[33] and so the most basic symptom of the dislocation of
this order, as one of domination—of the need to secure the
dependence of others.[34] Augustine's own sense of personal
dependence on God is particularly acute, it provides what is,
perhaps, the sharpest note in his *Confessions:* 'Let the proud
of heart deride me, and all who have never been brought
low and broken by Thee unto salvation. . . . For, without
Thee, what am I but a guide to my own destruction? Or at
my best what am I but an infant suckled on Thy milk and
feeding upon Thee. . . . What indeed is any man, seeing
that he is a man? . . .'[35] For such a man, the only Fall
could be one that upset this relationship of omnipotence and
dependence. Thus, first the Devil, then Adam, chose to live
on their own resources; they preferred their own *fortitudo,*
their own created strength, to dependence upon the strength
of God.[36] For this reason, the deranged relationships between fallen angels and men show themselves in a constant

SUBMISSIVE UNITY VS. MASTERING DISPERSION

effort to assert their incomplete power by subjecting others
to their will.[37] This is the *libido dominandi,* the lust to dominate, that was once mentioned in passing by Sallust, as an
un-Roman vice, typical of aggressive states, such as Assyria,
Babylon, and Macedon;[38] and was fastened upon by Augustine as the universal symptom *par excellence* of all forms of
deranged relationships, among demons as among men. Seen
in this bleak light, the obvious fact of domination, as a feature
of political society, could make the world of states appear
as a vast mental hospital, ranging from the unhealthy self-
control of the early Romans to the *folie de grandeur* of a
Babylonian tyrant. This was a bitter pill, which many lay
rulers were forced to swallow in later ages. But, as always
with Augustine, the outward expression of this 'lust' in the
form of organized states is merely a symptom. The extent,
and even the admitted injustice of the state-building that Augustine observed, and commented on in blistering terms, was
of purely secondary importance. A *libido,* for Augustine, was
a desire that had somehow got out of control: the real problem, therefore, was why it had got out of control, what deeper
dislocation this lack of moderation reflected. So, to say, as
Lord Acton would, that 'all power tends to corrupt, and absolute power corrupts absolutely', would have struck Augustine as being rather like saying that a man got measles from
having spots.

We emphasize this aspect of Augustine's thought because
we tend to treat the state in isolation. But this is something
which Augustine never did, at any time. The object of his
contemplation, the aspect of human activity that he sought to
make intelligible and meaningful, is not the state: it is something far, far wider. For him, it is the *saeculum.* And we
should translate this vital word, not by 'the world', so much
as by 'existence'—the sum total of human existence as we
experience it in the present, as we know it has been since
the fall of Adam, and as we know it will continue until the
Last Judgement.[39]

For Augustine, this *saeculum* is a profoundly sinister thing.
It is a penal existence, marked by the extremes of misery
and suffering,[40] by suicide,[41] madness,[42] by 'more diseases
than any book of medicine can include,'[43] and by the in-

explicable torments of small children.[44] It is also marked by
a disquieting inanity. Like a top set off balance, it wobbles
up and down without rhyme or reason. Huge states can just
happen, 'like a passing mist';[45] a gang of slaves almost over-
turns the Roman Republic at its height;[46] elderly bishops,
vowed to poverty, are tortured by their conquerors for buried
treasure they have no part in.[47] There are no verbs of historical movement in the *City of God,* no sense of progress
to aims that may be achieved in history.[48] The Christians
are members of a far country. Even to call them 'pilgrims'
somewhat weakens the impact of Augustine's terminology:
they are *peregrini* in the full classical sense; they are regis-
tered aliens, existing, on sufferance, *in hoc maligno saeculo.*
Above all, they are in the *saeculum,* as in a vast experimental
laboratory: to bring this point home, Augustine uses the familiar image of an olive press, squeezing the olives for oil.[49]
The religious life of all members of the Christian Church is
quite inconceivable for Augustine without this constant
pressura—this constant pressing—inside the *saeculum.* It is
important to note this. A whole study of the relations between
the Catholic Church and society might be written around
changes in the meaning of this one word, *saeculum.* For
Augustine, it is all-embracing and inescapable: for other writers, it can become narrow, it can stand for a 'lay world' outside the Church, as a sort of primeval swamp of unregenerate
politics that demands reclamation by the Catholic Church.
This last view would contradict Augustine's most firmly held
assumptions on the religious life: the true Christian was here
to be pressed in the selfsame press as the bad; to suggest anything else would be like suggesting that, in our experimental
laboratory, the guinea pigs should take over control of the
tadpoles.[50]

The most obvious feature of man's life in this *saeculum*
is that it is doomed to remain incomplete.[51] No human potentiality can ever reach its fulfilment in it; no human tension
can ever be fully resolved. The fulfilment of the human personality lies beyond it; it is infinitely postponed to the end of
time, to the Last Day and the glorious resurrection. Whoever
thinks otherwise, says Augustine: 'understands neither what
he seeks, nor what he is who seeks it.'[52]

For Augustine, human perfection demands so much, just because human experience covers so very wide an area, a far wider area than in most ethical thinkers of the ancient world. It includes the physical body: this dying, unruly thing cannot be rejected, it must be brought into its proper place and so renewed.[53] It includes the whole intense world of personal relationships:[54] it can only be realized, therefore, in a life of fellowship, in a *vita socialis sanctorum*.[55] It is inconceivable that such claims can be met in this world; only a morally obtuse man, or a doctrinaire, could so limit the area of human experience as to pretend that its fulfilment was possible in this life. Thus, in opening his nineteenth book of the *City of God* by enumerating and rejecting the 288 possible ethical theories known to Marcus Varro as 'all those theories by which men have tried hard to build up happiness for themselves actually within the misery of this life,'[56] Augustine marks the end of classical thought. For an ancient Greek, ethics had consisted of telling a man, not what he ought to do, but what he could do, and, hence, what he could achieve.[57] Augustine, in the *City of God*, told him for what he must live in hope. It is a profound change. In substituting for the classical ideal of an available self-perfection, the idea of a man, placed as a stranger in an uncomprehending land, a man whose virtue lies in a tension towards something else, in hope, in faith, in an ardent yearning for a country that is always distant, but made ever-present by the quality of his love, that 'groans' for it, Augustine could well be called the first Romantic. Thus we should never isolate Augustine's reflections on the state and society. They are part of an anxious search for at least some echo, for some stunted analogy, that might lead men, in the misery of this life, to share with him some appreciation of the fulfilment of the human being that will be achieved beyond the *saeculum*. Anyone who reads the whole of Book Nineteen of the *City of God*—and it can be done with a most intelligent translation in Barrow's *Introduction to St. Augustine, The City of God*—will realize this immediately. It will be a salutary lesson in the true perspective of Augustine's thought.

Augustine attempts deliberately and persistently to see in human society the expression of the most basic and fundamental human needs. For only when he has hit upon what is truly fundamental in this life, can he feel that he has caught a partial hint of how these needs will reach fulfilment in his 'most glorious City'. For this reason, he is impatient with classical Roman theories of the state: these exclude too much of the realities of human behaviour. Augustine's political theory, therefore, is marked by the search for an all-embracing lowest common denominator of human needs that seek realization in social life. It is concerned with what is fundamental.

He finds this fundamental need in the human desire for peace. 'So great a good is peace', he writes, 'that even in earthly and mortal conditions to hear of it is pleasant, and nothing more desirable can be desired, nothing better, in fact, can be found. I should like to speak a little longer about this, and I think I shall not burden the reader: I do it because peace is the end of the city which I am describing, and also because of its inherent attractiveness, since peace is dear to all of us.'[58] This *pax,* for Augustine, means far more than tranquillity, unity, and order. These things are only preconditions for its attainment. For Augustine, the obverse of peace is tension—the unresolved tension between body and soul and man and man, of which this life is so full. Peace, therefore, is the avoidance, and in its final form, the resolution of these tensions. Such a meaning of peace is characteristic of Augustine. He was a sensitive man, with an acute sense of violence and tension. His concern with peace as something absolutely fundamental to human happiness made him welcome any feature of organized society that might at least cancel out some of those tensions of which he was so intensely conscious.[59]

For this reason, Augustine could accept the domination of man over man that had arisen from the Fall. This domination at least cancelled out certain tensions: although at a terrible cost, as anyone who has witnessed judicial torture and executions would admit if he had any sense of human dignity.[60] But at least an ordered hierarchy of established powers can canalize and hold in check the human lust for domination and vengeance. For Augustine, like Hobbes, is a man for whom a sense of violence forms the firmest boundary stone of his political thought. The North Africa of his age was a notoriously 'tough' province. Augustine narrowly escaped assassination by his ecclesiastical rivals.[61] What Augustine feels particularly acutely is the manner in which violence is a two-way affair, as demoralizing for the avenger as for the victim.[62] It is this that shocks him in the lynching of the commander of the garrison at Hippo. *Ordinata est respublica* he says: 'The state is an ordered affair'; if he was wicked, let him be executed by a properly vested, impersonal authority, and not by the most degrading of all forms of action for all who take part in it, *privata licentia*, taking the law into one's own hands by mob violence.[63] It is a deep-seated and lasting anxiety. We in England, who can only bring ourselves to kill a man by hanging him decently in impersonal surroundings, are the direct heirs of this, Augustine's antiseptic theory of the state.

The weakness of Augustine's position is, of course, that it implies a very static view of political society. It is quite content merely to have some of the more painful tension removed. It takes an ordered political life for granted. Such an order just happens among fallen men. Largely because he feels he can take it for granted, Augustine can dismiss it. For him, it is a 'peace of Babylon' that should only be 'used' by the citizens of the Heavenly City. Like the Jews, they are 'captives' in this Babylon, although they are urged, as Jeremiah urged the Jews, to *Let its peace be your peace.*[64] Even in a model prison all the inmates can do is to accept, gratefully, whatever benefits may come their way.

But this is only the most negative facet of his attitude. The structure of political society, its vested order of command and obedience, is what Augustine would take for granted: what really interested him deeply was the quality of such ordered societies, above all, the quality of the reasons for their coherence. He, therefore, rejects as too narrow the classical definition of the *respublica:* such a definition would make it appear as if political society were a mere structure designed to protect certain rights and interests. For Augustine, this misses the point. Men, because they are men, just do cohere and work out some form of normative agreement—an *ordinata concordia.* What cannot be taken for granted is the quality of this ordered life; and, for Augustine, this means the quality of the motives and aims of its individual members. 'Suppose therefore', he writes, 'that a different definition of *populus* is proposed . . . like this: A people is a gathering of a multitude of rational beings united in fellowship by sharing a common love of the same things. In that case, to see the character of each people, you have to examine what it loves . . . it is a better or a worse people as it is united in loving higher or lower things.'[65]

This definition is typical of Augustine. It is deliberately fundamental and all-embracing. Such a definition is so wide that it could include a football crowd on a Saturday afternoon; indeed, the atmosphere of the Roman circuses, with their amazing manifestations of mob psychology, is never far from Augustine's discussion of the motives of human groups.[66] It hits upon a fundamental motive: *dilectio,* which, for Augustine, stands for the orientation of the whole personality, its deepest wishes and its basic capacity to love, and so it is far from being limited to purely rational pursuit of ends. It is dynamic: it is a criterion of quality that can change from generation to generation. 'History tells us', he writes, of how the quality of the Roman Republic did change, 'what were the things the Roman people loved in its earliest days, and in its later days.'[67] In short, Augustine's definition deliberately focuses attention upon that 'middle distance' of human habits, values, and instincts, which, far more than its structure, remains the greatest mystery of political society.

Today, perhaps, we can appreciate the importance of this shift of emphasis. Previously, it could be assumed that political theory was a matter of structure, in an almost mechanical sense. In discussing this structure, we had tended to analyse it into its component parts, and, hence, to isolate the individual on the one hand, and the state, on the other, as the only two parts whose relations are relevant to thought on political society. In fact, this isolation is a deliberately self-limiting myth. So much of our modern study in sociology and social psychology has shown the degree to which political obedience is, in fact, secured, and political society coheres by the mediation of a third party, of a whole half-hidden world of irrational, semiconscious, and conscious elements that can include factors as diverse as childhood attitudes to authority,

SEARCH FOR A METHOD

crystallized around abiding inner figures, half-sensed images
of security, of greatness, of the good life, and, on the conscious plane, the acceptance of certain values.[68] These make
up an orientation analogous to Augustine's *dilectio*.

The problems which this perspective poses, therefore, cannot be ones of structure, so much as of the quality of the
needs that seek expression in obedience and coherence.
Viewed in such a way, the state becomes a symbol: it is one
of the many moulds through which men might be led to
express needs and orientations that lie deep in themselves; and
the expression of these needs through an organized community provides a far more tenacious bond of obligation than
the purely rational agreements of a social contract. For Augustine, this need to express loves through political society
can be very sinister, just as human loves can be sinister: 'the
earthly (or fallen) city worships its own strength in its rulers.'[69] But it can also provide his successors with the foundations of a theory of the Christian state. For, as it was expressed at the time, and in the middle ages, this emphasis
on quality, on the direction of a *dilectio,* as the criterion
of an organized society, appealed to very different preoccupations than that of a modern sociologist. It offered a way to
re-create the link between a given form of political structure
and what could be broadly called a civilization—a set of traditionally accepted values. Augustine is content, in Book Nineteen, to demonstrate that the quality of a state ultimately
depends upon the values of its members; but the natural inference, drawn throughout the Augustinian tradition in the
middle ages, was that the state exists precisely in order to
maintain specific values, to preserve the true ends and loves
dictated by the Christian religion.[70] Augustine did not draw
this conclusion in the *City of God,* partly, I suspect, because
he could, by that time, take such an inference for granted.

The Christian emperors of his generation had made the
possibility of an official Christian state seem quite natural
to Augustine. They were proud to be 'limbs of the Church'
as well as Roman emperors.[71] They indulged in spectacular
acts of piety, the penance of Theodosius before St. Ambrose,
told in a surprising number of Christian sources, had already
begun a popular image of Christian kingship that would have

a long future.[72] Above all, they had suppressed pagans and heretics. Augustine was deeply involved in this last change. He is the only bishop in the early Church whom we can actually see evolving, within ten years, towards an unambiguous belief that Christian emperors could protect the Church by suppressing its rivals. He is the only writer who wrote at length in defence of religious coercion; and he did this with such cogency and frequency that he has been called *le prince et patriarche des persécuteurs*.[73]

Augustine is also a crucial figure in the symbiosis between bishop and politician that is the most obvious feature of fifth-century life.[74] The provincial governors who came from Ravenna to Carthage, most of them good, Catholic Christians, would have found themselves obliged both to praise 'the solicitude of the bishops' in massive edicts against heretics, and, from 415 onwards, they were expected to read presentation copies of instalments of the *City of God*. Augustine could write to one such man: 'I tell you this: If your administration, inspired as it is by the qualities I have just mentioned, is limited to the one aim that men should suffer no inconveniences in their material life, and if you do not think that it is your business to be concerned with the end . . . to which they relate this quiet, that is, to put it bluntly, how they should worship the true God, in Whom lies the fulfilment of all quiet in this life, all such hard work on your part cannot advance you to the blessed life. . . .'[75] Here we have, already in Augustine's correspondence, the subtle and all-important difference between reading the *City of God* for oneself, and being told it by a bishop. In later centuries, in a society where the external role of the Church will become more explicit, Augustine's subtle, dynamic doctrine in which values form a field of forces, linking what men really want in their hearts with what they want from a state, will settle down as a static hierarchy of duties. In the letter of Pope Gregory the Great to Queen Brunhilde, the *dilectio* of Augustine has become, quite simply, *dilectio sacerdotum*,[76] and 'love,' 'love of the see of S. Peter.'[77]

Augustine would not have said this. We are left with a dichotomy: an acute awareness of the actual condition of man in this *saeculum;* and a yearning for a City far beyond it. Augustine never overcame this dichotomy. And for this reason, his most considered reflections on political society, as they appear in the *City of God*, are no more than the anxious questioning of a shadow; they are a hint of a full peace and of a full realization of hidden loves, in the Heavenly Jerusalem, whose name signifies *'Visio pacis.'* In a sermon which he preached at Carthage in the same year as he sat down to write the *City of God*, we can see, better than anywhere else, the force and the true direction of the momentum that led Augustine to pile up this great work for future ages to puzzle on: 'When, therefore, death shall be swallowed up in victory, these things will not be there; and there shall be peace—peace full and eternal. We shall be in a kind of City. Brethren, when I speak of that City, and especially when scandals grow great here, I just cannot bring myself to stop.'[78]

1. 'Mentitur qui te totum legisse fatetur,
   Aut quis cuncta tua lector habere potest?'
Lines placed above the cupboard containing the works of Augustine
in the library at Seville. Migne, *Patrologia Latina*, 83 col. 1109,
cf. Possidius, *Vita Augustini*, xviii, 9.

2. See H. I. Marrou, *St. Augustine and his influence through
the ages* (Men of Wisdom), New York–London, 1957, for a suc-
cinct summary of Augustine's life, thought and influence, and a
full table of the usual editions and of English translations of his
works, pp. 183–86. C. Andresen, *Bibliographia Augustiniana*,
Darmstadt, 1962, is a full bibliography, and E. Lamirande, 'Un
siècle et demi d'études sur l'ecclésiologie de S. Augustin', *Revue
des Etudes augustiniennes*, viii, 1, 1962, 1–124, covers exhaustively
all studies of Augustine's views on Church and State. Of innumerable editions and translations of the *De civitate Dei*, the best
edition is in the *Corpus Christianorum*, Series Latina, xlvii and
xlviii, 1955 (cited here by book, chapter, line and page), and the
best bilingual text, that of the *Bibliothèque augustinienne*, vols.
33–36. R. H. Barrow, *Introduction to St. Augustine, The City of
God*, London, 1950, contains a summary, commentary and thought-
ful translations of select passages, to all of which I am particularly
indebted.

3. *Gloriosa dicta sunt de te, civitas Dei*, Ps. lxxxvi, 3. Augustine
deliberately chose this title, rather than the classical word for a just
community, *res publica: De civ. Dei*, ii, 21, 116 (p. 55).

4. Augustine's qualities as a writer, and the literary taste of his
age, have been brilliantly characterized by H. I. Marrou, *St. Augustin et la fin de la culture antique*, Paris, 1938, esp. pp. 39–76
(with handsome modifications, pp. 665–72). J. C. Guy, *Unité et
structure logique de la 'Cité de Dieu'*, Paris, 1961, is an excellent
introduction to the shape of the work.

5. *De civ. Dei*, xix, 21, 2 (p. 687), of a promise made in ii,
21 (pp. 52–55), transl. Barrow, pp. 110–18.

6. This has been done, admirably, by J. N. Figgis, *The Polit-
ical Aspects of St. Augustine's 'City of God'*, London, 1921, and
N. H. Baynes, 'The Political Ideas of St. Augustine's 'De civitate
Dei', *Historical Association Pamphlet*, No. 104, London, 1936 =
Byzantine Studies and Other Essays, London, 1955, pp. 288–306.
See also H. A. Deane, *The Political and Social Ideas of St. Au-
gustine*, New York-London, 1963. Recent studies have emphasized
the manner in which Augustine's thought on this, and on every

other subject, was constantly changing: See F. E. Cranz, 'The Development of Augustine's Ideas on Society before the Donatist Controversy', *Harvard Theological Review*, xlvii, 1954, pp. 255–316, [reprinted here pp. 336–403] and B. Lohse, 'Augustins Wandlung i. seiner Beurteilung d. Staates', *Studia Patristica*, vi, *Texte u. Untersuchungen*, 81, 1962, pp. 447–75.

7. *Ep.* 130, ii, 4, transl. Dods, *The Letters of Saint Augustine*, ii, Edinburgh, 1875, p. 145.

8. *Conf.* X, viii, 15: transl. F. J. Sheed, *The Confessions of St. Augustine*, London-New York, 1944, p. 147.

9. *Conf.* X, xxxii, 48: transl. Sheed, p. 194.

10. *Conf.* VII, vi, 10: transl. Sheed, p. 109.

11. *Prov.* 21, 1, in *De gratia et libero arbitrio*, c. 42 (426/7). In this, and other passages of his late works, Augustine appears to have deliberately made a study of the political history of the Old Testament, in order to show that it was God only who controlled the outcome of the policies and conscious intentions of the protagonists: see A. M. de la Bonnardière, in *Revue des Etudes augustiniennes*, ix, 1–2, 1963, pp. 77–85.

12. *Sermon* 169, c. 11.

13. *Rom.* xiii, 1 ff. By a characteristic slip, Augustine, quoting from memory, once wrote 'Omnis *ordo* a Deo', instead of 'Omnis *potestas . . .*': *De vera religione*, xli, 77; *Retractationes*, i, 12, 8.

14. *De cathecizandis rudibus*, xiv, 20. The citation—*Prov.* xix, 2—recurs when Augustine discusses his own dealings with the Imperial authorities on behalf of a town which had been severely punished for rioting: *Ep.* 104, iii, 11.

15. *Contra litteras Petiliani*, II, xcii, 211.

16. *Sermon* 302, 10–17.

17. *Hsiao Ching*, ed. Creel, Chang and Rudolph, 'Literary Chinese by the Inductive Method', Chicago, 1948[2], p. 68.

18. For the complex idea of *ordo* as it affects Augustine's ethical thought, see two brilliant studies, J. Burnaby, *Amor Dei*, London, 1938, esp. pp. 113–37, and R. Holte, *Béatitude et Sagesse:* St. Augustin et le problème de la fin de l'homme dans la philosophie ancienne, Paris-Worcester (U.S.A.), 1962, esp. pp. 193–300. The essentially dynamic and interior nature of this idea is well stressed by G. Madec, in *Revue des Etudes augustiniennes*, ix, 1–2, 1963, p. 140: 'Or il me semble que la spéculation augustinienne ne s'appuie sur la base statique d'un univers hierarchisé que pour s'épanouir en recherche de Dieu par l'ascension spirituelle'.

19. *De vera religione*, xli, 77.

20. *Sermon* 158, 7.

21. *Sermon* 169, 14.

22. The classic summary of this idea is in *De doctrina Christiana*, I, xxii, 21; transl. D. Robertson, *Saint Augustine, On Christian Doctrine*, The Library of Liberal Arts, New York, 1958, p. 19.

23. *De quantitate animae*, xxxiii, 72.

24. *De civ. Dei*, V, 13 (pp. 146–47). Characteristically, Augustine allows a classical author, Sallust, *Catilina*, vii, 6, to provide the material for this description; see F. G. Maier, *Augustin u. das antike Rom*, Stuttgart, 1955, a sound, if studiously negative treatment.

25. *De civ. Dei*, V, 19, 50–51 (p. 155): *secundum quandam formam terrenae civitatis*. The translation of Barrow, p. 56, 'if judged by the rough standards of the earthly city', misses the sharpness of the word *forma* cf. *Sermon*, 268, 2: a baptized Christian outside the Church is like a perfectly formed, but dead, amputated limb.

26. *De civ. Dei*, V. 18 (pp. 151–54).

27. *De civ. Dei*, IV. 5, 19 sq. (p. 102).

28. esp. the sketchy and superficial panegyric of Theodosius the Great: *De civ. Dei*, V. 26 (pp. 161–62).

29. *De civ. Dei*, V, 24 (p. 160): transl. Barrow, pp. 58–60.

30. *De civ. Dei*, V, 24, 6 (p. 160).

31. *De civ. Dei*, V, 25, 1–14 (pp. 160–61). For the difficulty experienced by his first biographer, Bishop Eusebius of Caesarea, in fitting Constantine into the stereotype of a pious man, see A. D. Momigliano, 'Pagan and Christian Historiography in the Fourth Century A.D.', *The Conflict between Paganism and Christianity in the Fourth Century*, ed. Momigliano, Oxford, 1963, pp. 93–94.

32. Thus, a promise of a book dedicated to the nature of the two 'cities' caused by the Fall of the Angels is contained in Augustine's commentary on Genesis: *de Genesi ad litteram*, XI, xv, 20. For this reason, I would reject, with Guy, pp. 9–10, the widespread and facile opinion that the *City of God* was provoked entirely by the Sack of Rome, in 410: a 'City of God' might well have been written by Augustine without such an event.

33. esp. *De Genesi ad litteram*, VIII, vi, 12.

34. esp. *De Genesi ad litteram*, XI, xv, 20.

35. *Confessions*, IV, i, 1: transl. Sheed, p. 45.

36. See the massive summary in *De civ. Dei*, XII, 6, 1–14 (pp. 359–60): transl. Barrow, pp. 30–32.

37. *De civ. Dei*, XIV, 28 (pp. 451–52): transl. Barrow, pp. 36–38.

38. Sallust, *Catilina*, ii, 2, in *De civ. Dei*, III, 14, 50 (pp. 76–77).

39. This aspect of Augustine's thought is made particularly clear by H. I. Marrou, *L'Ambivalence du Temps de l'Histoire chez S. Augustin*, Montreal-Paris, 1950.

40. *De Genesi ad litteram*, XI, xxxv, 48: *omnis contritio saeculi*, above all, *De civ. Dei*, XXII, 22 (pp. 842–45).

41. *De civ. Dei*, XIX, 4, 110–31 (pp. 666–67).

42. *De civ. Dei*, XIX, 4, 43–61 (p. 665).

43. *De civ. Dei*, XXII, 22, 89–94 (p. 844).

44. See a moving passage in *Contra Julianum*, V, i, 4: 'There is no other reason why the mass of Christians detest your new-fangled ideas [the Pelagian denial of collective punishment for an Original Sin] . . . but that they think of God as both the Creator of men and as absolutely just, and then witness with their own eyes the sort of agonies suffered by their own little babies. . . .'

45. *De civ. Dei*, IV, 5, 19 (p. 102).

46. *De civ. Dei*, IV, 5 (p. 102).

47. *De civ. Dei*, I, 10, 70 ff. (p. 12).

48. Augustine's view was not shared by other Christian writers of his century: v. E. Th. Mommsen, 'St. Augustine and the Christian Idea of Progress', *Journ. of the History of Ideas*, xii, 1951, 346–74 = *Medieval and Renaissance Studies*, ed. E. F. Rice, jr., Ithaca-New York, 1959, pp. 265–88.

49. *Sermon* 19, 6.

50. This alternative is dismissed as irrelevant: *de Trinitate*, III, iv, 9: 'But since we have not reached that state [in which 'the government and direction of human affairs are in the hands of men who are devoutly and perfectly submissive to God'] (for we must be exercised in this exile after the manner of mortal men, and be forcibly instructed by scourges in meekness and patience), let us think of that higher and heavenly country itself, from which we are separated during this exile', transl. Stephen McKenna, 'Saint Augustine's *The Trinity*', Catholic University of America, Washington, D.C., 1963, p. 103.

51. See Burnaby, pp. 53–60, for a brilliant evocation of Augustine's attitude.

52. *De consensu Evangelistarum*, II, 20. The statement is all the more poignant as Augustine in his early days had once hoped for just such fulfilment; see Burnaby, pp. 35–36.

53. *Sermon* 115, 15. 'Take away death, the last enemy, and my own flesh shall be my dear friend throughout eternity'.

54. *De civ. Dei*, XIX, 8 (pp. 672–73): transl. Barrow, pp. 78–80.

55. *De civ. Dei*, XIX, 5, 5–6 (p. 669): transl. Barrow, p. 70.

56. *De civ. Dei*, XIX, 1, 4 ff. (p. 657).

57.   Max Pohlenz, *Die Stoa,* i, Göttingen, 1948, p. 111.

58.   *De civ. Dei,* xix, 11, 26 ff. (p. 675): transl. Barrow, p. 84.

59.   'His learning is too often borrowed, and his arguments are too often his own . . .', Gibbon, *Decline and Fall,* c. xxviii, note 79. The sources of Augustine's idea of peace have been exhaustively studied by M. Fuchs, *Augustin u. der antike Friedensgedanke,* Stuttgart, 1936. But the danger of treating the history of the idea *in vacuo* is that Augustine's concern, in Book XIX, is to persuade the reader of the Resurrection as a final resolution of tensions. H. J. Diesner, 'Die "Ambivalenz" des Friedensgedankens u.d. Friedenspolitik bei Augustin', *Kirche u. Staat im spätrömischen Reich',* Berlin, 1963, 46–52, in presenting this attitude as purely static and conservative, seems to have missed the subtle alchemy by which Augustine will transform a traditional *idée reçue* by incorporating it in a novel argument.

60.   *De civ. Dei,* XIX, 6 (pp. 670–71), transl. Barrow, pp. 72–76.

61.   Possidius, *Vita Augustini,* xii, 2.

62.   *Sermon,* 302, xi. 10.

63.   *Sermon,* 302, xiv, 13–17.

64.   *Jerem.* xxix, 7 in *de civ. Dei,* XIX, 26 (pp. 695–97): transl. Barrow, pp. 126–28.

65.   *De civ. Dei,* XIX, 24, 1–3 (p. 695): transl. Barrow, p. 124, *rationalis* in this case means 'possessing reason', as distinct from a herd of animals.

66.   *Confessions,* VI, viii, 13: transl. Sheed, pp. 90–91, for an acute description of this reaction of his friend, Alypius, to the gladiatoral shows—'He was no longer the man who came there, but one of the crowd to which he had come, a fit companion for those who had brought him'. In *De doctrina Christiana,* I, xxix, 30: transl. Robertson, pp. 24–25, he can explain the Christian fellowship in terms of the fan-club of an actor!

67.   *De civ. Dei,* XIX, 24, 11–16 (p. 695): transl. Barrow, p. 124.

68.   Among many abstract treatments, see esp. the precise study of I. Menzies, 'A Case Study of the Functioning of Social Systems as a Defence against Anxiety: A Report on a Study of the Nursing System of a General Hospital'. *Human Relations,* xiii, 1960, pp. 95–121.

69.   *De civ. Dei,* XIV, 28, 7–12 (p. 451): transl. Barrow, p. 36.

70.   esp. H. X. Arquillière, *L'Augustinisime politique,* Paris, 1955.[2]

71.   *De civ. Dei,* V, 26, 47 (p. 162).

72.   *De civ. Dei,* V, 26, 50 ff. (p. 162).

73. This evolution took place less abruptly and with far less hesitation than many commentators would admit. See R. Joly, 'S. Augustin et l'intolérance religieuse', *Revue belge de philologie et d'histoire*, xxxiii, 1, 1955, 263–94, and P. R. L. Brown, 'The Attitude of St. Augustine to Religious Coercion', *Journal of Roman Studies*, 54 (1964), pp. 107–16.

74. P. R. L. Brown, 'Religious Coercion in the Later Roman Empire: the case of North Africa', *History*, xlvii, 1963, pp. 283–305.

75. *Ep.* 155, 10.

76. Greg., *Reg.* VIII, 4.

77. Greg., *Reg.* VI, 5. See Arquillière, pp. 131–41.

78. *Ennaratio in Ps.* lxxxiv, c. 10.

14

The Development of Augustine's Ideas on Society before the Donatist Controversy

F. EDWARD CRANZ

In the Preface to the Retractationes, Augustine suggests: "Perhaps whoever will read my works in the order in which they were written will discover how I made progress while writing them."[1] The present essay is an attempt to carry out this suggestion of Augustine, with particular attention to his ideas on society, from the earliest Dialogues of 386 up to the time, shortly after A.D. 400, when the Donatist controversy introduces a new period in Augustine's thought.[2]

The material has been grouped into four sections: I. The early ideas as stated in the language of Greco-Roman philosophy. II. The early ideas as stated in biblical and ecclesiastical language. III. The development of Augustine's ideas from 393 through the Ad Simplicianum of 396. IV. The elaboration of the new position of the Ad Simplicianum in the writings from 396 through 400.

Sections I and II overlap chronologically, but they have been separated since exposition is easier when texts using the same terminology are grouped together, e.g. those which speak of the intelligible world as against those which speak of the heavenly Jerusalem. It is however always assumed that Augustine's thought for any given period should be studied as a coherent unity. His statements in the language of Plato must therefore ultimately receive their meaning in the con-

Reprinted, by permission of the author and the publisher, from *Harvard Theological Review* 47 (1954), pp. 255–316. Copyright 1954 by the President and Fellows of Harvard College.

text of his contemporary statements in the language of the Bible and vice versa.

The main works to be considered, with their probable dates,[3] are:

1. Contra Academicos (c. Acad.). 386. Corpus Scriptorum Ecclesiasticorum Latinorum (= CSEL) LXIII, 3–81.
2. De beata vita (b. vit.). 386. CSEL LXIII, 89–116.
3. De ordine (ord.). 386. CSEL LXIII, 121–85.
4. Soliloquia (sol.). 386. J.-P. Migne, Patrologiae Cursus Completus, Series Latina (= PL) XXXII, 869–904.
5. De moribus ecclesiae catholicae et de moribus Manichaeorum (mor. eccl. cath.). 387–88, probably revised later. PL XXXII, 1309–78.
6. De animae quantitate (anim. quant.). 388. PL XXXII, 1035–80.
7. De libero arbitrio (lib. arb.). 388–c.95.[4] PL XXXII, 1221–1310.
8. De Genesi contra Manichaeos (Gen. c. Man.). 389. PL XXXIV, 173–220.
9. De musica (mus.). 387–89, Book VI revised later. PL XXXII, 1081–1194.
10. De magistro (mag.). 389. PL XXXII, 1193–1220.
11. De vera religione (ver. relig.). 389–90. PL XXXIV, 121–72.
12. De sermone Domini in monte (serm. in mon.). 393–94. PL XXXIV, 1229–1308.
13. Expositio quarundam propositionum ex Epistola Apostoli ad Romanos (exp. prop. Roman.). 394. PL XXXV, 2063–88.
14. Expositio Epistolae ad Galatas (exp. Galat.). 394. PL XXXV, 2105–48.
15. De diversis quaestionibus LXXXIII (div. quaest. 83). c. 389–c95. PL XL, 11–100.
16. Ad Simplicianum (Simplic.). 396. PL XL, 101–48.
17. De doctrina Christiana (doctr. Christ.). I–III, 25, §35. 396–97. PL XXXIV, 15–122.
18. Confessiones (conf.). 396–97. ed. Skutella (Leipzig, 1934).
19. Contra Faustum Manichaeum (c. Faust.). c. 400. CSEL XXV, 1 pp. 251–797.
20. De catechizandis rudibus (catech. rud.) c. 400. PL XL, 309–48.
21. De consensu evangelistarum (cons. evang.). c. 400. CSEL XLIII.
22. Retractationes (retract.). 426–27. CSEL XXXVI.

Some additional material for the period A.D. 386–400 is found in the following collections:

1. Sermones (serm.). PL XXXVIII–XXXIX; ed. G. Morin, Miscellanea Agostiniana (Rome 1930–31), Vol. I. For the dating, see A. Kunzelmann, "Die Chronologie der Sermones des hl. Augustinus" *ibid.,* Vol. II, 417–520.

2. Epistulae (epist.). CSEL XXXIV; XLIV; LVII. For the dating see CSEL LVIII, 12–63.

3. Enarrationes in Psalmos (en. in psalm.). PL XXXVI–XXXVII. For the dating, see H. Rondet, Recherches de Science religieuse XXXVII (1950) 628–33, with the references to the articles of S. Zarb.

I.   THE EARLY IDEAS AS STATED IN THE LANGUAGE OF GRECO-
     ROMAN PHILOSOPHY.

The main theme of Augustine's first Dialogues is the quest for wisdom. As a Christian, he is sure that he will never depart from the authority of Christ; as a Platonist he is confident that reason will find in Platonism what agrees with Christianity.[5] But while Augustine thus recognizes two ways to wisdom, through authority and through reason, it is the method of reason which dominates the early writings.[6] In working out the method of reason Augustine centers his attention on the individual Christian thinker, and society plays only a subordinate role. There are nevertheless several points at which Augustine works out ideas on society which are significant for his later development.

In a number of passages, Augustine uses the metaphor of the fatherland (patria) to describe the blessed life; this is the earliest form of his continuing conviction that man's destination is, in one form or another, a heavenly society. He first mentions the fatherland in the Contra Academicos, and his argument illustrates the typical synthesis of Christianity and Platonism. The one discipline of most true philosophy, maintains Augustine, has finally appeared. "For it is not the philosophy of this world, which our sacred rites most properly detest, but of that other intelligible world. And yet the most subtle reason would never have called souls back to the intelligible world, souls blinded by the manifold darkness of error and made forgetful by the deepest stains of the body, unless the highest God, with a kind of clemency for the many (populari quadam clementia) had lowered the authority of the divine intellect as far as the human body itself. Thus souls which had been aroused, not only by its precepts but also by its acts, might even without argument and disputation return to themselves and regain (resipiscere) the fatherland."[7] In several other passages Augustine explains that the fatherland, or proper region of the soul, is God.[8]

In the De beata vita, Augustine develops the metaphor of the fatherland at greater length and combines it with the important concept of pilgrimage. All souls begin their lives as pilgrims; they are far from the fatherland and tossed about on the stormy sea of the world. The fortunate ones are able to steer themselves to the harbour of philosophy, or they are blown to it by the winds of fortune. From here, if they can avoid the dangerous mountain of vainglory, they may reach the quiet and tranquillity of the fatherland.[9]

While the heavenly society of the fatherland receives only brief treatment in the early works, Augustine has a good deal to say about human society in this world. Admittedly, human society is not of great value in itself, and the wise man should beware of too great attachment to it. Nevertheless a proper attitude toward society is a stage on the way to wisdom, and even the philosopher must know how to live with his fellow men.

In his theoretical analysis of human society, Augustine makes use of two somewhat different approaches. In the first he studies society under the aspect of image, and he argues that human society as part of the sensible world should be a copy or image of the intelligible world which is its exemplar. In the second he studies society under the aspect of order, and he argues that human society, as part of God's universal order, should itself be ordered through the supremacy of things intelligible and the subordination of things sensible. Roughly speaking, the image argument is more important in the earliest period, and the order argument later gradually displaces it; however, no rigorous separation of the two is possible.

In the Dialogues of 386 Augustine on several occasions discusses human society as the image of a higher, intelligible reality. In the Contra Academicos, for example, he summarizes Plato's doctrine of the two worlds. The intelligible world is true; the sensible world is only an image of the true world and only like-the-true (veri similem). "Whatever is done in this world through the so-called civil virtues (which virtues are only like-the-true virtues, while the true virtues are unknown to all but the few who are wise) cannot be called anything more than like-the-true."[10] Somewhat later Augustine says of moral judgments, "He rightly tests the image who contemplates the exemplar."[11]

In other Dialogues Augustine describes law in terms comparable to those used of the civil virtues. He prays to God "from whose kingdom law is copied down (describitur) even into these kingdoms," and he goes on to explain that God's kingdom is "the whole world which sense does not know."[12] He maintains that the law of God "which always remains fixed and unshaken in Him (apud eum) is as it were transcribed into wise souls."[13]

The order argument receives its fullest statement, as the title would suggest, in the De ordine.[14] There is a universal order, and everything which God made is moved in accord with it. In this all-inclusive order even evils are seen to be necessary. Human society is of course part of the order, and as evils are necessary in the universe, so executioners and prostitutes are necessary and proper in a well-ordered city.[15]

The universal order is not only all-embracing; it is also everywhere accessible to the mind of man. Augustine and his friends are led to meditate on a cockfight which had distracted them from their studies. "Where is there not law? Where is not the power of command owed to the better? Where is there not the shadow of constancy? Where not the imitation of that most true beauty? Where is there not mode?"[16]

Under these conditions the duty of man, and of the wise man in particular, is to comprehend the order in all things and to rise to the contemplation of its highest mode. Here is the vantage point of wisdom, and from here, even while involved in human affairs, the wise man can so look down upon them and so understand them that their apparent irregularity leaves him unmoved.[17]

Against this background of an individualist and intellectualist transcending of society and the world, Augustine includes in the De ordine a brief and traditional summary of social ethics. The wise man should, for example, regard as his own family all those over whom he has power. He should so serve that men shame to rule him and so rule that men delight to serve him. In all human contacts, let him hold to the familiar proverb: Don't do to others what you don't wish done to you. He ought not to administer the republic until he is perfect, and he should hasten to become perfect.[18]

Thus as early as the Cassiciacum Dialogues of 386, Augustine introduces a few significant ideas on society. However, he does little to develop them, and his main interests evidently lie elsewhere. Wisdom is found in the contemplation of the exemplar, not in the study of the image. The wise man delights in the comprehension of the universal order; he is not primarily concerned with its parts.

Augustine's position does not change radically during the years immediately following. Nevertheless the problems of ethics and of society become more important, and the early ideas on society are worked out in greater detail. Three arguments from the period 387–90 may be singled out for special analysis: the discussion of law in Book I of the De libero arbitrio, and the sections on society in the De musica and in the De vera religione.

Augustine's aim in Book I of the De libero arbitrio is to discover the nature of sin and wrongdoing. His conclusion is that sin is a violation of God's order in which things eternal should be superior and things temporal subordinate. "All sins are contained in this one category, that someone turns away from the things which are divine and truly permanent and turns toward the things which are mutable and uncertain. For while these things are rightly ordered in their own place and exhibit a certain beauty of their own, it is the action of a perverse and disordered soul to follow, and thus be subject to, the things which, by divine order and right (ius), it should command and lead at will."[19]

In the course of the argument Augustine introduces an

important discussion of law. The eternal law, which is God's highest reason, reigns over all things, and by this law it is just that all things should be most ordered. The eternal law is impressed on man's mind, and it commands that he should turn his love from things temporal to things eternal and that within man reason (or mind or spirit) should be supreme over the body and over the irrational parts of the soul.[20]

In addition there is a temporal law which is derived from the eternal law and dependent on it.[21] In human society the temporal law aims at peace, and it represses, as far as possible, the crimes which threaten peace. "What do you think the temporal law orders, unless that the things which may temporarily be called ours . . . should be possessed in accord with that right (eo jure) by which human peace and society are preserved, as much as they can be preserved in such things?"[22] Augustine lists, as subject to the temporal law, the body and its goods, liberty from human domination, the family, the city, and lastly wealth. These things, and only these, are controlled by the temporal law "by which earthly peoples and cities are governed."[23]

As these are two classes (genera) of things, temporal and eternal, and two corresponding laws, so there are two classes of men. The first love temporal things, and the temporal law is imposed on them; the second love things eternal, and they act of themselves under the eternal law.[24] By the definition of the De libero arbitrio, the first are the sinners, the second the just.

This is the first appearance of a motif which will become steadily more important in Augustine's thinking, that human society is in some way divided into two classes or two groups or two cities. It is therefore particularly important to notice the form of the division as we find it in the De libero arbitrio. In the first place, while the two classes are the sinners and the just, the argument of the De libero arbitrio is that it rests with the free choice of the individual to which group he shall belong. There is a right order; man chooses or he does not choose to accept it freely; as a result of the one choice or the other, there are constituted two classes of men.[25] In the second place, at this period Augustine feels that the whole universe, both in its obvious order and in its apparent disorder, calls upon man to make the right choice and proves its rightness. His mood can be illustrated from Book II of the De libero arbitrio where he writes that wisdom shows herself joyously in the way and meets you in all providence. "Wherever you may turn yourself, she speaks to you through the traces she has impressed on her works, and when you fall into outer things, by the very forms of the outer things, she calls you back within."[26]

The second work to be noticed here, the De musica, is one of a projected series of books on the liberal arts. The aim of the series is to demonstrate how man's reason can move "as it were by sure steps from things corporeal to things incorporeal."[27] The special aim of the De musica (in particular of Book VI) is to do this through the "numbers" of rhythm and to show "how from corporeal and spiritual, but mutable, numbers one reaches the immutable numbers which exist in immutable truth itself, and so the invisible things of God are clearly seen as they are understood through the things which are made (Romans I, 20)."[28]

The sight of the invisible things of God involves the comprehension of His universal order, and De musica VI is in large part a discussion of this order. Here for the first time Augustine makes extensive use of the simple schematic description which will be basic in his later writings: order is the proper hierarchy of God, souls, and bodies. "For the soul should be ruled by what is above it; the soul should rule what is below it. Above it is only God; below it is only body. . . ."[29] In this context Augustine offers a systematic analysis of the way in which sin produces disorder in society and of the way in which virtue preserves and restores order.

Sin in the De musica, as in the earlier works, is primarily man's choice of what is temporal as against what is eternal. More specifically, sin results from the soul's preoccupation with actions which involve the body. In this way the soul falls into pride, through which vice the soul would rather imitate God than serve Him.[30] Or it may be guilty of apostasy as it pursues some private work to the neglect of universal law.[31]

Within human society sin perverts the order of rule and subjection. By God's universal law, the rational soul receives command only over the souls of beasts. Through pride it wrongly desires to rule and dominate other rational souls, who should rightly be its fellows and consorts under the same law. But sinful souls who refuse obedience to God and who try to impose obedience on their fellows are properly punished when they themselves have difficulty in commanding their own passions and their own bodies.[32]

In contrast, virtue, the proper order of the soul, is prerequisite to the proper order of society. Justice, for example, is the order "by which the soul serves none but God, by which it wishes to be equal to none but the purest souls and to dominate none but bestial and corporeal natures."[33] Or, in terms of love: "The soul holds its order when with its whole self it loves what is above it, that is God, and when it loves its fellow-souls as itself."[34]

In society, the ordered soul will act upon human bodies for the sake of their welfare (salus), not for its own pleasure. It will act upon other souls for their utility, not for its own proud excellence.[35] Thus man enters into proper relationship with his neighbor, the neighbor whom he should love as himself because of the natural bond of a common law (juris).[36] And if Augustine in the De musica by no means regards life in society as an end in itself, nevertheless this ordered love of neighbor is a most certain step on the way to the goal "that we may cling to God, that we may not merely be held by His ordering (ordinatione) but also ourselves hold our own order in certainty and steadfastness."[37]

In the second part of the De vera religione,[38] the part based on the method of reason, Augustine reasserts the main position of the De musica and develops some points more fully. The general aim is the same: "Let us see how far reason can make progress from things visible to things invisible, ascend from what is temporal to what is eternal."[39] And Augustine concludes the long argument with the vision of that form (speciem) "in comparison with which are ugly even those things which by its bounty are fair. 'For the invisible things of God are clearly seen as they are understood from the creation through the things that are made, both His sempiternal power and His divinity.' (Romans I, 20). This is the return from things temporal to things eternal, and the reformation from the life of the old man into the new man."[40]

From the standpoint of this comprehensive intellectual optimism, Augustine develops at some length the thesis that man is called back to the blessed life even through his vices. "What remains then, whence the soul cannot recall that first beauty which it deserted, when it can do so even through its own vices?"[41] Augustine groups the vices, as often in his later writings, under the three main heads of lust (libido), pride, and curiosity (curiositas).[42]

The discussion of pride is essentially an analysis of government and society: how pride corrupts them and how even pride points to the source of their reformation. Man in his desire for nobility and excellence wishes to be the One to whom all things are subject, and this is a perverse imitation of God. But if he would rightly imitate God as God's subject, then all other things would be subject to man.[43] Man wishes to be unconquered, and properly, for this belongs to the soul after God in whose image the soul was made. But he who refuses to obey God will be conquered not only by other men but even by his own vices.[44] If he would be truly unconquered, let him love only that which cannot be taken away from him; he does this when he loves God with all his soul and his neighbor as himself. In a somewhat extreme argument, Augustine maintains that the proper love of neighbor is a love of human nature without fleshly limitation (sine carnali conditione) and that such human nature cannot be taken away from its lover.[45]

Thus the wise man is properly related to all his fellows. He uses a friend for the repaying of favors, an enemy for the exercise of patience, whomever he can as a recipient of good deeds, and all as objects of good will. And while he does not love temporal things, he uses them rightly and gives temporal help to those with whom he is associated.[46] Augustine concludes the section with a restatement of his thesis. "Consequently, if pride itself is a shadow of true liberty and of the true kingdom, then divine providence reminds us even through our pride what we betoken (significemus) when we are vicious and whither we ought to return when we are corrected."[47]

We have now noticed the main early ideas of Augustine on society, insofar as they appear in the language of Greco-Roman philosophy. These ideas on society receive only limited emphasis in the early writings, and Augustine's orientation remains individualist and intellectualist.

At the center of his thought, Augustine places the concept of a universe which is ordered through the hierarchies of sensible and intelligible, of bodies, souls, and God. Man comprehends the universe only as he sees it in its eternal and intelligible aspects, but the universe leads him to this comprehension through all its temporal and sensible aspects. Freely to accept the order of the universe is justice; to reject it is sin. But not even sin can escape the order, and even sin leads man back to the order.

Human society, as part of the universe, must be ordered in terms of the same hierarchies of sensible and intelligible, of bodies, souls, and God. As sin cannot destroy or make incomprehensible the universal order, so the sins of society such as pride are reintegrated into the universe by their punishment and they image the proper order even in their sin.

As human society is sensible and temporal, the wise man must detach himself from it even while he aids in its ordering. From the standpoint of the universal order, society must always appear on the subordinate level of means and needs. The wise man shows detachment even in his love of neighbor, for he loves not the particular individual but that part of man which should be capable of the same detachment from what is temporal and sensible.

All in all, this remains a Greco-Roman universe and a Greco-Roman solution. Man has within himself and in his power all that is necessary for the right decisions and the right choices. He rises by reason through ordered stages to his goal. And his goal is integration at the level of comprehension with a universe which is in all its essential aspects comprehensible.

II. THE EARLY IDEAS AS STATED IN BIBLICAL AND ECCLESIASTICAL LANGUAGE.

In the writings so far noticed, Augustine makes primary use of the language of Greco-Roman philosophy. In other contemporary works he makes primary use of the language of the Bible and of the church. The change in language need not in itself involve changes in Augustine's ideas. As we have seen in the Contra Academicos, he was sure that what he found in Platonism would not be out of harmony with the Christian mysteries.[48]

Nevertheless the form of the biblical and ecclesiastical statement is very different. Accordingly our first task is to study certain new concepts and to relate them to the ideas already discussed.

How does Augustine in his earliest period understand such central Christian concepts as sin, Christ, and the ecclesia? His general method is to explain them as different ways of stating the same world-view which we have already seen expressed in the language of Greco-Roman philosophy. Sin, as noted above, is the free turning away from things which are divine and truly permanent and the turning toward things which are mutable and uncertain.[49] Christ appears primarily as teacher and example; both by his precepts and his acts, he calls men back from sin and demonstrates to them the way to the intelligible world.[50] The ecclesia, in turn, is essentially a place of instruction where men are taught the way to blessedness, whether on the higher level of reason or on the popular level of authority.[51] In Augustine's Platonism, the basic ethical distinction is between things sensible and things intelligible; he now uses this to explain the biblical distinction between the flesh and the spirit.[52]

Augustine admits that there are some Christian dogmas, such as original sin and the resurrection of the flesh, which he accepts willingly but without full understanding.[53] Perhaps in such cases there are potential contradictions between his Platonism and his Christianity. But in terms of Augustine's own awareness, insofar as this is accessible to us in his writ-

ings, there appear to be no serious tensions within his general
unity of true religion and true philosophy.

A similar harmony prevails in the more limited area of his
ideas on society. As man's destination is the fatherland and
the intelligible world, so it is the heavenly Jerusalem and the
house of God. And when Augustine explains the biblical
phrases he frequently uses the terms and the ideas of his
philosophic works. In Sermo CCXVI (A.D. 391), for example,
Augustine urges his audience to be weary of their Babylonian captivity. "Behold, Jerusalem, the heavenly mother,
meets you in the ways and joyously summons you. . . ."[54]
The passage is in part a reminiscence of Wisdom VI, 7: Wisdom shows herself joyously to them in the way, and she
meets them in all providence. Augustine uses the same text
three times in a philosophic context in the roughly contemporary De libero arbitrio II, and in each case he keeps wisdom
as the subject.[55] We may conjecture that in the sermon he
could substitute Jerusalem as the subject because in his thinking it makes no essential difference whether one refers to
man's destination as the harbour of wisdom or as God's heavenly city. Likewise, in the same sermon, Augustine starts from
the biblical "house of God" and goes on to speak, in the
manner of his philosophic works, of the "blessedness of this
region and habitation."[56]

In Sermo CCLIX (A.D. 393), the heavenly Jerusalem appears in the context of a brief universal history. Six ages of
human history are to be followed by a chiliastic seventh age;
the saints and the just men of God will enjoy their sabbath on
earth. The eighth age will be one of eternal rest, and Augustine interprets this as a cyclic return to the starting point.
"Then, as it were, one returns to the beginning (ad caput).
Just as when these seven days have been accomplished, the
eighth is the same as the first, so when the seven ages of
the transient world have been finished and accomplished, we
shall return to that immortality and blessedness from which
man fell."[57] Meanwhile we labour in the night and wander
in the desert until we come to the celestial Jerusalem, like
the land of promise flowing with milk and honey. Here again
Augustine understands the Bible in such a way that it is in
harmony with his Platonist statement. The heavenly Jerusa-

lem is like the timeless intelligible world which is the fatherland of the soul, and the goal is restoration to the eternity
which man had once participated.

There are a few other scattered references to the heavenly
Jerusalem and the city of God in the writings from 388 to
about 393.[58] However the concept receives little emphasis,
and it shows no tendency to expand or develop.[59]

In contrast, Augustine in his biblical and ecclesiastical
statement has a good deal to say about human society in
the world. His most significant ideas appear in areas where
the Bible forces him to consider new problems. The Platonist
statement can, for example, largely ignore history, since its
interest centers on the individual's typical and timeless ascent from the sensible to the intelligible world. A biblical
statement, however, must justify the ways of God in time
toward the whole human race, and it must make understandable the history of the Old and the New Testaments.

Here again, however, Augustine's solution reconciles Plato
and the Bible, for his method is to identify the stages of God's
providence in history with the stages of the Platonist ascent.
He mentions, for example, the distinction between the Jews
as carnal and the Christians as spiritual, and he maintains
that the same distinction can be seen within each individual.
"And thus it is most fitting (pulcherrimum) that what happens in one rightly trained man by the order of nature and
by instruction, the same happens and is arranged in the whole
human race by divine providence."[60] Likewise when Augustine would explain the biblical contrasts between the carnal
man and the spiritual man, the earthly and the heavenly
man, or the old and the new man, he starts from the Platonically understood contrast between the outer man and the inner man.[61] He writes in the De diversis quaestionibus
LXXXIII, for example, of the differences "between the two
men, the old and the new, the outer and the inner, the
earthly and the heavenly, that is between him who pursues
carnal earthly goods and him who follows after eternal
spiritual goods."[62]

In the context of these identifications, Augustine rethinks
a traditional Christian theory of the six ages of history.[63]
In the tradition, there are five ages of Old Testament history,

each containing either ten or fourteen generations; the sixth and last age of history begins with the coming of Christ. Further each age corresponds not only to one of the days of creation but also to one of the stages in the life of an individual. Augustine first develops such a scheme of history in the De Genesi contra Manichaeos,[64] and he later works it out more carefully, though without reference to the days of creation, in the De vera religione.

Augustine in the De vera religione first lists the stages in the physical life of an individual from infancy to old age. "This is the life of man living from the body and bound up with the desires of things temporal. He is called the old man, the outer man, and the earthly man, even though he may obtain what the many (vulgus) call happiness in a well-established earthly city . . . and indeed even he has his certain mode of beauty."[65] Some people never lead any life but this of the old man. "Some of necessity begin life with him, but they are reborn within. . . . Such a one is said to be the new man, the inner man, and the heavenly man."[66]

Like the old man, the new man has his stages, and Augustine describes them largely in the language of philosophy. The new man begins with the examples of useful history, but already in the second stage he "trusts himself to the steps of reason toward the highest immutable law."[67] In the third and fourth stages he learns to control his carnal appetites and to live unshaken by the storms of the world. The fifth age is one of perfect peace "in the riches and abundance of the immutable kingdom of the highest ineffable wisdom." In the sixth age the new man moves in all his aspects toward eternal life; he approaches the perfect form, made in the image and likeness of God, and he reaches the point of total forgetfulness of the temporal life. Finally, the seventh age is eternal quiet and perpetual blessedness. "As the end of the old man is death, so the end of the new man is eternal life. For the former is the man of sin, the latter the man of justice."[68]

The two men, the old and the new, have their analogies in the human race, "whose life is as it were the life of one man from Adam to the end of the world."[69] Mankind is thus divided into two classes (genera). One is the throng of the impious, who bear the image of the earthly man from the

beginning to the end. The other is the lineage of the people
of God, and this second class is further divided into an earlier
and a later stage. From the time of Adam to John the Baptist,
it lives the life of the earthly man with a kind of servile justice, "and its history is called the Old Testament, as promising
an earthly kingdom, and the whole history is nothing but the
image of the new people and of the New Testament promising the heavenly kingdom."[70] The later stage, the life of the
new people, begins with the coming of the Lord, but it remains a temporal life to the last judgment, when the pious
people will completely transform its relics of the old man into
the new.

Augustine in the De vera religione thus combines a Jewish-
Christian theory of the successive stages in God's providential
dealing with mankind and a Greco-Roman theory of the successive stages in man's ascent from the sensible to the intelligible world. The result is an outline of history in terms of
universal progress, for history is God's gradual education of
the whole human race.

The ideas on society which appear in this history do not
differ fundamentally from those of the De libero arbitrio,
though the typical contrast between the lovers of the temporal
and the lovers of the eternal has become the historical contrast between the Jews and the Christians.[71] In the De libero
arbitrio temporal law, imposed on lovers of the temporal,
rules earthly cities and peoples; in the De vera religione the
Jews, under the constraint of a servile justice, are an earthly
people and possess an earthly kingdom. As in Augustine's
Platonism, things sensible are images of things intelligible, so
Jewish history is an image of the Christian people and of
their heavenly kingdom.

Augustine harmonizes his Christianity and his Platonism
not only in his theory of history but also in his exegesis of
biblical passages on the proper order within man and society.
In the De sermone Domini in monte, for example, he explains
the beatitude: Blessed are the peace-makers (Matthew V, 9).
The peace-makers, declares Augustine, are those who in themselves subordinate all the movements of their soul to reason,
that is, to mind and spirit. They thus "become the kingdom of
God in which all things are so ordered that what is outstand-

ing and preeminent in man commands the parts which he has in common with the beasts and that these parts obey without resistance. In turn, what is preeminent in man, that is, mind and spirit, is subject to what is higher (potiori), which is truth itself, the only-begotten Son of God."[72] From this most peaceful and most ordered kingdom the devil has been cast out, who rules only those who are perverse and disordered.

Augustine in his biblical and ecclesiastical statement continues to discuss society primarily in terms of utility and welfare (salus).[73] The love of neighbor is still highly detached. The Christian loves his enemies, but even in his family he "hates the things which are transient in those who, he hopes, will come with him to the things which remain always."[74] The Christians are subject to all powers which are given men for the rule of the commonwealth; they give to Caesar what is Caesar's and to God what is God's.[75]

To a first approximation then we may say that Augustine's ideas on society, like his other ideas, are until about A.D. 393 characterized by a harmonious synthesis of his Christianity and of his Platonism. We may leave open the question to what extent the synthesis is Augustine's own and to what extent he received it from earlier Christian thinkers. If we ask which phase of his thought, Platonist or Christian, is the more important, the general answer is that his Platonism is in this period the major partner. If we compare Augustine's writings first with a typical Neoplatonist work and second with the New Testament, the form of his thought appears closer to the Neoplatonist work. And within his own writings it is generally true that philosophical concepts, such as order, give new meaning to biblical texts, while the biblical texts, by and large, simply reenforce meanings, such as order, which are already present.

But in the long run Augustine's synthesis is precarious. He has tried to harmonize two bodies of thought which are essentially disparate. He has tried to express his own Christian experience in a language which is basically alien to it. Already in 393 there are some slight signs of emerging tensions; in the next few years fundamental changes will occur with extraordinary rapidity.

III. THE DEVELOPMENT OF AUGUSTINE'S IDEAS FROM 393
     THROUGH THE AD SIMPLICIANUM OF 396.

To a first approximation, the broad outline of Augustine's
thought remains unchanged from 386 to about 393. He is
trying, particularly in the first years, to achieve a philosophic
statement of his position. He is also trying, particularly toward the end of the period, to achieve a biblical and ecclesiastical statement of his position. The two statements are felt
to be in harmony, and it does not appear that Augustine
markedly modifies either after his first presentation of it.

In the years following 393, however, Augustine moves
rapidly to the new position of the Ad Simplicianum. The
background of the change is seen in the gradual abandonment or weakening of the general assumptions of the old
solution. Meanwhile the actual working out of a new solution
takes place in terms of certain specific problems which dominate Augustine's thinking at this time.

On the general level, Augustine after 393 slowly abandons
his original high estimate of man's intellectual and moral
capabilities. Augustine's intellectual goal is still the comprehension of the universe and the sight of the invisible things of
God, but he is increasingly doubtful whether man can ever
achieve the goal except through God's grace and whether he
can ever achieve it at all in this life.[76] Similarly in his analysis
of morality, Augustine places more and more emphasis on
the continuing consequences of sin and on the absolute need
for grace.[77]

At the same time, Christ and the ecclesia begin to play a
larger role in Augustine's thought, and their functions are
reinterpreted. Christ is not only the teacher and an example
of the way to salvation; He is also the God through whose
death man is saved.[78] The ecclesia is not only the school of
God; it is also the place of the sacraments of grace.[79]

The special problems which concern Augustine during the
crucial years 394–96 center about his search for a new statement of God's public providence as seen in the history of
mankind. His solutions take the form of biblical exegesis,

particularly of St. Paul (see nos. 13, 14, 15 in part, and 16 of the list above).

The selection of the problems and the preoccupation with St. Paul are both understandable in terms of the orientation of Augustine's thought at this time. In the years from about 390 through 393 Augustine had worked mainly at the biblical and ecclesiastical statement of his position. In this statement a theory of history as universal progress occupies a central place; it not only serves as a main organizing principle but it also makes possible the harmony between Augustine's interpretation of the Bible and his philosophy. Now, however, Augustine's new understanding of sin and grace threatens to undermine this theory of history, and it is clearly essential for him to reconsider the whole problem. In such a situation Augustine naturally seeks help in Paul. On the general level Paul offers, or Augustine can read into Paul, a solution which is a possible end-point of tendencies already present in Augustine's thinking: a total denial of man's ability to do anything toward salvation on his own. On the particular level, Paul's analysis of the relation between the Jewish Law and Christianity is clearly relevant to Augustine's search for a more adequate explanation of God's providence in history.

Augustine's development after 393 starts from the theory of history which he had worked out earlier in the De Genesi contra Manichaeos and in the De vera religione. Augustine had here taken a traditional scheme of six ages and had combined it with a doctrine of gradual progress through God's education of the whole human race. The older theory reappears essentially unchanged in some of the earlier writings of the period 393–96, though it is nowhere stated at length.[80] Soon however the context of gradual progress is dropped, and while Augustine continues to make use of the six ages, the Old Testament periods serve merely as convenient chronological divisions.[81] We may conjecture that Augustine begins to be dissatisfied with the theory of the De vera religione because it does not sufficiently emphasize grace and because the assumption of gradual and regular progress seems inconsistent with his increasingly absolute contrast between sin and salvation.

In the Expositio quarundam propositionum ex Epistola

Apostoli ad Romanos Augustine makes use for the first time of another traditional scheme of history.[82] According to this scheme, history is divided into four ages: 1. before the law. 2. under the law. 3. under grace. 4. in peace. The four ages, like the earlier six ages, correspond to stages in the life of the individual.[83] Augustine probably prefers the scheme of the four ages since it better brings out the crucial importance of grace. In general, he has little to say of the first age, and human history has two main divisions, the Jews under the law and the Christians under grace.

Under these circumstances Augustine is forced to attempt a more careful statement of the relation between Judaism and Christianity. His first answers do not differ materially from what he had said in the De vera religione: Judaism and Christianity are two stages, the less perfect and the more perfect, on the way to eternal life.[84] Augustine develops the idea in terms of various contrasts such as between things carnal and things spiritual, between fear and love, between slavery and liberty.[85]

Gradually, however, Augustine's thinking comes to center on the absolute contrast between the sinners and the saved, and in consequence he begins to abandon the whole idea of a series of steps or stages on the way to salvation. The movement of his thought is clearly reflected in his changing attitudes first, toward the law of the Old Testament and second, toward the Jews. In the first instance, the law of the Old Testament becomes, not a stage on the way to the law of Christ, but the same thing as the law of Christ. The Mosaic Law is spiritual, even though the Jews were carnal and failed to understand it. "It is manifest that the scripture which was given the earlier people (sc. the Jews) is the law of Christ, which he came to fulfil with love. The same scripture and the same commandment is the Old Testament when it oppresses slaves clinging to earthly things, and it is the New Testament when it raises up free men who burn for things eternal."[86] In the second instance, the Jews as a people are depressed to the level of the heathen, and they no longer form a special stage in the universal progress of mankind. They are sinners who serve the spirit of slavery which has the power of death.[87]

Augustine effects the same revision in relation to the Christians and the New Testament. On the one hand, the newness of the Christian people becomes almost accidental in the face of an eternal decree. "The people of the New Testament is a new people, and yet its predestination in God (apud Deum) is ancient (antiqua) and so is the heavenly Jerusalem itself."[88] On the other hand the worthies of the Old Testament are more and more assimilated to the saints of the New Testament. Men like Abraham received as individuals the same grace which Christ later granted generally.[89]

Thus not only the "six ages" but also the "four ages" lose their original significance; they are no longer the important stages in a universal history of mankind's providential progress.[90] Augustine has accordingly set the stage for the Ad Simplicianum, where he will develop a new and profound interpretation of history to replace the traditional theories which are no longer adequate for him.

The Ad Simplicianum climaxes Augustine's development from 393 to 396 not only on the special level of history but also on the general level of grace. On this general level it represents a radicalization of tendencies already present in Augustine's thinking. He had, for example, earlier concluded that mankind after Adam was a "mass of sin" (massa peccati), and the mass of sin becomes the new universal concept in place of the "whole human race" of the De vera religione.[91] Similarly he had decided that grace is absolutely necessary for the moral reformation and salvation of sinners and that God predestines the sinner's salvation.[92]

Despite these tendencies, Augustine before the Ad Simplicianum still preserves some small area of human freedom in man's relation to salvation. While grace is absolutely necessary to all sinners, grace is given to those who merit it by faith, and faith, in turn, is a free choice of the individual. Not even God's predestination can annihilate this freedom, since God predestines men to salvation on the basis of His foreknowledge of their free choice of faith.[93]

In the Ad Simplicianum[94] divine omnipotence overwhelms these last barriers. God chose Jacob and rejected Esau. He did so not by foreknowledge of their works and by the same token not by foreknowledge of their faith. God's election is finally of wills. "But the will itself, unless there be something which attracts and delights the soul, cannot in any way be moved. And that something of this sort should present itself is not within the power of man."[95] God chooses His elect on the basis of His foreknowledge of His determination of their wills. Those He chooses are called; they have faith; they are justified; and they are glorified.

Against the background of this radicalization of the need for grace, Augustine introduces in the Ad Simplicianum his new interpretation of history. On the basis of Pauline texts (e.g. Romans IX, 24 f.) he first points out that God did not call all the Jews or all the Gentiles but that He called some from each race. "For after Adam there is one mass of sinners and of the impious, in which, without grace, Jews and Gentiles belong to the same leaven (conspersionem)."[96] All are sinners, but not all are saved; and God's providence must be understood in terms of the absolute contrast between those who are saved and those who are not.

Augustine then elaborates his ideas on providence in the form of a commentary on Ecclesiasticus XXXIII, 10–15.[97] This passage, declares Augustine, is "most necessary for the problem we are considering and marvellously confirms what has just been discussed."[98]

Augustine finds in Ecclesiasticus first an account of man's exclusion from Paradise. God changed men's ways and they became mortal. "Then was made the one mass of all, arising through the transmission of sin and the punishment of mortality."[99] The universal starting point is the mass of sin.

From the mass of sin which is mankind, God blessed some and God cursed some. In the words of Ecclesiasticus: From them He blessed some and exalted them; He sanctified them and drew them to Him. From them He cursed some and dashed them down; He turned them toward their own strife" (XXXIII, 12). Augustine in his commentary relates the passage to Paul's metaphor of the potter and the clay; God does with man what He will. Nevertheless neither God's justice nor His providence may be denied, and the just punishment of the damned is of providential service to the saved.

Thus the lesson of history is the general lesson of the Ad Simplicianum. The better are such only through grace, not through their works but by God's mercy. The whole purpose of Paul, and of all teachers of grace, is that whoever glories should glory in the Lord.[100]

And the pattern of history, as it emerges from Ecclesiasticus, is no longer the gradual stages of progress of the De vera religione;[101] it is the absolute contrast between the damned and the saved. Again in the words of Ecclesiasticus: "The opposite of evil is good, and the opposite of life is death; so too the sinner is the opposite of the just man. And in the same way, look at all the works of the Almighty: two by two, the one opposite the other" (XXXIII, 15).

In the Ad Simplicianum Augustine has accordingly achieved a clear and coherent solution to his questions on grace and history. He first developed the solution in a series of biblical commentaries, and he appears to have thought out the problems almost entirely in terms of a biblical and ecclesiastical statement. Nevertheless, because of the original equivalence of Augustine's Christianity and his Platonism, changes in the one necessarily imply changes in the other. And even in the Ad Simplicianum itself Augustine indicates something of the extent to which his new position on grace in history must lead to modifications of his earlier philosophic statement.

On the negative side the most important point is that the movement of thought culminating in the Ad Simplicianum leaves unchanged Augustine's description of the proper structure of the universe and of society. By 396 Augustine maintains that all mankind, the "mass of sin," has fallen into disorder, and that no man can win his way back to order except by God's grace. But there is no sign that Augustine has new ideas on the characteristics of the proper order. God's order —the hierarchy of God, souls, and bodies—still exists, and Augustine continues to describe it as he had earlier.

Augustine speaks, for example, of the goodness of God's creation, a goodness which even sin cannot destroy. He mentions the figure and structure of the body, the vital spirit which gives life to the earthly members, "and the whole nature of man, marvellously tempered through the rule of the soul and the service of the body."[102] Or as he phrases the point in an earlier passage of the Ad Simplicianum, "The soul is more excellent than the body; God who is the maker and creator of both, is more excellent than either body or soul, and He hates nothing in man but sin. Sin then is the disorder and perversity of man, that is his turning away from the more excellent creator and his turning toward the less excellent creature."[103]

Similarly, from the standpoint of an image theory, Augustine preserves his older description of human justice. He now argues, in contrast to his earlier position, that sinful men without God's grace could only wither away before they would thirst for justice. Nevertheless when he speaks of justice in human society, he describes it, as in his earlier writings, as a kind of image or vestige of divine justice.[104]

On the positive side the most important point is that Augustine now places the old ideas in a very different context. The will of sinful man cannot accept the order and image of justice; the mind even of the just man cannot comprehend them.

On the simplest moral level, this has already been seen in Augustine's new doctrine of grace and sin. Though the order is still existent, sinful man is out of relation with it, and action in terms of it is impossible for him.

A comparable change, and perhaps a more profound one, occurs on the intellectual level, and Augustine now feels that the total order of justice is beyond human comprehension. Human justice, for example, is just, because it is an image of divine justice; divine justice, however, is "a hidden equity not to be searched out by mere human measure."[105] God is certainly just, but Augustine can no longer comprehend the grounds of the justice. "Thus in some God punished impiety by damnation and in some He removes it by justification, according as He judges through His inscrutable judgments what should be done."[106]

Ultimately, though Augustine may maintain continuity on the descriptive level of order and image, the new insights of the Ad Simplicianum imply a total reorientation of his worldview. Augustine's early doctrine of human wisdom and self-sufficiency had been strictly correlative with his early doctrine of the rational comprehensibility of the universe. Now that he has totally denied human self-sufficiency, he must also deny the comprehensibility of the universe. He does so in the important closing section of Book I of the Ad Simplicianum. "Let us believe, though we cannot grasp it, that He who made

the whole creation, both spiritual and corporeal, disposed all
things in number and weight and measure (Wisdom XI, 21).
But inscrutable are His judgments, and His ways are past
searching out (Romans XI, 33).[107]

And from the standpoint of the new world-view, Augustine
must now rethink almost all of his early ideas on society.
How, for example, is the Christian to know of the fatherland
and of the heavenly Jerusalem, and how is he related to them?
What is the mode of existence of a Christian or of a Christian
society on earth? Augustine himself appears early to have
recognized the need for thinking out the answers to such
questions. The writings from 396 to about 400, notably the
Confessiones, may be regarded from one aspect as a brilliantly
successful attempt to meet the need.

IV. THE ELABORATION OF THE NEW POSITION OF THE AD
SIMPLICIANUM IN THE WRITINGS FROM 396 TO 400.

The Confessiones[108] tower above the other writings of the
years following the Ad Simplicianum. They are the most important statement of Augustine's general position, and they
also provide the most significant elaboration of his new ideas
on society.

The general approach of the Confessiones is suggested in
the opening biblical quotations where Augustine praises God
and declares: "Of Thy wisdom there is no number (Psalm
CXLVI, 6)."[109] This is the position of the Ad Simplicianum,
and it is a far cry from the claim of the early De musica to
see clearly the immutable numbers which exist in immutable
truth itself.[110] Augustine in the Confessiones meditates on
the relations between Christians and a God whose saving
providence exceeds their comprehension; the saved participate
eternity in some way but Augustine no longer hopes to
grasp it.

The two main divisions of the Confessiones are Books
I–IX (X),[111] which deal with Augustine himself, and Books
XI–XIII, which deal with God's universal government from
the creation of the world through the final rest of the saints.
The two divisions correspond to the two aspects of God's

providence, private and public; first we have an account of His dealing with Augustine as an individual and then an account of His dealing with all mankind.[112] In the Confessiones the two aspects are organically connected since both Augustine's own story and God's public providence culminate in the heavenly Jerusalem.

Books I–IX contain comparatively little that is directly relevant to Augustine's ideas on society. In Book VII, Augustine tells of his reading of the "Platonists"; his comments, like much of the Confessiones, constitute as it were a "retractatio" of his earlier philosophic statement. From the standpoint of man's heavenly destination, the Platonists failed, according to Augustine, because while they could see the fatherland (patria) they could not see Christ the Mediator who is the only way to it.[113] The turning point in Augustine's story is of course the scene in the garden (VIII, 12, §28 f.), and we may regard it as an autobiographical statement of the conclusion of the Ad Simplicianum: wills are chosen.

The culmination of Augustine's experience, as he tells it in the Confessiones, is the dialogue with Monica at Ostia. Earlier, after reading the Platonists, Augustine had achieved at least briefly the sight of the invisible things of God (Romans I, 20). However he had been unable to continue in the vision, and his reaction was one of disillusion and dissatisfaction.[114] At Ostia the circumstances are different. Augustine and Monica do not seek a direct vision of God. ". . . forgetful of things past, and stretching out (extenti) to the things which are before (Philippians III, 13), we were enquiring between ourselves . . . of what sort the eternal life of the saints was to be. . . ."[115] The quest is successful. They are granted a foretaste of the Christian heavenly society as they attain to that "region of neverfailing plenty where Thou feedest Israel with the food of truth."[116] There they had "touched" eternal wisdom, and there they had left bound up the first-fruits of the spirit. In contrast to the mood following the Platonist visions, Augustine now achieves peace, and he is confident, even after the return to this world of time and change, that his long search is ended. His final destination is God's heavenly Israel. This is the closing note of Book IX as Augustine requests prayers for Monica and Patrick. May his readers remember those who were "his parents in this transitory light, his brethren in our Catholic mother under Thee our Father, and his fellow-citizens in the eternal Jerusalem, for which the pilgrimage of Thy people sighs, from their going out to their final return."[117]

Membership in the eternal Jerusalem has set the seal on Augustine's individual story, and in Books XI–XIII he goes on to meditate on universal history under the same aspect of God's heavenly city. He would consider "the marvellous things of Thy law from the beginning (principio) in which Thou madest heaven and earth through to the perpetual reign with Thee of Thy holy city."[118] Universal history will in turn further reveal the significance of Augustine's own story, and Augustine prays to Christ the Mediator, "Thy Word, through whom Thou madest all things, and among them, me also; Thy Only-begotten, through whom Thou callest to adoption the believing people, and in it, me also."[119]

In Book XI Augustine begins with the creation, but he quickly moves to the main topic of the book, the problem of time.[120] What is the relation between the eternity of the Creator and the time of the creature? The analysis is developed brilliantly, and Augustine's answer constitutes another "retractatio" of his earlier philosophic statement. In the first writings, a main theme was that even in temporal things man can find vestiges of the eternal and that through these vestiges he is always being called back through regular stages and steps to the eternal intelligible world which is his fatherland.[121] But Augustine now sees very differently man's involvement in time and the possible conditions of his escape. Time, which is in the soul, represents merely dispersion and dissipation, what Augustine will call "distention." If man is to be saved, God's grace must somehow make it possible for him, as at Ostia, to touch eternity.

The crucial argument, for our purposes, is found in the last sections of Book XI. Time in the soul appears as past, present, and future; the soul remembers the past, attends the present, and expects the future. But all three levels lack unity and reality. What is present has no quantity (spatium), and the soul loses its unity as it is stretched (distenditur–extenditur–tenditur) into both past and future. Augustine illustrates his argument in terms of a memorized poem. "Before I begin my expectation is stretched (extenditur) over the whole, but when I have begun, however much of it I shall separate off into the past, by so much is my memory stretched out (tenditur). Thus the life of this action of mine is distended or stretched out (distenditur) into memory, because of what I have already said, and into expectation, because of what I am still to say."[122] And what happens in the "life" of the poem also happens "in the whole life of a man, whose parts are all the actions of a man, and in the whole 'world' (saeculo) of the sons of men, whose parts are all the lives of men."[123]

But Augustine escapes this tragic involvement in time, as at Ostia, through the experience of his heavenly destination, and in his escape he comes to full realization of the involvement. "But because Thy mercy is better than all lives, behold, my life is (nothing but) distention, and (yet) Thy right hand took me up in my Lord the Son of Man, the Mediator between Thee the One and us the many in our manynesses (nos multos, in multis per multa)."[124] Again as at Ostia, Augustine uses Philippians III, 13 f. to explain his experience: 13 . . . forgetting the things which are behind, and reaching forward (extentus) to the things which are before, 14. I follow on intently (secundum intentionem). . . ." In a difficult passage, he combines this Pauline terminology with his own terminology of distention: ". . . forgetful of what is past, not distended but extended, and not to those things which shall come to be and pass away but to those things which are before, I follow on, not through distention but through intention, after the reward of my heavenly calling, where I may hear the voice of praise and contemplate Thy delight which neither comes to be nor passes away."[125] Augustine has achieved his unity through the grace of eternity, and from this vantage point he can look back with new insight to his former state. "I had burst asunder (dissilui) into times, whose order I do not know."[126] He closes the book with another confident statement on the relation of the eternal God to His society. "Oh, how high art Thou, and yet the humble in heart are Thy house, for Thou raisest up those that are bowed down, and they fall not whose elevation Thou art."[127]

In Book XII Augustine goes on to analyze more carefully the nature of the heavenly society to which he is called. He starts from the "heaven of heaven" (caelum caeli) of Psalm CXIII, 6. This he explains as "some intellectual creature, which though in no way coeternal unto Thee the Trinity, yet participates Thy eternity. Through the sweetness of that most blessed contemplation of Thyself, it strongly restrains its mutability; without any fall since its first creation, by clinging to Thee it rises above all the rolling vicissitudes of times."[128] The heaven of heaven neither expects the future nor conveys what it remembers into the past; "it is not altered by any change, and it is not distended (distenditur) into any times."[129]

Augustine has thus made plain the two main theses of Book XII. First, man's heavenly destination is not an eternal intelligible world, as in the early writings; it is a creature of the creator. Second, though a creature, it neither has fallen nor will it ever fall into the mutability of time.

Augustine goes on to describe the heaven of heaven with the traditional biblical terms. It is God's house, which is "most harmoniously one through that established peace of the holy spirits, the citizens of Thy city in the heavenly places which are above the heavens we see."[130] Augustine sighs in his pilgrimage, "remembering Jerusalem with his heart stretched (extento) above to it, Jerusalem the fatherland, Jerusalem the mother, and Thyself that rulest over it."[131] There are his first-fruits[132] of the spirit; thence he is certain of these things; and thither he would be collected from his dispersion and deformity.

In Books XI and XII of the Confessiones Augustine analyzes a few problems exhaustively and with a full discussion of other possible solutions. By the end of Book XII, however, he realizes that such an approach cannot be continued if he is to treat God's universal law within the limits of a single work.[133] Accordingly the tempo changes, and in a single book Augustine completes his meditation on the whole history of God's providence.

Book XIII is the most wide-ranging portion of the Confessiones. In form, the bulk of the Book is a free allegory on the opening chapters of Genesis, but there is often only a

very tenuous connection between the text and the explanation. No brief account can be adequate to the multiplicity
and profundity of Augustine's thought, and the following discussion attempts only to point out some of the main phases of
the argument.

Augustine's starting point, and a continuing theme, is the
total dependence of the creature on the creator. This is true
even of the heaven of heaven, the spiritual creature which
is the celestial Jerusalem. "Angels fell away, and man's soul
fell away. They pointed out the abyss of the whole spiritual
creature in deepest darkness, unless Thou hadst said in the
beginning, 'Let there be light' and there was light, and unless
every obedient intelligence of Thy heavenly city clung to Thy
spirit and rested in it."[134]

The blessed heavenly city was made light, without interval
of time, at the moment of its creation. The story of human
salvation, in contrast, is the story of an alteration between
darkness and light. "We were darkness, and we are being
made light."[135]

The starting point of human history is thus universal darkness and the mass of sin.[136] Through Adam's fall, there
flowed from him "the brackishness of the sea, the human race
so profoundly curious (curiosum) and so tempestuously ar-
rogant and so changeably lax (instabiliter fluvidum)."[137]
Throughout Book XIII, the sea will symbolize sinful mankind, "the embittered ones" (amaricantes).[138]

Yet even the sea of sinful mankind is subject to God's
order. He brings the impious together into one society, for
they all aim at the same goal of temporal and earthly happiness; God's gathering of the waters, not human bitterness,
constitutes the sea. God restrains man's evil desires and imposes limits on them, "and so Thou makest the sea by the
order of Thy empire over all things."[139]

Over against the sea, God creates the land, which symbolizes the souls who thirst after Him and who appear before Him.[140] He separates these souls from the society of
the sea, and they bring forth their fruit according to their
kind.

Above both land and sea, God placed the firmament of
the Scriptures.[141] The firmament will play an important role

in Augustine's allegory, for it marks the distinction between
the spirits of the heaven of heaven and the Christians here
on earth. The supercelestial peoples, above this visible heaven,
have no need of the Bible, for they see God directly. Christians on earth, the lower peoples, see God's eternal word
only in the riddle (in aenigmate) of the clouds and in the
glass (per speculum) of the firmament.[142]

On land the soul first brings forth works of mercy "according to its kind" (secundum genus). Here man loves his
neighbor in relieving his carnal necessities and in giving him
protection.[143] Above this lower stage of action, there is the
higher stage of contemplation. Man learns in the Bible to
separate things sensible from things intelligible and to distinguish between men attached to the one or the other. Through
the Spirit, some receive the word of wisdom (sapientiae),
some the word of science (scientiae), and some the other
gifts of the spirit. Wisdom is the food of the spiritual ones
of the ecclesia; science and the other gifts of the spirit aid
the carnal ones.[144]

The sea in turn brings forth its works. God's holy men
bring his sacraments into the "world," and these are sym-
bolized by the "moving creature that hath life" and the "fowls
that fly above the earth" (Genesis, I, 20). Augustine contrasts
the bodily sacraments, which vary in time, with unchanging
and certain knowledge like the lights of wisdom and knowledge in the firmament. But the bodily sacraments are nevertheless necessary because of the sea, the peoples who are
alienated from the eternity of God's truth.[145]

Augustine continues with a second and fuller account of
the works of the earth; his starting point in the text is now
the "living soul" (Genesis I, 24). Such a soul no longer needs
baptism, though by God's ordinance there is now no other
entrance to the kingdom of heaven. But it continues to use
the eucharist, which is the "fish" brought up from the sea
to nourish the land, and the "fowl that fly over the land,"
which are God's ministers to the faithful.[146]

By imitating these ministers in their actions, the faithful
are virtuous "according to their kind." They reform themselves from the triple lust of the world: the cruelty of pride,
the sloth of pleasure, and the vain name of knowledge (a

fallaci nomine scientiae).[147] They may then go on to the higher insights of contemplation, where men no longer live merely "according to their kind" but where they are reformed in God's image and no longer need live by any human authority.

Such are the spiritual Christians. They have power "over the fish of the sea and over the fowls of the air, and over all cattle and wild beasts and over all the earth and over every creeping thing" (Genesis I, 28). They do not judge of the spiritual truths of the Bible nor of its dark places nor of the distinction between those who are spiritual and those who are carnal nor of the eventual fate of the disordered peoples of the world. But they do judge of the rightness and wrongness of the sacraments, of the interpretation of the Bible, of the acts and morals of the faithful, and of pious thoughts about things we know through the senses.[148]

This is the life of the spiritual man who judges all things, and it is the highest life possible on earth. But Augustine no longer expects an intellectual vision that will take man out of grace and time. God in his firmament most wisely disputes with His faithful "so that we may discern all things with marvellous contemplation, although still in signs and in times and in years."[149] Augustine reaches eternity in his thought when he realizes that through grace God's eternal revelation in some way coincides with Augustine's temporal understanding of it. God tells him: "Thus the things which you see through my spirit, I see, and the things which you say through my spirit, I say. And so, although you see them temporally, I do not see them temporally, and although you say them temporally, I do not say them temporally."[150]

Augustine has accordingly used the opening chapters of Genesis as an allegorical basis for his description of the sea of sinners, the land of the pious, and the firmament of the scriptures. As a theory of history, Book XIII of the Confessiones agrees in general with the Ad Simplicianum. The basic contrast is again between the sinners and the just, between the sea and the land. The contrast is an abiding pattern of history, not merely a means of distinguishing epochs of progress.

Book XIII of the Confessiones also agrees with the Ad

Simplicianum in repeating the early philosophic description
of the proper order in society and in man. God is said, for
example, to form the "living soul" of the faithful Christian
through ordered affections. "And after that, the mind subject
to Thee alone and needing to imitate no human authority
hast Thou renewed after Thy image and likeness, and didst
subject its reasonable action to its dominant intellect. . . ."[151]
Augustine praises the earth and its creatures, most particularly man "created after Thy image and likeness, and even
through that Thy very image and likeness (that is, the power
of reason and of understanding) set over all irrational
creatures."[152]

More clearly than in the Ad Simplicianum, Augustine in
the Confessiones defines the two groups of men, the sea and
the land, entirely in terms of man's relation to God through
grace; they cannot be identified with disorder and order on
the descriptive level since the sea sometimes achieves order
in part and the land sometimes fails to achieve it completely.
Many men, for example, are able to see that God's creation
is good, but they necessarily fall into sin when they try to
enjoy it rather than use it. It is quite another matter "that
when a man sees something to be good, God should in the
same man see that it is good, in such a way namely that God
should be loved in that which He made, Who cannot be loved
except by the Holy Spirit which He gave."[153] Similarly, to
contain oneself from the world is of no use to any but the
faithful.[154] And if the faithless try to aid God's servants in
some need of the present life, they of the sea cannot feed
them of the land, who are to be fed only by the land's
fruits.[155]

Book X of the Confessiones stands somewhat apart from
the rest of the work and is perhaps a later addition.[156] It
falls into two main sections. In the first Augustine questions
what he loves when he loves God, and in his answer he
reevaluates the older Platonist ascent from things corporeal
to the sight of the invisible things of God. He concludes that
while the things of the world do proclaim God as their creator, sinful man cannot hear their message because he is himself subject to these corporeal things through his disordered
love.[157] Augustine continues his search for God with his

celebrated analysis of memory, and he finally concludes that
God is known to Augustine only insofar as He has told Augustine of Himself. "See, what a space I have gone over in
my memory, seeking Thee, O Lord; and I have not found
Thee outside it. Nor have I found anything concerning Thee
but what I have kept in memory, ever since I learnt
Thee."[158] To describe the origin of this memory Augustine
must, as in the dialogue at Ostia and in his intention of his
heavenly calling, transcend his self and its powers. "Where
then did I find Thee that I might learn Thee, but in Thee
above me?"[159]

The second main section of Book X of the Confessiones
is devoted to another treatment of the theme of the three
lusts.[160] In the De vera religione Augustine had used the
topic to show that even through his vices man is called back
to virtue; the argument attempted to maintain, for an extreme case, the comprehensible order of the universe.[161]
Such ideas play no part in the discussion of the Confessiones;
Augustine attempts on the contrary to show how the three
lusts appear even in the life of the Christian destined for
salvation and how they are a threat even to him.

The discussion of pride is, as before, the one most important for Augustine's ideas on society. God alone, he declares, rules without arrogance (sine typho), and Augustine
doubts that he can ever escape this third group of temptations.
There are certain functions of human society (humanae societatis officia) which make it necessary for men to be loved
and feared by their fellowmen.[162] It appears that these functions are common, to use the language of Book XIII, to both
sea and land. There is however always the danger that even
men of the land will wish to receive this fear and love not
on God's behalf but in place of God, and Augustine can
never be sure that he has himself escaped the danger.

In summary, Augustine's Confessiones, notably Books XI–
XIII constitute a remarkable statement of the new position
on society implied by the insights of the Ad Simplicianum.
In this fuller statement the similarities and contrasts between
the new position and the position of 386 through 393 appear
more clearly.

As in his early writings, Augustine still maintains that man's destination is a heavenly society. However the society is no longer the intelligible world which is eternal in its own right. The heavenly Jerusalem is a creature of the creator, even though it is one which through God's grace totally escapes the mutability and distention of time. Further Augustine no longer thinks that any man can return to the fatherland by gradual steps through his own powers; all sinners are inextricably involved in the dispersion of time. Only grace permits the saved Christian to have his first-fruits in Jerusalem, and he does not reach the heavenly city by the steps of reason but when time "touches" eternity or coincides with it.

As in his early writings, Augustine in the Confessiones holds that God's governance embraces all mankind and all history. However the governance in history does not lead to a regular and universal progress which man can comprehend. God's providence, known only to faith, lies in the dualist contrast between the sea and the land, between the damned and the saved.

When Augustine in the Confessiones discusses the life of the Christians within the society of the land, we again find similarities with the descriptions of the philosopher in the early writings. In general, Augustine still concentrates his attention upon an elite rather than upon the whole society; he mentions the carnal ones of the ecclesia, but they play only a subordinate role in his allegory. Further his ultimate values still lie in contemplation rather than in action, and religious insight receives far more emphasis than love or charity.

But as against the early writings, grace is the crucial factor even in the life of the intellectual and spiritual Christian; Augustine denies that grace ever, in this life or the next, leads to a situation where grace is no longer necessary. By and large, neither the sacraments nor the ecclesia appear to play a dominant role in the life of the spiritual Christian, though both are prerequisite to his existence. Such a spiritual Christian, to judge from Book XIII of the Confessiones, draws his religious values primarily through the Scriptures. He does not, as the philosopher in the early writings, achieve a direct vision of eternity; the high point of his experience is the realization that his own temporal understanding of the Bible in some way embodies and coincides with God's eternal word.

Lastly, Augustine in the Confessiones both preserves and modifies his earlier order and image theory. On some points he must deny the old position. If "wills are chosen," Augustine can no longer maintain that the universe is a comprehensible order in such a way that man can reach his destination by himself and through his own powers. The older theory must therefore be abandoned as a basis of salvation; it must be "secularized" or, perhaps, "creaturized." But if this change is accepted, Augustine does not seem to wish any others. He still describes the old hierarchy of God, souls, and bodies, and within souls there is still the old hierarchy of the contemplative and active parts.

After the Confessiones, Augustine next presents a comparable general statement of his ideas on society and history in the De catechizandis rudibus. In several other works of about the same period, however, he introduces discussions of special aspects of society, and these will be noticed first.

Some of the most significant material is found in the Contra Faustum Manichaeum libri XXXIII. Faustus uses as his main argument the standard Manichaean attack on the contradictions between the Old Testament and the New, and Augustine replies with a restatement of the position of the Ad Simplicianum. The Jewish Law, far from contradicting the law of Christ, is essentially identical with it. "For the very same law, which was given by Moses, was made truth and grace by Christ."[163]

Faustus in his special polemic devotes a great deal of attention to the alleged immorality of the patriarchs, and Augustine's answer takes up the whole of Book XXII, the longest in the Contra Faustum. Augustine starts from the eternal law as his main point of reference, and he makes repeated use of a standard definition. "The eternal law is divine reason or the will of God ordering that the natural order be preserved and forbidding that it be perverted."[164]

The form of the definition does not differ markedly from that found in the early De libero arbitrio, though the new phrasing is more easily harmonized with a sharp contrast between God and the creature, between the creator and the natural order.[165] But in the Contra Faustum, as in the Ad Simplicianum, Augustine departs from his early position when he emphasizes that God's actions in the context of the natural order are incomprehensible to man. God's sending the demons into the herd of swine illustrated a "hidden but everywhere just government."[166] Man's ignorance and his weakness result from the inscrutable judgments of God, and while the Christian has no doubt that all things are done by God's mercy and judgment, "the measures and weights and numbers by which all things are ordered are hidden."[167]

In this context man's duties within the natural order are made totally dependent upon God. Sometimes the individual may know the natural order only through God's revelation, and yet in no case should he use human reason to resist God's commands. In his discussion of the Israelites' thefts from the Egyptians, Augustine remarks, "It may be that there are other most hidden reasons, why this command was divinely given them: but we must yield to the divine commands with obedience, not resist them with argument."[168] Such an approach threatens to deny any fundamental permanence to the natural order and to make any rational comprehension of it impossible, and in a later book of the Contra Faustum, Augustine declares: "God the founder and creator of all natures, does nothing against nature, for that will be "natural" to anything which He shall have done to it, from Whom is all mode, number, and order of nature."[169]

But again, if Augustine in the Contra Faustum modifies the theological aspects of his older order theory, it does not appear that he wishes to change it insofar as it simply describes the proper structure in man or in society. Man consists of soul and body, and there can be no doubt that the soul is by the natural order placed before the body. Similarly within the soul, the reason (ratio) is placed by the law of nature before those parts which even the beasts possess. Finally, within reason, contemplation is without doubt to be placed before action.[170]

Similarly, Augustine speaks of a natural order in society which is adjusted to the peace of mortals. Such an order defines the relations between a prince and his soldiers in terms of "peace and the common welfare (salus)."[171] The order holds whether the ruler is pagan or Christian, and even the faithful are sometimes obligated to fight in the army of a sacrilegious ruler to preserve "the order of civic peace."[172] On this point the ideas of the Contra Faustum are in agreement with Augustine's earlier exegesis of Romans XIII in the Pauline commentaries.[173]

As in his earlier writings, so in the Contra Faustum Augustine assigns to society only the limited values of peace and welfare. Nevertheless he does not doubt that man is a social as well as a rational creature[174] and that kingship ranks among the goods divinely established. He argues, for example, that the period of the Old Testament was necessary "so that it might first appear that even earthly goods pertain only to the power and decision of the one true God, earthly goods among which are included human kingdoms and victories over enemies, for the sake of which things particularly the city of the impious . . . makes supplication to idols and demons."[175]

In addition to the account of the eternal law and of the natural order, two other developments of the Contra Faustum are relevant to Augustine's ideas on society. In the first, Augustine clears up an ambiguity in his interpretation of the contrast between the outer and the inner man. It will be remembered that in the early works he had identified the contrast with such other contrasts as that between the old man and the new; further he had used all these contrasts to point out the main stages of individual and universal progress.[176] Later Augustine had abandoned many of these ideas as he worked out a new interpretation of providential history in terms of the absolute distinction between the damned and the saved. He had however not explained just how the contrast between the outer and inner man was related to his new view.[177]

Faustus seems to deserve the main credit for making Augustine think through his new position on this point. In an interesting argument, The Manichaean had maintained with the use of Pauline authorities that the outer and the inner man are actually two men and that of the two God created only the inner man.[178] Augustine replies that Paul wishes the inner man to be understood as the spirit of the mind and the outer man as in the body and in this mortal life. They are not two men, but two parts of one man, and God made the whole man.[179] On the other hand, the contrast between the earthly and the heavenly man is between what we are in Adam and what we shall be in Christ;[180] the contrast between the old man and the new is between righteousness (iustitiam) and unrighteousness (iniustitiam). Hence, concludes Augustine, "man as a whole, that is in his inner as well as his outer part, became the old man (inueteravit) through sin."[181] The Christian is now being renewed in the inner man in the image of God, and after the resurrection even the outer man, with a spiritual body, will receive the dignity of a heavenly dwelling place.

Augustine's differing interpretations of the outer and inner man may serve as a paradigm for his whole development. He originally gives the contrast a meaning consonant with the main tradition of Greco-Roman philosophy, and he argues that salvation lies in turning away from the outer man and toward the inner man as a special case of the turn away from the sensible to the intelligible, away from the temporal to the eternal. In the early period he further understands the biblical contrasts, e.g. between the old man and the new, in the same sense. In the course of the movement of thought leading to the Ad Simplicianum, Augustine takes the biblical contrasts out of this context of stages and uses them to point to the absolute contrast between the damned and the saved. Possibly Augustine might have reinterpreted the contrast between the outer and the inner man in the same way but here, as in the case of ideas of order, he is dealing with terms which to him still seem to have useful descriptive meanings. He accordingly separates the contrast between inner and outer man from the biblical contrasts such as between the old man and the new: both inner and outer man are damned (i.e. are the old man) and both inner and outer man are saved (i.e. are the new man).

Thus Augustine in his early writings begins with the assumption that there are stages leading to salvation. By about 400, if the stages still appear, as in the inner and outer man, they have been reduced to the level of description and do not define salvation. If it is a question of salvation, as in the case of the old man and the new, Augustine finds not stages but an absolute contrast.

A second significant development of the Contra Faustum is the new sense of Christian triumph arising out of the conversion of the Roman Empire. At one time the kings of this world (huius saeculi) had persecuted the Christian religion, but now the kings of the earth (terrae) are subject to Christ's Empire.[182] Augustine thus sees in his own time the fulfillment of the prophecy of Psalm LXXI, 11: And all the kings of the earth shall adore him, and all nations shall serve him. The nations have been led to the cult of the one true God by Christian empire (imperio Christiano), and the whole inhabitable world has been conquered not by war but by truth. Augustine can even write that Christian emperors, with full confidence of Christian piety, have won most glorious victories over sacrilegious enemies who placed their trust in the sacraments of idols and demons.[183] Something of the same attitude appears in the roughly contemporary De consensu evangelistarum. The Jews, though worshipping the true God, were conquered by the Romans, but God subjected the Roman Empire to His name through Christ the King and He converted the Empire to the destruction of idols.[184]

After the Contra Faustum, the De doctrina christiana is among the works of this period the most illuminating for Augustine's ideas on society. In the opening sections of Book I Augustine makes considerable use of the old metaphor of the fatherland (patria); for the most part what he says differs little from the early De beata vita.[185] But the early ideas fall far short of solving Augustine's problem at this time, and in the Confessiones, as we have seen, he had attacked the Platonists for seeing only the fatherland and not Christ as the way to the fatherland. How is he now to explain the relation of Christ to the fatherland, and in what sense is Christ the way to it?

Augustine in the De doctrina christiana presents a fundamentally new solution to these problems: in the Incarnation the fatherland and the way are united. He first states the point in terms of God's Wisdom: "While therefore Wisdom is the fatherland (patria), Wisdom also made itself for us the way (viam) to the fatherland."[186] Later he rephrases the point in terms of the Christ who appeared in space and time.

The believer in Christ both begins with what is temporal and also transcends what is temporal.[187]

The new solution of Augustine on the relation between the fatherland and the way is admirably adapted to the previous development of his thought and experience. In his early works he had seen salvation (for example in the De musica[188]) as the ascent by gradual stages from what is temporal to what is eternal; under such conditions there is evidently no reason for thinking of an identification of the eternal fatherland with the temporal way. Later however he had abandoned the theory of salvation through stages, and he had come to place his emphasis on the total gulf between the creator and the creature, between eternal and temporal, a gulf which disappears only in the coincidence of the eternal and the temporal effected by grace. In the Confessiones he had worked out some of the implications of this position in the area of knowledge. He had come to feel that nowhere in this life will the Christian see God directly. His vision is mediated by the "firmament" of the Bible, and Augustine's highest intuition is that his own temporal understanding of the Scriptures coincides with God's eternal statement of them. If Augustine is now to rethink in terms of these new insights his older idea of man's goal as the eternal fatherland, he must say, as he does in the De doctrina christiana, that faith in Christ is an experience both of the way and of the fatherland. He no longer moves on the level of society from temporal to eternal, but through grace the two coincide. In the De doctrina christiana, as in the De beata vita, one feels that the metaphor of the fatherland still serves to explain a primarily individual and intellectual experience. If, however, the fatherland is considered as the heavenly ecclesia or as Jerusalem or as the body of Christ, then important social consequences are immediately apparent.

In addition to these new ideas on the fatherland, Augustine introduces in the De doctrina christiana the concept of a common society of fallen angels and of sinful men. The various rites of superstition result from such a fellowship, for the demons, led by their prince the devil, endeavor in every way to make it impossible for men to achieve the return to the fatherland.[189]

On the level of the proper order of society, Augustine in the De doctrina christiana again repeats essentially unchanged the ideas of the early writings. Man should love his neighbor as himself, but through vice men try to lord it over their fellows while they themselves deny obedience to God.[190] It is true that after Adam the spirit struggles against the flesh, but the struggle is necessary only because of the consequences of Adam's sin; the aim of the spirit is simply to check all disordered motion and to restore the "natural order."[191]

Augustine continues to picture the Christian as accepting the existing order of society on the human level. "The Christians do not neglect those human institutions which are valuable for a common society in view of the needs of the present life."[192] Augustine hopes for the reform of individuals within existing institutions; he does not envisage a change in the institutions.

The last work of the period we are studying is the De catechizandis rudibus. Here Augustine presents a very simple statement for those who are only beginning to study Christianity; we must not expect the subtlety or the profundity of the Confessiones. Nevertheless this simple statement consolidates and codifies some of the most important results of the developments we have analyzed, and the doctrine of the two cities, which first appears here, may be regarded as the endpoint of all the previous tendencies toward a dualistic theory of society.

The most important part of the De catechizandis rudibus is an outline of history from the creation through the kingdom of the just in heaven. More clearly and simply than in the Ad Simplicianum or in the Confessiones Augustine now explains all history in terms of a contrast between two societies, here called the two cities. "Thus there are two cities, one of the wicked and the other of the holy, which endure from the beginning of the human race even to the end of time, and which, moreover, are to be separated in body also on the day of judgment. For all men who love pride and temporal dominion together with empty vanity and display of presumption and all evil spirits who set their affections on such things and seek their own glory by the subjection of men are bound fast together in one fellowship (societate); and even though they frequently fight with one another for these ends, still they are flung headlong by an equal weight of desire into the same abyss, and are united to one another by the likeness of their ways and their deserts. And again all men and all spirits who humbly seek God's glory, not their own, and who follow Him in godliness, belong to one fellowship."[193]

This description of the two cites carries further in several respects the dualistic tendencies of Augustine's previous ideas on society. There are now only two societies, and they include all men and all spirits; both are present from the creation of man to the end of history. Augustine in the De doctrina christiana had argued that in Christ the fatherland and the way are identical;[194] he now goes on to argue that the angels in heaven and the Christians on earth form one society. Through faith the Christians here and now *are* the heavenly city. Augustine as early as the Expositio epistolae ad Galatas had assimilated the Jewish heroes to the New Testament Christians; he now goes on to state that they are members of the same society with the Christians and the angels.[195] And as a result of these developments Augustine can make the city of the holy synonymous with the ecclesia and with the body of Christ.[196] On the other side, Augustine had earlier abandoned the theory that the Jewish people represented a special stage in the progress of mankind; he now places the Jews as a people on the side of the city of the wicked.[197]

Augustine in the De catechizandis rudibus then uses these ideas in his outline of universal history. God created man and placed him in Paradise, but Adam fell and here was the real beginning of human history. "For by the most just laws of God, all were condemned."[198] Nevertheless Adam's sin could not frustrate God's purpose and a new city of God emerged within the race of sinful men.

Augustine continues with a summary of some of the high points of Old Testament history. He mentions the traditional five ages but he attaches little importance to them, and there is no suggestion of the older theory that they mark stages in the universal progress of mankind. Indeed the contrast between the two cities so dominates Augustine's thinking that he now has little interest in Jewish history as such. As we have seen, the Jewish heroes have no special place since they are members of the ecclesia, the body of Christ, and the city of the holy; the mass of the Jews have no special place since they belong to the city of the wicked. What remains unique in Jewish history is simply its prophetic character. As Augustine had said in the De consensu evangelistarum, the fact that the Romans conquered the Jews after the coming of Christ showed that "the kingdom of that nation, its temple, its sacrifices, and its mystic unction . . . existed for no purpose but the foretelling of Christ."[199]

Of the various prophetic aspects of Jewish history, the Babylonian captivity is the most significant for Augustine's ideas of society. Jerusalem symbolizes the society of the holy and Babylon the society of the wicked. Consequently the primary figurative meaning of the captivity is the future subjection of the ecclesia to the kings of this world (sub regibus hujus saeculi). But Augustine also notes that through the captivity some earthly kings (terreni reges) were converted to the worship of the true God and granted temporal peace to the Christians. Thus the Christians were enabled to carry on Christian missionary work, which now extends over the whole world with the permission of Christian kings (cum pace regum Christianorum).[200] Augustine supports his reading of the allegory by such New Testament texts as Romans XIII, 1, and I Timothy II, 1. Christians are to be subject to their temporal rulers (dominis). If the rulers remain wicked, the Christians will finally judge them; if the rulers are converted, the Christians will finally reign with them.[201]

In the De catechizandis rudibus, as in the earlier works, earthly kingship and temporal rule appear as goods which are independent of the contrast between the two societies into which mankind is divided. This appears in the account of the Jewish kingdom[202] and it was implied in the account of the Babylon captivity. In his discussion of the New Testament he mentions earthly kingship among the goods which Christ spurned.[203] In the same passage Augustine writes that Christ was born in Bethlehem, a city so small that it was finally classified as a mere village (villa): "He did not wish anyone to glory in the sublimity of any earthly city (de cuiusquam terrenae civitatis sublimitate)."[204]

Thus Augustine in the De catechizandis rudibus confirms on a simpler level the pattern established by the earlier works. In the Ad Simplicianum and in the Confessiones, he had moved toward a dualist interpretation of history and of society, but the older philosophic statement on the proper order of society remained valid as description. So in the De catechizandis rudibus he achieves the consistent dualism of the two cities, but earthly kingship and earthly cities remain, as before, goods which are neutral in relation to the absolute contrast between the two cities.

The preceding analysis of Augustine's changing ideas on society suggests certain more general, and also more tentative, conclusions.

The first and most evident conclusion is that Augustine's thought does indeed develop significantly during the period from 386 to about A.D. 400. Further, from a historical standpoint, there is no justification for restricting this development to a "theological" in contrast to a "philosophical" aspect. In Augustine's early writings, "philosophy" and "theology" form a rational unity, and the breakdown of this unity is in itself an important philosophic development.

In the tracing of the development, Augustine's ideas on society supply a thread of continuity, perhaps the most convenient one. In the early works, though society is relatively unimportant, Augustine explains with some clarity how it fits into his whole world-view. During the transition period from about 393 through 396, certain problems of history and society are in the foreground of Augustine's interest. And in such later works as the Confessiones or the Contra Faustum Augustine continues to discuss many of these same problems.

How can we best characterize the general course of Augustine's development? We must, I think, start from the fact that Augustine's early thought represents an attempted synthesis of Greco-Roman and of Christian ideas and that at this time the Greco-Roman elements are dominant. Later Augustine becomes aware of the tensions within the synthesis. He accordingly rethinks his Christian ideas from the standpoint of their unique values and works out a new position.

Most simply, Augustine in his early period argues that man through his own powers ascends by gradual stages to his destination, the vision of eternal truth. He later denies man's ability to do this. Man's salvation rests on the eternal, incomprehensible choice of a God who from the sinful mass of mankind chooses some, whom He saves.

But if Augustine denies his early position as a doctrine of salvation, it is almost equally important for the historian of his thought that he preserves a large part of it on the "secular" or "creaturely" level. Intellectually, man is still able to achieve some vision of eternity, though he is not saved by it.[205] Morally, Augustine still affirms the old order of body and mind, of things sensible and things intelligible, but man cannot realize the order or, if he can, this does not in itself lead to salvation.

On the positive side, Augustine in his later position emphasizes the total gulf between the temporal and the eternal, between the creature and the creator; not even grace creates intermediate stages here. At the same time he sees Christian experience as a transcending of the gulf. His general explanation, though not yet codified or systematized, is that the Christian experience, in contrast to the Greek movement away from the temporal to the eternal, represents a coincidence of the temporal with the eternal. Christ is both in time and above time; he is the way and at the same time the fatherland.

Augustine's general development is reflected in his changing ideas of society. He begins in the early period with a properly ordered human society as a sure stage on the way to eternity and the fatherland. There are also stages in the universal progress of mankind in history. In his later position he abandons these stages in favor of dualistic contrasts. The crucial point about human society is the absolute division between those who are to be damned and those who are to be saved, between the city of the wicked and the city of the holy; the crucial point about history is not universal progress but again the absolute and abiding contrast of the two cities.

Nevertheless Augustine does not abandon his early ideas on how a human society should be properly ordered; these ideas persist but they are "secularized" and made neutral in relation to the dichotomy between the two cities. And insofar as Augustine has thus established a gulf between God and society, he again finds that Christianity transcends the gulf. Through faith the believer in his heavenly calling participates in a society which never falls into the mutability of time; the believer, though himself in time, is already a member of the eternal city.

One special feature of the development deserves note. Augustine starts with two large bodies of ideas, his Platonism and his Christianity, and he uses them both to say the same thing. Later he develops the Christian ideas, as we have seen, into the one true doctrine of salvation, and he reduces the Greco-Roman ideas to the secular level. As a result the Christian propositions may become statements *about* the Greek propositions with which they were originally identified. For example, the old man and the new were once identified with the outer man and the inner man. Later Augustine uses "old" and "new" to point out the relation of the whole man to eternal damnation or salvation, and he uses "outer" and "inner" to describe the parts of the whole man. Similarly the two cities of the wicked and the holy served to make statements *about* an earthly city and an earthly kingship which are neutral with respect to the eternal dualism of the two cities of damnation and salvation.

A second group of conclusions deal with the reasons for Augustine's development as these are revealed in his writings. Here we are on even more uncertain ground, and several negative observations may preface the attempt to reach some positive conclusions.

Augustine nowhere in this period seems troubled about his own individual salvation. The triumph of the Ad Simplicianum is not a "Now I am saved" but a "Now I see what I believe about how any man is saved, though I cannot grasp it."

Further, Augustine's thought does not in this period appear to have developed through any increasing concern with the ecclesia as an institution or with its sacraments or with Augustine's own office as priest or bishop. The argument is essentially *ex silentio,* but there appears to be adequate material to validate the argument.[206]

Finally, Augustine does not develop the contrast between the two cities through fear of Rome nor through enmity toward the Empire. At about the same time that he first introduces the contrast, he also expresses in the Contra Faustum a strong Christian and imperial optimism.

On the positive side, the general conclusion is, I think, that Augustine's thought develops because as a Christian intellectual he aims to state, and as far as possible to understand, what he believes and what he has experienced. He begins as a Christian and a Platonist. Why did he move away from this first position? To a first approximation, because he found that the Greco-Roman forms of thought which dominated his first position were not adequate as a statement of his own commitment and of his own experience. Why did he move to his later position on salvation? Again to a first approximation, because certain of the Christian writings available to him, and which he had always willingly accepted as authority, did to some extent offer a better statement of his commitment and his experience. It is perhaps impossible to say how far the Christian writings, notably the letters of Paul, at this stage gave something radically new and how far they merely helped him to formulate what he had already experienced. But against any thesis that Augustine is totally dependent on Paul, two main points must be made. First, there are a great many ideas in Paul, and Augustine is highly selective; second, there are a great many ideas in Augustine, and only some of them can be found also in Paul. In very oversimplified statement, Paul is primarily engaged in a Christian transformation of an earlier Judaism; Augustine is primarily engaged in a Christian transformation of an earlier Hellenism. But while Paul "secularizes" *and* relativizes the Jewish Law, Augustine secularizes but does not relativize the natural order. Augustine can make no statement about the natural order which corresponds to Paul's "Circumcision is nothing; uncircumcision is nothing." (1st. Corinthians VII, 19). Lastly, why did Augustine even in his later development continue to make such extensive use of Greco-Roman forms of thought on the descriptive level? One might suggest that he

had only recently been strongly committed to them, that his
new theory of salvation had not given him any other answer
on this level, and that one cannot live or think merely in
terms of the eternal contrast between damnation and salvation.

One last question may be raised, on the relation between
Augustine's position of about A.D. 400 and his still later position in the *De civitate Dei*. The full answer is extremely complex, but one crucial difference may be noted. In the two
cities doctrine of the De catechizandis rudibus, the earthly
cities and the Roman Empire are neutral in relation to the
absolute contrast between the cities of the wicked and of the
holy. In the *De civitate Dei*, however, the earthly city (terrena
civitas), which is often represented by the Roman Empire,
loses its neutrality, and Augustine organizes a dualistic history
around the contrast between it and the city of God. The new
terminology produces many problems for Augustine and
many difficulties for his commentators. Perhaps the best approach to these problems and difficulties is to see that Augustine's position of about A.D. 400 is both the end-point of one
development and the beginning of another. And as the earlier
development modifies without totally abandoning the ideas
of A.D. 386–93, so the later development of the *De civitate Dei*
modifies without totally abandoning the ideas of A.D. 400.

1. retract., prol. §3.
2. There appears to be no earlier treatment of this exact topic. Valuable material may be found in many works dealing with related subjects.

A. Works not limited to Augustine's early period. K. Adam, Die geistige Entwicklung des heiligen Augustinus (Augsburg, 1931); H. Arendt, Der Liebesbegriff bei Augustin (Berlin, 1929); F. Hofmann, Der Kirchenbegriff des hl. Augustinus in seinen Grundlagen und in seiner Entwicklung (München, 1933); K. Holl, "Augustins innere Entwicklung" in his Gesammelte Aufsätze zur Kirchengeschichte (Tübingen, 1928) Vol. III, 54–116; A. Pegis, "The Mind of St. Augustine" Mediaeval Studies VI (1944) 1–61; J. Ritter, Mundus Intelligibilis (Philosophische Abhandlungen VI) Frankfurt, 1937; O. Scheel, Die Anschauungen Augustins über Christi Person und Werk (Tübingen, 1901); W. Theiler, Porphyrios und Augustin (Schriften der Königsberger Gelehrten Gesellschaft, geisteswiss. Kl., XI, 1 [1933]).

B. Works dealing with the period A.D. 386–400. P. Alfaric, L'évolution intellectuelle de saint Augustin (Paris, 1918); H. Becker, Augustin. Studien zu seiner geistigen Entwicklung (Leipzig, 1908); P. Courcelle, Recherches sur les Confessions de saint Augustin (Paris, 1950) with full bibliography; A. Guzzo, Agostino dal 'Contra Academicos' al 'De vera religione' (Firenze, 1925); G. Hultgren, Le commandement d'amour chez Augustin. Interprétation philosophique et théologique d'après les écrits de la période, 386–400 (Paris, 1939); K. Janssen, Die Entstehung der Gnadenlehre Augustins (Rostock, 1936); H. Lother, "Augustins Entwicklung als Christ" Neue Kirchliche Zeitschrift XXXVII (1926) 429–42; 449–74; A. Pincherle, La formazione teologica di Sant'-Agostino (Roma, 1947); W. Thimme, "Augustins geistige Entwicklung in den ersten Jahren nach seiner Bekehrung," Neue Studien zur Geschichte der Theologie und der Kirche III (1908).

The present article is not concerned with the problem of Augustine's specific sources. A good brief account, with bibliography, of his relation to the Greco-Roman tradition may be found in B. Capelle, "Augustinus" Reallexikon für Antike und Christentum, Fasc. VII (1944) 981–93. Two significant later articles should be added; P. Courcelle, "Plotin et saint Ambroise" Revue de Philologie LXXXVI (1950) 29–56; R. Lorenz, "Die Herkunft des augustinischen FRUI DEO," Zeitschrift für Kirchengeschichte LXIV (1952–53) 34–60.

For works dealing with Augustine's theory of the two cities, see note 193, below.

3. The dates given are those of G. Bardy in his edition of the Retractationes in the Oeuvres de Saint Augustin (Bibliothèque Augustinienne) Vol. XII (Paris, 1950). There is in some cases dispute about the absolute dating, but the relative order is well-established. For a fuller discussion of the chronology of Augustine's writings, see S. M. Zarb, "Chronologia Operum S. Augustini," Angelicum X (1933) 359–96; 478–512; XI (1934) 78–91. For a bibliography of textual studies, see Clavis Patrum Latinorum (Sacris Erudiri III, 1951) 50–74.

4. For the dating of the various parts of the lib. arb., see W. Thimme, op. cit. (note 2 B.) p. 6–10.

5. c. Acad. III, 20, §43; compare c. Acad. II, 2, §5, and ver. relig. 5, §8. Sic enim creditur et docetur, quod est humanae salutis caput, non aliam esse philosophiam, id est sapientiae studium, et aliam religionem. . . .

6. c. Acad. III, 20, §43 ita enim iam sum affectus, ut quid sit uerum non credendo solum sed etiam intelligendo apprehendere impatienter desiderem. Compare c. Acad. II, 2, §4 f.; lib. arb. I, 2, §4 f., II, 2, §5 f.

7. c. Acad. III, 19, §42. For the return to heaven, compare II, 1, §2 ergo non erumpet aliquando ista uirtus et . . . rursus proiecto totius corporis onere recurret in caelum. II, 8, §22 de uita nostra de moribus de animo res agitur, qui se superaturum inimicitias omnium fallaciarum et ueritate comprehensa quasi in regionem suae originis rediens triumphaturum de libidinibus atque ita temperantia uelut coniuge accepta regnaturum esse praesumit securior rediturus in caelum. In the retract. I, 1, §3 Augustine observes that he should have said *iturus in caelum* and not *rediturus*.

8. anim. quant I, §2 utrumnam quasi regionem ejus (sc. animae) et patriam, unde huc venerit, nosse desideras . . . Propriam quamdam habitationem animae ac patriam, Deum ipsum credo esse a quo creata est. Compare mag. 8, §21 . . . vires et mentis aciem, quibus regionis illius, ubi beata vita est, calorem ac lucem non modo sustinere, verum etiam amare possimus. In lib. arb. III, 9, §27–28 Augustine speaks of the *habitatio caelestis* of the soul; in sol. I, 1, §4 he prays to God as . . . domus mea, patria mea, salus mea.

9. b. vit. I, §1–2. The *portus philosophiae* appears also in c. Acad. II, 1, §1; for the *portus sapientiae,* see c. Acad. I, 1, §1 and III, 2, §3. For the notion of pilgrimage, compare anim. quant. 31, §63, where Augustine urges the soul not to plunge too deeply into the senses, donec corrigas firmesque vestigia, quae usque ad ipsum

deum animum ducunt: ne ab illo secretissimo et tranquillissimo mentis habitaculo, a quo nunc, dum haec incolit, peregrina est . . . avertaris; epist. II (A.D. 386–87) . . . ut se totus animus, etiam dum hoc corpus agit, in ea quae semper eiusdem modi sunt neque peregrino pulchro placent, feratur atque aestuat. In b. vit. 1, §2 (possibly in sol. I, 1, §1) Augustine speaks of the *cives* of the fatherland.

10. c. Acad. III, 17, §37. The *civiles virtutes* are not mentioned again in the early works. For an interesting later usage see epist. CXXXVIII, 3, §17.

11. c. Acad. III, 18, §40. Compare lib. arb. III, 9, §28 Ideo quanquam orbis iste terrenus rebus corruptibilibus deputatus sit, tamen servans quantum potest imagines superiorum, exempla nobis et indicia quaedam demonstrare non cessat; div. quaest. 83, §53, 2.

12. sol. I, 1, §3. For Augustine's later revision of these statements, see retract. I, 4, §2. Compare also ord. I, 11, §32 esse autem alium mundum ab istis oculis remotissimum, quem paucorum sanorum intellectus intuetur, satis ipse Christus significat, qui non dicit, "Regnum meum non est de mundo," sed: "Regnum meum non est de hoc mundo." Here too Augustine later revises his statement, retract. I, 3, §8.

13. ord. II, 8, §25.

14. For some useful comments on the organization of the De ordine, see A. Dyroff, "Über Form und Begriffsgehalt der augustinischen Schrift De Ordine" in: Aurelius Augustinus, Festschrift der Görresgesellschaft zum 1500 Todestag des hl. Augustinus (Köln, 1930) 15–62. For the concept of *ordo* here, see Hultgren, *op. cit.* (note 2 B.) p. 25 f.

15. ord. I, 7, §18; II, 4, §12.

16. ord. I, 8, §26.

17. ord. II, 5, §14.

18. ord. II, 8, §25. There is a somewhat cryptic reference to Pythagorean politics at the very end of the De ordine. II, 20, §54 . . . mirari et paene cotidianis, ut scis, ecferre laudibus soleo, quod regendae rei publicae disciplinam suis auditoribus ultimam tradebat iam doctis iam perfectis iam sapientibus iam beatis.

19. lib. arb. I, 16, §35. Compare §34 utrum sit aliud male facere, quam neglectis rebus aeternis, quibus per seipsam mens fruitur, et per seipsam percipit, et quas amans amittere non potest, temporalia et quae per corpus hominis partem vilissimam sentiuntur, et numquam esse certa possunt, quasi magna et miranda sectari. Nam hoc uno genere omnia malefacta, id est peccata, mihi videntur includi.

20. lib. arb. I, 6, §15. For a useful description of Augustine's

texts on the eternal law, see A. Schubert, Augustins Lex-aeterna-Lehre (Beiträge zur Geschichte der Philosophie des Mittelalters XXIV, 2 [1924]). Augustine does not at this time appear to have any separate concept of a *lex naturalis;* compare div. quaest. 83, §53, 2.

21. E.g., lib. arb. I, 6, §15. Simul etiam te videre arbitror in illa temporali (sc. lege) nihil esse justum atque legitimum, quod non ex hac aeterna sibi homines derivarint; I, 15, §31; ver. relig. 31, §58.

22. lib. arb. I, 15, §32. Compare I, 5, §13. Ea enim vindicanda sibi haec lex populi assumit, quae satis sint conciliandae paci hominibus imperitis, et quanta possunt per hominem regi.

23. lib. arb. I, 15, §32. It is not clear what Augustine thinks of the implied contrast with *celestial* peoples and cities. In lib. arb. III, 20, §57 he mentions *civitatis beatissimae gloriam,* but this is in a later section of the De libero arbitrio, dated by Thimme in Augustine's priesthood, *op. cit.* (note 2 B.) p. 9.

24. lib. arb. I, 16, §34 et rerum duo genera, aeternarum et temporalium, duoque rursus hominum, aliorum aeternas, aliorum temporales sequentium et diligentium, satis aperteque distincta sunt. Compare I, 15, §31. Cum igitur manifestum sit alios esse homines amatores rerum aeternarum, alios temporalium . . . nam beatos illos ob amorem ipsorum aeternorum sub aeterna lege agere existimo, miseris vero temporalis imponitur. In the last part of the argument Augustine seems to be thinking not so much of the law of human society as of the law of God's providence which is imposed on those who will not accept it freely. See, e.g., mus. VI, 10, §30, where the sinner, Turpis enim factus est voluntate, universum amittendo quod Dei praeceptis obtemperans possidebat, et ordinatus in parte est, ut qui legem agere noluit, a lege agatur. Compare also en. in Psalm. I, §2; div. quaest. 83, §27; mus. VI, 14, §48.

25. Compare lib. arb. I, 16, §34. quid autem quisque sectandum et amplectandum eligat, in voluntate esse positum consistit, nullaque re de arce dominandi rectoque ordine mentem deponi nisi voluntate.

26. lib. arb. II, 16, §41. The reference to wisdom is a reminiscence of Wisdom VI, 17; for other similar reminiscences, see lib. arb. III, 16, §42 and 17, §45. For the general approach, compare ord. I, 8, §25 quid enim non ambiunt, qua non peragrant oculi amantum, ne quid undeunde innuat pulchritudo rationis cuncta scientia et nescientia modificantis et gubernantis, quae inhiantes sibi sectatores suos trahit quacumque atque ubique se quaeri iubet?

27. retract. I, 5, §6 (=ed. Maur. I, 6) Augustine here speaks

of moving *quibusdam quasi passibus certis*. His more usual expression is that found e.g. in mus. VI, 1, §1 ut . . . non praepropere, sed *quibusdam gradibus* a sensibus carnis . . . avellerentur.

28. retract. I, 10, §1 (ed. Maur. I, 11, §1).

29. mus. VI, 5, §13. Compare anim. quant. 36, §80. Deus igitur summus et verus lege inviolabili et incorrupta, qua omne quod condidit regit, subjicit animae corpus, animam sibi, et sic omnia sibi . . . ; serm. CCXIV, 2 (A.D. 391) Haec omnia fecit omnipotens, mediis ima et summa conjungens.

30. mus. VI, 13, §40 Generalis vero amor actionis quae avertit a vero, a superbia proficiscitur, quo vitio Deum imitari quam Deo serviri anima maluit.

31. mus. VI, 14, §48; VI, 16, §53. Compare lib. arb. I, 6, §14 Porro si paulatim depravatus idem populus rem privatam rei publicae praefert . . . II, 16, §41 ut non jam privato suo gaudeat quod implicavit rebus transeuntibus sed exuta omnibus temporum et locorum affectionibus apprehendat id quod unum atque idem semper est; ver. relig. 46, §88. The contrast is developed at length in the probably later div. quaest. 83, §79, 1.

32. mus. VI, 13, §41.

33. mus. VI, 15, §50.

34. mus. VI, 14, §46. Compare §43.

35. mus. VI, 14, §45. Augustine makes the statement in terms of the technical distinction between the four "numbers" of rhythm, but he actually organizes his ideas around a triple classification of the lusts (see note 42 below). . . . homo . . . qui omnes illos numeros qui sunt de corpore, et adversus passiones corporis, et qui ex his memoria continentur, non ad carnalem voluptatem sed ad salutem tantum corporis refert: omnesque illos qui de adjunctis animis operantur, vel qui ad adjungendas exseruntur (see mus. VI, 13, §41–42 for the distinction) non ad superbam excellentiam suam, sed ad ipsarum animarum utilitatem redigit. . . .

36. mus. VI, 14, §45. For the notion of a common bond, see ord. II, 12, §35; epist. XXXIII, 1.

37. mus. VI, 14, §46. Compare mor. eccl. cath. I, 26, §48 . . . ut nullus certior gradus ad amorem Dei fieri posse credatur, quam hominis erga hominem charitas; De utilitate credendi 10, §24 CSEL XXV, 1 p. 30; Contra Adimantum §6 CSEL XXV, 1 p. 126.

38. On the De vera religione, see H. Dörries, "Das Verhältnis des Neuplatonischen und Christlichen in Augustins 'De vera religione'" Zeitschrift für die neutestamentliche Wissenschaft XXIII (1924) 64–102 and W. Theiler, *op. cit.* (note 2 A.) p. 7 f.

39. ver. relig. 29, §52. In a part of the section closer to the terminology of the De musica, Augustine declares: In quorum con-

sideratione non vana et peritura curiositas exercenda est, sed gradus ad immortalia et semper manentia faciendus.

40. ver. relig. 52, §101. Compare ord. II, 19, §51. . . . promitti nobis aspectum pulchritudinis, cuius imitatione pulchra, cuius conparatione foeda sunt cetera.

41. ver. relig. 39, §72.

42. ver. relig. 38, §69 Serviunt enim cupiditati triplici, vel voluptatis, vel excellentiae, vel spectaculi. §7 . . . vel libidine, vel superbia, vel curiositate damnati. In §70 Augustine uses I John II, 16 as biblical authority and in §71 he links the classification to the triple temptation of Christ. For a philosophic derivation of it, see lib. arb. II, 19, §53 with parallels in mus. VI, 14, §45. On occasion, Augustine links the lusts with certain of the animals of the creation story, e.g. Gen. c. Man. I, 23, §40; en. in Psalm. VIII, 13. See W. Theiler, *op. cit.* (note 2 A.), p. 36 f.

43. ver. relig. 45, §84.

44. ver. relig. 45, §85; compare 52, §101.

45. ver. relig. 46, §86 f. §89 ipsa igitur natura humana sine carnali conditione diligenda est, sive sit perficienda sive perfecta. For a penetrating analysis of Augustine's thought in this area, see H. Arendt, *op. cit.* (note 2 A.).

46. ver. relig. 47, §91. Et quamquam temporalia non diligit, ipse recte utitur temporalibus, et pro eorum sorte hominibus consulit.

47. ver. relig. 48, §93.

48. See p. 338 above.

49. See p. 341 above. Compare Gen. c. Man. I, 3, §6 Illud autem lumen non irrationabilium avium oculos pascit, sed pura corda eorum qui Deo credunt, et ab amore visibilium rerum et temporalium se ad ejus praecepta implenda convertunt. Quod omnes homines possunt si velint. . . .

50. See p. 338 above. Compare div. quaest. 83, §25. Sapientia Dei hominem ad exemplum, quo recte viveremus, suscepit.; §43; In ver. relig. 16, §32–17, §33 Augustine explains the Incarnation as illustrating disciplina morum, disciplina naturalis, and disciplina rationalis. Valuable material on the problem may be found in O. Scheel, *op. cit.* (note 2 A.) p. 1–149.

51. Compare the use of *schola Dei* in serm. II, 4, §5 (c. A.D. 391) and in serm. CCXCII, 1, §1 (A.D. 393–405). For an analysis of Augustine's thought about the ecclesia in this period see F. Hofmann, *op. cit.* (note 2 A.) p. 36 f.

52. E.g. mag. 12, §39 Namque omnia quae percipimus aut sensu corporis aut mente percipimus. Illa sensibilia, haec intelligibilia, sive, ut more auctorum nostrorum loquar, illa carnalia,

haec spiritualia nominamus. Compare De duabus animabus §12
CSEL XXV, 1 p. 66.

53. E.g. mor. eccl. cath. I, 22, §40. Sed inter omnia quae in hac
vita possidentur, corpus homini gravissimum vinculum est, justis-
simis Dei legibus, propter antiquum peccatum, quo nihil est ad
praedicandum notius, nihil ad intelligendum secretius. Compare
anim. quant. 28, §55; 33, §76.

54. serm. CCXVI, 4, §4.

55. See note 26 above.

56. serm. CCXVI, 1, §1 . . . ut inhabitem in domo Domini
omnes dies vitae meae. Atque hujus regionis et habitationis beati-
tudinem explanans. . . . Compare the probably contemporary
serm. CCXIV, 8–9 for similar expressions, and see note 8 above.

57. serm. CCLIX, 2–3. If Augustine had written retractationes
on the sermons he would probably have changed the *rediemus* of
§2, as in the contra Academicos he changed *rediturus in caelum*.
See note 7 above. For the eighth day as a return *ad caput*, see serm.
in mon. I, 4, §12. For chiliastic parallels, see div. quaest. 83, §57, 2;
en. in Psalm. VI, 1 f.

58. Compare, for example, serm. CCXIV, §11 (A.D. 391) Sanctam quoque ecclesiam matrem vestram, tanquam supernam Jerusalem sanctam civitatem Dei honorate, diligite, praedicate;
CCCLIII, 2, §4 (A.D. 391–96); CXC, 3, §3 (A.D. 391–400); CCLII,
7, §7 (A.D. 396). There are also a few references in other writings,
e.g. lib. arb. III, 20, §57. God prepares, civitatis beatissimae
gloriam triumphantibus de illo qui primum hominem ad istam mis-
eriam perduxit.; Gen. c. Man. II, 10, §13; De fide et symbolo 6,
§13 CSEL XLI, 15; serm. in mon. I, 15, §41; II, 25, §84; en. in
Psalm. XV, 3.

59. It appears that in this period Augustine usually speaks of
the ecclesia simply as a preparation for the heavenly city of God;
he does not identify the ecclesia with the heavenly city. Compare,
e.g. en. in psalm. V, 8 . . . quibus civitas illa constabit, quam nunc
parturit et paulatim parit ecclesia; exp. Galat. §24 (with the variant
readings); div. quaest. 83, §61, 2. Whether Augustine does or does
not call the ecclesia on earth a city of God is perhaps merely a
question of style. In serm. L, 8, §11 (A.D. 394–95) there is an account of three "houses" of the Lord: . . . in domo ejus, id est in
ecclesia, ... Prima enim domus, id est, cives terrenae Jerusalem. . . . ad aeternam gloriam domus novissimae. It would seem
to take no more than a change in terminology to make this a doctrine of three "cities." It would take more than a change of terminology for Augustine at this time to speak of a *single* society which
includes both the angels in heaven and the Christians on earth; for

this development see the discussion of the De catechizandis rudibus, p. 378 below. Serm. XV, 3 (before A.D. 400) illustrates the later approach; however the argument of the sermon is close to that of the Contra Faustum (see below p. 375 f.), and it should not be dated much before 400.

60.   div. quaest. 83, §49.

61.   div. quaest. 83, §64, 2 . . . quoniam omnia visibilia ad exteriorem hominem pertinent, quibus christiana disciplina renuntiatur. . . . quoniam et nobis vocatis a Christo visibilium delectatio minuitur, ut invisibilium amore homo interior recreatus, ad interiorem lucem quae numquam occidit, revertatur; en. in Psalm. I, 4 . . . quia ut haec terra visibilis exteriorem hominem nutrit et continet, ita illa terra invisibilis interiorem hominem; ver. relig. 39, §72; mag. 1, §2.

62.   div. quaest. 83, §36, 2; §64, 2; ver. relig. 26, §48–49; mor. eccl. cath. I, 19, §36.

63.   On this theory, see H. Scholz, Glaube und Unglaube in der Weltgeschichte (Leipzig, 1911) p. 154 f.; Oeuvres de Saint Augustin (Bibliothèque Augustinienne) Vol. XI (Paris, 1949) 552–54. Most of the extensive bibliography of Augustine's ideas of history deals only with his later position; however there is an excellent statement of the differences between the De vera religione and the De civitate Dei in the important work of W. Kamlah, Christentum und Geschichtlichkeit, 2nd ed. (Stuttgart, 1951) p. 302 f. and particularly 311 f.

64.   Gen. c. Man. I, 23, §35 f.

65.   ver. relig. 26, §48.

66.   ver. relig. 26, §49.

67.   ver. relig. 26, §49. Augustine on a number of occasions works out schemes of progress and ascent, and many of these show similarities with the schemes of the Gen. c. Man. and of the ver. relig. Compare for example anim. quant. 33, §70 f. and doctr. christ. II, 7, §9 f. On the general topic, see E. Hendrikx, Augustins Verhältnis zur Mystik (Cassiciacum I, 1936) p. 110–23; J. Pépin, "Primitiae Spiritus. Remarques sur une citation paulinienne des 'Confessions' de saint Augustin" Revue de l'histoire des religions CXL (1951) 155–202 p. 193 f. with note 2.

68.   ver. relig. 26, §49. It must be remembered that Augustine still defines sin as in the passages cited note 19, above.

69.   ver. relig. 27, §50. At about this time, Augustine frequently distinguishes the two aspects of God's providence, individual and public. Compare ver. relig. 25, §46. Quoniam igitur divina providentia non solum singulis hominibus quasi privatim, sed universo generi humano tanquam publice consulit.; div. quaest. 83, §44 aliud

enim est quod divina providentia quasi privatim cum singulis agit, aliud quod generi universo tanquam publice consulit.

70. ver. relig. 27, §50.

71. For the lib. arb., see p. 342 above. The distinction between the impious and those devoted to the true God is not utilized in Augustine's outline of history, and he treats the Jews and the Christians as if together they constituted the human race. In ver. relig. 28, §51 he remarks of the prophets, Quisquis autem populi terreni temporibus usque ad illuminationem interioris hominis meruit pervenire, *genus humanum* pro tempore adjuvit . . .

72. serm. in mon. I, 2, §9. Compare with the *homo ordinatissimus* of lib. arb. I, 8, §18 f.

73. E.g., ver. relig. 28, §51 Non enim honoribus suis vanis consulunt et inanibus laudibus, sed utilitati eorum cum quibus societatem vitae hujus inire meruerunt; Gen. c. Man. I, 25, §43 propter utilitatem fraternae societatis; mor. eccl. cath. I, 26, §48.

74. serm. in mon. I, 15, §41.

75. ver. relig. 55, §111. Compare en. in Psalm II, 9.

76. E.g. De utilitate credendi 12, §27 CSEL XXV, 1 p. 34; exp. Galat. §36; Contra Epistulam Fundamenti 4, CSEL XXV, 1 p. 196. On the general development see F. Hofmann, *op. cit.* (note 2 A.) p. 99 f.

77. Compare serm. in mon. I, 12, §34; Contra Fortunatum Disputatio §22, CSEL XXV p. 104 f. On the development, see K. Janssen, *op. cit.* (note 2 B.) p. 96 f.

78. Compare O. Scheel, *op. cit.* (note 2 A.) p. 79 f.

79. Compare F. Hofmann, *op. cit.* (note 2 A.) p. 76 f.

80. E.g. div. quaest. 83, §58, 2; §64, 2; serm. CCLIX, 2 (c. A.D. 393); contra Adimantum 2 CSEL XXV, 118.

81. The most important texts are listed in H. Scholz, *op. cit.* (note 63) p. 154 f.

82. exp. prop. Roman §13–18 with frequent later allusions: §30, 35, 45–46, 51, and 53. Compare also exp. Galat. §46 and §61; div. quaest. 83, §61, 7 and 66, 3. On Augustine's use of this scheme of history, see P. Platz, Der Römerbrief in der Gnadenlehre Augustins (Cassiciacum V, 1938) p. 123 f.

83. div. quaest. 83, §66, 3 Ex quo comprehendimus, quatuor esse differentias in uno homine quibus gradatim peractis in vita aeterna manebitur. Augustine appears in this scheme to have placed the Jews in *pueritia* and the Christians in *juventus;* see div. quaest. 83, §44, §49; exp. Galat. §28; retract. I, 25, §44 (= ed. Maur. I, 26).

84. See above, p. 350 f.

85. mor. eccl. cath. I, 28, §56; ver. relig. 4, §9; 17, §33; serm.

in mon. I, 1, §2; de utilitate credendi 3, §9 CSEL XXV, 12; exp. Galat. §19, §22; div. quaest. 83, §61, 1.

86. exp. Galat. §58. Compare §7 non per illam spiritualem legem quam acceperunt Judaei. . . . Lex enim spiritualis est nec carnaliter se cogit intelligi, sed illorum vitium est, qui et illa quae acceperunt carnaliter sentiunt.

87. exp. prop. Roman. §52. Augustine does not wish to set up a merely comparative distinction between the Jews (spiritus servitutis) and the Christians (spiritus adoptionis). Nam si spiritum servitutis ipsum spiritum hominis intellexerimus, incipit spiritus adoptionis ipse intelligi tanquam in melius commutatus.

88. exp. Galat. §40. It will be noted that Augustine does not yet say what he does in the De baptismo contra Donatistas (A.D. 401) I, 15, §24 CSEL LI, 168 Ecclesia uero, quod est populus Dei, etiam in istius uitae peregrinatione antiqua res est. . . .

89. exp. Galat. §23. On the general problem, see J. Beumer, "Die Idee einer vorchristlichen Kirche bei Augustinus" Münchener Theologische Zeitschrift III (1952) 161–75.

90. For explicit statements of Augustine's changed attitude toward the six ages, compare the later texts: Quaestionum Libri VII, VII, §49 CSEL XXVIII, 2 p. 500. . . . ex omnibus quippe aetatibus ecclesia congregatur. In Joannis Evangelium, Tract. IX, 6 PL XXXV, 1461. Illa ergo tempora sex, quasi articulis distributa atque distincta, quasi vasa essent inania, nisi a Christo implerentur.

91. *massa peccati* is used div. quaest. 83, §68, 3 . . . et omnes una massa luti facti sumus, quod est massa peccati.

92. exp. prop. Roman. §44, §55.

93. exp. prop. Roman. §55; §60 f.

94. Augustine was well aware of the importance of the Ad Simplicianum in his development. Compare retract. II, 27, §3 (= ed. Maur. II, 1, §1) in cuius quaestionis solutione laboratum est quidem pro libero arbitrio uoluntatis humanae, sed uicit dei gratia . . . ; De praedestinatione sanctorum 4, §8 (PL XLIV, 965 f.) Videtis certe quid tunc (= exp. prop. Roman.) de fide atque operibus sentiebam, quamvis de commendanda gratia Dei laborarem: in qua sententia istos fratres nostros esse nunc video; quia non sicut legere meos libros, ita etiam in eis curaverunt proficere mecum. Nam si curassent, invenissent istam quaestionem secundum veritatem divinarum Scripturarum solutam in primo libro duorum, quos ad beatae memoriae Simplicianum scripsi . . . ; De dono perseverantiae 20, §52 (PL XLV, 1026).

95. Simplic. I, 2, 22.

96. Simplic. I, 2, 19.

97. Augustine cites the passage as follows: Et omnes homines

de solo, et ex terra Adam creatus est. In multitudine disciplinae Dominus separavit eos, et immutavit vias eorum. Et ex ipsis benedixit et exaltavit, et ex his sanctificavit et ad se applicavit, et ex ipsis maledixit et humiliavit: et convertit illos ad dissensionem illorum. Quasi lutum figuli in manu ipsius plasmare illud et disponere, omnes viae ejus secundum dispositionem ejus; sic homo in manu illius qui se fecit, et reddet illi secundum judicium suum. Contrarium malo bonum est, et contra mortem vita est; sic et contra virum justum peccator. Et sic intuere in omnia opera altissimi: duo, duo; unum contra unum.

98.   Simplic. I, 2, 20.

99.   *Ibid.*

100.   Simplic. I, 2, 20–21.

101.   See above, p. 349 f.

102.   Simplic. I, 2, 20. Similar statements are found in the roughly contemporary Contra Epistulam Fundamenti §33 (CSEL XXV, 236–37) applied to a prince of the Manichaean realm of evil. Lauda tu mecum speciem, distinctionem, ordinationem, pacem, unitatem formarum, membrorum congruentias et numerosas parilitates, uitalia spiramenta et nutrimenta, temperamentum salutis, regimen et moderamen animae famulatusque corporis, . . . adtendite quanta laudabilia remanebunt: compago corporis, membrorum hinc atque inde congruentia, formae unitas et pax contextarum inter se partium, animae regentis et uegetantis famulantisque et uegatati corporis ordo et dispositio.

103.   Simplic. I, 2, 18. Compare the definition of sin with that given above p. 341 and note 19; there is a new emphasis on the contrast between creator and creature as fundamental.

104.   Simplic. I, 2, 16.

105.   Simplic. I, 2, 16. In ipsis rebus humanis terrenisque contractibus . . . in quibus nisi supernae justitiae quaedam impressa vestigia teneremus, numquam in ipsum cubile ac penetrale sanctissimum atque castissimum spiritualium praeceptorum nostrae infirmitatis suspiceret atque inhiaret intentio. . . . Haec imago vel, ut supra dixi, vestigium negotiis hominum de fastigio summo aequitatis impressum est. For a similar passage, probably somewhat earlier, see div. quaest. 83, §53, 2. Ex hac igitur ineffabili atque sublimi rerum administratione, quae fit per divinam providentiam, quasi transcripta est naturalis lex in animam rationalem, ut in ipsa vitae hujus conversatione moribusque terrenis homines talium distributionum imagines servent.

106.   Simplic. I, 2, 16 . . . quod Deus "cujus vult miseretur et quem vult obdurat," hoc est, cujus vult miseretur et cujus vult non miseretur, esse alicujus occultae atque ab humano modulo investi-

gabilis aequitatis. . . . Eorum autem non miseretur, quibus mis-
ericordiam non esse praebendam, aequitate occultissima et ab humanis sensibus remotissima judicat. Inscrutabilia enim sunt judicia
ejus, et investigabiles viae ipsius (Romans XI, 33).

In the writings of the preceding period Augustine sometimes
speaks of "hiddenness" in a similar context but its meaning is
different: e.g. div. quaest. 83, §68, 4 Prorsus cujus vult miseretur
et quem vult obdurat; sed haec voluntas Dei injusta esse non potest.
Venit enim de occultissimis meritis . . . ; exp. prop. Roman. §63;
possibly serm. CCXIV, 3 (A.D. 391). Here it is the "facts" which
are hidden, and if Augustine knew them he would understand the
Why of God's action; in the case of Jacob and Esau, there are no
facts, and the Why of the action must remain incomprehensible.

The notion of incomprehensibility as it appears in the Ad Simplicianum should, I think, be distinguished from Neoplatonist un-
knowability as it is found in the De ordine II, 16, §44; 18, §47 in
relation to God. Similarly this "measure" which cannot be grasped
is to be distinguished from the "measure without measure" of De
Genesi ad Litteram IV, 3, §7. On this last, see J. Ritter, *op. cit.*
(Note 2 A.) p. 11.

107.   Simplic. I, 2, 22. In contrast, compare the early ord. II,
7, §24. et tamen etiam ista omnia, quae fatemur esse peruersa, non
esse praeter diuinum ordinem alta quaedam et a multitudinis uel
suspicione remotissima disciplina se ita studiosis et deum atque
animas tantum amantibus manifestaturam esse promittit, ut non
nobis summae numerorum possint esse certiores.

108.   On the Confessiones in general, see P. Courcelle, *op. cit.*
(note 2 B.) with full bibliography; F. Cayré, "Le sens et l'unité des
Confessions de saint Augustin" L'année théologique augustinienne
XIII (1953) 13–32.

109.   conf. I, 1, §1. There are some comments on the interpretation of Psalm CXLVI, 6 in en. in Psalm. CXLVI, §11. Ergo intelli-
gentiae ejus non est numerus. Conticescant humanae voces, requies-
cant humanae cogitationes: ad incomprehensibilia non se extendant
quasi comprehensuri, sed tanquam participaturi; . . . dictum est de
Jerusalem, cujus dispersiones colligit, dictum est de illa quiddam
magnum: Jerusalem quae aedificatur ut civitas, cujus participatio
est in idipsum. (Psalm CXXI, 3).

110.   See p. 343 f. above.

111.   Book X stands somewhat apart from the rest of the work
and will be treated separately; see p. 368 below.

112.   For the distinction, see note 69, above.

113.   conf. VII, 20, §26; 21, §27.

114.   conf. VII, 17, §23; 20, §26.

115. conf. IX, 10, §23. On the vision at Ostia, see P. Courcelle, *op. cit.* (note 2 B.) p. 222 f.; J. Pépin, *op. cit.* (note 67, above).

116. conf. IX, 10, §24.

117. conf. IX, 13, §33.

118. conf. XI, 2, §3 et considerem mirabilia de lege tua ab usque principio, in quo fecisti caelum et terram, usque ad regnum tecum perpetuum sanctae civitatis tuae. Compare X, 43, §70. ecce domine, iacto in te curam meam, ut vivam et considerabo mirabilia de lege tua.

There has been surprisingly little scholarly study of Books XI–XIII of the Confessiones. See however W. Lipgens, "Die Bekenntnisse Augustins als Beitrag zur christlichen Geschichtsauffassung" Münchener Theologische Zeitschrift (II [1951] 164–77); J.-M. Le Blond, Les Conversions de Saint Augustin (Paris, 1950) Part III.

119. conf. XI, 2, §4.

120. On Augustine's doctrine of time, particularly in the Confessiones, see P. Brunner, "Zur Auseinandersetzung zwischen antikem und christlichen Zeit- und Geschichtsverständnis bei Augustin" Zeitschrift für Theologie und Kirche N.F. XIV (1933) 1–25; J. F. Callahan, Four Views of Time in Ancient Philosophy (Cambridge, 1948), Chapter IV; C. Rau, "Theories of Time in Ancient Philosophy" Philosophical Review LXII (1953) 514–25.

121. Compare p. 343 f. above, on the De musica, and mus. VI, 11, §29.

122. conf. XI, 22, §38.

123. *Ibid.*

124. conf. XI, 29, §39.

125. conf. XI, 29, §39 . . . praeterita oblitus, non in ea quae futura et transitura sunt, sed in ea quae ante sunt non distentus sed extentus, non secundum distentionem sed secundum intentionem sequor ad palmam supernae vocationis . . . Augustine's experience of his eternal calling to the heavenly Israel seems regularly to be stated through some use of Philippians III, 12–14. Compare e.g. conf. IX, 10, §23 (see p. 361 above); conf. XII, 16, §23 . . . et recordans Hierusalem extento in eam sursum corde . . . ; doctr. christ. I, 34, §38 (see p. 375 below). For other possibly contemporary interpretations of the text, see serm. CCLV, 6, §6 (A.D. 418, but see Kunzelmann, *op. cit.* [p. 338 above] p. 479.); serm. Denis XVIII, 2 (at latest A.D. 399).

It will be noted that Paul has a simple contrast between the things which are past and the things which are before, and the things which are before serve to express man's heavenly calling. Augustine's scheme is more complicated. He has the contrast between past and future and the corresponding actions of memory and expectation. However both memory and expectation are grouped together as distention, and Augustine's distention in time is contrasted with his intention (sometimes extention) on his eternal calling.

In his early period, Augustine makes use of a simpler interpretation which harmonizes well with his Platonism of the time: Gen. c. Man. II, 9, §12. . . . anima quae debet in ea quae anteriora sunt se extendere, id est, in Deum, et ea quae posteriora sunt oblivisci, id est, corporeas voluptates.

126.   conf. XI, 29, §39 at ego in tempora dissilui, quorum ordinem nescio, . . .

127.   conf. XI, 31, §41.

128.   conf. XII, 9, §9.

129.   conf. XII, 11, §12.

130.   conf. XII, 11, §12.

131.   conf. XII, 16, §23.

132.   See the account of the dialogue at Ostia, p. 361 f. above.

133.   conf. XII, 32, §43.

134.   conf. XIII, 8, §9; compare XIII, 2, §3.

135.   conf. XIII, 10, §11.

136.   conf. XIII, 14, §15.

137.   conf. XIII, 20, §28. It will be noted that Augustine is making use of the triple classification of the lusts; see note 42 above.

138.   conf. XIII, 17, §20.

139.   conf. XIII, 17, §20.

140.   conf. XIII, 17, §21. In conf. XIII, 23, §33 Augustine identifies the land with the ecclesia.

141.   conf. XIII, 15, §16.

142.   conf. XIII, 15, §18.

143.   conf. XIII, 17, §21.

144.   conf. XIII, 18, §23. In XIII, 20, §27, Augustine groups *sapientia* and *scientia* together in contrast to *operationes corporales*.

145.   conf. XIII, 20, §27.

146.   conf. XIII, 21, §29.

147.   conf. XIII, 21, §30–31. Particularly interesting is Augustine's statement on "knowledge": §31 . . . et serpentes boni non perniciosi ad nocendum, sed astuti ad cavendum et tantum explorantes temporalem naturam, quantum sufficit, ut per ea quae facta sunt, intellecta conspiciatur aeternitas. In the early works (see e.g. p. 343 above) such an ascent leads to the highest point of the Christian's life on earth; here in the Confessiones, it has in some way been "secularized."

148. conf. XIII, 23, §34.

149. conf. XIII, 18, §23.

150. conf. XIII, 29, §44. Compare XIII, 18, §22. Tu autem idem ipse est et in annis tuis qui non deficiunt, horreum praeparas annis transeuntibus.

151. conf. XIII, 34, §49.

152. conf. XIII, 32, §47.

153. conf. XIII, 31, §46.

154. conf. XIII, 21, §29.

155. conf. XIII, 27, §42.

156. For its place in the whole work and the argument that Book X is a later addition, see E. Williger, "Der Aufbau der Konfessionen Augustins" Zeitschrift für die neutestamentliche Wissenschaft XXVIII (1929) 81–106.

157. conf. X, 6, §10. sed amore subduntur eis et subditi iudicare non possunt. Contrast this with the earlier account of Romans I, 20 in ver. relig. 52, §101. Imo vero commemorati ab iis quae judicamus. . . .

158. conf. X, 24, §35.

159. conf. X, 26, §37.

160. Compare notes 42 and 137 above. For a comparison of the argument in the conf. with that in the ver. relig. see W. Theiler, op. cit. (note 2 A) p. 40 f.

161. See above p. 344 f.

162. conf. X, 36, §59. For the phrase humanae societatis officia, see mor. eccl. cath. I, 26, §49.

163. c. Faust. XV, 8; compare XVII, 6; XIX, 7; XXII, 6. For an assimilation of the Old Testament heroes to the Christians, see XIX, 14; for the absence of any emphasis on the progressive character of the five ages, see XII, 8 and 14.

164. c. Faust. XXII, 27, 28, 30, 43, 61, 73, and 78.

165. One might here notice the contrast between the earlier statement of the De ordine II, 18, §47 hic est ordo studiorum sapientiae, per quem fit quisque idoneus ad intelligendum ordinem rerum, id est ad dinoscendos duos mundos et ipsum parentem uniuersitatis . . . and div. quaest. 83, §81, 1 Omnis sapientiae disciplina, quae ad homines erudiendos pertinet, est creatorem creaturamque dignoscere, et illum colere dominantem, istam subjectam fateri. Compare note 119, above.

166. c. Faust. XXII, 72. Compare XXI, 2–3.

167. c. Faust. XXII, 78.

168. c. Faust. XXII, 71.

169. c. Faust. XXVI, 3.

170. c. Faust. XXII, 27.

171.   c. Faust. XXII, 75.

172.   c. Faust. XXII, 75. Compare XXII, 74 . . . salutis publicae defensores; XXII, 31 . . . in caeteris actibus ad humanam
pacem pertinentibus.

173.   Compare e.g. exp. prop. Roman, §72, §74. exp. Galat.
§28.

174.   c. Faust. XIX, 24 et diligamus inimicum propter id quod
in eo bonum est, id est, socialem rationalemque creaturam.

175.   c. Faust. XXII, 76. Compare XII, 32 . . . quia ecce con-
spicimus leges ipsas regni terreni quae aduersus Christum ante
fremuerant, nunc jam perempta feritate dulcedini evangelicae
praedicandae etiam munimenta praebere.

In the passage quoted in the text, Augustine speaks of the *civitas
impiorum*. There are other passages in which Augustine indicates
that he is still making use of a dualist interpretation of history;
see for example the contrast between *corpus diaboli* and *corpus
dominicum* in XXII, 93. However there was no need to emphasize
this dualism in answering the Manichaean arguments, and Augustine may have deliberately avoided it as dangerously close to the
Manichaean argument on two kingdoms.

176.   See above p. 349 f.

177.   There are a few passages before the Contra Faustum
which suggest that Augustine has modified his earlier position; e.g.
conf. XIII, 14, §15 speaks of *interius nostrum tenebrosum et
fluvidum*. In div. quaest. 83, §64, 2 Augustine still writes, Et quoniam exterior est homo vetus, et novus interior.

178.   c. Faust. XXIV, 1. Compare with Faustus' position the
earlier statement of Augustine himself, div. quaest. 83, §36, 2. Tunc
jam persuadendum est fidelibus praecedentibus regenerationis sac-
ramentis, quae necesse est plurimum moveant, quid intersit inter
duos homines, veterem et novum, exteriorem et interiorem . . . ;
§51, 1.

179.   c. Faust. XXIV, 2 Paulus quidem apostolus interiorem
hominem per spiritum mentis, exteriorem uero in corpore atque
in ista mortali vita uult intelligi; non tamen utrumque horum
simul duos homines eum dixisse aliquando in eius litteris legitur,
sed unum, quem totum Deus fecerit, id est, et id, quod interius
est, et id, quod exterius.

180.   c. Faust. XXIV, 2 item cum de terreno et caelesti homine
dissereret idem Paulus inter mortalem immortalemque discernens,
inter id quod in Adam sumus, et illud quod in Christo erimus. For
Augustine's earlier use of the outer-inner contrast in this same
context, see div. quaest. 83, §51, 1.

181.   c. Faust. XXIV, 2 ergo totus ille homo, id est, et interiore et exteriore sui parte, inueteravit propter peccatum . . .

182.   c. Faust. XIII, 7. Compare XIII, 9 . . . Domini, qui per reges terrae, secundum eandem prophetiam, iam sibi seruientes seque adorantes, seuerissimis legibus terram confringit, id est, terreni cordis frangit audaciam; XXII, 38. serm. XLIV, 2 (c. A.D. 400).

183.   c. Faust. XII, 42; XXII, 60, 76.

184.   cons. evang. I, 13, §20.

185.   doctr. christ. I, 4, §4–10, §10. Compare with p. 339 above and with c. Acad. II, 1, §1.

186.   doctr. christ. I, 11, §11 Cum ergo ipsa sit patria, viam se quoque nobis fecit ad patriam.

187.   doctr. christ. I, 34, §38 Christ . . . non solum pervenientibus possessionem, sed etiam viam praebere se voluit venientibus ad principium viarum. . . . There are close connections between the argument here and the analysis of time in Book XI of the Confessiones. Compare conf. XI. 29, §39 with doctr. christ. I, 34, §38. Apostolus igitur, quamvis adhuc ambularet in via et ad palmam supernae vocationis sequeretur vocantem Deum, tamen ea quae retro sunt obliviscens et in ea quae ante sunt extentus (Philipp. III, 12–14), jam principium viarum transierat; hoc est, eo non indigebat a quo tamen aggrediendum et exoriendum iter est omnibus qui ad veritatem pervenire, et in vita aeterna permanere desiderant. The notion of Christ as both *patria* and *via* appears in a number of sermons dating roughly c. A.D. 400: serm. XCII, 3, §3 (A.D. 391–405); serm. Denis VIII, 1 (A.D. 393–405). For an early statement of the same point in terms of time and eternity, see cons. evang. I, 35, §53. For a discussion of Augustine's later use of the idea, see M. Comeau, "Le Christ, chemin et terme de l'ascension spirituelle d'après saint Augustine," Recherches de Science Religieuse XL (1952) 80–89.

188.   See p. 343 f. above.

189.   doctr. christ. II, 23, §35 f.; 39, §58 f.

190.   doctr. christ. I, 23, §23.

191.   doctr. christ. I, 24, §25.

192.   doctr. christ. II, 39, §58; 25, §38 f.

193.   catech. rud. 19, §31. I have in general followed the translation by J. P. Christopher in his edition in the Catholic University of America Patristic Studies, Vol. VIII (Washington, 1926). Another general statement on the two cities, possibly almost as early as that of the De catechizandis rudibus is found in De Genesi ad Litteram XI, 15, §20 (CSEL XXVIII, 347 f.).

The bibliography on Augustine's theory of the two cities is very

extensive, but most of the writings concentrate their attention on
the De civitate Dei. Some discussion of the earlier period may be
found in the following. H. Scholz, Glaube und Unglaube in der
Weltgeschichte (Leipzig, 1911); W. Kamlah, Christentum und
Geschichtlichkeit, 2nd ed. (Stuttgart, 1951); E. Gilson, Les
metamorphoses de la cité de Dieu (Paris, 1952); G. Bardy, "La
formation du concept de 'Cité de Dieu' dans l'oeuvre de saint Augustin" L'année théologique augustinienne XII (1952) 5–19; A.
Lauras and H. Rondet, "Le thème des deux cités dans l'oeuvre
de saint Augustin" in Études Augustiniennes, H. Rondet etc.
(Paris, 1953) 99–160. An article by Ratzinger, "Les origines de
l'idée des deux cités et la notion des deux cités chez st. Augustin"
was published in the Congrès International Augustinien (September 1954).

194.   See p. 375 above.

195.   catech. rud. 19, §33. neque tunc sane defuerunt justi qui
Deum pie quaererent, et superbiam diaboli vincerent, cives illius
sanctae civitatis . . . Ex quibus Abraham pius . . . For the earlier
development in exp. Galat., see p. 356 above.

196.   Compare catech. rud. 3, §6 ecclesia id est populus Dei per
omnes gentes, quod est corpus ejus; adjunctis etiam et annumeratis
omnibus sanctis, qui etiam ante adventum ejus in hoc saeculo
vixerunt . . . ; 19, §33.

197.   catech. rud. 19, §33.

198.   For the six ages, see 17, §28 and 22, §39.

199.   cons. evang. I, 13, §20.

200.   catech. rud. 21, §37. For the general exegesis, compare c.
Faust. XII, 36.

201.   catech. rud. 21, §37.

202.   See catech. rud. 20, §36.

203.   catech. rud. 22, §40.

204.   catech. rud. XXII, 40. An identification of *Babylon* with
terrena civitas is found in the Adnotationum in Iob Lib. I:3 (CSEL
XXVIII, 2 p. 511); compare 6 (p. 519). This is exceptional for
the period 386–400, and it will be remembered that Augustine does
not revise nor take responsibility for the work: see retract. II, 39, 1
(= ed. Maur. II, 13).

205.   It is difficult to determine just what Augustine's position
on this point is in about 400. Sometimes he seems to admit the
vision and deny that it saves; sometimes he seems to deny the vision
and admit that it saves. Compare, for example, doctr. christ. I, 4,
§4; conf. VII, 20, §26; X, 6, §10; XIII, 21, §31; De Trinitate IV,
16, §20 f. (PL XLII, 901 f.) For the early dating of this book, see
E. Hendrikx, "La date de composition du De Trinitate de S. Au-

gustin" L'année théologique augustinienne XII (1952) 305–16 part. 309–10.

206. For the place of the ecclesia and the sacraments, compare Simplic. I, 2, 2 and 2, 22; conf. XIII, 21, §29; on the ecclesia and rule, compare conf. XIII, 23, §33.

15

De Civitate Dei, XV, 2, and Augustine's Idea of the Christian Society

F. EDWARD CRANZ

St Augustine devotes a work of twenty-two books to the defense of the city of God, and in his other writings he often assumes his readers to be familiar with this heavenly city of which they are members.[1] It is consequently surprising that scholars have found his account of it ambiguous and that they have been so little able to reach agreement as to just what the city of God is.[2]

Some of their difficulties have resulted from trying to answer questions which Augustine had not considered and which, indeed, he could not consider in his own terminology. We must not, for example, expect to find in his writings a solution to the problem of 'church' and 'state,' for this is a modern question and its terms are incommensurable with those of the fifth century. Our account of the city of God must be placed in an Augustinian context, and our analysis should ultimately admit translation into Augustinian Latin.

Even with such an approach we are still faced by the difficulty that Augustine never discusses the city of God in quite the way we as historians might wish. He tells us a great deal about it, but he does not define it. In part this is because the concept is familiar and traditional. More significantly, it is because the city of God, like grace, is for him so immediately bound up with the Christian experience that it hardly admits of definition. Augustine perhaps comes closest to direct com-

Reprinted, by permission of the author and the publisher, from *Speculum* 25 (1950), pp. 215–25.

munication with his audience when he simply speaks of the
city of God in the first person plural.[3]

There is nevertheless one chapter (Book XV, 2) of the
De Civitate Dei, in which, if Augustine does not define the
city of God, he at least states with precision certain of its
relationships to Israel and the earthly city. The chapter has
long been regarded as important, but the key passages seemed
susceptible of various interpretations and among early scholars there was little agreement as to the conclusions to be
drawn.[4] In 1925, however, Hans Leisegang proposed a consistently Platonist (or Neoplatonist) interpretation, and his
thesis has been widely accepted.[5]

The first purpose of the present article is to suggest a simpler, more literal exegesis of the chapter in question. This
exegesis will then be related briefly to the general social
thought of Augustine. Finally, to throw the Augustinian position into clearer relief, the ideas of Augustine will be compared with the sharply divergent views of Eusebius of
Caesarea.

The place of *De Civitate Dei*, xv, 2, in the argument of
the whole work may be briefly indicated. In Books XI through
XIV Augustine deals with the origins of the earthly and heavenly cities, and in Book XV he begins his account of their
progress in human history. In Chapter I he restates the general contrast between the two cities and exemplifies them in
Cain and Abel. Cain, the citizen of earth, was the first born,
and so are all men born in sin and only later saved by grace.
Cain founded a city but Abel did not, for the saints belong
to a heavenly city even though it has citizens on earth in
whom it is pilgrim until the time of its eternal reign shall
arrive. In Chapter II Augustine then considers the way in
which this heavenly city was foreshadowed on earth. The
chapter is brief and it will be well to have the main passages
before us.

De Civitate Dei, xv, 2.   Dombart-Kalb, ii, 60 f.
    Umbra sane quaedam civitatis huius et imago pro-
  phetica ei significandae potius quam praesentandae ser-
5 vivit in terris, quo eam tempore demonstrari oportebat,
  et dicta est etiam ipsa civitas sancta merito significantis

imaginis, non expressae, sicut futura est, veritatis. De
hac imagine serviente et de illa, quam significat, libera
civitate sic Apostolus ad Galatas loquitur: *Dicite mihi*
10 inquit *sub lege volentes esse legem non audistis?* . . .
(Augustine then quotes in full Galatians, iv, 21–31)
                                        Haec forma intel-
30 legendi de apostolica auctoritate descendens locum nobis
p. 61 aperit, quem ad modum scripturas duorum testamentorum,
veteris et novi, accipere debeamus. Pars enim quaedam
terrenae civitatis imago caelestis civitatis effecta est, non
se significando, sed alteram, et ideo serviens. Non enim
5 propter se ipsam sed propter aliam significandam est in-
stituta, et praecedente alia significatione et ipse prae-
figurans praefigurata est. Namque Agar ancilla Sarrae
eiusque filius imago quaedam huius imaginis fuit; et quoniam transiturae erant umbrae luce veniente, ideo dixit
10 libera Sarra, quae significabat liberam civitatem, cui rursus alio modo significandae etiam illa umbra serviebat:
Eice ancillam et filium eius; non enim heres erit filius
ancillae cum filio meo Isaac, quod ait Apostolus: *Cum*
filio liberae. Invenimus ergo in terrena civitate duas
15 formas, unam suam praesentiam demonstrantem, alteram
caelesti civitati significandae sua praesentia servientem.
Parit autem cives terrenae civitatis peccato vitiata natura,
caelestis vero civitatis parit a peccato naturam libe-
rans gratia; unde illa vocantur vasa irae, ista vasa miseri-
cordiae. . . .

Let us now notice the interpretation of Leisegang. His general thesis is that Augustine, despite the appeal to the authority of St Paul, has substituted a Platonic hierarchy or
Stufenreich for the simple Pauline contrasts.[6] In this hierarchy of societies he finds three stages:

1. Exemplar: the *civitas Dei* in heaven.
2. Image: the *civitas Dei* on earth. Sarah (also Isaac) as
   its representative.
3. Image of the image: the *civitas terrena* in the stricter
   sense. Agar (also Ishmael) as its representative.

As names for the three stages Leisegang suggests:

1. *civitas caelestis spiritalis.*
2. *civitas terrena spiritalis.*
3. *civitas terrena carnalis.*[7]

In the series of societies, the city of God on earth is an image of the city of God in heaven, and the earthly city in the stricter sense is an image of the city of God on earth.[8]

The most useful criticism of Leisegang's interpretation is a careful analysis of the meaning of *De Civitate Dei,* xv, 2, for such an analysis will show that this hierarchy or *Stufenreich* is a construction without foundation in the text. Augustine introduces the chapter, as we have seen, when he is about to begin the human history of the earthly and heavenly cities. He must first solve the preliminary question: how is Israel of the Old Testament related to these two cities? The answer of the chapter is that Israel occupied a unique position. In itself it was a part of the earthly city, but as a prophecy it was related to the city of God.

In the first section (p. 60, lines 3–7), Augustine declares that a shadow and a prophetic image of the heavenly city existed on earth as long as such an image was necessary. In other words, the historical Jerusalem foreshadowed the city of God until the coming of Christ; then Jerusalem and the Jewish kingdom were destroyed by the Romans.[9]

Augustine quotes as apostolic authority for this position the Pauline allegory of Sarah and Agar as found in Galatians IV, 21–31. He then relates the doctrine of the prophetic character of Jerusalem both to his own theory of the two cities and also to the symbolism of St Paul in Galatians.

In the first place (p. 61, lines 2–6), Augustine says that a part of the earthly city became an image of the heavenly city. Since it existed not for its own sake but merely to symbolize another, it was in bondage.[10] In other words, the historical Israel, despite its prophetic character, was still a part of the earthly city.[11]

In the second place, Augustine works out a complicated inter-relationship between the symbolism of the earthly Jerusalem and the earlier symbolism of Sarah and Agar. 1. Sarah, as well as the earthly Jerusalem, symbolizes the heavenly city (p. 61, lines 10–11). 2. Agar symbolizes the earthly Jerusalem. Since the earthly Jerusalem was itself an image of the true city of God, Agar is an image of an image (p. 61, line 8). 3. The relationship between Sarah and Agar is an image of the relationship between the two cities which they respec-

tively symbolize. The earthly Jerusalem is in bondage because
it exists merely to symbolize the city of God and not for
itself; Agar is in bondage to Sarah. The earthly Jerusalem,
the shadow city, was destroyed after the appearance on earth
of Christ and the pilgrim city of God; Agar's son Ishmael
was cast out after the birth of Sarah's son Isaac (p. 61, lines
8–11).

Finally, Augustine resumes his main thesis. We find in the
earthly city two parts. There is the earthly city in itself, without symbolic significance. There is Israel, a divinely ordained
image of the city of God.

It is clear, therefore, that *De Civitate Dei*, xv, 2, provides
no basis for the hierarchic imagery suggested by Leisegang.
Only Agar, and not any society, is the image of an image.
Only Israel, and not the earthly city in any other sense, is
an image of the heavenly city. And Augustine does not say
that the pilgrim city of God on earth is related as an image
to the city of God in heaven.

If *De Civitate Dei*, xv, 2, does not justify the imposition
of a Neoplatonist pattern on the doctrine of the two cities,
it nevertheless gives us precise information about certain
inter-relationships of the city of God, the earthly city in general, and the earthly city in its special function as Israel.
How can we relate this information to the general social
thought of St Augustine?

In the first place, Augustine here reasserts the fundamental
thesis of *De Civitate Dei* that there are in the final analysis
not more than two cities.[12] From one point of view the aim
of the chapter is simply to show that the special position of
Israel is perfectly consistent with this dualism, for Israel can
be explained as a part of the earthly city which was made
a prophecy of the city of God.

In the second place, contrary to the interpretation of Leisegang, Augustine here denies that these two cities are related
as exemplar and image. Admittedly Israel is a prophecy, and
therefore an image, of the city of God, but this relationship
does not hold of the earthly city in general, which symbolizes
nothing beyond itself.[13]

These two propositions go far toward determining the main

outlines of Augustine's social thought. To realize their full
force, we must realize that while in *De Civitate Dei* they appear in a city terminology, Augustine can elsewhere phrase
them in terms of other key concepts. What we have seen as
a doctrine of two cities can also be stated as a doctrine of
two kingdoms, and the earthly Jerusalem can be explained
not only as a prophecy of the city of God but also as a
prophecy of the *ecclesia*.

The best illustration of a parallel to *De Civitate Dei*, xv,
2, in the terminology of kingdom is found in the *Enarratio
in Psalmum CXIX*, where Augustine again discusses Isaac
and Ishmael and again uses Galatians as his authority. 'The
old testament is from God, and the new testament is from
God, as both Isaac and Ishmael were sons of Abraham. But
Ishmael pertains to the earthly kingdom and Isaac to the
celestial kingdom. Therefore, the old testament has earthly
promises, an earthly Jerusalem, an earthly Palestine, an
earthly kingdom, earthly salvation, the subjugation of enemies, an abundance of sons and fruitful harvests. All of these
are earthly promises. As symbols (*in figura*) they are understood spiritually, just as the earthly Jerusalem was a shadow
of the heavenly kingdom and as the earthly kingdom was a
shadow of the kingdom of heaven.'[14] The theory of kingdoms, like that of cities, involves no hierarchy of societies.
Only the kingdom of Israel, not human kingship in general,
is an image of the heavenly kingdom. In its non-symbolic
form the earthly kingdom is a perversion of the divine order
rather than a reflection of it. Even the empire of Augustine's
own time remains a part of the earthly kingdom, and those
Christians who serve as its officials are in bondage to
Babylon.[15]

In *De Civitate Dei*, xv, 2, Sarah and the earthly Jerusalem
are prophecies of the city of God, but there are many other
passages in which Augustine explains the prophecy in terms
of the *ecclesia*. In *De Catechizandis Rudibus*, for example,
he says that the captivity of Jerusalem in Babylon was a symbol of the captivity of the *ecclesia* under the kings of this
world.[16] Earlier in the same work we find a passage in which
Israel is prophetic in the three terminologies of *ecclesia*, heavenly kingdom, and heavenly city. 'And so through many and

varied signs of things to come—things which it would take
a long time to enumerate completely and which we now see
fulfilled in the *ecclesia*—that people was led to the land of
promise, where it might reign in a temporal and carnal manner after the measure of its desire; which earthly kingdom
however was an image of the spiritual kingdom. There Jerusalem was built, the most illustrious city of God, which in her
bondage was a sign (*in signo*) of that free city which is
called the heavenly Jerusalem.'[17]

We have seen that Augustine in presenting the ideas of
De Civitate Dei, xv, 2, refers to the specifically Christian
society either as city of God or as heavenly kingdom[18] or
as *ecclesia*. Such usage shows that the three concepts are to
some extent interchangeable. Furthermore, Augustine on occasion explicitly equates them. In the *De Civitate Dei*, for
example, he speaks of the philosophers 'against whom we are
defending the city of God, that is His *ecclesia*';[19] he refers
to the many prophecies 'concerning Christ and the kingdom
of heaven, which is the city of God';[20] and he declares
'Therefore, even now the *ecclesia* is the kingdom of Christ
and the kingdom of heaven.'[21] Such equations are regularly
introduced parenthetically, but this is no justification for denying that Augustine uses all three terms to refer to the same
society. He has no reason to labor the point with an audience
which already felt themselves members of that society.

Modern scholars have not in general accepted these statements of Augustine at their face value but have instead set
up distinctions such as that between the 'church' and the city
of God.[22] Additional proof, however, that such distinctions
are not Augustinian may be found in the fact that Augustine himself expresses his basic generalizations about the
Christian society in all three terminologies. In each, members
of the Christian society appeared on earth before the coming
of Christ as head and king of the society.[23] In each case,
whether as city of God or kingdom of God or as *ecclesia*,
the Christian society on earth is a mixture of the good and
the bad.[24] Finally, and most important, in each terminology
there is always a sharp contrast between the present earthly
mode of the Christian society and its final glory. For example,
the pilgrim city of God, captive to the earthly city and existing

only by faith, is contrasted with the heavenly city above.[25]
But there is the same contrast between the *ecclesia* and the
kingdom of God as they now are and as they will be.[26]

From *De Civitate Dei*, XV, 2, as a starting point, we have
reached the basic categories of Augustine's social thought.
He feels himself a member of a Christian society which from
various aspects may be called the city of God or the kingdom
of God or the *ecclesia*. This society is heavenly in essence
and destination, but it was foreshadowed on earth by Israel
and a part of it has been given earthly reality by Christ. Over
against this true Christian society, there is human society in
general, the earthly city and the earthly kingdom. This society,
which includes human kingship and empire, has no positive
relation, in particular no relation of image, to the Christian
society of heaven. Nor has the coming of Christ and the
spread of Christianity destroyed the continuity of the earthly
city and its kingship; the Roman empire is still Babylon.

There are many thinkers with whom we might compare
Augustine to illumine his position. Eusebius of Caesarea[27]
best serves this purpose, for he is concerned with the same
basic question as Augustine but gives a sharply contrasting
answer. The *De Civitate Dei*, though the sack of Rome in
A.D. 410 was its immediate occasion, is fundamentally a solution to the older problem of the relation of Rome and Christianity. Augustine's answer is that Roman empire and Christian *ecclesia* are not essentially connected. Eusebius, on the
other hand, sees the achievement of a unified Christian empire as the goal of all history. Even in his early writings, he
insists on the mutual support of Christianity and Rome, of
the monarchy of Christ and of the monarchy of Augustus.
For him, Roman empire and Christian *ecclesia* are not only
essentially connected; they move towards identity.

The key concepts of his social thought are, therefore, differently interrelated. He begins in the same way with a Christian society which may be called city of God or kingdom of
God or *ecclesia*.[28] Unlike Augustine, however, Eusebius does
not find in history a persistent contrast between this Christian
society and human society in general; history is rather an
account of Christian triumph and of the raising of all society
to a Christian form. The triumph has two aspects. Pagan

polytheism disappears in the face of Christianity and the *ecclesia*. And since human kingship must also be transformed and Christianized, particularism and polyarchy disappear in the face of a providentially ordained Roman empire.[29] As against the Augustinian distinction within human society between earthly and heavenly cities, earthly and heavenly kingdoms, Eusebius can say that the city of earth has become the city of God[30] and that the monarchy of Constantine brings the kingdom of God to men.[31]

The Christian society on earth, which Eusebius tends to identify with the *oikoumene*,[32] is for him an image of the exemplar which is the Christian society of heaven. The *ecclesia*, as the city of God on earth, stands forth as an image of the city of heaven.[33] The kingdom and empire of Constantine is resplendent as an image of the kingdom of heaven.[34] Consequently, the final synthesis of Eusebius, in contrast to that of Augustine, unites rather than separates Rome and Christianity; it culminates in the vision of a single society which is both Roman and Christian, the earthly model of an heavenly original.

If we look for an explanation of this sharp contrast between Augustine and Eusebius, it is to be found in their relation to the earlier tradition of Christian social thought. They present the two general answers which result from the attempt to apply, in a newly Christianized world, the ideas of the first three centuries. Up to the time of Constantine, the Christians had thought of themselves as members of a society in some way like that of Rome; they, too, were a city and a people and a kingdom. But at the same time, they had sharply distinguished themselves from a Rome which was pagan; there were two distinct societies, and the city of God was not the city of the world. The general conversion of the Romans forced a rethinking of the tradition. One might on the one hand suppose that by its conversion Rome had become the city of God and that the contrast between the two cities had disappeared. Or one might maintain that the contrast was fundamental, and that it persisted even in a Christianized empire. Eusebius chose the first alternative, Augustine the second.

Neither was trying to answer any question about the 'state.'

The concept of the state is a product of the late mediaeval development and presupposes the separation of the 'supernatural,' which is specifically Christian, from a 'natural,' which is valid even though non-Christian. Neither Augustine nor Eusebius knows this form of thought, nor can we translate what they say about the Roman empire into such terms. For Augustine, the empire is too low and represents a perversion of the Christian and natural order. For Eusebius, it is too high and represents an earthly manifestation of the kingdom of God.

The contrast between Eusebius and Augustine is historically significant as broadly typical of the contrast between Greek East and Latin West. In Byzantium, and even in later Russia, men thought fundamentally in terms of a single, all-embracing Christian society under the headship of emperor or czar. But in the West, throughout the ancient period, the city of God and the empire were kept distinct. Pope Gregory I (A.D. 590–604), for example, echoes Augustine when he explains that a Christian who serves as imperial official is in bondage to Babylon.[35] It is true that even in the West men finally came to feel that the city of God had absorbed the earthly city and earthly kingship and that it was dominant in human society. History became the story not of two cities but of one.[36] From this new approach we can date the beginning of the 'Middle Ages,' and the social thought of the mediaeval West as well as of the Byzantine East may, therefore, be related to a sense of the victory of the Christian society. But we must not suppose that in the West this victory meant the introduction of a Eusebian view of the Christian society. Augustine had seen a city of God which transcended any human kingship, any human order of rule and subjection, and even in the new unified society his vision remained a powerful ferment. Neither kings nor popes in the West were ever able to establish an all-embracing, monistic rule like that of the Eastern emperors, nor were thinkers of the West, whether royalist or papalist, ever able to prove that Christianity directly determines human government and kingship. Ultimately it remained true, even for the period of the 'Middle Ages,' that the basic contrast lay, on the one hand, between a Byzantium which defined the Christian society after the manner of Eusebius and, on the other, a Western Europe which defined it in the light of what St Augustine had said about the city of God.

1. Cf. *Enarrationes in Psalmos*, LXI, §7 (*Patrologia Latina* [henceforth *P.L.*] XXXVI, 754): 'Delectat enim me pauca adhuc loqui vobis de civitate hac dulci. . . . Dicam ergo quod agnoscatis, quod approbetis: commemorabo quod nostis; non docebo quod ignoratis.' *Ibid.*, CXXXVI, §1 (*P.L.*, XXXVII, 1761): 'Oblitos vos esse non arbitror, commendasse nos vobis, imo commemorasse vos, quod omnis eruditus in sancta ecclesia nosse debet unde cives sumus . . .'

2. The evidence for this statement would be a bibliography of modern writings on the *De Civitate Dei*. The most important works are listed in E. Gilson, *Introduction à l'étude de saint Augustin* (2nd ed., Paris 1943), pp. 338–40.

3. E.g., *De Civitate Dei* (henceforth *C.D.*) X, 7 (ed. Dombart-Kalb, Leipzig, 1928–1929), I, 412: 'Cum ipsis enim sumus una civitas Dei, cui dicitur in psalmo; *Gloriosissima dicta sunt de te, civitas Dei;* cuius pars in nobis peregrinatur, pars in illis opitulatur.' XIX, 23 (II, 399). 'Huius autem praeclarissimum atque optimum sacrificium nos ipsi sumus, hoc est civitas eius . . .' *Enarrationes in Psalmos*, LXXXVI, §1 (*P.L.*, XXXVII, 1100f.) 'Civitas quaedam in isto psalmo cantata et commendata est, cujus cives sumus in quantum christiani sumus; et unde peregrinamur, quamdiu mortales sumus; . . .'

4. Some used the chapter to prove the subordination of the state to the church, as H. Reuter, *Augustinische Studien* (Gotha, 1887), p. 145, note 3. Others saw in it the view that the city of God on earth is an image of the heavenly city, as E. Bernheim, *Mittelalterliche Zeitanschauungen* (Tübingen, 1918), I, 20. The most detailed of the earlier interpretations was that of H. Hermelink in his article 'Die *civitas terrena* bei Augustin,' *Festgabe A. v. Harnack* (Tübingen, 1921) p. 320, note 1, and p. 310 with note 1. Hermelink's main thesis was that the part of the earthly city which served as an image of the heavenly city was in the first place the state of the Jews and in the second place the state in general.

5. Hans Leisegang, 'Der Ursprung der Lehre Augustins von der Civitas Dei,' *Archiv für Kulturgeschichte*, XVI (1925), 127–58. The material of the article was originally presented in lecture form, and a summary may be found in *Verhandlungen der 55. Versammlung Deutscher Philologen und Schulmänner in Erlangen* (Leipzig, 1926), pp. 31–32. For illustration of the use of Leisegang's conclusions cf., e.g., E. Lewalter, 'Eschatologie und Weltgeschichte in der Gedankenwelt Augustins,' *Zeitschrift für Kirch-*

engeschichte, LV (1934), 12–17; P. Brezzi, 'La concezione agostiniana della città di Dio e le sue interpretazione medioevali,'
Rivista Storica Italiana, Ser. V, Vol. 3, Fasc. 3 (1938), 78–86.
Particularly among German scholars, there has been a tendency to
erect further constructions on the basis of Leisegang's thesis: e.g.,
V. Stegemann, *Augustins Gottesstaat* (Heidelberger Abhandlungen zur Philosophie und ihrer Geschichte, XV; Tübingen, 1928),
pp. 49–52; C. V. v. Horn, *Beiträge zur Staatslehre St. Augustins
nach De Civitate Dei I* (Breslau, 1934), pp. 20–24. A more independent interpretation but one of the same type may be found in
G. Tellenbach, *Libertas, Kirche und Weltordnung im Zeitalter
des Investiturstreits* (Forschungen zur Kirchen- und Geistesge-
schichte, VII, Stuttgart, 1936), Excursus II, pp. 202–4.

6. Leisegang, 'Der Ursprung . . . ,' p. 133.

7. *Ibid.,* p. 134. No Augustinian texts are cited in support of
the assertion.

8. In the later part of the article (pp. 136 f.) Leisegang discusses the sources of the view of society which he finds in *De
Civitate Dei,* XV, 2; he concludes that these sources are St Ambrose directly and Philo ultimately.

9. For Jerusalem as an *umbra* and *figura* of the heavenly city
cf. *Enarrationes in Psalmos,* LXXXVI, §5 (*P.L.,* XXXVII, 1105):
'. . . loquitur autem iste de civitate quadam, quam spiritualiter
intelligit, cujus umbra et figura erat illa terrena.' *In Joannis Evangelium,* Tractatus XI, 2, §8 (*P.L.,* XXXV, 1479): 'Ideo illa Jerusalem in terra, umbra erat caelestis Jerusalem matris omnium
nostrorum, quaet in caelo.' *Sermo* IV, §8(9) (*P.L.,* XXXVIII, 37):
'Cum enim Jerusalem quae fuit in terra, pertineat ad Vetus
Testamentum, imaginem habet ad Jerusalem quae est in coelo, et
pertinet ad Novum Testamentum.' For a general statement of the
prophetic character of Israel as a whole and its consequent destruction after the appearance of Christ, who proclaimed what it
had foreshadowed cf. *De Consensu Evangelistarum,* I, 11(17)–
14(22) (*Corpus Scriptorum Ecclesiasticorum Latinorum* (henceforth *CSEL*), XLIII, 17–21; *P.L.,* XXXIV, 1050–52.

10. For this doctrine of mere symbolism as bondage cf. *De
Doctrina Christiana,* III, 5(9) f. (*P.L.,* XXXIV, 68 f.), part. 9(13) c.
70: 'Sub signo enim servit qui operatur aut veneratur aliquem
rem significantem, nesciens quid significat . . .'

11. Augustine uses three approaches to the historical Israel in
the *C.D.* In itself it is a part of the earthly city. Cf. *C.D.,* XVII, 4 (II,
205): 'Haec dicuntur adversariis civitatis Dei ad Babyloniam per-
tinentes . . . ex quibus sunt etiam carnales Israelitae, terrenae
Hierusalem, cives terrigenae.' XVII, 16 (II, 239 f.): Augustine is

discussing the significance of the *regina* mentioned in Psalm
XLIV, 10. 'Ipsa est Sion spiritaliter. . . . Ipsa est et Hierusalem
eodem modo spiritaliter . . . Eius inimica est civitas diaboli Babylon, quae confusio interpretatur; ex qua tamen Babylone regina
ista in omnibus gentibus regeneratione liberatur et a pessimo rege
ad optimum regem, id est a diabolo transit ad Christum. . . .
Cuius civitatis impiae portio sunt et Israelitae sola carne, non
fide; inimici etiam ipsi magni huius regis eiusque reginae.' But
Israel is also, as we have seen, a prophecy of the city of God.
Finally, it contains certain early members of the city of God. *C.D.*,
XVI, 3 (II, 127) 'In quo (sc. populo) Dei civitas et in sanctis pere-
grinata est, et in omnibus sacramento adumbrata.'

12. *C.D.*, XII, 1 (I, 511–12); XIV, 1 (II, 3); XV, 1 (II, 58);
Enarrationes in Psalmos, LXI, §6 (*P.L.*, XXXVI, 733): 'Quid est, una
civitas et una civitas? Babylonia una; Jerusalem una. Quibuslibet
aliis etiam mysticis nominibus appelletur, una tamen civitas et una
civitas; illa rege diabolo, ista rege Christo.'

13. *C.D.*, XV, 2 (II, 61 lines 14–15): 'Invenimus ergo in terrena civitate, duas formas, unam suam praesentiam demonstrantem . . .'

14. *Enarrationes in Psalmos*, CXIX, §7 (*P.L.*, XXXVII, 1603).
For the Jewish kingdom as a symbol of the heavenly kingdom cf.
Contra Faustum Manichaeum, XIII, 4 (*P.L.*, XLII, 283): '. . . no-
menque ipsum Christi, quod non scimus nisi in regno Judaeorum in
sacerdotibus et regibus institutum, ut non solum ille aut ille homo,
sed universa gens totumque regnum prophetia fieret Christi Christi-
anique regni.' *C.D.*, XVII, 6 (II, 218): 'Regnum quoque isto modo
etiam Saulis ipsius, qui certe reprobatus atque reiectus est, futuri
regni erat umbra in aeternitate mansuri . . .' *De Cathechizandis
Rudibus*, XX, 36 (*P.L.*, XL, 336): '. . . quod tamen regnum terrenum, regni spiritualis imaginem gessit.' *De Vera Religione*, XXVII,
50 (*P.L.*, XXXIV, 144) '. . . cujus historia Vetus Testamentum vocatur, quasi terrenum pollicens regnum; quae tota nihil aliud est
quam imago novi populi et Novi Testamenti pollicentis regnum
coelorum.'

15. For a general statement of the two kingdoms, cf. *Enarrationes in Psalmos*, LI, §4 (*P.L.*, XXXVI, 602): 'Est ergo regnum
terrenum . . . hodie in isto saeculo, ubi est et regnum coeleste.
Peregrinos habet cives suos utrumque regnum, regnum terrenum
et regnum coeleste, regnum eradicandum et regnum in aeternum
plantandum. Modo in hoc saeculo cives utriusque regni permixti
sunt: corpus regni terreni et corpus regni coelestis commixtum est.
Regnum coeleste gemit inter cives regni terreni et aliquando . . .
quodammodo regnum terrenum angariat cives regni coelorum; et

regnum coeleste angariat cives regni terreni.' The argument continues through §6 (c. 604) where imperial service is described as 'aliqua gerere Babyloniae negotia.' In the *Enarrationes in Psalmos*, LXI, §8 (*P.L.*, XXXVI, 735–36) the doctrine of the forced service imposed by each kingdom on the citizens of the other appears in a terminology of cities. 'Videamus si et nunc cives bonae civitatis administrent quosdam actus malae civitatis. Terrena omnis respublica, quandoque utique peritura; cujus regnum transiturum est . . . terrena ergo respublica habet cives nostros administrantes res ejus. Quam multi enim fideles, quam multi boni et magistratus sunt in civitatibus suis, et judices sunt, et duces sunt, et comites sunt, et reges sunt? Omnes justi et boni, non habentes in corde nisi gloriosissima quae de te dicta sunt, civitas Dei (*Psal.* LXXXVI, 3). Et quasi angariam faciunt in civitate transitura . . .'

16. *De Catechizandis Rudibus*, XXI, 37 (*P.L.*, XL, 337). Cf. also XIX, 33 (*P.L.*, XL, 334).

17. *Ibid.*, XX, 36 (*P.L.*, XL, 336).

18. It will be seen from the passage from *Enarrationes in Psalmos*, LI, cited in the previous note, that 'regnum coeleste' is synonymous with 'regnum coelorum.' Augustine also identifies 'regnum coelorum' with 'regnum Dei'; cf. *De Gestis Pelagii*, v, 15 (*P.L.*, XLIV, 329): 'Non enim aliud est regnum Altissimi quam Dei regnum, aut quisquam contendere audebit, aliud esse Dei regnum, aliud regnum coelorum.' In the remainder of the article I have used 'kingdom of God,' as the most common term. The phrase is more dynamic in Latin (and Greek) than in English, and perhaps 'reign of God' is a more accurate translation.

19. *C.D.*, XII, 16 (I, 574). Cf. also *C.D.*, VIII, 24 (I, 360); XVI, 2 (II, 124); *Enarrationes in Psalmos*, XCVIII, §4 (*P.L.*, XXXVII, 1261). Many other passages might be added in support of this identification; I know of no passage in which Augustine denies it.

20. *C.D.*, XVII, 1 (II, 198); cf. *Enarrationes in Psalmos*, CXLVI, §9 (*P.L.*, XXXVII, 1904).

21. *C.D.*, XX, 9 (II, 429). Cf. also *Quaestiones in Heptateuchum*, VII, 49 (*P.L.*, XXXIV, 821): 'Tunc tradet regnum Deo et Patri. (I Cor. XV, 24): Quod regnum ipsa ecclesia est, rex ipse cujus figuram vovens ille (sc. Jephte) gestabat.' *Sermo*, CCLI, §4 (*P.L.*, XXXVIII, 1169): '. . . *minimus vocabitur in regno coelorum.*' (Matthew, v, 19): 'Sed in quo regno coelorum? In ecclesia quae modo est, quia et ipsa vocatur regnum coelorum.' This identification of the *regnum Dei* and the *ecclesia, qualis nunc est*, is better understood in the light of Augustine's explanation of the meaning of *regnum Dei*. Cf. *De Diversis Quaestionibus*, LXIX, §3 (*P.L.*, XL, 76): 'Regnum ejus sunt in quibus nunc regnat per fidem. Aliter

enim dicitur regnum Christi secundum potestatem divinitatis, secundum quod ei cuncta creatura subjecta est; et aliter regnum ejus
dicitur ecclesia, secundum proprietatem fidei quae in illo est.' *In
Joannis Evangelium,* Tractatus cxv, §2 (*P.L.,* xxxv, 1939): 'Quid
est enim ejus regnum nisi credentes in eum . . . ?' *Sermo* viii, §1
(*P.L.,* xxxviii, 67): 'Virga significat regnum Dei: idemque regnum
Dei esse utique populum Dei.'

One is conscious of a certain tension in those passages such as
C.D., xx, 9, where Augustine argues that even the *ecclesia* as it
now is should be called the kingdom of God. However, the tension
results not from ambiguity in Augustine's position but from fear
of misunderstanding. As we shall see (cf. note 26 *infra*) the Christian society has two sharply contrasted parts, what it is now on
earth and what it is and will be in heaven. 'Ecclesia,' without qualification will usually be understood of its earthly form; 'regnum Dei'
without qualification will usually be understood of heaven and the
world to come. Cf. e.g. *Sermo* ccli, §2 (*P.L.,* xxxviii, 1168):
'Super numerum modo in ecclesiam intrare possunt, in regnum
coelorum non possunt.' Consequently, when the two general concepts are identified, there is always danger that the ecclesia, *as it
now is,* will be confused with the kingdom of God, *as it will be.*

But this fear of misunderstanding does not lead Augustine to
abandon the identification. In the first place, such Biblical passages
as Matthew, v, 19, compel him to admit that the kingdom of God
includes those who break Christ's commandments, so he cannot
separate the kingdom, as perfect, from the *ecclesia,* as imperfect.
In the second place, and more important, the identification seems
to follow from the basic orientation of Augustine's thought. For
him the Christian society on earth, whatever its failings, *is* the
Christian society, and he has no other way of thinking of it. His
thought is most easily understood in the terminology of the *C.D.,*
for here there was little question of the famous *exegetische Not-
wendigkeit.* There is really only one Christian society, the city of
God. It has two parts, what it is now on earth and what it is and
will be in heaven. Though these are clearly separated as the pilgrim
city of God on earth and the city of God in heaven, Augustine
nowhere denies that even the pilgrim city *is* the city of God.

22. Cf. Gilson, *op. cit.* (note 2), p. 238. Gilson's reasoning is
instructive and may be noted briefly. '. . . l'Église n'est pas la Cité
de Dieu, car cette cité est la société de tous les élus passés, présents
ou futurs; or il y a manifestement eu des justes élus avant la constitution de l'Église du Christ; il y a maintenant, hors de l'Église
et peut-être jusque parmi ses persécuteurs, de futurs élus qui se
soumettront a sa discipline avant de mourir; enfin et surtout il y a

dans l'Église beaucoup d'hommes qui ne seront pas du nombre des
élus: *habet secum, quamdiu peregrinatur in mundo, connexos com-
munione sacramentorum, nec secum futuros in aeterna sorte sanctorum.*' But Augustine believes that there were members of the
ecclesia before the time of Christ; cf. *Sermo* IV, §11 (*P.L.*, XXXVIII,
39). He also believes that the *pilgrim* city of God has future citizens among its apparent enemies and that some apparently connected with it by the sacraments will not share in its final glory.
Cf. *C.D.*, I, 35 (I, 51). The subject of the passage from this chapter
cited by Gilson (*habet secum* etc.) is *Dei civitas.*

The general significance of Gilson's argument is that it represents an attempt to translate Augustine into a different terminology,
though one linked to that of Augustine by a historical development. Where Augustine knows an *ecclesia* which appears both as
peregrina and *coelestia* (cf. *Sermo* CCCXLI, §9 (11) (*P.L.*, XXXIX,
1500), Gilson's *l'Église* is apparently restricted to the former.
Where Augustine knows a *civitas Dei* which is both pilgrim on
earth and also established in heaven, Gilson's *Cité de Dieu* seems
to have the marks only of the latter. Such translation of Augustine's
thought into a different terminology, even when done as accurately
as possible, probably hinders rather than helps our historical understanding of him.

23.   For the city of God cf. *C.D.*, XVI, 3 (II, 127); *Enarrationes
in Psalmos*, LXI, §4 (*P.L.*, XXXVI, 732). For the kingdom of God
cf. *C.D.*, XVII, 10 (II, 229). For the *ecclesia* cf. *C.D.*, XVIII, 51 (II,
337); *Enarrationes in Psalmos*, CXXVIII, §2 (*P.L.*, XXXVII, 1689–
90); *ibid.*, XC, *Sermo*, II, §1 (*P.L.*, XXXVII, 1158 f.). The same idea
can also be explained in terms of the body of Christ, e.g. *De Catechizandis Rudibus*, III (6) (*P.L.*, XL, 313 f.).

24.   For the city of God cf. *C.D.*, I, 35 (I, 51); *Enarrationes in
Psalmos*, C, §13 (*P.L.*, XXXVII, 1292–93). For the kingdom of
God cf. *C.D.*, XX, 9 (II, 428 f.); *In Joannis Evangelium*, Tractatus
LXVIII, §2 (*P.L.*, XXXV, 1814 f.); CXV, §2 (*P.L.*, XXXV, 1939 f.).
For the *ecclesia* cf. *Enarrationes in Psalmos*, CXXVI, §8 (*P.L.*,
XXXVII, 1673). Other passages may be found in the Migne index
s.v. ecclesia (*P.L.*, XLVI, 267).

25.   E.g., *C.D.*, I, *Praef.* (I, 3).

26.   *C.D.*, XX, 9 (II, 428–29). For the kingdom of God cf. also
In Joannis Evangelium, Tractatus LXVIII, §2 (*P.L.*, XXXV, 1814 f.)
and CXV, §2 (*P.L.*, XXXV, 1939 f.). For the *ecclesia* cf. *Enchiridion*,
LVI (*P.L.*, XL, 258 f.); *Enarrationes in Psalmos*, CXXXVII, §4 (*P.L.*,
XXXVII, 1776); *Sermo* CCCXLI §9 (11) (*P.L.*, XXXIX, 1499 f.).

27.   For a general introduction to the writings of Eusebius, with
full bibliography cf. B. Altaner, *Patrologie* (Freiburg, 1938),

pp. 141–47; some additional material may be found in the Italian translation (Rome, 1944), pp. 151–56. In recent years there has been considerable interest in the social and political ideas of Eusebius; cf. N. H. Baynes, 'Eusebius and the Christian Empire,' *Mélanges Bidez* (Annuaire de l'Institut de philologie et d'histoire orientale, II, Brussels, 1934), pp. 13–18; E. Peterson, *Der Monotheismus als politisches Problem* (Leipzig, 1935), pp. 71 f.; H.-G. Opitz, 'Euseb von Cäsarea als Theologe,' *Zeitschrift f. NTliche Wissenschaft,* XXXIV (1935), 1–19; H. Eger, 'Kaiser und Kirche in der Geschichtstheologie Eusebs von Cäsarea,' *ibid.,* XXXVIII (1939), 97–115; H. Berkhof, *Die Theologie des Eusebius von Caesarea* (Amsterdam, 1939).

28. Cf. e.g., *Commentaria in Psalmos,* LXXXVI (*Patrologia Graeca* [henceforth *P.G.*], XXIII, 1045; *ibid.,* LXIV (*P.G.,* XXIII, 625).

29. On this development in Eusebius cf. Peterson, *op. cit.,* pp. 71 f.

30. Cf. *Commentaria in Isaiam,* XIX, 18 (*P.G.,* XXIV, 232); *ibid.,* I, 27 (*P.G.,* XXIV, 100).

31. *Oration to Constantine,* II, §2 (ed. I. A. Heikel in: *Die Griechischen Christlichen Schriftsteller,* VII, Leipzig, 1902), p. 199.

32. Cf. e.g., *Commentaria in Psalmos,* LXXXVIII (*P.G.,* XXIII, 1089–92); *ibid.,* XCII (*P.G.,* XXIII, 1185–88); *ibid.,* LXXI (*P.G.,* 801–5); *Oration to Constantine,* XVI (ed. Heikel, pp. 248–54).

33. Cf. the passages cited in note 28; also *Commentaria in Isaiam,* XLIX, §11 (*P.G.,* XXIV, 436) and LI, §17 (*P.G.,* XXIV, 449).

34. The most important passages will be found in the *Oration to Constantine,* I, 6–III, 5 (ed. Heikel, pp. 198–201).

35. Gregory I, *Register,* VIII, 33 (*Monumenta Germaniae Historica,* Epistolae II, 35). For the parallels in Augustine cf. the passages mentioned in note 15, *supra.*

36. The classic mediaeval statement is that of Otto of Freising, *Chronica sive Historia de Duabus Civitatibus,* V, Prologue (ed. A. Hofmeister, Hanover-Leipzig, 1912), p. 228.

354	Augustine born at Thagaste, North Africa.
371	Goes to Carthage to complete his education.
384	to 386 Becomes professor of rhetoric at Milan; encounters bishop Ambrose and circle of Christian Platonists at Milan; reads some "Platonist" literature; retires to Cassiciacum; writes earliest surviving dialogues.
387	Baptized in Milan.
388	Returns to Africa, via Rome. More "philosophical" dialogues.
391	Ordained priest in Hippo, North Africa. Continues writing. Drawn into affairs of North African church; Donatist schism.
395	Consecrated bishop of Hippo. Attends Church councils, travels, preaches, continues to write, etc.
397	to 401 *Confessions.*
399	to 419 *De Trinitate.*
401	to 414 *De Genesi ad litteram.*
410	Alaric and his Visigoths enter Rome.
413	to 427 *De Civitate Dei.*
411	First encounter with Pelagius.
429	Vandals invade North Africa.
430	Augustine dies in Hippo.

NOTE ON FURTHER READING

AUGUSTINE'S WORKS: the standard complete edition is that by the Benedictines of St. Maur (1679–1700), reprinted in J. P. Migne, *Patrologia latina*, Vols. 32–47. Modern critical editions of many works exist; for details consult E. Dekkers and A. Gaar, *Clavis patrum latinorum*, 2a ed. (Bruges, 1961).

ENGLISH TRANSLATIONS exist of most works; details in the Appendix (by J. J. O'Meara) in Marrou, *Saint Augustine,* or Brown, *Augustine of Hippo* (see below). Translations of some works of special

---

* This table includes only the barest essentials. Of Augustine's writings only those likely to be of most interest to the student of philosophy are mentioned.

interest to the student of philosophy: *Earlier writings* (incl. *De Magistro, De Libero Arbitrio*), trans. J. H. S. Burleigh (Library of Christian Classics, Vol. 6, 1953); *Later Writings* (incl. *De Trinitate* [parts]) trans. J. Burnaby (Library of Christian Classics, Vol. 8, 1954). Of the *Confessions* and *The City of God* there are a number of useful translations, as well as the bilingual editions in the Loeb Classical Library.

GENERAL WORKS ON AUGUSTINE: Peter Brown, *Augustine of Hippo: a Biography* (1967), and Gerald Bonner, *St Augustine: Life and Controversies* (London, 1963), are the best full accounts. On a smaller scale, H. I. Marrou, *Saint Augustine and His Influence Through the Ages* (English Translation, London, 1957).

GENERAL EXPOSITIONS OF AUGUSTINE'S PHILOSOPHY: The only serviceable full-scale exposition is E. Gilson, *The Christian Philosophy of Saint Augustine* (English Translation, London, 1961). For shorter accounts, see R. A. Markus, "Marius Victorinus and Saint Augustine," Part IV, in *Cambridge History of Later Greek and Early Medieval Philosophy*, ed. A. H. Armstrong (Cambridge, 1967) 327–420, and R. A. Markus, "Augustine," Ch. 5, in *Critical History of Western Philosophy*, ed. D. J. O'Connor (New York and London, 1964) 79–97.

BIBLIOGRAPHY: The field is vast, and none of the bibliographies available is adequate. For a beginning: F. M. Sciacca, ed. *Augustinus* (Bibliogaphische Einführungen in das Studium der Philosophie, 10. Bern, 1948). There is a useful select bibliography in C. Andresen, ed. *Zum Augustingespräch der Gegenwart* (Wege der Forschung, 5. Darmstadt, 1962). Current bibliographical reports appear regularly in *Revue des études augustiniennes*, and notices in the philosophical bibliographies.